THE CLARENDON EDITION OF THE
WORKS OF JOHN LOCKE

GENERAL EDITOR: JOHN W. YOLTON

SOME THOUGHTS CONCERNING
· EDUCATION

SOME THOUGHTS CONCERNING EDUCATION

by

JOHN LOCKE

Edited with Introduction, Notes,
and Critical Apparatus
by

John W. and Jean S. Yolton

CLARENDON PRESS · OXFORD

Oxford University Press, Walton Street, Oxford OX2 6DP

Oxford New York Toronto
Delhi Bombay Calcutta Madras Karachi
Petaling Jaya Singapore Hong Kong Tokyo
Nairobi Dar es Salaam Cape Town
Melbourne Auckland

and associated companies in
Berlin Ibadan

Oxford is a trade mark of Oxford University Press

Published in the United States
by Oxford University Press, New York

© Oxford University Press 1989

First published 1989
Reprinted 1990

British Library Cataloguing in Publication Data
Locke, John, 1632–1704
Some thoughts concerning education.—(The Clarendon
edition of the works of John Locke).
1. Moral education
I. Title II. Yolton, John W. (John
William), 1921–   III. Yolton, Jean S
370.11′4
ISBN 0–19–824582–3

Library of Congress Cataloging in Publication Data
Locke, John, 1632–1704
Some thoughts concerning education/by John Locke;
edited with introduction, notes, and critical apparatus
by John W. and Jean S. Yolton.
p.   cm.—(The Clarendon edition of the works of John Locke)
Includes index.
1. Education—Philosophy—Early works to 1800.
2. Locke, John, 1632–1704. I. Yolton, John W.
II. Yolton, Jean S., 1924-   III. Title.
IV. Series: Locke, John, 1632–1704. Works. 1975.
LB 475.L6S65 1989 370′ 1dc 19 88–28218 CIP
ISBN 0–19–824582–3

Set by Joshua Associates Limited, Oxford
Printed in Great Britain by
The Alden Press, Oxford

TO
E. S. DE BEER

CONTENTS

LIST OF PLATES

ABBREVIATIONS AND SYMBOLS

Corr. *The Correspondence of John Locke*, ed. E. S. de Beer (Clarendon Edition of the Works of John Locke, Oxford, 1976–); cited by letter-number, volume and page

DNB *Dictionary of National Biography*

Essay *Essay concerning Human Understanding*, ed. P. H. Nidditch (Clarendon Edition of the Works of John Locke, Oxford, 1975); cited by book, chapter, and section

H   Harvard College Library MS Eng. 860

K   British Library Add. MS 38771

LL   *The Library of John Locke*, by John Harrison and Peter Laslett (2nd edn., Oxford, 1971)

NA   'I' edition (1693)

NN   'I my' edition (1693)

OED *Oxford English Dictionary*

T   *Two Treatises of Government*, ed. P. Laslett (2nd edn., Cambridge, 1967); cited by treatise and section

1   1693 editions (NN and NA)

3   Third edition (1695)

4   Fourth edition (1699)

5   Fifth edition (1705)

Where manuscript transcriptions are given in the text or in notes, we have employed the signs and abbreviations used by P. H. Nidditch for his transcripts of Drafts A and B of the *Essay*, as follows:

` ´   scribal (author's and/or copyist's) interlineation
[ ]   scribal deletion
⟦ ⟧   scribal cancellation by superimposition of correction
⟨ ⟩   editorial insertion or substitution
{ }   editorial deletion
...   illegible or indecipherable

INTRODUCTION

A. CONTENT

JOHN LOCKE, medical doctor, psychologist, economist, biblical exegete, naturalist, amateur scientist, may also with some careful qualification be called an 'educationist'. He published a book, *Some Thoughts concerning Education* in 1693, but he had been writing on the subject of education from at least 1684 when in Holland (where he had prudently retreated after the statesman he worked for, Lord Shaftesbury, was charged with treason) he was asked by his friends Mr and Mrs Edward Clarke for recommendations on how best to rear and educate their young son. While Locke did later agree to publish these letters to the Clarkes, with some revisions and expansions (they span the years 1684–91), the letters and the book are not, and do not pretend to be, a systematic treatise on or a theory of education. The title of the published version, *Some Thoughts*, indicates Locke's view of that work. Many of his books carry similar modest titles: *A Letter concerning Toleration* (1689), an *Essay concerning Human Understanding* (1690), *Some Considerations of the Consequences of the Lowering of Interest and Raising the Value of Money* (1692). His political work was more definite: *Two Treatises of Government* (1690).

Despite the origin of *Some Thoughts*, and despite the modesty of Locke's claims about it, it does occupy a central place in his thought and writing. The themes of the origin and growth of knowledge, the development of awareness, the formation of character, virtue, and social responsibility: these themes span much of his writing. The links between *Some Thoughts* and *Two Treatises* are especially important; the former provides a training and educational programme for the development of a moral person, the latter places that person in the political arena. The rationale of Locke's civil society is the protection of property: the possessions, the life, the individuality of the person. The list of virtues praised by Locke in *Some Thoughts* includes some individual-oriented properties (e.g., industriousness, prudence), but also contains social virtues (e.g., kindness, generosity, civility). The individualism of his philosophy is nicely balanced by his twin concepts of the community of mankind and the civil polity. The person as a moral being belongs to both communities; both communities set the standards for and preserve the values of Locke's morality. Locke's person is, in short, a socialized and Christianized individual. The *Essay* guides us through the distinction between man and person, *Some Thoughts* gives parents a very specific manual on how to guide and mould their children into moral, social persons. Seen in this light, Locke's work on education acquires the significance and importance it deserves.

In noting the interconnections of Locke's various books and in appreciating the rich relation between his work on education and *Two Treatises*, we must be careful not to saddle him with more systematic theory than is found in his writing. In his approach to the issues, problems, and themes discussed in his writings, we can discern similarities with the scientific attitudes of Locke's contemporaries. Thomas Sprat tells us that the Royal Society believed that 'the true Philosophy must be first of all begun, on a scrupulous, and severe examination of particulars'.[1] Sprat warns against letting general theories turn into metaphysical systems unchecked by reference to things themselves. Sprat (with some reservations) spoke for the scientists of the Royal Society. Locke was one of them, a member from 1668, strongly in agreement with the methods and attitudes of its members. That attitude of working with particulars rather than with general theories, of starting with concrete and known facts, is exemplified in most of Locke's writings, no less in *Some Thoughts concerning Education* than in the *Essay concerning Human Understanding* or *Two Treatises of Government*. Most of his writings were the result of some question, problem, or concern which arose from his own experience. What are the limits of our knowledge? How do ideas arise in the mind? How can we formulate the knowledge that experimental scientists are acquiring of the world? What can we say about the nature of things themselves? How can the acquisition of private property be accounted for and our right to it defended? What is the relation between parental and political power? What will motivate men to pursue virtue? These are the kinds of specific questions to which Locke addresses himself in different writings, the bases from which he carried on his careful and detailed analyses of related concepts. He does not, in other words, start with a systematic philosophy and then fit his thoughts on government, society, or education into that framework.

This is not to say that Locke did not have some general beliefs

[1] Thomas Sprat, *The History of the Royal Society of London, For the Improving of Natural Knowledge* (London, 1667), p. 31.

about the world and man, beliefs that influenced his accounts of the areas on which he directed his questions. One area in particular where his beliefs and convictions are readily apparent is in the rearing and educating of children. A close examination of *Some Thoughts*, of his recommendations for working with children so that they acquire the virtue and wisdom necessary for living in the world, reveals a complex and detailed set of beliefs about adults and children. There are some important continuities between this aspect of that work and his account of civil society in *Two Treatises*. As will be suggested later, education for Locke provides the character-formation necessary for becoming a person and for being a responsible citizen. Too much should not be made of the distinction between a philosophy of human nature (a systematic theory) and a set of beliefs about man and his nature, but the consequences of these two approaches differ markedly, for example in the detailed, descriptive method of the latter, as opposed to the more general and abstract tenor of the former. Locke's approach to most problems and questions favours careful observation and description.

Locke, then, did not start with a system of thought, though like all thinkers he of course worked within specific conceptual boundaries. He was, nevertheless, systematic and thorough in his analyses. The total result may even be a system in the sense that philosophy of man, theory of knowledge, and ethical and political doctrines are inter-related. What we must guard against is forming an interpretation of some passage in one book based on what is said in another; for example, that since Locke held such-and-such views in the *Essay* or *Two Treatises*, his meaning in some troublesome passage in *Some Thoughts* must be such-and-such. Nina Reicyn is right in saying that we should not view *Some Thoughts* as 'une entreprise systématique destinée à déduire de la philosophie de l'*Essai* les applications éducatives qu'elles comportent'.[1] Reicyn conjectures that when Locke wrote his letters on education to Edward Clarke, 'il ne faisait, sciemment, aucun rapport entre sa philosophie et les conseils qu'il adressait à son ami'. In attempting 'à établir un lien entre la totalité de l'*Essai* et l'*Œuvre pédagogique de Locke*, on risque d'interpréter d'une façon trop large'.[2] Nevertheless, we need to remember that Locke's advice to the Clarkes was written against a background of years of reading, note-taking, and writing on such topics as religious toleration; the nature of

---

[1] Nina Reicyn, *La Pédagogie de John Locke* (Paris, 1941), p. 59.
[2] Ibid., p. 207.

the family; the formation of civil society; the connection between language, thought, and reality; knowledge and belief; medicine and science generally; Christianity and the Bible. Locke published nothing until he was fifty-eight years old; but the years between 1689 and 1693 saw five books issue from his pen. There was a backlog of knowledge and ideas upon which he drew in a flurry of major publications. Out of a rich context of thought, *Some Thoughts* took its place with these other publications. His reading, writing, and thinking were not rigidly compartmentalized; there are continuities and interrelations between his books.

Still, Reicyn is right to warn against too detailed and specific connections, without careful textual support. Another danger in the history of thought is to use labels as a means of uncovering what an author meant. In dealing with his psychology and his educational remarks, the *tabula rasa* concept has obscured what Locke really said about the powers of the mind in acquiring ideas, or about the tempers of the child which must be recognized by the tutor. One commonplace is, as Peter Gay remarks, 'that Locke was an empiricist', but Gay, like others, hardly pauses to ask whether his account of knowledge and awareness in the *Essay* fits that label, or how and in what ways.[1] It is easy to say, but not always as easy to argue, that 'Locke's philosophy as expressed in the *Essay* coloured his ideas about education, and must be taken into account when analysing the *Thoughts*'.[2] It is somewhat extravagant to claim, as Gay has, that Locke's *Essay* 'laid the psychological groundwork for modern educational theory', even more so to say without qualification or specific claims that *Some Thoughts* 'applied his philosophy specifically to pedagogy'. Gay is correct, of course, to say that Locke did not develop his pedagogical programme in isolation, but it is highly questionable to add that the programme was developed 'as part of a total view of the world'.[3] Systems tend to emerge out of, rather than control, what Locke writes. Too much can

---

[1] *John Locke on Education*, ed. Peter Gay (Classics in Education, 20, New York, 1964), p. 5. Gay says that 'by insisting on empiricism, Locke imported Newton's scientific method into philosophy', but it is very doubtful that Newton had much influence on Locke's *Essay*. The science of nature Locke took as his model was that practised by people such as Robert Boyle, Robert Hooke, and Thomas Sydenham—those who stressed the need for gathering data and building natural histories of phenomena. For a corrective to the supposed influence of Newton on Locke, see G. A. J. Rogers, 'Locke's *Essay* and Newton's *Principia*', *Journal of the History of Ideas*, 39, no. 2 (Apr./June 1978), 217–32.

[2] S. J. Curtis and M. B. Boultwood, *A Short History of Educational Ideas*, 4th edn. (London, 1966), p. 226.

[3] Gay, op. cit., pp. 1, 5.

be made of interconnections between works. Too little can also be made of obvious parallels and assumptions that carry over from one work to another. One simply has to read carefully, keeping in mind the total body of Locke's writing while examining any one book.

The impetus for *Some Thoughts* was a request from Locke's close friend, Edward Clarke and his wife, for some advice on rearing their son. That was not the only request Locke received for such advice. When another close friend, William Molyneux, learned of Locke's writing on education, he asked Locke to allow him to read it. Molyneux's brother Thomas had learnt of Locke's writing on education when he talked with Locke in Holland.[1] William Molyneux was looking for a method of instruction for his son. In another letter, Molyneux details for Locke the progress of his son, then five years old, following Locke's method.[2] In a still later letter, he speaks of the 'Extraordinary Effects your Method of Education has had on my little Boy', and in another letter also of 1695, Molyneux describes some of the subjects learnt by his son under the influence of Locke's recommendations.[3] Locke also tells us in the 'Epistle Dedicatory' to Clarke which accompanied the publication of *Some Thoughts* that 'I my self have been consulted of late by so many, who profess themselves at a loss how to breed their Children.'[4]

Locke and Children

Why should married people approach a bachelor for advice on raising and educating their children? While there are a number of references to infants and children in his *Essay* (which form the basis for a preliminary genetic psychology), and some discussion of parents and children in *Two Treatises*, nothing Locke published before 1693 suggests that he was especially knowledgeable about children or their breeding and education. The question, what led parents to seek Locke's advice in these areas, has been raised in the past. The Revd Evan Daniel, in the detailed Introduction and Notes to his popular 1880 edition of *Some Thoughts*, cites Hallam's remark about Locke's *Some Thoughts* and Rousseau's *Émile*: 'If they have both the same defect, that their authors wanted sufficient observation of children, it

[1] Letter of Molyneux to Locke, no. 1609, 2 Mar. 1693, in *Correspondence*, ed. E. S. de Beer, iv. 649.   [2] No. 1748, 2 June 1694 (v. 70–1).
[3] Nos. 1896, 7 May 1697, and 1936, 24 Aug. 1695 (v. 363, 428–9).
[4] The word 'breed' and 'breeding', a word often used in other writings at that time, carries the sense of 'rearing', as well as 'teaching' or 'instructing'.

is certain that the caution and sound judgment of Locke has rescued him better from error.'[1] Mr Daniel makes no comment on this opinion, apparently concurring with it. But sound judgement hardly seems a sufficient basis for the breeding of children, at least, not sound judgement isolated from close contact with an understanding of children, their natures, their motives, their desires. The detailed description of children's behaviour found in Locke's *Some Thoughts* suggests more than a passing acquaintance with children. The fact is that Locke was apparently fascinated with children and liked by them. His correspondence is filled with many references to the children of his friends.

Mrs Anne Grigg writes in 1676 to Locke about her son, Honest Will, remarking that he 'is at Bristoll [i.e. at home] where he prospers mightyly', indicating that she intends 'to leave him there till he be fit to busle with the hardships of a bording scoole'. Will often mentions Locke 'as his friend'.[2] Another friend, Dr David Thomas, adds a note at the end of a letter in 1677, saying that 'your godson [their son John] is well'.[3] Dr Denis Grenville tells Locke that his sister 'could never forget your extraordinary kindnesse to her selfe, and troublesome child last winter'.[4] This child, 'Our little Demoiselle', sends Locke her thanks for the favours he has done her, though the father is sceptical about her sincerity. In a letter in 1680, Sir Anthony Ashley Cooper thanks Locke 'for your care about my Grandchild', the future third Earl, who was then nine years old.[5] James Tyrrell thanks Locke for 'the little grammer for Jemmy, and the instructions you give me about his learneing';[6] the child was then six years old. Still another friend, Thomas Stringer, tells Locke that 'my little boy [then five years] says he is much at your Commands'.[7]

These samples from Locke's correspondence are reinforced by *Some Thoughts*, which contains many references to occasions when Locke has observed specific behaviour by children, and parents' attitudes towards them. Section 18 relates one occasion when Locke

---

[1] Quoted from Hallam's *Literary History*, iv. 183, by the Revd Evan Daniel, in his edition of *Some Thoughts* (London, 1880), p. 10. Daniel has a long introduction and extensive notes.

[2] No. 319, 13 Sept. 1676 (i. 460). Mrs Grigg discusses details of her son's education in other letters, e.g. no. 689 (ii. 491–2). For an account of the family, see *Corr.* i. 334 n. 2.

[3] No. 345, 21 July 1677 (i. 500). The child was between one and two years old.

[4] No. 357, 19 Nov. 1677 NS (i. 522).

[5] No. 532, 20 Mar. 1680 (ii. 160).

[6] No. 554, 9 July 1680 (ii. 211).

[7] No. 631, 12 Mar. 1681 (ii. 390).

'lived in an House, where, to appease a froward Child, they gave him *Drink* as often as he cried; so that he was constantly bibbing: And tho' he could not speak, yet he drunk more in Twenty four Hours than I did.' This could have been a reference to Locke's experiences in Benjamin Furly's house in Amsterdam, where Locke lived for two years (1687–9) during the period when some of his letters to Clarke were being written. The Furlys had five children, the youngest of whom, Arent, became especially attached to Locke. Arent was only two at that time.[1] Living with families permitted Locke to observe children in their natural setting. In another passage in *Some Thoughts* he remarks on a 'great Mistake I have observed in People's breeding their Children ... That the Mind has not been made obedient to Discipline, and pliant to Reason', a favourite topic with Locke (§ 34). In still another passage, he says: 'I have seen Children at a Table, who, whatever was there, never asked for any thing, but contentedly took what was given them: And at another Place I have seen others cry for every Thing they saw, must be served out of every Dish, and that first too' (§ 39). Again, 'A prudent and kind Mother, of my Acquaintance' is the occasion for a description of the way that mother coped with stubbornness, by whipping—not Locke's preferred way of disciplining children but on some occasions a necessity (§ 78). Under the topic of 'the self-will and love of dominion of children' Locke remarks, with the clear ring of one closely acquainted with children, 'We see Children (as soon almost as they are born, I am sure long before they can speak) cry, grow peevish, sullen, and out of humour, for nothing but to have their *Wills*' (§ 104). He goes on to remark on their love of dominion and their self-will:

He, that has not observed these two Humours working very betimes in Children, has taken little notice of their Actions: And he, who thinks that these two Roots of almost all the Injustice and Contention, that so disturb humane Life, are not early to be weeded out, and contrary Habits introduced, neglects the proper Season to lay the Foundations of a good and worthy Man. (§ 105.)

[1] For an account of Locke's stay in the Furly household, see Cranston's biography, p. 280. Cf. also M. G. Mason, 'John Locke's Experience of Education and Its Bearing on His Educational Thought', *Journal of Educational Administration and History* (University of Leeds), 3, no. 2 (June 1971), 1–8. When Locke returned to England, he lived in the Masham household, where he was closely involved with the rearing of Lady Masham's son Francis. Earlier, when Locke worked for Shaftesbury, he was in charge of Shaftesbury's son's education. During a two-year period while he travelled in France, Locke was tutor to the son of Sir John Banks. So the evidence is strong for Locke's continual involvement with children and young people, always with an eye, it would seem, upon breeding.

We hear in this last comment a basic theme with Locke: childhood as the basis for forming the man. Another observation of children he has known enables Locke to give a graphic account of the crying and screaming of children, to distinguishing two kinds of crying: 'either *stubborn* and *domineering*, or *querulous* and *whining*' (§ 111; cf. §§ 112–14). Only someone often exposed to such behaviour as is described in these sections could have given such an analysis of that behaviour. Similarly, having as he says, 'frequently observed in Children, that when they have got possession of any poor Creature, they are apt to use it ill', Locke gives a convincing account of their treatment of animals and their motives which lead to such cruelty, which Locke strongly deplored (§ 116). He also noted and disapproved the attitudes expressed by children towards servants: 'It is not unusual to observe the Children in Gentlemens Families, treat the Servants of the House with domineering Words, Names of Contempt, and an imperious Carriage; as if they were of another Race, and Species beneath them' (§ 117).

Earlier Treatises on Education

It is the wealth of detail on these and many other topics relating to the growing up of children in families that attests to Locke's first-hand observations of the children of his friends. This attention to specific behaviour distinguishes Locke's treatise on education from most others at that time. But in writing about the education of children, especially of the children of gentlemen's families, Locke did not invent a new subject-matter. There were many treatises, from as early as the sixteenth century, which addressed themselves to that topic. A number of the themes found in *Some Thoughts* is present in these earlier treatises.

One of the earliest such treatises, one cited often in the histories of education, is Thomas Elyot's *The Boke Named the Gouvernor* (1531), written for children of gentlemen who were going to govern politically, and have authority over the public weal. Some of the topics discussed were choosing a tutor or master, the rearing of the child, specific subjects to be taught and their order. One topic of great importance for Locke is found here: the virtues a gentleman should have, such as justice, fortitude, patience. Roger Ascham's *The Scholemaster* (1570) was primarily directed towards teaching Latin (also a concern of Locke's), but its subtitle spoke of the 'private bringing up of youth in gentlemens and Noblemens houses'. Ascham's preface raises questions about discipline and punishment of children, another topic on which Locke held firm views. Ascham says that some people believe too much beating can cause the child to hate learning. The whole of the first part of Ascham's work is concerned with ways to encourage the child while learning Latin in particular, but generalized to all learning. Ascham shows a genuine concern for the child, an attitude which Locke shares.

The Compleat Gentleman (1622) by Henry Peacham is another example of a book of advice for gentlemen. Specific chapters deal with the duty of parents to their children's education. Learning is, Peacham says, an essential part of nobility; it enables princes to govern better. Recognizing that children differ, that they have a variety of different natures (a point stressed by Locke), he urges the tutor to accept the fact that 'one and the selfesame Method agreeth not with all alike' (p. 22). He also speaks against cruel and harsh treatment of the pupil: '*Correction without instruction is plaine tyrannie*' (p. 23). There 'ought to bee a reciprocale and a mutuall affection betwixt the Master and Scholler' (p. 24). He criticizes the master as well as parents who lack this sympathetic attitude towards learning. Praise is given for the methods used in the Low Countries, where interspersed with formal instruction are informal walks and talk.

A more important work for its extensive treatment of themes to be found in Locke's *Some Thoughts*, especially for the stress placed on moral education, is Jean Gailhard's *The Compleat Gentleman* (1678). The difference in the 'tempers' of children (a term to be used by Locke too) is given prominence by Gailhard. The rules given in this work will, he says, 'afford variety of things for several sorts of persons'. He tends to find the different tempers falling along class lines: 'men of superior orb' are contrasted with 'the multitude', or a 'countryman' with a 'gentleman'.[1] We all have a role or a part to play: 'For my part I look upon this world as a stage, and I value men only according as they act their part in it' ('To the Reader'). While birth, place, and authority ought to be respected, 'Vertue alone makes men be esteemed'. Gailhard believes that most men are 'usually affected to evil', only a few have good 'Inclinations, and do good Actions'. The stress on virtue becomes very strong with Locke. Another theme often found in these works on education, and again with Locke, is the importance of

[1] Cf. *Some Thoughts*, § 217: 'Besides that, I think a Prince, a Nobleman, and an ordinary Gentleman's Son, should have different ways of Breeding.'

education for society. The main part of Gailhard's study opens on that theme: 'To have Youth well brought up, is so necessary to Humane Society, that all Nations ought to make it one of their chief cares' (p. 1). Education is said to be a 'second nature', it makes a difference between men; it can also reform 'what is amiss in nature' (p. 3). Within the family, children's tempers can be influenced: 'Let Nature be what it will it may be changed by Education.' Breeding should begin as soon as the child is born. But a warning, also found in Locke, is issued against the bad influences of nurses and servants on the infant and child: preferably, the mother rather than a wet nurse should suckle the infant as a way of bypassing the potentially bad effects of a nurse. Gailhard recommends a healthy, jovial, and virtuous woman for a nurse, remarking on the habits of some nurses to frighten children with stories, causing the child to fear the dark. Locke makes much of these habits in the *Essay*. It must have been a common practice of nurses and servants, or at least a common complaint of parents.

Gailhard recommends that the child should first learn piety, then morality, and later acquire erudition (pp. 11–16). The character of the tutor is also important, as Locke was to stress in many sections of *Some Thoughts*. Learning, Gailhard believes, should be made interesting and appealing, not forced upon the child. He speaks against the master who frightens his pupils with too much severity. The advantages of learning are several. It 'instructs ones understanding, because it teaches us to know things by their causes, effects, definitions, descriptions and attributes' (p. 27). It instructs the will and enables us to act on an informed basis with sound judgement. It also helps us to master the passions. 'Men who are acted by sensual principles, aim at the satisfaction of their senses; but they who have learned and felt the corruption of these, will fence against, and bridle them' (p. 29). Control of our passions and desires is again a central concern for Locke.

Gailhard devotes some attention to such different subjects as logic, natural philosophy, ethics, and history, but these remarks stay rather general, as do also his comments on breeding the young child. In these ways, his study differs from Locke's. The similarities lie with the tone and sentiments towards children. These same similarities are present also in the popular work by Obadiah Walker, *Of Education, Especially of Young Gentlemen* (1673). Identifying three main prerequisites for learning as (1) 'naturall ability, power or capacity', (2) 'Art, or instruction', and (3) 'Exercise and practice' (p. 1), Walker perhaps over-formalizes his summary statement: 'The Educator prescribeth his *end*; gives him *rules* and *precepts*, presents him *examples* and *patterns*; and then *sets him to act* according to what was before taught him' (p. 9). Walker also writes 'Of the Duty of Parents in Educating their Children', remarking that some parents neglect or even refuse to give training and education to their children (p. 13). Like Gailhard, Walker warns against nurses, 'the foolish, vaine, or evil conversation of those about them' (p. 18). The effects of such an influence are long-lasting, they 'leave such impressions even upon their *Infancy*, as are difficultly defaced' (p. 18). He quotes Quintilian's warning, not to put the infant out to 'an hired Nurse'.

Recognizing different dispositions in children, Walker observes that not all dispositions are good, but even the worst can be reformed by the educator (p. 22). Close supervision by parents is urged, even when they use a tutor or nurse. Parents are also urged to guide their children 'as much as is possible, with *kindnes* and *affection*, endeavouring to convince and *perswade* them' (p. 24). Like Locke, Walker devotes a chapter to the educator, urging him to watch the disposition of the child and 'to know what it will produce' (p. 26). The educator should be gentle and persuasive in correcting the child, to improve 'his natural parts as much as he shall be able' (p. 34).

Walker gives great importance to laying 'the foundation of Religion and virtue' and, like Locke again, gives close attention to 'diverse passions, inclinations and dispositions' and the 'wayes to rectify and order them'. He speaks of anatomizing the soul (p. 71),[1] distinguishing two powers in it, a 'cognoscitive' power for knowledge and a motive power for action. Anticipating Locke in another way, Walker suggests that we can best discover the inclinations of children by watching them at play (p. 77). There is an extended analysis of a long list of passions and inclinations, with ways to control them.

There were other treatises which dealt with some of these same themes in a more minor way, treatises having a 'how to' quality: how to be a courtier, a councillor, a soldier, or even, as in Stephen Penton's *The Guardian's Instruction; Or, The Gentleman's Romance* (1688), on how to be a gentleman. Penton's book contains a section on 'General Directions for the better Education of a Child of Great Quality': parents are urged to get 'a grave, experienc'd, well-temper'd Person to manage him', and there is the usual talk of virtue. But his work is more superficial than those discussed above. The tone, however, is the

[1] This is an interesting medical analogy which reappears in Hume and Pope.

same: encourage the child rather than punish or frighten him. Some of the other 'how to' manuals pay more attention to the outward appearance of virtue rather than with being virtuous, the latter being the stress in the more serious tracts.

Locke's Place in This Tradition

Locke's *Some Thoughts* fits into this well-established tradition of advice to parents and tutors, as well as advice for the young men who were to be pupils. Just who the reading public was for these tracts on education, we do not know; but since some of them were often reprinted (Locke's went through four editions during his life), they were certainly bought and presumably read. Perhaps they became part of the home libraries, in much the way that in our day books on the care and rearing of children are found in our homes. Some of these tracts fall into the category of 'inspirational' literature, in the language used to urge parents to provide good breeding for their children, and especially in the encomia on the importance of education for the nation. There is this quality to Locke's *Some Thoughts* too: 'The well Educating of their Children is so much the Duty and Concern of Parents, and the Welfare and Prosperity of the Nation so much depends on it' ('Epistle Dedicatory'). But Locke's work falls much closer to the 'how to' manuals. The difference between these and Locke's lies in the seriousness with which Locke pursues his subject and in the details of his instructions on how to train the child in virtue, how to get him to love learning, how to correct his faults (in learning *and* in manners), how to select a good tutor. In all these areas, Locke goes in detail beyond anything to be found in these earlier writings.

These British writings on breeding and training children provide the specific background for Locke's *Some Thoughts*. Before he published his thoughts on education, all his friends had to go on, if they sought advice on how to raise their children (usually their sons), was the group of books discussed above. There is one other author, not British, who is usually cited as an influential predecessor of Locke on education, Montaigne. Coste noted many particular similarities between *Some Thoughts* and Montaigne's *Essais*, drawing up a list for the third edition of his French translation of parallel passages. The scattered essays of Montaigne are not systematized into a book on education, but they do view children in much the same way as do Locke and the British writers before him. The same subjects and themes are found: father–son relation, selection of a tutor, relations between tutor and pupil, teaching and learning Latin, what food to give the child, recommendations for cold water as a way of developing physical hardiness, and for encouraging some of the same virtues (civility, love, respect).

Confronted with these extensive similarities, similarities not only of theme and subject but of the language used to discuss them, Nina Reicyn draws the conclusion that Locke consciously borrowed from Montaigne. She goes so far as to conclude that the long list of quasi-identical passages in *Some Thoughts* and the *Essai* clearly indicates that 'il n'est pas douteux que Locke doive toute sa prétendue originalité aux *Essais*.'[1] Locke owned copies of the 1669 French edition of Montaigne and of the 1603 English translation by Florio. The similarities of language cited by Reicyn are certainly striking. She stops just short of charging Locke with plagiarism, following in the end Villey's more conservative analysis.

Il est probable que quand il a abrodé son élève, il s'était assimilé la méthode de MONTAIGNE; il en avait l'esprit rempli; ses réflexions et ses tentatives ont été commandées par ses souvenirs de l'*Essai de l'Institution.* Il a été ainsi amené, très probablement d'ailleurs sans en avoir une pleine conscience, à en éprouver la valeur pratique, à les vérifier, expérimentalement, si l'on peut dire. Puis, comme il en avait oublié l'origine véritable, comme il en avait pris possession par ses observations personnelles, il a exprimé à sa manière, ses mêmes idées, et d'une manière toute différente de MONTAIGNE, dans un ordre tout autre. . . .[2]

Villey's analysis needs to be viewed in the context of the British authors discussed above, for those books remind us of the British tradition out of which Locke's thought also grew. While Locke's library did not contain all these British writings on education, it did have sufficient numbers to indicate his general knowledge of that literature.[3] As with his other books, so with *Some Thoughts*, Locke read widely, absorbed tradition, but moulded and extended the ideas, the doctrines, and even the language found in his predecessors. What is unique with Locke is the sense we get of an intimate first-hand

---

[1] *Pédagogie*, p. 136.

[2] Ibid., p. 171, from P. Villey, *L'Influence de Montaigne sur les idées pédagogiques de Locke et de Rousseau* (Paris, 1911), pp. 97–9.

[3] For a discussion of other writers in this tradition, the tradition of 'courtly educational theory', and for the case that Locke's work belongs to this tradition, see R. C. Stephens, 'John Locke and the Education of the Gentleman', *University of Leeds Institute of Education Research Studies*, 14 (1956), 67–75. Stephens points out that many of the similarities between Locke and Montaigne stem from this courtly tradition.

knowledge of children. It would be rash to deny that his account of their motives, of their interests, of what will motivate them and shape them in the ways of virtue was influenced by Locke's own views of human nature. Nevertheless, the wealth of observations and recommendations found in *Some Thoughts*, as well as the biographical facts of his acquaintance with and study of children, support the impression of a close understanding of children.

Metaphysical Particulars and Civil Persons

There is one concept fundamental to Locke's general thought which is found in the *Essay* and in *Some Thoughts*: the concept of particulars. Locke accepted the principle that 'all that exists is particular'. What this expression means within his general system was that there are no natural classes. He did not mean there are no similarities between objects; it was the observable qualities which provide the bases for forming classifications of use. Classes are, on this account of reality, man-made. Locke's commitment to particularity has many forms, including the disavowal of talk of a common human nature shared by all men. There is no property or characteristic that I have which is *essential* to me, or more strictly, the *Essay* says, all my characteristics are equally essential: essential for me as an individual, the particular being that began to exist at a specific time, that has had the experiences I have had, that is shaped and formed as I am. Locke does not take this particularist view of man to the extreme of saying (as Leibniz did later) that the loss or alteration of any single feature would result in a different particular individual: the time and place of the beginning of my existence fixes my identity as *this* man. Along with the individuating beginning of existence there also goes a functioning biological and physiological mechanism. So long as the same continuous life unites the parts of this mechanism together, I am the same man.

The centrality given by Locke to particulars in his metaphysical system is reflected in his account of persons and in his work on education. Each child is to be dealt with individually; children have particular traits, biases, humours, tempers, a bent and tendency of their minds. Locke urged the tutor and the parents to pay careful attention to these natural dispositions, for they must be reckoned with in rearing children. Some can be altered to some extent, others can perhaps be replaced, but by and large the tutor must work around them. Thus a child may be gay, pensive, modest, timorous, confident, obstinate, or curious. It is not clear whether Locke considered these qualities to be born with the child, but that is how he tends to talk about them. Just as we have certain faculties which can be used later, so we have certain traits which will be manifested in behaviour. They are not especially good or bad, although some of them pose more of a problem than others for the objective of moral education.

Despite the stress upon particularity, Locke's notion of man did contain some common elements. Each of us has a set of psychological or mental faculties (reason, understanding, sensation, memory), and every human being has certain desires and aversions: the desire for pleasure and the aversion to pain are explicitly described as innate practical principles. Locke does not pay much attention to desires and emotions, save to urge their control by reason. Present desires may close future options, the desire for immediate pleasure may stand in the way of future (and especially of eternal) happiness. Reason was for Locke the preferred faculty, rationality the urgent goal. Rationality and morality were closely linked, in part because he viewed reason as natural revelation and revelation as 'natural *Reason* enlarged by a new set of Discoveries communicated by GOD immediately' (*Essay*, 4. 19. 4). What is important about natural revelation (other writers used the phrase 'light of reason' or 'of nature') is that it can (so Locke hoped) reveal God's moral laws, the laws of nature or of reason. The faculty of reason does not, however, play its role of natural revelation unaided and untrained. Education helps to shape the psychological and motivational structure of the child, enabling him to attain rational control of his life.

Locke's *Essay* contains a developmental psychology, the infant is traced from its first experiences of warmth in the womb to its first post-natal sensations, and to its first ideas and truths. The adult of the *Essay* is the scientific observer, careful and precise in recording experiences and uniformities, Locke's objective being to systematize experience so as to understand and control his environment. Locke sketches for us the dangers and pitfalls of careless attention to objects and events, and to imprecise and confused use of language. We are urged to be as careful in our use of language as we are in our scientific endeavours. Control of language and experience is the goal. The acquisition of ideas and knowledge of ourselves and our world is traced from infancy to adulthood. The child begins without any information of self or world, but possessed of the necessary faculties and tendencies to learn about the world and to form a responsible self.

Locke's political work, *Two Treatises of Government*, contains a move parallel to the child's transition from innocence to knowledge or from man to person, the move from pre-civil to civil society. There are in that work two components in this social maturation: one from the state where there is no private property, no 'private dominion' over land and what it produces or the beasts it feeds to ownership of land and possessions, the other from the state of nature or the community of mankind to the civil society. This latter component is especially important for an understanding of Locke's views on education. His objective in *Two Treatises* was in part to explain political power, its nature, jurisdiction, and origin. For an understanding of its origin we must, Locke says,

consider what State all Men are naturally in, and that is, a *State of perfect Freedom* to order their Actions, and dispose of their Possessions, and Persons as they think fit, within the bounds of the Law of Nature, without asking leave, or depending upon the Will of any other Man.[1]

Almost every phrase in this passage is important for the context of education: the notions of (*a*) ordering our actions, (*b*) disposing of our possessions and persons, (*c*) the law of nature, and (*d*) freedom from the will of others.

The skill and knowledge needed to order our actions in accordance with the law of nature, to treat our possessions and persons responsibly, and to avoid coming under the absolute control of others (a particularly frightening state for Locke in its threat to personal freedom) are major objectives for education. The particularity of Locke's metaphysics is echoed in his strong emphasis upon individual liberty in his political philosophy, but liberty for him is always correlative with law and order, the law and order of God's laws, of God's will. The state of liberty is not '*a State of Licence*', and the state of nature 'has a Law of Nature to govern it, which obliges every one' (TII: 6). The child born into this world has all the equipment and potential to become a member of the community of mankind. Membership in that community must, however, be earned. Training for membership is conducted by the family; the rearing of children is guided by that objective. The consequence of failing to meet the standards of that community are a slide down the chain of being to the ranks of the beasts.

There are some stark passages in Locke's discussions of the failure

---

[1] *Two Treatises of Government*, ed. P. Laslett (Cambridge, 1960), TII: 4.

to conform to the norm of humanity, that norm being conformity to the law or laws of nature. The exact content of the law of nature is not always specified by Locke, but it clearly contains most of the Christian moral values and injunctions, as to honour one's parents, help those in need, recognize God and ourselves as his workmanship. To transgress the law of nature is, Locke declares, to 'live by another Rule, than that of *reason* and common Equity, which is the measure God has set to the actions of Men, for their mutual security' (TII: 8). To do so makes such a man dangerous to mankind, 'a trespass against the whole Species', it turns him into, and he can be treated as, a wild savage beast. Such a transgressor of the law of nature can 'be destroyed as a *Lyon* or a *Tyger*' (TII: 11). So fragile is the boundary between man and beast, when that boundary is not secured by meticulous attention to moral education, the education which will prepare us for entry into the community of mankind, that Locke even says we have a right to kill a thief, since stealing my purse may only be a step towards the attempt at absolute dominion over me.

The value of civil society lies in the greater security and order provided by explicit laws, as well as the understanding and consent of its members. The state of nature is not a disorderly state, is not, as it was depicted by Hobbes, a war of all against all. The state of nature, whatever its status (whether real, imaginary, or conceptual), cannot quite be compared with the state of infancy, but there are some instructive parallels. Civil laws in the political society, based as they are on the laws of nature, provide a more secure environment for the acquisition of private property and the development of moral persons. The use of the term 'person' in the passage cited from *Two Treatises* about the state of nature had for Locke a special importance. He was careful to distinguish in his *Essay* between man and person. In discussing the nature of identity, person-identity (the identity of persons) is distinguished from the identity of man. The latter is the sameness of life in a biological organism, but identity of a person is an identity acquired through awareness of one's actions and thoughts, through a concern one takes in one's life, in one's rationality and morality. The term 'person' is, says Locke,

a Forensick Term appropriating Actions and their Merit; and so belongs only to intelligent Agents capable of a Law, and Happiness and Misery. This personality extends it *self* beyond present Existence to what is past, only by consciousness, whereby it becomes concerned and accountable, owns and imputes to it *self* past Actions, just upon the same ground, and for the same reason, that it does the present.[1]

Not only do we own (or 'own up to') our actions, if we are to be morally responsible; we also own and have property in our person: 'Though the Earth, and all inferior Creatures be common to all Men, yet every Man has a *Property* in his own *Person*' (TII: 27). Since the protection of private property is one of the main functions of civil society, the protection of the person, of the morally responsible person, comes under that function as well.

If civil society has the task of *protecting* the person, education has the task of *producing* persons. As with Aristotle, so with Locke, education and politics go closely together. One of the ways these are linked is revealed in the account of property given in *Two Treatises*, an account founded on the premise that we all have property in our persons. Education takes place within the family; it consists primarily in turning children into persons, into persons who embody natural laws and the rationality on which civil society and civil laws (as well as the community of mankind) are based. How is this transformation accomplished?

Moral Education: Motivating and Producing Persons

It would be only a slight exaggeration to say that Locke's *Some Thoughts* is mainly a treatise on moral education. Virtue is the health of the soul, the aim of education is to produce a healthy, virtuous person. While Locke writes about educating the son of a gentleman, his treatise is less about gentlemen than it is about developing a moral character. Morality was not limited to gentlemen, although there is greater importance for such persons to be virtuous. The connection between virtue and being a gentleman was clear for him: if those in 'the Gentleman's Calling' are 'by their Education once set right', that is, are 'vertuous, useful, and able Men', then they will 'quickly bring all the rest into Order' ('Epistle Dedicatory'). Locke's concept of man and his views about right conduct are most strongly revealed in this work. *Some Thoughts* is in effect a manual on how to guide the child to virtue. Close to half of its total sections are concerned with this topic.

The notion of *moral man* was an important one in the *Essay*, linked as it was with Locke's novel account of 'person' as a forensic term, in

---

[1] *Essay*, 2. 27. 26.

other words as a term for identifying the locus of responsibility. The morality assumed in the *Essay*, and clearly cited in several places, was that of natural law, God's laws. Those laws also play a role in *Two Treatises*. One can build up some of the specific content of those laws, of that morality, from what Locke says in those works (and also, of course, from what he says in the *Reasonableness of Christianity* and his *Paraphrases of the Epistles of St. Paul*; cf. the early unpublished *Essays on the Law of Nature*), but it is his *Some Thoughts* which gives us the most particular and detailed account of Locke's concept of morality and of a virtuous person. There is no other work in the seventeenth century that gives such a detailed account of moral man, and of how to develop that man into a responsible person. Locke works with the metaphor of children as 'Travellers newly arrived in a strange Country, of which they know nothing' (§ 120). Like strangers in any country, these new arrivals must learn the customs and habits of the country. In time, they will become citizens. Another revealing metaphor is found in Locke's advice on how to waken a sleeping child:

great Care should be taken in waking them, that it be not done hastily, nor with a loud or shrill Voice, or any other suddain violent Noise. This often affrights Children, and does them great harm. And sound *Sleep* thus broke off, with suddain Alarms, is apt enough to discompose any one. When Children are to be waken'd out of their *Sleep*, be sure to begin with a low Call, and some gentle Motion, and so draw them out of it by degrees, and give them none but kind words, and usage, till they are come perfectly to themselves, and being quite Dressed, you are sure they are throughly awake.   (§ 21.)

Helping the child move from being an individual, a man, to being a person requires the same kind of care and skill specified in this passage for waking him. The objective of a tutor is

to fashion the Carriage, and form the Mind; to settle in his Pupil good Habits, and the Principles of Virtue and Wisdom; to give him by little and little a view of Mankind; and work him into a love and imitation of what is Excellent and Praise-worthy; and in the Prosecution of it to give him Vigour, Activity, and Industry.   (§ 94.)

Love of virtue must be instilled in the child. Outward behaviour is insufficient, acting in accordance with virtue is only a start: 'he that is a good, a vertuous and able Man, must be made so within' (§ 42). Locke is very clear about the role of education in that process.

And therefore, what he is to receive from Education, what is to sway and influence his Life, must be something put into him betimes; Habits woven into the very Principles of his Nature; and not a counterfeit Carriage, and dissembled Out-side, put on by Fear, only to avoid the present Anger of a Father, who perhaps may dis-inherit him.   (Ibid.)

The child enters both a family and a nation (as well as what Locke calls in *Two Treatises* the community of mankind), the family's duty being slowly to awaken the child to virtue. Each of these communities should be guided by moral laws, laws derived from the laws of nature which are God's laws. Some of these are cited in *Two Treatises*, a few in the *Essay*, but Locke nowhere gives any systematic list of them. He is emphatic, though, that the true touchstone and standard for morality is God's laws (*Essay*, 2. 28. 8). A basic principle for civil society (for government) is that it must be consistent with natural law. What is the content of that law? If there is no list of moral rules, and no firm set of natural laws, how are we to know what we ought to do? How are we to identify moral actions? There are sufficient examples of rules or laws labelled 'natural law', 'laws of nature', 'law of reason', or 'God's laws' (which are all the same thing) to indicate that the content of that law speaks of more than self-preservation. The examples turn out to be rather familiar moral rules from the Christian and even classical traditions. It was symptomatic of Locke's partiality to reason and rationality that he suggested in his *Essay* that a demonstrative morality was possible,[1] but it was also indicative of his belief in the limitations of human reason that in the end he tells us to look to revelation in the Bible for our moral rules. It is even more typical that Locke insists that, just as one cannot learn a language by first learning the rules, so we become moral, as Aristotle said, through custom and habit.

The aim of education is identified as 'Vertue . . . direct Vertue', the 'hard and valuable part', harder to be acquired than 'a Knowledge of the World' (§ 70). To set the mind of the child right is to set it through training to be 'disposed to consent to nothing, but what may be suitable to the Dignity and Excellency of a rational Creature' (§ 31). Locke does not overlook the non-rational side of human nature, for it is most important for the tutor to be able to work with the emotions and desires of children. The non-rational side of children is part of human nature.

We must look upon our Children, when grown up, to be like our selves; with the same Passions, the same Desires. We would be thought Rational Creatures,

---

[1] Sometimes the demonstrative morality suggestion is taken to be a claim for a deductive derivation of moral rules. The more likely meaning is simply the demonstration of conceptual connections between moral ideas.

and have our Freedom; we love not to be uneasie, under constant Rebukes and Brow-beatings; nor can we bear severe Humours, and great Distance in those we converse with. (§ 41.)

Passions and desires, however, are defects, or at least forces which must be controlled, though they can be used and manipulated in moral education. Perhaps Locke wished we did not have passions and desires, but since we do, and since this is God's world and we are his workmanship, they have a purpose: 'the great Principle and Foundation of all Vertue and Worth, is placed in this, That a Man is able to *deny himself* his own Desires, cross his own Inclinations, and purely follow what Reason directs as best, tho' the appetite lean the other way' (§ 33). He did not rule out the possibility that reason might authorize the satisfaction of some desires, but 'the Principle of all Vertue and Excellency lies in a power of denying our selves the satisfaction of our own Desires' (§ 38). The importance for Locke of this principle is indicated by his repetition:

He that has not a Mastery over his Inclinations, he that knows not how to *resist* the importunity of *present Pleasure or Pain*, for the sake of what Reason tells him is fit to be done, wants the true Principle of Vertue and Industry; and is in danger never to be good for any thing. (§ 45; cf. §§ 52, 200.)

The time to begin mastering our desires is infancy: 'Children should be used to submit their Desires, and go without their Longings, even *from their very Cradles*' (§ 38). Locke admits that the denial of desires is 'contrary to unguided Nature' (§ 45), but the tutor and the parents should guide the child in learning how to modify his basic nature so that reason will take control. Reason and morality are closely connected. One positive result of denying children's appetites is to teach them modesty (§ 107), but it is clear that the greater virtue lies in acquiring mastery over our desires: that is a first step towards becoming virtuous. Reason is not and should never be, as Hume was to call it, the slave of the passions. Morality for Locke lies in reversing this relation.

At the same time, Locke recognized the power of desires, they have a power which can be turned to good, in motivating us to action. Our unguided nature will not help us pursue virtue: 'I grant, that Good and Evil, *Reward* and *Punishment*, are the only Motives to a rational Creature; these are the Spur and Reins, whereby all Mankind are set on work, and guided, and therefore they are to be made use of to Children too' (§ 54). But we must choose motivating desires carefully, using those that work on the intellect, not the body. Children 'are to be treated as rational creatures'. Not rewards such as sweets and punishments or threats and bodily blows, but *esteem* and *disgrace*, these are 'the most powerful incentives to the Mind' (§ 56). Children are to be shamed out of their faults (§§ 58, 60, 78). While Locke is very clear that the true principle and measure of virtue is 'the Knowledge of a Man's Duty, and the Satisfaction it is to obey his Maker, in following the Dictates of that Light God has given him', he sees reputation, the reputation the child has in the eyes of parents and tutor, as a help to virtue because it is 'the Testimony and Applause that other People's Reason, as it were by common Consent, gives to vertuous and well-ordered Actions' (§ 61).

Some Thoughts is filled with very specific suggestions for bringing the child's behaviour and character into harmony with what reason, the reason of adults, approves. A very ingenious method for moral education is suggested in an earlier section, the use of case studies: 'Especially in Morality, Prudence, and Breeding, Cases should be Put to him, and his Judgment asked' (§ 98). The tutor and the parents will also set the example by their behaviour and by the way they treat the child. Locke also gives illustrations of ordinary situations, and of others designed by the tutor, which show how dealing with the child in the way Locke recommends will, over time, produce some particular virtue. How many of these situations Locke depicted were witnessed by him, or whether he actually was able to apply, or to get parents to try, the methods he recommends, we do not know. That his account of child behaviour was in many cases based on first-hand observation has been indicated above. It is clear that Locke's own notion of morality and gentlemanly virtues is put to work in his examples. That morality was the common one accepted by most of Locke's acquaintances, based on Christian notions, with a strong conviction in the good of self-denial. A quick search through the sections of *Some Thoughts* will confirm this fact.

Praiseworthy Traits	*Negative Traits*
civility § 145	captiousness § 143
feeling of humanity § 117	censoriousness § 143
generosity § 110	clownish shamefacedness § 142
gracefulness of voice and gestures	contempt § 143
§ 143	craving § 39
honour § 56	cruelty § 116

Praiseworthy Traits	*Negative Traits*
humility § 145	domineering § 103
industry §§ 70, 94	hasty judgement § 122
kindness § 139	hypocrisy § 50
love of God § 136	indolence § 123
love of study § 128	lies §§ 131, 133
modesty § 70	malice § 100
politeness § 117	negligence § 141
prudence § 91	rashness § 115
reverence § 44	sheepish bashfulness § 141
self-control § 48	stubbornness §§ 111, 112
self-denial § 45	timidity § 115
self-restraint §§ 38, 39	

Moral Man

The list of virtues culled from *Some Thoughts* is very traditional. Few of Locke's readers would have rejected any on this list. Where some disagreement might have entered was about two questions: (1) were any of these virtues innate; (2) was man by nature inclined towards virtue rather than towards vice? To the first question, Locke had given a comprehensive 'no', but in returning that answer he was careful to specify just what was being denied.

I deny not, that there are natural tendencies imprinted on the Minds of Men; and that, from the very first instances of Sense and Perception, there are some things, that are grateful, and others unwelcome to them; some things that they incline to, and others that they fly: But this makes nothing for innate Characters on the Mind, which are to be the Principles of Knowledge, regulating our Practice. (*Essay*, 1. 3. 3.)

Nature, not custom, 'has put into Man a desire of Happiness, and an aversion to Misery'. These desires 'do continue constantly to operate and influence all our Actions, without ceasing'. The role of custom and habit in the breeding of children is to use those desires as motives, as well as to free the faculty of reason from the control of those desires. Thus, Locke's answer to the second question is also 'no': a tendency or inclination towards happiness but not towards virtue.

Professor John Passmore has called attention to a clear confirmation of this second negative answer in one of Locke's marginal comments in his copy of one of Burnet's pamphlets.

Men have a natural tendency to what delights and from what pains them. This universal observation has been established past doubt. But that the soul has such a tendency to what is morally good and from evil has not fallen under my observation, and therefore I cannot grant it.[1]

This denial of a natural tendency towards moral goodness and away from evil allows for two interpretations. Passmore concludes that Locke rejected the doctrine of original sin. He sees this rejection as one of the more important features of *Some Thoughts*. A study by Dr William Spellman has shown, however, that Locke did accept a version of original sin.[2] It was because he believed man is always close to evil that Locke stressed the importance of training for virtue. Just how much malleability Locke thought there was in human nature is not always clear from his religious writings, but he placed his hopes in proper and effective education. Burnet and other writers thought they discerned in the *Essay* a commitment to an amoral, if not hedonistic, human nature; they preferred to believe in innate moral principles as a hedge against evil.

Whether we read Locke's rejection of a natural tendency towards virtue as Passmore does (the child is neither virtuous nor evil by nature) or as Spellman does (sin threatens to negate our efforts to mould the child), it is clear that Locke's concept of human nature was firmly planted in the midst of his acceptance of a traditional doctrine of natural law and right, of laws and rights stemming from God. More than once in his writings, natural inclinations are linked with rights. In *Two Treatises*, self-preservation is both an inclination we all have and a right. *Some Thoughts* links love and duty: 'They love their little ones, and 'tis their Duty' (§ 34). 'Honour thy Father and Mother' is an eternal law prescribing this parent–child relation (TI: 64). Children have a right to inherit the goods and possessions of their parents; that right is one aspect of the natural law that commands parents to provide for their children (TI: 88). The correlative right for children is that they should be 'nourish'd and maintained by their Parents' (TI: 89). In these passages Locke was speaking specifically of 'Possessions and Commodities of Life valuable by Money', not of 'that Reverence, Acknowledgment, Respect and Honour that is always due from Children to their Parents' (TI: 90). A man also has a right to be cared

---

[1] John Passmore, 'The Malleability of Man in Eighteenth Century Thought', in Earl R. Wasserman (ed.), *Aspects of the Eighteenth Century* (Baltimore, Md., 1965), p. 24.
[2] W. M. Spellman, *John Locke and the Problem of Depravity* (Oxford, 1988).

for and maintained by his children when he needs it. In contrast to Filmer, Locke emphasized that 'All that a Child has Right to claim from his Father is Nourishment and Education, and the things nature furnishes for the support of Life: But he has no Right to demand *Rule* or *Dominion* from him' (TI: 93). Locke also declares that 'a Father cannot alien the Power he has over his Child, he may perhaps to some degree forfeit it, but cannot transfer it' (TI: 100).

Locke's concept of freedom and law linked them together; a lawless man is not free. 'For *Law*, in its true Notion, is not so much the Limitation as *the direction of a free and intelligent Agent* to his proper Interest' (TII: 57). The virtuous man is a free man. The child is an apprentice to freedom and reason. While children are not born in 'the full state of *Equality*', they are nevertheless born to it (TII: 55). The natural right children have for tuition and guidance gives parents the obligation to educate their children. 'He that *understands* for him, must *will* for him too; he must prescribe to his Will, and regulate his Actions' (TII: 58). After the child has reached the age of reason, he is free and equal: 'after that, the Father and Son are equally *free* as much as Tutor and Pupil after Nonage' (TII: 59). Age and education generally bring reason and the ability to govern oneself (TII: 61). One of the criteria for the age of reason is understanding 'that Law he is to govern himself by', meaning the law of nature or reason or, derivative from this law, civil law. Parental power (and educational or tutorial power) is 'nothing but that, which Parents have over their Children, to govern them for the Childrens good, till they come to the use of Reason' (TII: 170). To guide one's self by the law of nature and reason is not merely to live an orderly and virtuous life: it is to have the very essence of humanity. To turn the child 'loose to an unrestrain'd Liberty, before he has Reason to guide him, is not the allowing him the privilege of his Nature, to be free; but to thrust him out amongst Brutes, and abandon him to a state as wretched, and as much beneath that of a Man, as theirs' (TII: 63). Education literally humanizes the child by bringing him to reason and virtue, the defining marks of man and of that community of mankind which was so important for Locke.

When we remember that Locke described reason as 'natural revelation', we get a reinforcement of his strong views on the need for a careful training of the child in the ways of reason and virtue. The 'naturalness' of reason is not independent of training and culturation. We must learn how to make use of the faculties God has given us. The significance of training for virtue in *Some Thoughts* has not always been placed in the context of Locke's concept of reason and the community of mankind. The 'moral man' of the discussion in the *Essay* of personal identity and the forensic term 'person' reinforce the point that the consciousness which for Locke constitutes identity of person is meant to include a strong moral content. That moral awareness has to be cultivated and inculcated by education; that is what good breeding does. Locke was, it could be argued, more moralistic, more prescriptive, than his more traditional contemporaries, who were content to settle for innate moral truths and religious dictates. The traditional morality which Locke also accepted was placed in an even more compelling context, what it is to be human. Moreover, Locke not only insisted upon the importance of virtue, he set to work in *Some Thoughts* to chart the ways of helping children become moral persons. It was the negative aspects of Locke's response to the traditional morality—no innate idea of God, no innate moral truths, not even a natural inclination to virtue—which his contemporaries saw as a secularization of human nature. Without those built-in moral components, how was man to become moral, how was he to recognize the obligation which even Locke stressed to obey God's laws?

Locke's answer to the question, 'How is man to become moral?', was 'through education'. Some readers of Locke interpret his emphasis upon reason and rationality as an attempt to discover through reason alone how to be moral. Even if that could be done for each individual, we must recognize that Locke's reason is closely linked with revelation: it is natural revelation. Locke's answer to the question, 'How am I to recognize the obligation to obey God?', is that reason tells us we are God's creatures and hence should obey his laws. Revelation supports reason (being indeed described as 'natural reason'), and the prospect of eternal punishment or reward gives an incentive towards virtue. Locke may be seen as a transition figure from the traditional belief in innate truths implanted by God to the various secular views of man in the eighteenth century, secular views which struggled to explain how self-interest was compatible with concern for others. After Locke, attention was focused on human nature. With the theological basis for morality weakened, but with a strong concern to reject the Hobbesian view that all the desires of the person reduce to self-love, eighteenth-century writers talked of a moral sense as part of man's nature (Hutcheson, Hume, Shaftesbury), of a natural fittingness of things and actions (Samuel Clarke, Wollaston), or of a natural sympathy for others (Hume). To what extent the moral sense, or Hume's 'sentiment common to all mankind, which recommends the same object to general approbation',[1] were products of education induced in each generation from considerations of utility, is a question some of these writers discussed. Whatever the answer, the dominant account of human nature in eighteenth-century Britain and France leant towards finding that nature essentially good, inclined towards virtue, at least open to being formed into a virtuous person. The 'malleability of man' (Passmore's phrase) characterizes the eighteenth-century concept of man, a malleability which education and society can pervert from its 'natural' proclivity towards virtue, but which, in the fashion of Rousseau, education freed from the distortions of society can develop properly.

Locke's education of children is rooted in his civil society: he saw no need to break out of the social mould and rear children outside the traditional norms. Locke was in this respect very tradition-oriented, especially with respect to virtue. With his strong prescriptive instruction on moral education, with his definition of man as both rational *and* moral, the amoral aspect of his concept of man is greatly reduced in significance. What is important is that the child is malleable, that he can be trained to be virtuous. Thus, while Locke may have disagreed with the claims made later by Rousseau—that 'il n'y a point de perversité originelle dans le cœur humain', that 'les premiers mouvemens de la nature sont toujours droits'[2]—the main difference between Locke and Rousseau (and many other eighteenth-century writers on education and morality) lies in the primary role given by these writers to the passions, to sentiments, rather than to reason. Hume's extended discussion of the source of morality—whether it is reason or the passions[3]—deals with most of the answers to that question. Hume does not tell us how to train the passions, how to allow the sentiment of humanity to surface, other than advising us not to be bewitched by reason and the claims of philosophers. Rousseau's *Émile* attempts to chart some of the ways in which a tutor can guide the child away from the perversions of reason and bad education. Locke, too, writes with a firm understanding of the different tempers and passions of children, trying to suggest to parents and tutors various ways in which they can

[1] David Hume, *An Enquiry concerning the Principles of Morals*, ed. L. A. Selby-Bigge, 3rd edn. rev. P. H. Nidditch (Oxford, 1975), § IX, pt. i (p. 272).

[2] J. J. Rousseau, *Émile, ou de l'éducation*, in *Œuvres complètes*, ed. B. Gagnebin and M. Raymond (Paris, 1959–69), iv. 322.

[3] Hume, *A Treatise of Human Nature*, ed. L. A. Selby-Bigge, 2nd edn. rev. P. H. Nidditch (Oxford, 1978), bk. III, pt. i, § 1.

be harnessed and used in the moulding of a virtuous character. The apparent opposition between Locke and other writers on education and morality in the eighteenth century may be less than we first believe, since all these authors (Locke included) gave attention to the non-rational side of human nature. They were interested in the moral man, and with ways in which the morality of man was linked with and supported society. In one way or another, moral education was believed to be possible.[1]

Principles of Learning

In his specific comments on teaching and learning in *Some Thoughts*, Locke is more concerned with general methods and rules of thumb than with subject-matter and curriculum. He is never far from his constant stress upon virtue in the education of children. Virtue is a more important aim of education for Locke than specific instruction in subjects, and he never tires of stressing this point. In § 70 he suggests that parents have 'a strange value for words, when preferring the Languages of the Ancient *Greeks* and *Romans*, to that which made them such brave Men', and warns against hazarding 'your Son's Innocence and Vertue, for a little Greek and Latin'. Foreign languages and the contemporary teaching techniques for learning languages typified for Locke the wasteful preoccupation by tutors and parents with subject-matter rather than with the training of character. Some of Locke's de-emphasizing of particular subjects clearly arises because of the seventeenth-century notion of a young gentleman. The studies to which he is set are more designed as 'Exercises of his Faculties, and Imployment of his Time, to help him from Sauntering and Idleness' than for specific instruction (§ 94). No one expects the young gentleman to become 'an accomplished Critick, Orator, or Logician' or be a master of science or history. But along with these socially determined ideas of a gentleman's education, Locke's remarks show a more general appreciation of the importance of good character and a

[1] Among the less well-known 18th-c. writers on education who carry forward these themes of moral education, many either using Locke or showing his influence, are John Clarke, *The Foundation of Morality in Theory and Practice* (1726?) and *An Essay upon the Education of Youth* (1720); I. Watts, *A Treatise on the Education of Children and Youth* (2nd edn., 1769); Thomas Sheridan, *British Education: Or, The Source of the Disorder of Great Britain* (1756); James Burgh, *The Dignity of Human Nature* (1754); J. P. de Crousaz, *Traité de l'éducation des enfans* (1722). For a discussion of the knowledge of most such works, including Locke's *Some Thoughts*, in America, see Jay Fliegelman, *Prodigals and Pilgrims: The American Revolution against Patriarchal Authority, 1750–1800* (Cambridge, 1982).

recognition that the learning of a method of study related to what each person's own industry can achieve is of greater value than factual knowledge. The tutor's goal 'is not so much to teach him all that is knowable, as to raise in him a love and esteem of Knowledge; and to put him in the right way of knowing, and improving himself, when he has a Mind to it' (§ 195). One of the reasons Locke was opposed to large classes (a school in the seventeenth-century sense) was that these goals depend upon personal tuition: 'The forming of their Minds and Manners requiring a constant Attention, and particular Application to every single Boy' (§ 70). In a school or class of fifty or one hundred, the only successful instruction is book learning.

Locke may have been too pessimistic about what can be accomplished in large classes. What he has to say about teaching—his commonsense psychology of learning—has value beyond the small context he had in mind for the Clarkes. The constant stress upon and the priority given to virtue and good character has, so Locke claimed, even a practical pedagogic value. 'The more this Advances, the easier way will be made for all other Accomplishments, in their turns. For he that is brought to submit to Vertue, will not be refractory, or resty, in any thing, that becomes him' (§ 70). If once a 'right disposition' has been acquired, 'though all the rest [specific subjects] should be neglected', that right disposition 'would, in due time, produce all the rest' (§ 177). A virtuous character, carrying with it all the proper tempers of mind, is not only a condition for humanity: it is a condition for learning as well.

Just as there are some general principles for Locke's account in the *Essay* of the order of acquiring ideas, so there are a few advisory rules that he recommends to the teacher and tutor. The right way to teach children specific subjects is 'to give them a Liking and Inclination to what you propose to them to be learn'd' (§ 72). What is to be taught should not be presented as a task or burden or duty. Even play can become hated if children are made or forced to play (§ 73). The notion of forcing children to play is almost contradictory, force and play being incompatible. Similarly, Locke is suggesting that if not incompatible, the notion of forcing children to learn is at least impracticable. Another rule is not to attempt to get children to do even the things for which they have an inclination except when they 'have a Mind and *Disposition* to it' (§ 74). The changes of temper in children should be carefully studied so that instruction can fit the 'favourable *Seasons of Aptitude and Inclination*' (ibid.). More can be learnt in this way, and less time spent; in addition, more time for play can be allowed. Locke criticized contemporary educational methods for ignoring this psychological fact, as he thought it was. The rod is no substitute and should be used only in very special and recalcitrant cases, and then in careful and limited ways. Following these two rules of instruction, Locke thought, would enable teachers to make learning as much recreation as children's play is, thereby creating a motive to learn. Men will not follow virtue out of a knowledge of it; and, similarly, children will not learn without an activating motive. Pleasure and pain (more the former than the latter) function in both the acquisition of virtue and the learning of specific subject-matter. The goal of teaching is to get the child to ask to be taught.

Along with these two rules, Locke mentions two cautions. First, we may miss the seasons of aptitude through carelessness and inattention, or those seasons may not occur as often as they should in some particular child. We may in consequence confirm a child in habitual idleness. Second, we can help the process of learning if we are able to teach the student how to gain mastery over himself, how to be able, upon choice, to study some subject (§ 75). Control and even alteration of our desires is necessary for both virtue and learning. This sort of training or guidance in how to learn to study may be part of the psychology of learning, since it is not instruction in a particular subject but training for learning. For this, we should sometimes try to make the child 'buckle to the Thing proposed' when he is 'by Laziness unbent, or by Avocation bent another Way' (ibid.).

Locke does not give much specific advice on how to bring out these learning tempers, though he does offer a few suggestions. In § 76 he points out the effectiveness of the example of others whom the child esteems; in § 148 he cites the case of a boy whose reluctance to learn to read was overcome by the parents and Locke talking among themselves in the child's presence of 'the Privilege and Advantage of Heirs and Elder Brothers, to be Scholars; ... And that for Younger Brothers, 'twas a Favour to admit them to Breeding', but that they could, if they pleased, 'be ignorant Bumpkins and Clowns'. Envy and a feeling of exclusion from privilege seem to have operated in this instance. The natural curiosity of children can also be used to lead the child to want to learn: it is nature's device for removing ignorance. As a way of cultivating this natural curiosity, Locke cites a few simple rules: do not check the child's questions, do not laugh at his questions, explain in his own terms, and never give deceitful answers (§§ 118,

120). Commending the child and frequently bringing strange and new things to his attention are other ways to encourage and use curiosity (§§ 119, 121). Whether or not these suggestions for bringing the child to want to learn are useful, they at least show that Locke's principles of learning were not meant to lead the tutor to stand idly by and wait for the seasons of aptitude to come. Learning is not to be permissive, but the guides and controls ought to be child-centred: they ought to arise from the child's own character and motivational structure, subtly manipulated by the tutor.

Another more general learning principle is that 'Care must be taken with Children, to begin with that, which is plain and simple, and to teach them as little as can be at once' (§ 180). In this passage Locke is speaking specifically of teaching astronomy, but I think he would take this principle as having a wider use, as the alternative formulation in the language of ideas clearly indicates: 'Give them first one simple Idea, and see that they take it right, and perfectly comprehend it before you go any farther, and then add some other simple Idea which lies next in your way to what you aim at, and so proceeding by gentle and insensible steps.' The natural temper of children is that their minds wander, but also think about one thing at a time (§ 167). Just as the order of time (the chronology) must be followed in studying and teaching history and the order of nature carefully observed and recorded in physical science, so there is an order of learning and knowledge natural to the mind (§ 195). That order is 'from the knowledge it stands possessed of already, to that which lies next, and is coherent to it, and so on to what it aims at, by the simplest and most uncompounded parts it can divide the Matter into' (ibid.). The notion of one piece of knowledge or idea being 'coherent' with another is important. Locke's notion of demonstration set out in the *Essay* was that of showing the conceptual relations of ideas. What the teacher does is to demonstrate the connections one idea has with another within any given subject-matter. More importantly for Locke's conception of a curriculum, the connection of ideas is carried over into the relations between one subject and another. One of the most interesting features of Locke's account of the curriculum—a feature I do not think was stressed by other writers at this time—is the careful use he makes of the interconnection of subject-matter. Just as there is an order of acquiring ideas, both a temporal and a conceptual one, so there is for Locke an order in learning. The order in learning across the curriculum is not only a temporal one, though he does specify the order of instruction in this way: the curriculum order is also a *content* order.

The Curriculum

The standard curriculum of spelling, reading, writing, and foreign languages was integrated, in that reading and writing skills were to be exercised by copying and reading the material in Latin or French. Locke follows the latest trend in language learning by downgrading grammar and stressing oral instruction.[1] He also testifies from his own experience that having a child read from a Latin Bible, where the syllables have been marked for pronunciation, will in a short time produce some understanding of the Latin. The same technique, together with the use of interlinear Latin and English, can be used with Aesop's *Fables* and other books of interest (§ 177).[2] Skill in reading one's native language is thus put to use and paired with reading another language. That process is also aided by having the child copy the interlinear books which he had been reading (§ 167). Skill in writing can also be enhanced by drawing, which is therefore to be encouraged in the child (§ 161). Facility in Latin or French can in turn be used for learning geography, astronomy, chronology, anatomy, history, and other sciences (§ 166). In this way, the child will improve his knowledge of those languages and acquire some knowledge of those specific disciplines as well (§ 178).

Within the specific disciplines, Locke recommends a definite order of learning based upon natural connections of subject-matter. Geography is the first of these disciplines to be taught. 'For the learning of the Figure of the *Globe*, the Situation and Boundaries of the Four Parts of the World, and that of particular Kingdoms and Countries, being only an exercise of the Eyes and Memory, a child with pleasure will learn and retain them' (§ 178). Locke believed that 'Children may be taught any thing, that falls under their Senses, especially their sight, as far as their Memories only are exercised' (§ 181). That is why

[1] 'After the Restoration the practice of talking Latin, always difficult to enforce, was dying out, although some educationists like Charles Hoole, John Locke and John Aubrey advocated that boys should learn Latin by speaking the language and hearing others speak it.' (W. A. L. Vincent, *The Grammar Schools: Their Continuing Tradition, 1660–1714* (London, 1969), p. 76.)

[2] For an account of Locke's role in the publication of just such an edition of Aesop, see James Axtell, *The Educational Writings of John Locke* (Cambridge, 1968), p. 271 n. 2. See also Robert H. Horwitz and Judith B. Finn, 'Locke's Aesop's Fables', in *The Locke Newsletter*, 6 (1975), 71–88.

geography comes first in this order. The study of geography is not exhausted by the knowledge of the main physical divisions and characteristics of the globe, but this will be the child's first learning in this field. He learns these geographical facts by sight and by rote, rather than reasoning. Arithmetic, the next subject in Locke's order, introduces the child to abstract reasoning (§ 180). With the rudiments of counting, addition, and subtraction, further progress can be made in geography by teaching the child '*Longitude* and *Latitude*, and by them be made to understand the use of Maps, and by the Numbers placed on their Sides, to know the respective Situation of Countries, and how to find them out on the Terrestrial Globe' (ibid.). From them, the tutor can progress to the figure and position of the constellations, to the nature of our solar system, and then to an outline of the Copernican system. By this progressive and interdisciplinary process, the child can be prepared 'to understand the Motion and Theory of the Planets, the most easy and natural Way'.

Geometry is a natural step after the child has acquired some knowledge of the globe, the equator, and the meridians. The first six books of Euclid can be taught at this stage. Another closely related subject to geography is chronology. These subjects go hand in hand (§ 182). They are prerequisites for history, the next subject in Locke's integrated curriculum. Without these prerequisites, 'History will be very ill retained, and very little useful; but be only a jumble of Matters of Fact, confusedly heaped together without Order or Instruction' (ibid.). Latin can also be put to use by giving the child some Latin history, starting with the easiest and going to 'the most difficult and sublime', Cicero, Virgil, and Horace (§ 184). Ethics and civil law will emerge from some of this historical reading, and English law can also be easily introduced at this point (§§ 185–7).[1]

Locke's curriculum goes on to include rhetoric, logic, and natural science, as well as art and dancing. It was a typical gentleman's education. What is of interest is his attempt to show how learning in one area can aid and be used in other areas. While he does not assign ages to the features of his curriculum, he clearly worked with a notion of

---

[1] Ethics as a subject in the curriculum must be distinguished from the moral training that Locke emphasized as a preliminary to any learning and as the way to lead students to become moral. The training of the child in virtue seeks to habituate him to right conduct, in accordance with the laws of nature. It is hoped that along with these habits will go some beliefs about what is right and wrong. The study of ethics would be the examination of previous systems of laws and beliefs about right and wrong. There is no suggestion that Locke intended the study of ethics to make the student moral.

development. The rudimentary developmental psychology of the *Essay* is matched by his commonsense recognition of the ways in which the child's interest and skills in one area can be stepping stones for another. He saw and stressed the difference between learning by heart (as the child should learn languages, his first geography, the Lord's Prayer, the Creeds, and the Ten Commandments, §§ 157, 177–8), learning to read (which requires understanding), and learning to reason (as he begins to do in arithmetic). Throughout his outline of the curriculum, Locke illustrates the learning principles that he accepted. The general principle—to make learning play and recreation—is stated in his discussion of reading (§ 148). Some methods of carrying out this principle are the device of putting letters, syllables, and pictures of animals on the child's toys (§§ 151–3), and encouraging the child to read by giving him books that will catch his interest (§ 156). The device of using pictures of objects for teaching their names was urged as a way of making sure that when the child hears visible objects talked of he has clear ideas of those objects, 'those Idea's being not to be had from Sounds; but from the Things themselves, or their Pictures' (ibid.).[1] The constant stress in Locke's account of the science of nature in the *Essay* was laid upon the same way to clarity of ideas, on going to the things themselves and observing and recording precisely and carefully. The move away from scholastic verbiage and from sounds without meaningful ideas—a move characteristic of the century—is reflected in *Some Thoughts* by injunctions for making sure that children acquire clear and distinct ideas of the objects discussed in the various disciplines.

Interpretations of Locke

Writers on the history of education tend to praise or criticize in the light of the concepts, issues, and debates current when they write.

---

[1] A prospectus for a school at Tottenham High Cross in Middlesex promised that, among many other useful aids, 'Repositories for Visibles shall be immediately provided, out of which may be produced, Herbs, Drugs, Seeds, Mineral Juices, Metals, precious Stones, Birds, Beasts, and Fishes, that cannot be produced in Specie, shall be shewed in their Pictures.' (Quoted by Vincent, op. cit., p. 200.) Comenius, of course, stressed the value of pictures in teaching, but not before 1649; about 1635, John Frooke criticized his *Janua Linguarum*, suggesting that its defects 'might be overcome if an "Encyclopaedia of Sensuals" was combined with the *Janua*, complex pictures being particularly valuable as showing both physical characteristics and relationships, operations and degrees of phenomena' (Charles Webster (ed.), *Samuel Hartlib and the Advancement of Learning* (Cambridge, 1970), p. 20). Cf. Locke's suggestion for a natural history dictionary with little pictures, *Essay*, 3. 11. 25.

Such a tendency is natural enough; any historian is apt to use his own perspective in this way. Examining some of the analyses of Locke found in some of the standard writings in this area can be useful in aiding us to form a more balanced understanding and evaluation of Locke's *Some Thoughts*. Even where obvious misreadings have been made, the various accounts do manage to highlight most of the main pedagogic issues raised by Locke.

The Senses, Reason and Play. The feature of *Some Thoughts* not discussed in this introduction, that portion dealing with the care of the child's body and bodily health, was of great interest to nineteenth-century writers. R. H. Quick's edition of Locke's book contained extensive notes at the end made by Dr J. Payne on Locke's advice on these matters.[1] Payne attempted to assess the wisdom of Locke's regimen in the light of medical knowledge. The fact that Locke was trained in medicine is frequently noted as the probable cause for this interest on his part.[2] While William Boyd oddly finds that Locke's stress on training the body leads to a separation of mind and body and a failure to recognize the need to train the senses,[3] J. W. Adamson credits Locke with the principle 'so frequently repeated since his time, that the sense-organs of children should be exercised in school', that 'the learning of young children should be acquired by the active employment of the organs of sense rather than through information supplied by books or teachers'.[4] The senses are an important link between mind and body in Locke's general philosophy, and *Some Thoughts* does stress the usefulness of getting to the mind through the senses, but Fliegelman's recent study overdoes that stereotype of Locke's thought, 'sensationalist epistemology'.[5]

For Locke, the healthy body is of much less importance, though a necessary condition, for education than a sound mind. That the soundness of the child's mind is heavily dependent upon virtue in Locke's account is generally recognized, though not always analysed. Curtis and Boultwood claim, as late as 1965, that Locke's arguments for 'the necessity of moral education might have been written yesterday,

---

[1] Quick's edition was published by the Cambridge University Press in 1880, with extensive notes by Dr J. Payne.

[2] See Curtis and Boultwood, *Short History*, p. 225. They suggest that these ideas originate from Comenius, rather than from Locke's medical interests.

[3] William Boyd, *From Locke to Montessori* (London, 1914), pp. 22–3.

[4] J. W. Adamson, *The Educational Writings of John Locke* (Cambridge, 1922), pp. 11, 15.

[5] See Fliegelman, *Prodigals and Pilgrims*, ch. 1.

especially those dealing with the decay in religion and morals of the times'.[1] However, Locke's training for virtue was not just a matter of making the child moral. The cultivation of virtue was, as Reicyn remarks, 'le dessein unique qui doit guider l'éducateur', she reminds us, but virtue consists in following reason instead of the emotions or appetites.[2] The rationality of morality does not embody quite the same concept of reason as Locke's stress upon teaching the child to reason does. Curtis and Boultwood claim that Locke's 'contention that children should be treated as rational creatures is one of Locke's greatest contributions to educational thought',[3] but Quick holds that Locke overplays reason to the detriment of affections, feelings, and imagination.[4] Not only is Locke criticized for emphasizing some mental faculties at the expense of others, he is also charged with 'understanding little of normal child nature'.[5] Boyd says that in the *Essay*, Locke takes the adult, not the child, as his example in discussing the origin of ideas and the nature of the understanding, apparently overlooking the many passages in that work which treat of the early development of the child. The curriculum of studies, Boyd says, is 'based on adult needs rather than on childish capacities'.[6]

M. V. C. Jeffreys expresses just the opposite view to Boyd, claiming that Locke was one of 'the originators of *child centred education*'.[7] Quick thinks that Locke errs too much on the side of individuality, tending to ignore 'our nature'.[8] A number of commentators call attention to Locke's concern with observing the child at play, with using play as a way of teaching, and with working from the interests of the child. Reicyn points out the obvious similarities between Locke's recognition of the importance of interest and the project-method of the Montessori techniques: 'Et en apprenant à étudier le caractère propre de chaque enfant, ses appétits, ses goûts, en essayant, à l'école ou à la maison, d'adapter l'enseignement à chaque individu, on a trouvé le principe de l'éducation attrayante.'[9] Reicyn calls attention to a paper of Locke's on recreation, in which he takes an instrumentalist attitude

---

[1] *Short History*, p. 240. [2] *Pédagogie*, pp. 59–60. [3] *Short History*, p. 241.
[4] R. H. Quick, *Essays on Educational Reformers* (London, 1902), p. 222. Much has been made by literary people of Locke's apparent insensitivity to literature, to imagination, and to the creative activity of the mind. See e.g. N. Frye, *Fearful Symmetry* (Boston, Mass., 1962), ch. 1. This belief about Locke needs to be corrected by reference to the very active role the mind plays in his account of the origin of all ideas. *Essay* 2. 11. 2 also has an interesting comment on wit, metaphor and allusion.
[5] Curtis-Boultwood, *Short History*, p. 248. [6] *From Locke to Montessori*, p. 27.
[7] M. V. C. Jeffreys, *John Locke, Prophet of Common Sense* (London, 1969), p. 51.
[8] Quick, *Essays on Educational Reformers*, p. 230. [9] Reicyn, *Pédagogie*, 112.

towards play: 'recreation being a thing ordained, not for itself, but for a certain end, that end is to be the rule and measure of it'. The end of play, says Locke, is 'to restore the mind or body, tired with labour, to its former strength and vigour, and thereby fit it for new labour.'[1] Play as a restorer is an important feature in Locke's use of play for educational purposes.

The Child's World. The fact that play, unlike work, is freely consented to is an equally important feature for Reicyn in Locke's concept of play. Instead of suppressing play, Locke urges us to replace it with educative play, a substitution that does not reject effort but only constraint.[2] A number of commentators have noted the passage in *Some Thoughts* (§ 125) where Locke talks of observing the child at play, unnoticed by the child. That passage was no afterthought; it marks a basic ingredient in his advice on how to learn how to help the child learn.[3] Reicyn makes much of the point that the child has a world of his own which the educator must understand and penetrate. 'L'observation de l'enfant est, en effet, le moyen unique qui soit à notre disposition pour nous permettre de pénétrer dans le monde particulier où l'enfant évolue.'[4] More recent writers on education have stressed the need for a phenomenological description of the child's world.[5] The child's thought differs from that of the adult's in structure, interests, even in logic. Adult thought, Reicyn remarks, is

une pensée socialisée, une pensée qui—généralement—se règle sur un modèle externe, qui a acquis, à force de frottements, une certaine forme, une certaine consistance aussi, qui la rendent compréhensible à tout autre adulte parlant la même langue. La pensée de l'enfant est bien différente, et plus que la pensée,

[1] Locke, 'An Essay concerning Recreation', in Lord King, *The Life of John Locke*, 2nd edn. (London, 1830), vol. ii, p. 165, quoted by Reicyn, p. 216.

[2] Reicyn, *Pédagogie*, pp. 118, 123, 130.

[3] In his recent study, Nathan Tarcov, *Locke's Education for Liberty* (Chicago, 1984), characterizes the secret observation of the child at play as 'spying' and 'concealment', taking this as part of a general programme of using and teaching the child to use deceit, lies, and dissimulation (pp. 175, 182, 253 n. 180).

[4] Reicyn, *Pédagogie*, p. 73.

[5] See e.g. M. J. Langeveld, 'Some Recent Developments in Philosophy of Education in Europe', pp. 81–101, in *Philosophy and Education*, Proceedings of the International Seminar, March 23–25, 1966. Monograph Series, no. 3 (Toronto, 1967). Langeveld criticizes the 'adultolatry' in our approach to education. He urges us to replace this approach with an 'anthropological' study of the child and his world. The world, he suggests, has different meanings for us at different stages in our lives. Piaget's earlier studies on child development are well known. For a general account of Piaget's work, see J. H. Flavell, *The Developmental Psychology of Jean Piaget* (Princeton, 1963). The work of L. Kohlberg, especially in moral education, is also relevant.

le mode d'expression. Contrairement à la pensée de l'adulte, celle de l'enfant correspond à un 'modèle interne'. . .[1]

Locke's goal was to replace that internal model with a socialized one which would in time be internalized. This Piagetian recognition of the structural differences between adult and child could not, of course, have been made with any precision by a writer in the seventeenth century, but it is to the credit of Locke to have seen the general truth about this difference. Reicyn agrees that Locke saw this fact, although he made only a beginning.[2]

One of the products of a careful observation of growing children is an analysis of their stages of growth and of the different abilities and capacities they have at different points in their development. To enter into the world of the child is to discover those features of growth. For us, after Piaget, an adequate psychology of learning would, as Reicyn says, have to 'nous donner une description des étapes que parcourt l'enfant de sa naissance à son adolescence'.[3] It is too harsh to say, as Reicyn does, that Locke 'n'a pas eu la curiosité de scruter le développement interne de nos facultés et de nos organes', since that is precisely what the *Essay* was endeavouring to do. That Locke did have some notion of child development is shown by his attention to the time-order of ideas in his account of idea-genesis in the *Essay*. There is a clear genetic strain in his account of the human understanding. Quick was easily put off by the *tabula rasa* metaphor (as others have been too), taking that as evidence that Locke had no idea of an organism growing and developing.[4] Jeffreys repeats this obviously false remark.[5] The developmental psychology offered by Locke is sketchy and incomplete, but it is far from being non-existent.

---

[1] Reicyn, *Pédagogie*, p. 124.

[2] Cf. James Axtell (ed.), *The Educational Writings* (Cambridge, 1968), and his reference to Ariès's well-known book on the so-called discovery of the child and his world, *L'enfant et la vie familiale sous l'ancien régime* (Paris, 1960). A corrective to Ariès, and to most other writers on attitudes towards children in the 17th and 18th cc., has recently been issued: Linda A. Pollock, *Forgotten Children: Parent–Child Relations from 1500–1800* (Cambridge, 1983).

[3] Reicyn, *Pédagogie*, p. 92.

[4] Quick, *Essays on Educational Reformers*, p. 230. For an account of Locke's genetic psychology, his development of awareness in children, see my *Locke, An Introduction* (Oxford, 1985), pp. 124–31.

[5] Jeffreys, *Prophet*, p. 55. Curtis–Boultwood misunderstand the nature of the innate theory Locke was attacking. They claim that 'Locke contradicts one of his former contentions in asserting that men are born with different capacities and aptitudes' (p. 232). The *tabula rasa* doctrine was of course about ideas and propositions, not about faculties, capacities, or tempers.

The Social Context of Education. One feature of a growth theory that Locke does little to delineate is the acquisition of beliefs.[1] The physiognomy of the mind outlined in a number of passages in the *Essay* does include some beliefs such as 'that this stranger is not my mother', but there is no explicit social psychology in that work or in *Some Thoughts*. Nor are the details of the curriculum refined to the point where the beliefs and customs of the society become a part of the child's education. R. S. Peters has stressed that one fundamental feature of education (as opposed to training) is 'the transmission of what is worth-while' in a society.[2] The curriculum specified by Locke does not include (nor does it consciously exclude) this feature of education, but his concern with the moral education of the child has a clear social backing. His concern with this aspect of education was not only motivated by a conviction that virtue is important for gentlemen; it also had the deeper and far more dynamic motive that virtue was the very fabric and basis for humanity. Man's humanity is achieved within civil society. It is not just the civil laws and customs of a society that constitute this humanizing framework: the laws of nature (inchoate and imprecise as they are in Locke's writings) constitute for him the more important standards of conduct. Within these laws and what they implied for one who accepted these seventeenth-century renditions of Christian morality is to be found what is considered worthwhile for society. It is of the utmost importance to see that Locke's stress upon virtue in *Some Thoughts* has this sort of cultural foundation. Moral training of the child would inevitably produce beliefs, not just habits of behaviour. The transition from man to person, in the technical sense given to it in Locke's account of personal identity, produces a socialized person sharing the customs and beliefs of the society in which the educative process occurred.

There have been two ways in which the cultural background inherent in Locke's account of education has been overlooked. Writers have missed the connection between the doctrine of laws of nature and the socialization process, failing to see that the specific content of the law of nature captures the customs, values, and norms of the society Locke envisaged. From the fact that the law of nature is not mentioned in *Some Thoughts*, Tarcov[3] seems to conclude that it is not relevant to

---

[1] He did, however, pay some attention to the nature of and grounds for belief and assent. For an enlightening discussion of this feature of Locke, see H. H. Price, *Belief* (London, 1969), pp. 130–56.

[2] R. S. Peters, *Ethics and Education* (London, 1966), p. 45. See also his 'Aims of Education—A Conceptual Inquiry', *Philosophy and Education*, pp. 1–16.

[3] Tarcov, op. cit.

that work. His is a strange study in many ways, but nowhere more so than in its failure to place Locke's early *Essays on the Law of Nature* (together with the frequent use of the law of nature in the *Essay*, *Reasonableness*, and *Two Treatises*) in the context of the moral education depicted in *Some Thoughts*. There have been two extremes in the interpretation of Locke on this point. One (represented by John Dunn's monograph[1]) takes Locke's talk of the possibility of a demonstrative morality as the claim that reason alone can derive moral laws through some sort of deduction. When Locke fails to produce such a derivation of the laws, Dunn concludes that reason has failed Locke, finding in that failure the threat of relativism and subjectivism. The other extreme (represented by Tarcov) ignores the laws of nature, plays up Locke's account of mixed modes as ideas or words not dependent upon any objective standards (they are ectype ideas), and reaches a similar conclusion: that Locke's morality is personal, subjective, and rather Hobbesian in content. The mixed mode concept in Locke's account contrasts with the ideas of physical objects and events where careful observation and the following of nature is in order. Mixed modes are ideas of our own construction, but not, on Locke's recommendation, relativized to each individual. There are, both in society and in the Christian religion that Locke endorsed, rules and standards which we must follow. Civil laws must be based upon and not clash with these natural or divine laws for action. What the moral education of *Some Thoughts* does is to guide the child in conformity with these Christian values and Christian virtues, which in turn constitute the moral fabric of society.

The second way in which the cultural background of *Some Thoughts* has been overlooked is in concentrating upon the fragmented developmental psychology found in Locke's writings, primarily a psychology of ideas and knowledge; this has led readers to miss his clear acceptance of the value and necessity of those absolute moral truths articulated in the laws of nature and exemplified in the attitudes and beliefs of most of Locke's contemporaries. R. S. Peters links Locke's account of the development of mind with the sensory-based stereotype of 'British empiricism': 'the development of the individual mind is regarded as a slow process by means of which generalized beliefs are acquired as a precipitate of individual experience. Atomic sense data, it was argued, are admitted through the inlets of sense.'[2]

---

[1] Dunn, *Locke* (Past Masters, Oxford, 1984).
[2] Peters, *Ethics and Education*, p. 47.

This particular stereotype needs to be corrected by taking cognizance of the activity of the mind in the acquisition of ideas and by augmenting the *tabula rasa* slogan with a recognition of the faculties and the many mental processes in his account of the mind. One other correction needed is in the account of Locke's notion of the child's relation to his society during his growth and maturation. Peters wishes to stress that

The ideas and expectations of an individual centre of consciousness, however, do not develop as deposits out of an atomic individual experience. This is one of the misleading features of the empiricist account. On the contrary they are the product of the initiation of an individual into public traditions enshrined in the language, concepts, beliefs, and rules of a society.[1]

Whether Peters has correctly characterized the views held by any of those called 'empiricists' is doubtful, but he has certainly missed much in Locke's explicit account and even more in the background doctrines found in the *Essay*. Locke was a very tradition-oriented man, albeit sometimes a tradition modified. He would especially have agreed with Peters' repeated insistence that the mind's structure 'develops out of and as a response to public traditions enshrined in language'.

Locke's acceptance and use of this notion that tradition is captured by thought and language is found in a number of doctrines in his *Essay*. His view of language and meaning is conventionalist, and he insists that language is for communication. Language is a social instrument whose value is relative to its appropriateness as a way of expressing and communicating ideas about ourselves and our world. His distinction between the nominal and real essence of objects was designed to show that those Schoolmen who claimed a knowledge of real essence were wrong and that all our knowledge of objects starts with the classification of the things marked out in our language. Peters is unknowingly paraphrasing Locke's doctrine of nominal essence when he writes: 'The objects of consciousness are first and foremost objects in a public world that are marked out and differentiated by a public language into which the individual is initiated.'[2] Locke saw that any attempt to uncover the nature of objects as they are by themselves was doomed to failure. Even to raise the question about the real essence of gold or lead already makes use of nominal concepts for indicating the kind of objects we are talking about. 'What is the nature

[1] Ibid., pp. 48–9; cf. p. 51.
[2] Ibid., p. 50.

of X?' presupposes a location of X in our classification of the kinds of objects in our world. Locke accepted the corpuscular theory as a likely account of the nature of body apart from our awareness and our language, but he did not think that theory could be confirmed, nor that the acceptance of that theory altered our ordinary notions of what objects there are or of what properties they have.

It was quite easy for Locke to hold to a realism in his ontology while underscoring the perceiver-dependence of our knowledge of objects. Even more interesting than his recognition of the way in which language captures and controls our knowledge of the world of objects is his insistence upon the similar role language and thought play in human action.[1] The actions a man can perform are circumscribed by the concepts and words that his society has in its vocabulary. A man can do only actions for which he has words and concepts. When Peters says: 'For in a language is distilled a view of the world which is constituted by' the purposes, standards, feelings, and beliefs of a society, he is again expressing a view endorsed by Locke, though perhaps not developed or expressed in quite the same way.[2] Locke's general view of man's world is governed by the acceptance of a physical world independent of but causally interacting with us. Progress in science, he believed, will mainly be made (certainly for a time) not by attempting to uncover the corpuscular nature of each object (a task which he thought very likely impossible) but in making more careful observations of coexisting qualities and of the behaviour of objects as experienced. For that description, we can use only the concepts and language at our disposal. Even if we find it necessary to coin new words for some of our ideas, we are still working from within our thought about the world. Locke sees science not as determining what objects there are, but rather as recording, more carefully than had been done until then, the objects already accepted and specified in our language. The 'mixed mode' words for human actions are a more explicit adoption of the same language- and thought-governed notion, though here observation is not a necessary guide to which descriptions we will accept, as it must be with physical knowledge. The notion that the modes of action are determined by the stock of descriptions in our

---

[1] Language and thought work together in Locke's account, but thought is in some ways independent of language. Even if we find we cannot in fact think without language, Locke believes that some ideas arise before language. He also believes it possible, with effort, to think without language, though he recognizes that this is unusual (*Essay*, 4. 6. 1, 4. 5. 3, 4. 5. 5).

[2] Peters, *Ethics and Education*, p. 53.

language is augmented by Locke's acceptance of a doctrine of laws of nature. It is in the philosophy of action in particular that Locke agrees with the point of view expressed by Peters. In encouraging the virtue of the pupil, the tutor is working with the accepted mixed modes of his society and imparting that aspect of the culture to the child.[1]

Conclusion

In interpreting Locke's *Some Thoughts* one must always be careful not to blow it up beyond its own proportions. It was a treatise limited to a time and place, and even to a particular child. He has, he tells us at the very end of that work, given here 'only some general Views, in reference to the main End, and aims in Education, and those designed for a Gentleman's Son' (§ 217). He disclaims having written 'a just Treatise on this Subject' of education. There are few hints about what he would have done differently, were he writing a 'just Treatise'; but it is symptomatic of his thought that in this concluding section he tells us that, for a proper treatment of the subject, 'There are a thousand other things, that may need consideration; especially if one should take in the various Tempers, different Inclinations, and particular Defaults, that are to be found in Children; and prescribe proper Remedies.' By ending on the need to particularize discussions on education to specific types of minds and abilities, Locke may be saying in effect that general treatises on education have limited value at best. The most effective approach to education is not through general theories and general rules, but through a careful study of individual persons. The most general goals of education are the training in virtue, the acquisition of a method of study, and lastly the imparting of specific subject-matter. These goals can be achieved, Locke firmly believed, only by fitting our techniques to the particular talents and potentialities of each individual. The tutorial method is especially appropriate just because it provides the context in which the child's tempers and frame of mind can most easily be understood. We today may often forget this simple truth, assuming (or being forced to assume) that the similarities among people provide a sufficient basis for educating in the mass. Locke's remarks on education may still have importance for us if they

---

[1] Locke had in mind not only local names and customs but also universal features of rational men. Travel is stressed at the end of *Some Thoughts* for the value it has in opening up for the student 'Tempers, Customs, and Ways of living different from one another, and especially from those of his Parish and Neighbours' (§ 212).

can remind us of the need to particularize our educational methods. Whether Locke has anything to offer us today by way of specific methods is doubtful, but he did succeed in locating and identifying goals of education that we should still accept. He also understood the fundamental importance of education for the individual and for society.

B. TEXT

I. Genesis

Locke's *Some Thoughts* is one of the earliest English treatises on the subject, certainly one of the most systematic. Edward Clarke of Chipley, near Wellington in Somerset, a friend of Locke, had married Locke's kinswoman, Mary Jepp, the niece of John Strachey, in 1675.[1] The work originated in a request from the Clarkes (in June or July 1684) for instructions in educating their son Edward 'and more generally of their other children'. The first of Locke's instructions survives in a letter dated 19 July 1684 NS.[2] Locke's earlier letters frequently contained medical recommendations, including prescriptions.[3] In late November 1684, Locke sent Clarke a long list of instructions, transcribed by his secretary Sylvester Brounower, presumably from the manuscript copy Locke kept by him; as he was later to write, 'For I doubt not but when I revise the foul copy, which I keep by me on purpose, I shall myself find occasion for additions or alterations.'[4]

The letter of November 1684 was a transcription of Locke's foul copy closed by a letter of transmittal in Locke's hand.[5] This draft, headed 'Of Education', known as the Nynehead version, was sold at Sotheby's on 23 June 1924, item no. 477. It has reached its ultimate resting-place in Harvard College Library (shelfmark MS Eng. 860), the gift of Mrs Donald Hyde, 26 December 1946.

Presumably this version had gone astray in the post. Locke's statement in a letter (no. 801) to Clarke dated 1 January 1685 NS implies its loss:

If you had receivd the dir . . . . . . pers at large concerneing the management of your sons health I sent about ⟨th⟩e end of November you would then have

---

[1] For a fuller description of her relationship to Locke, see *Corr.* ii. 479–80 and the folding genealogical chart at the end of vol. i.

[2] No. 782 (ii. 624–9).   [3] e.g. no. 762, 27 Mar. 1683 (ii. 587–9).

[4] No. 849 to Clarke, 4 May 1686 (iii. 1–4).

[5] Letters of transmittal transcribed in Appendix II (pp. 317–18 below); cf. nos. 791 (ii. 648), 804 (ii. 677).

seen a great part of my thoughts . . . much better then in stragling pages writ at distant times which you have received, which some times crosse out the and seeme to con   what was writ. If those be miscaried as your silence gives me reason to suspect, let me know, and then I shall repeat them again with my stragling additions and shall make this advantage of the losse that then you shall have all my thoughts togeather in that matter, and thus seeing them all togeather I shall be sure to make them of a peice.   (*Corr.* ii. 674–5.)

Another copy, slightly expanded, was sent to the Clarkes about 5 January 1685. Since neither manuscript is dated, two further letters help us: Mrs Clarke, in a letter to Locke of 16 January 1685 (no. 806), writes: 'now in perticuler I am to thanke you for the Great Care you have taken in writing and sending the directtions How to Bring up my Little Boy' (*Corr.* ii. 680). Further, Locke's letter to Clarke dated 'February' (no. 807) includes the statement: 'I am glad to hear by yours of 20th Jan. that my opinion on children has at last come to hand. But I hope you have ere this received a more perfect copy [of the portion] lost I took care to send you. Indeed I was in some trouble for several days [in trying to] find the original copy and so being [thereby able] to retrieve it again' (*Corr.* ii. 681). This later copy is now known as British Library Add. MS 38771. It was transcribed and edited by F. G. Kenyon with the title *Directions concerning Education*, and published for the Roxburghe Club in 1933; we therefore cite it as K, for Kenyon, though readings are taken from the original.

The Harvard manuscript occupies 30 leaves measuring 157 × 98 mm. It ranges from 28 to 32 lines to a page, both sides of each leaf being written on. The text is numbered into 65 sections; with some rearrangement they are almost identical in wording with the first published edition's §§ 1–5, 7, 9, 11–22, 29–36, 38–57, 63, 65–9, 88–9, 126–34, 138–47, 155–6. However there are many variant spellings and scribal abbreviations: beside the usual 'y^e', 'y^t', 'w^{ch}', 'w^t' (for 'the', 'that', 'which', 'what'), there are other less usual abbreviations: 'nev^r', 'bett^r', 'n$\overline{\text{aa}}$l', 'ph^{er}' (for 'never', 'better', 'natural', 'philosopher'). Spelling variants are 'sourse' for 'source', 'flixible' for 'flexible', 'happynesse', 'dispachtd', amid many others.

The British Library manuscript, on 52 leaves, measuring 109 × 77 mm, ranges from 18 to 23 lines to a page, with catchwords and signatures on a few leaves. The text is numbered in 82 sections, with one exception corresponding to the same published sections of the first edition as the Harvard manuscript. The exception relates to the addition of §§ 21–30, corresponding to the first edition's §§ 23–8, all concerning 'costiveness'. Otherwise, the greater number of sections is derived from introducing more section-numbers for the same material: e.g. § 11 in the Harvard manuscript becomes §§ 11–16 in the British Library manuscript (first edition §§ 13–18).

'Costiveness' occurs as the subject of Locke's letter to Clarke dated by de Beer to mid-November 1684, with an endorsement by Clarke: 'Received the 25th December, 1684.'[1] Its inclusion as a topic in the British Library manuscript thus implies the later dating for that draft.

Both the Harvard and British Library manuscripts are written in the hand of Sylvester Brounower, and both end with a letter of transmittal in Locke's handwriting. Both manuscripts exhibit corrections by Locke, including, oddly, an interlinear insertion in the same place. In § 7 of the first edition, concerning getting a child's feet used to cold water by wearing leaky shoes, both manuscripts have the sentence: 'but begin wth lukewarme & soe colder & colder every night til in a few days `y^{u} come to perfectly cold water & soe continue".[2] If Brounower was transcribing Locke's foul copy, it is surprising that Locke had to inset 'you come . . . continue' himself in exactly the same place, in both drafts.

Other interlinings are in Locke's hand in the Harvard manuscript, but normally present in the British Library one.[3] Except for the expansion on 'costiveness', they are almost word-for-word identical, except in spellings and abbreviations. 'You' and 'y^{u}', 'your' and 'y^{r}', 'ye' and 'the', 'w^{t}' and 'what' occur indiscriminately in either draft: where the British Library manuscript has 'y^{u}' in one line and the Harvard has 'you', or vice versa, in the next line they may both have 'you'. This random interchange of fully spelt-out or abbreviated words shows little or no pattern, except perhaps a slightly greater frequency of abbreviation in the later British Library manuscript. Sometimes Brounower accidentally omits from the latter a word present in the Harvard draft. The Harvard draft is a little more fully and carefully punctuated. Sometimes Brounower catches his own errors or omissions, but more frequently it is detectably Locke's hand that has made the correction. Footnotes in our edition showing the variations from the reading in these two manuscripts have ignored abbreviations and

---

[1] No. 799 (ii. 667–9).   [2] The interlinear passage is indicated by ` '.
[3] Correspondences between the letters, the two manuscripts and the text are shown in footnotes to the text. There is also a table which shows the development from the Harvard manuscript to the 5th edn. (pp. 72–5 below).

punctuation variants, but otherwise offer a word-for-word comparison between the manuscripts and the printed editions.

Locke continued to write to the Clarkes with further ideas on other topics as they occurred to him. Some letters in the series are undoubtedly lost. A fragment of a letter (no. 803) anticipates §§ 40 and 95 of this edition and deals with early childhood and familiarity. Letters of February 1685 NS (no. 807), 3 May NS (no. 822), 1 September (no. 829), 8 February 1686 NS (no. 844), 15 March NS (no. 845), 29 April 1687 NS (no. 929), 15 July NS (no. 943), 9 March 1688 NS (no. 1020), 9 March 1691 (no. 1370), and 16 March (no. 1376) deal with assorted topics such as crying, reading matter, curiosity, 'sauntering', a tutor, etc.

The transition from instruction by post to publication must have been an easy one. Not only did Locke have his foul copy by him, but he also seems to have kept drafts of his letters. Some of his letters only survive in manuscript drafts: e.g. nos. 752 to Damaris Cudworth, 503 to Dr Denis Grenville, 1165 to Mrs Jane Stringer. His statement in the Epistle Dedicatory, 'That if some, who having heard of these Papers of mine, had not pressed to see them and afterwards to have them printed, they had lain dormant still in that privacy they were designed for', seems no more than truth, if we look at his correspondence with William Molyneux. In a letter to the latter dated 20 January 1693 Locke refers to his 'method of learning' as to which 'I may entertain you more at large hereafter'.[1] In his reply of 2 March 1693, Molyneux writes of his son Samuel that 'my Whole Study shall be to lay up a Treasure of Knowledge in his Mind . . . And I have been often thinking of some Method for His Instruction, that may best obtain the End I propose. . . . And My Brother has sometimes told Me, that . . . you were upon such a Work as this I desire . . . Wherefore, Good Sir, let me most earnestly intreat you by no means to lay aside this infinitely Useful Work, till you have finishd it.'[2]

In a letter to Locke dated 2 March 1693 William Popple says he will 'be very glad to receive the Papers you mention, and to contribute what care I am capable of towards their publication'.[3] De Beer thinks this statement refers to the work on education, so that Locke had already decided upon its publication, before being importuned by William Molyneux. Certainly Popple seems to have acted as intermediary with the Churchills; and in a letter to Locke dated 18 May 1693 Popple stated that he would send Lady Masham 'the little Essay

[1] No. 1592 (iv. 627).   [2] No. 1609 (iv. 649).   [3] No. 1608 (iv. 646).

about an European Diet, through Mr Churchill's hands, together with some of your Proofs'.[1] Similarly, a letter from Benjamin Furly from Rotterdam,. dated 23 June 1693 NS, requests that Locke 'let Syl write me out a copy of those things writ by you, when here, to mr. Clark, about the education of children, and give Syl a guinny for his pains. I was to blame that I tooke not a copy of it when I had it'.[2]

II. Published Editions

Some Thoughts was advertised in the *London Gazette*, no. 2886, the issue for 6–10 July 1693. In a letter to William Molyneux, dated 15 July 1693, Locke states his hope that Molyneux will have received 'that which I promis'd you the beginning of this spring',[3] presumably *Some Thoughts*. Edward Clarke's letter of 22 July 1693 to Locke states 'This morning I Received . . . your Booke of Education for Madam, which I will deliver to Her this Evening, but I heare nothing of any more of them from Mr. Churchill'; since his copy was received 'by the handes of one Mr. Babb a Bookseller here' in Taunton,[4] it is fair to say that the book was published by mid-July 1693.

(a) The First Editions (1693)

Title in double rules: SOME THOUGHTS CONCERNING Education. *LONDON*, Printed for *A.* and *J. Churchill*, at the *Black Swan* in *Pater-noster Row*, 1693. 8° (laid paper 177 × 107 mm cut) A⁴ B–R⁸ S⁴; pp. *i* title, *iii–vii* The Epistle Dedicatory, 1–262 text, *263–4* 'The Contents of the Sections.'

Locke was a meticulous keeper of records, as has been and will be noted elsewhere. He kept a journal[5] in which he recorded his expenses, medical and culinary receipts, his travels, and, occasionally, his thoughts.[6] He kept a commonplace-book. With his collection of papers there are included lists of friends to whom he wanted to present copies of his works. According to one list,[7] the recipients of his work on education were as follows:

'Ld Keeper'	Sir John Somers of Evesham
'Ld Pembroke'	Thomas Herbert, eighth Earl of Pembroke and Lord Privy Seal

[1] No. 1630 (iv. 684).   [2] No. 1638 (iv. 691).
[3] No. 1643 (iv. 701).   [4] No. 1644 (iv. 701).
[5] In the process of publication; ed. Henry Schankula, for the Clarendon Edition of the Works of John Locke.
[6] Bodleian Library, MS Locke f. 1–10, British Library Add. MS 15642.
[7] From Locke's notebook, Bodleian Library, MS Locke f. 29, p. 144.

'L: Ashley'   Anthony Ashley Cooper, later third Earl of Shaftes-
                     bury
'L: Ch: Just Treby' Sir George Treby, Chief Justice of Common Pleas
                     from 1692
'Mr Clarke'   the dedicatee
'JL'   Locke himself
'Mr Freke'   John Freke, a barrister and member of the Middle
                     Temple
'Mr Popple'   London merchant, translator of Locke's *Epistola de
                     Tolerantia*
'S^r W Yonge'   Friend and MP
'L. Monmouth'   Charles Mordaunt, first Earl of Monmouth of 2nd
                     creation, later Earl of Peterborough
'ABp.'   John Tillotson, Archbishop of Canterbury
'B Furley'   Benjamin Furly, a Quaker and friend
'Dr Guenelon'   Peter Guenellon, medical graduate living in Amster-
                     dam
'M^r LeCler'   Jean Le Clerc, friend at Amsterdam, theologian and
                     biblical scholar, editor of the *Bibliothèque universelle*,
                     etc.
'Mr Daranda'   Paul d'Aranda, friend and correspondent of Le Clerc
'Mr Pawling'   Oxford mercer with whom Locke left papers and
                     clothes when he fled to Holland
'Mr Fermin'   Thomas Firmin, a Socinian, and friend of Tillotson
'Mr Molineux'   William Molyneux, friend, scientist, Irish MP, and
                     member of the Royal Society
'Dr Molineux'   Thomas Molyneux, brother of William, MD from
                     Dublin, later FRS
'J. Johnston'   James Johnstone or Johnstoun, nephew of Gilbert
                     Burnet and Secretary of State for Scotland, 1692–6
'Mr Bridges'   Brooke Bridges, Auditor of Imprest (Exchequer)
                     1682–1705, at one time with the East India Company
'Mrs Duke'   Sir Walter Yonge's sister
'Helmont'   Baron F. M. van Helmont of Rotterdam, friend and
                     medical writer
'L. Farfar'   Archibald Douglas, Earl of Forfar and Lord of Scots
                     Treasury
'J. Bonville'   Locke's cousin, and a pewterer

To these a second list adds 'Mrs Smith', a wealthy English widow
living in Utrecht when Locke was in Holland, and 'F Limborch' an
Amsterdam theologian Locke met when in Holland, but omits 'JL'.[1]

[1] In a collection of miscellaneous papers in the Bodleian Library, MS Locke c. 25, fo.
53.

SOME
THOUGHTS
CONCERNING
Education.

LONDON,

Printed for *A.* and *J. Churchill,*
at the *Black Swan* in *Pater-
noster-row,* 1693.

1*a*. Title-page of NN edition

SOME
THOUGHTS
CONCERNING
Education.

LONDON,

Printed for *A.* and *J. Churchill,*
at the *Black Swan* in *Pater-*
noster-row, 1 6 9 3.

1*b*. Title-page of NA edition

Of course Locke himself had copies of the anonymously published first edition. Two copies are recorded in his library catalogue: LL 1020 (shelfmark 53) and 1785 (183a). This latter copy is now in the Bodleian Library. So far there is no knowledge of the location of the other copy.

The first published edition of *Some Thoughts* is two editions: there is no second edition as such, but two lookalike editions. As the illustrations (Pls. 1*a*–1*b*) show, the title-pages differ only in that the three rows of ornaments in the middle have been more squarely aligned for the later edition, and the first set of double horizontal rules has been lowered 3 mm from 'Education'. Attention to the problem of these two editions was drawn first by Sir Frederick Kenyon while he was at work on the British Library manuscript draft. In *The Times Literary Supplement* for 20 April 1933 (no. 1629) he appealed (in vain) for the location of copies of the second edition. He was answered obliquely by D. Massey, who in the issue for 27 February 1937 (no. 1830) reported that his examination of copies of the first edition showed him there were 'two variant states of the work' which differed from each other throughout. 'Perhaps it can be assumed that one of these variants was intended to have taken the place of the second edition.'

A short note by John Eliot Alden in the *Papers of the Bibliographical Society of America*, 37 (1943), 309 distinguished the two editions, by noting that one group has the catchword 'I my' on the verso of leaf A2, the other group 'I'. He felt it difficult to assert which was the earlier edition, but inclined to the 'I' edition's being the second and later. This is the distinction used by antiquarian bookdealers generally when offering copies for sale.

The late Professor Peter Nidditch went into this problem in even greater detail in his pamphlet *A Bibliographical and Text-Historical Study of the Early Printings of John Locke's* Some Thoughts concerning Education (Sheffield, 1973). While examining the question of which is the true first edition, he distinguished the two as the 'NN' and 'NA' editions (corresponding respectively to the 'I my' and 'I' editions) from the spelling of the word '*Patronnge/Patronage*' on sig. A3^v, l. 19.[1] He seems to have been unaware of Alden's note in 1943.

The facts of the case are that there are two different typesettings of the work, both without author- or edition-statement, one a line-by-line reprint of the other. If we omit the title-page and the index in

---

[1] Perhaps he overlooked 'deferr/defer' on sig. A2^v, l. 3.

our reckoning, out of a total of 7,702 lines, there are seven lines that end differently, one because of a spelling error.[1]

There are other differences, roughly 530 in number, chiefly relating to punctuation and spelling. There are many italic colons in the NN edition,[2] probably because the printer was short of roman fount (at least 70 incorrect italic colons in NN). In NN there are 6 verbs, 15 nouns, 6 adjectives, one conjunction, and one adverb capitalized that have become lower-case in the NA edition. On the other hand, 98 nouns, 7 adjectives, 2 conjunctions, and 2 verbs are capitalized in NA but lower-case in NN. There are 94 occurrences in NA of punctuation added or corrected (chiefly commas added where there was none in NN), and 14 occasions where NN punctuation is wanting in NA. There are 28 typographical errors in NN which are corrected in NA, but NA introduces 14 new ones. There are 45 variant spellings in the two editions (usefull/useful, wilfull/wilful, easie/easy, imploy'd/employ'd, etc., NN spelling given first). There are also differences in the style of ligatures long s and t (e.g. ſt /ſt). If as a hypothesis we take the NN edition as the earlier, there is thus a very discernible tendency from NN to NA to capitalize nouns, to correct typographical errors (even when introducing new ones), to insert punctuation where it was omitted, and to remove capital letters from adverbs and verbs. Most of these, however, are accidental (or formal) variants.

There are substantive errors in the NN edition. In the following examples the NA reading is given within parentheses.

(1) For he that has been used to have his Will in every thing, as long as he was in Coats, why would (should) we think it strange, that he should desire it, and contend for it still, when he is in Breeches? (D2^r, ll. 22–7, § 35.)

(2) When constant custom has made any one thing easy and natural to them, and they practise it with (without) Reflection, you may then go on to another. (F1^v, ll. 24–8, § 64; 3rd edn. § 66.)

[1] The line-endings are as follows:

	NN	NA
A2^v, ll. 27–8	*to every* | *body*	*to eve-* | *ry body*
B3^v, ll. 26–7	wash-|ed	wa-|shed
C5^v, ll. 5–6	Per-|ristaltick	Pe-|ristaltick
E6^v, ll. 23–4	to | a Degree,	to a | Degree
L5^v, ll. 26–7	if he | persists	if| he persists
P4^v, ll. 4–6	fix it in his Me-|mory, and to in-courage him to go on, | as to set him	fix it in his|Memory, and to incour-age him to | go on, as to set him
Q4^v, ll. 9–10	Princi-|ples	Prin-|ciples

[2] Because of its ease and brevity I shall use Nidditch's terminology in distinguishing these two edns.

(3) To this purpose, their being in their presence, should be made easie to them; they shall (should) be allowed the liberties and freedom suitable to their Ages ... (F4^r, ll. 2–6, § 67; 3rd edn. § 69.)

(4) ... when, I say, by these Ways of Tenderness and Affection ... you have also planted in him a particular Affection for you ... and you have formed in his Mind that true *Reverence*, which is alway afterwards carefully to be increased and maintained in both the Parts of it, *Love* and *Fear*, as the great Principle ... to turn his Mind to the ways of Vertue of (and) Honour.   (I1^r, ll. 2–15, § 94; 3rd edn. § 99.)

(5) And if you carefully observe the Character of this (his) Mind now in the first Scenes of his Life ... (I2^v, ll. 3–5, § 97; 3rd edn. § 102.)

(6) But where that is wanting, unless it be in things absolutely necessary, it is better to let him pass them (pass them by) quietly, than to vex him about them to no purpose ... (N7^r, l. 29–N7^v, l. 4, § 153; 3rd edn. § 161.)

(7) In which abstract Speculations when young Men have had their Heads imploy'd a while without finding the Success and Imployment (Improvement) or Use of it which they expected, they are apt to have mean Thoughts ... (O3^r, ll. 14–19, § 157; 3rd edn. § 166.)

In each of these cases the NA edition is correct and the NN wrong. In the seventh example, a similar passage is found in the letter of 8 February 1686 NS (no. 844) to Edward Clarke; there the manuscript has 'Improvement'.[1] Further, the NA wordings are the ones followed in the third edition. There are two other cases where the differences between NN and NA are notable because the spelling used in one was an acceptable variant in the seventeenth century, though is so no longer. In § 72 (F7^v, ll. 3–6; 3rd edn. § 74) NN reads: 'The hardest Part, I confess, is with the first, or eldest; but when once he is set right, it is easie by him to lead the rest whether one will'; NA has the form 'whither' instead of 'whether'. And again, in § 143 (N2^r, ll. 18–20; 3rd edn. § 150) the word 'least' is changed in NA to 'lest' in the sentence: 'This being a play amongst you, tempt him not to it, least you make it Business; ...'. The only substantive error in the NA edition is the numbering of § 29 as § 22.

In the course of examining as many copies of both editions as we could find (some dozen of each were scrutinized in detail), we detected several stop-press corrections in NN, and none in NA. For such corrections the press is stopped in the course of printing to correct an error, the rest of the sheet (in the case of an octavo book, of eight pages on each side) not being disturbed. 'Founation' for 'Foun-

---

[1] *Corr.* ii. 775.

dation' (H6^r, l. 4) in § 91 (cf. below, on p. 158, l. 30) and *'familiarity'* for *'familiarly'* (H8^r, l. 20) in § 93 (3rd edn. § 97) must have been noticed very early in the press-run, perhaps by the printer himself: most copies have the correct word. The other three such corrections seem to have occurred late in the printing-run and survive in single copies, all others that we have seen having the incorrect word.

Locke was known to be fussy about the printing of his works. In a letter to Edward Clarke (no. 1557) dated 2 November 1692 Locke writes from Oates:

> I have this farther favour to beg of you that you would send for Mr Awnsham Churchill (to whom I have writ fower or five times to desire him to send me the sheets have been printed since I came out of town but can not receive a word from him) and tell him I would by noe means have him publish it till I have perused all the remaining sheets which I would have him send to me. I desire you would give your self this trouble. For I am concernd to see it before it goe abroad. (*Corr.* iv. 564.)

De Beer states that this section refers to *A Third Letter for Toleration*; he presumably based his decision on material in Locke's journal at the relevant period. Both Maurice Cranston and Peter Nidditch take it to refer to *Some Thoughts*. We agree with de Beer. However, it is informative of Locke's attitude toward his publications. In the case of *Some Thoughts*, we think the publisher went ahead and had the printing completed before Locke could peruse the sheets. Some of his works exhibit cancelled pages: the title-page for *A Letter to . . . the Bishop of Worcester*, is a cancel, replacing the original because it omitted the bishop's proper title, 'The Right Reverend the Lord Bishop'; pp. 3–4 of his *Vindication of the Reasonableness of Christianity*, where the marginal note on the cancellandum, p. 4, divulges the secret of the authorship of *The Naked Truth* ('Bishops Taylor and Crofts'). A more grievous case is that of the two issues of the first edition of Locke's *Two Treatises of Government* (1690): some issues have a corrected gathering Q, set chiefly in 31 lines to the page; the earlier ones (Laslett's 1X) have 29 lines throughout. Because of some textual omissions, the whole gathering (pp. 225–40) was reset with more lines to the page so as to insert matter omitted in the earlier issue (this corrected issue constitutes Laslett's '1R', for 'right'(?)). Thus the whole gathering is a cancel.

Another example of Locke's distress at the quality of the printing is shown by the following letter to Edward Clarke, dated 12 March 1694.

I had taken some pains to rectifie the faults yet remaining in the book you sent me, And to make the edition as good as may be: But there is noe contesting with ever lasting unalterable neglect. If I receive that other paper I sent for I shall goe on with it. If not I shall trouble my self noe more about it. Its fate is it seems to be the worst printed that ever book was, and tis in vain for any one to labour against it.[1]

In the case of the two 1693 editions of *Some Thoughts*, we think Locke was so incensed by the many errors that the whole printing was treated as a cancellandum, and a barely distinguishable new printing set in type. Because of the substantive errors in the NN and the stop-press corrections, it is obvious that the NN was the earlier or true first edition. In this connection it is worth noting that one of Locke's two copies, now in the Bodleian Library, is a mixed-sheet copy: that is, all gatherings except K (pp. 129–44) are of the NN edition, but K is of NA. Despite appeals to all libraries known to own the 1693 editions, this is the only mixed-sheet copy we have located. The only inference we can draw from this occurrence is that the two editions were printed within a short time one of the other: that is, the publisher still had sheets of the NN edition on hand when he printed the NA edition.

Further, the usual progression in publishing is from an incorrect (first) to an improved (second) to a further corrected (third) edition, and so forth. Many of the errors in the NN edition must also derive from the printer's difficulty in reading the 'foul copy'. Since it is not known to survive, we do not know if it was in Locke's or, as we suspect, Brounower's hand. Locke's correspondence is helpful in deciding which word is correct in the substantive errors listed above (see example 7).

Some of the errors in the NN edition Nidditch called 'verbal exchange errors', such as would arise from the printer's not hearing correctly the word read to him while setting type. He cited example 2 above, in addition to 'those/these' (E3^r, l. 19), 'your/you' (F5^v, l. 4), NN readings first. Locke's letter to Clarke of 29 April 1687 NS (no. 929) uses 'you grown men', not 'your grown men' (*Corr.* iii. 177) and 'whether' not 'whither' (iii. 178) in the phrase 'lead the rest whether one will'.

The evidence from presentation copies to the donors listed above is also ambiguous. Of all those copies only two are known to survive.

---

[1] No. 1719 (v. 30). De Beer states that Locke is here referring to the second edition of *Two Treatises of Government*.

A Texas bookseller, W. Thomas Taylor, recently acquired and offered for sale William Molyneux's presentation-copy, as well as some of Locke's letters to Molyneux. That copy is of the NA edition, as we learnt in correspondence. Professor Nidditch discovered and drew our attention to the one presented to Sir Walter Yonge, now in the University of Sheffield Library, in the pamphlet already cited. It too is an NA copy. His opinion was that that must be the true first edition, reasoning that authors presented their works to their friends before publication, and would wish them to have the first edition. Therefore Sir Walter Yonge's copy is the true first edition. He explains the NN edition by reasoning that the work was surprisingly popular, and therefore a hasty, careless reprint was immediately undertaken. Since the two editions are indistinguishable without a close examination, we are of the opinion that Locke preferred to present his friends with the more correct edition.[1]

We have already mentioned the first edition was published anonymously in mid-July 1693. 'The Epistle Dedicatory' in the third and fourth editions is signed 'John Locke' and dated '7 March. 1692' (i.e. 1693 Modern Style), though it was undated in the 1693 editions. The fifth and later editions print '1690' incorrectly; the incorrectness of this date is supported by the inclusion of material on 'sauntering' or idleness in letter 1370, dated 9 March 1691 (*Corr.* iv. 222–5), rewritten for the published edition as §§ 116–19 (3rd edn. §§ 123–6).

It is speculation at best to give the number of copies printed: a print-run of 200 or 500 copies was not unusual. The contract quoted below for the third edition between Locke and the Churchills speaks of 1,500 copies: we may assume an edition of any number between 200 and 1,500 for the first edition.

We have found no record of the price charged. However, a copy in Trinity College Library at Dublin is inscribed 'Char. Watts, 00:03:00, 1704', indicating he paid three shillings for his NA edition, a fairly usual price for an octavo book in the 1690s.

(b) *The Third Edition (1695)*

Title in double rules: SOME THOUGHTS CONCERNING Education. [Four lines of verse from Horace, *Odes*] Hor. *L.* IV. *Od.* 4. The Third

---

[1] Much of this information about the differences in the NN and NA edns. has been published by Jean S. Yolton in *Papers of the Bibliographical Society of America*, 74 (1981), 315–21, under the title: 'The First Editions of John Locke's *Some Thoughts concerning Education*'.

SOME

THOUGHTS

CONCERNING

Education.

Doctrina vires promovet insitas,
Rectiq; cultus pectora roborant :
Utcunq; defecere mores,
Dedecorant bene nata culpæ.

Hor. *L.* IV. *Od.* 4.

The Third Edition Enlarged.

LONDON,
Printed for *A.* and *J. Churchill,* at the
Black Swan in *Pater-noster-row,* 1695.

2. Title-page of third edition

Edition Enlarged. LONDON, Printed for *A.* and *J. Churchill*, at the *Black Swan* in *Pater-noster-row*, 1695. 8° (laid paper 173 × 105 mm cut) A⁴ B–2A⁸ B⁴; pp. *i* title, *iii–vii* dedication, 1–374 text, *375–6* contents.

When the publishers were running out of stock, they probably wrote to Locke to inform him and to enquire whether he wished to add or change anything before they went ahead with reprinting. Such a letter concerning reprinting the *Essay* survives.

I were lately at your Lodgings to speake with you about Reprinting your Book . . . I trouble you with this letter to acquaint you that the Impression of your Books are so neare sold that I am ready to Reprint it but thought it necessary to acquaint you first with it because you shewed me some altera- tions and Additions that you had made, and if you have finished what you intended, I desire you would be pleased to send it by the first oppertun- ity. . . .[1]

Further, a contract for a new edition of *Some Thoughts* survives. It reads:

Wee Awnsham & John Churchil o London Booksellers doe hereby oblidge ourselves to pay unto Mʳ Jnᵒ Locke Gent during his Life five pounds Sterl upon every Impression wee shall print or cause to be printed of his Booke called Some thoughts concerning education, and Ten shillings p sheet printed for all additions that he shall make to the same, the Impressions not to exceed fiveteen hundred Bookes. & to deliver him Twenty five bookes bound in Calve skin Lettʳᵈ on every Impression. Wee doe allso hereby oblidge & bind our selves heyrs Executors, Assʳˢ to the sᵈ John Locke. during his Life that neither wee nor they will or shall dispose of the right or Title to the Coppy of the said Booke to any person whatever without the Consent of the said John Locke Witniss our hands in London this Twenty day of June 1694

A. Churchil
John Churchill[2]

As the comparative table (pp. 71–5) shows, §§ 37, 62, 93–4, 98, 115, 117, 176, and 205 are new to this edition. Renumbering of sections was necessary chiefly from this new material, but also some sections in the 1693 editions were split: § 87 expanded into §§ 88–9, § 143 divided into §§ 150–1, § 157 into §§ 165–6, § 177 into §§ 188–90. But the first edition §§ 76–7 are combined into one, an expanded § 78, and there are two §§ 172 in the first edition. The 203 sections of the 1693 editions have become 216 sections in the third edition. The last

---

[1] Letter from Thomas Bassett, no. 1607 (iv. 645–6), dated 28 Feb. 1693.
[2] Bodleian Library, MS Locke b. 1, fo. 173.

section is numbered 217, but there is no § 213—not in the third, fourth, fifth, or later editions.

Parallel material occurring in letters to the Clarkes is indicated in a note at the head of the comparative table, witnessing to Locke's continuing concern to add to his material.

Apart from these major differences between the first and third editions, there are many minor differences: corrections of spelling and punctuation, and some expansions, often only a sentence or a phrase.

This edition was advertised for sale in the *London Gazette*, no. 3098, the issue for 18–22 July 1695, and was probably published in early July.[1] From the contract transcribed above, we would hazard an edition of 1,000 copies.

The list of presentation copies in Locke's notebook, headed 'Education Copys *95*', contains the following names (those also on the list for the first edition, are indicated by an asterisk).

*'Mr Bridges 1'	[deleted]
*'Mr Freke 1'	
'Mr Connier'	John Conyers, a second cousin of Sir Francis Masham and an MP, 1695–1725
*'Ld Ashley 1'	
*'E: Pembroke 1'	
'Mrs Pit 1'	Perhaps Martha, née Nourse, wife of Robert Pitt, MD, a member of the College of Physicians
*'Dr Guenellon 1'	
*'Lady Farfar 1'	
'Mr Lyddell'	Robert Liddell, younger son of Sir Thomas Liddell of Ravensworth Castle, Durham. One of 15 men chosen on 15 August 1694 to prepare by-laws for the Bank of England. First mentioned in Locke's journals 28 September 1694
'Mr Fletcher 1'	Andrew Fletcher of Saltoun, the Scots patriot
*'L. C. J. Treby 1'	
*'Mr Molineux 1'	
'Mrs Masham 1'	Lady Masham, née Damaris Cudworth, wife of Sir Francis Masham; a friend with whom Locke lodged in the 1690s until his death
'Monsr Coste 1'	Pierre Coste; came to England through friendship with Jean Le Clerc, as tutor to Lady Masham's son, Francis Cudworth Masham, and to translate Locke's *Essay* into French under Locke's supervision

[1] Cf. *Corr.* v. 393, 397nn.

'Mr Teute 1'	Person mentioned in letter 1918 (v. 397), to whom (or whose son) D'Aranda forwarded a book on Le Clerc's behalf
'Ld Chamberlain 1'	Charles Sackville, Lord Buckhurst, afterwards Earl of Dorset; also known for his munificence to men of letters
'Tyrrell 1'	James Tyrrell, the historian and political writer; a friend of Locke's
'Harley 1'	Possibly Robert Harley, first Earl of Oxford, the statesman; but more probably his father, Sir Edward Harley, MP for Herefordshire
*'Furly 1'	
'Marlow 1'	Unidentified
'Pepys'	The diarist, Samuel Pepys.
'Sr Fl. Sheppard'	Sir Fleetwood Sheppard, the poet and courtier; a fellow student of Locke's in the 1650s at Christ Church, Oxford; protégé of the Lord Chamberlain and one-time tutor to Nell Gwynn's son by Charles II, Charles Beauclerk
'Mr Ashley'	Perhaps a relative of Lord Ashley, the future third Earl of Shaftesbury
*'Mr Clarke'	
'L: Masham 25'	Another copy to Lady Masham; the 25th copy
'L: Chichley 26'	Perhaps Sir John Chicheley, Knight, son of Sir Thomas Chicheley, the former MP for Cambridgeshire; the 26th copy

This list occurs in Locke's notebook (Bodleian Library, MS Locke f. 29, p. 145). Another list of recipients, differently arranged, and headed 'Education 1695' occurs in a collection of manuscripts, giving the same names but with the inclusion of Mr Bridges and omitting Lord Chicheley.[1] However, this second list appears to have been written during or after 1695. The sheet has been folded in four to include lists of recipients for *Further Considerations concerning Raising the Value of Money* (1695), *Several Papers Relating to Money . . .* (1696), *Some Thoughts*, 1695 edition, and a copy of the 1693 list with some variations, third edition of the *Essay concerning Human Understanding* (1695), the first two 'Letters' to the Bishop of Worcester (1697), and the fourth edition of *Some Thoughts* (1699).

(c) The Fourth Edition (1699)

Title in double rules: SOME THOUGHTS CONCERNING Education. [Four lines of verse from Horace] Hor. *L.* IV. *Od.* 4. The Fourth Edition

---

[1] Bodleian Library, MS Locke c. 25, fo. 53.

SOME

THOUGHTS

CONCERNING

Education.

Doctrina vires promovet insitas,
Rectiq; cultus pectora roborant :
Utcunq; defecere mores,
Dedecorant bene nata culpæ.

Hor. *L.* IV. *Od.* 4.

The Fourth Edition Enlarged.

LONDON,

Printed for *A.* and *J. Churchill,* at the
Black Swan in *Pater-noster-row,* 1699.

3. Title-page of fourth edition

Enlarged. *LONDON*, Printed for *A.* and *J. Churchill*, at the *Black Swan* in *Pater-noster-row*, 1699. 8° (laid paper 189 × 112 mm cut) A⁴ B–2B⁸; pp. *i* title, *iii–vii* dedication, 1–380 text, *381–2* contents.

This edition was presumably published when the Churchills had used up their stock of the third edition. It was published about November 1698,[1] and is largely a reprint of the third, but new errors, especially of spelling, have been introduced, and variant punctuation supplied. It is not, in fact, as accurately printed as the third.

There are a few substantial changes: § 7 is expanded by one printed page, § 94 by a half-page, and §§ 192–3 are slightly rephrased. The only large addition occurs in § 167, the section headed 'Latin', where more details about the skills of a teacher or tutor needed to encourage and instruct his pupil occur.

A very short list of recipients from the author of this edition is listed in the Bodleian Library, MS Locke c. 25, fo. 53ᵛ: 'Du Bos', 'Dr. Moly-neux', and 'Mr Crell'. Du Bos is the Abbé Jean Baptiste Du Bos, a good friend of Nicolas Toinard, who introduced him (by letter) to Locke. He was known to be in England in May 1698. 'Mr Crell' is Samuel Crellius. He studied under Limborch—who introduced him (also by letter) to Locke—and himself became a notable theologian.[2]

We are fortunate to have evidence of the price of this edition. By request, the Churchills supplied over 100 volumes of recent publications in 1700 to James Logan in Philadelphia. The shipment included 6 copies of Locke's *Essay* at £4. 4s. 0d. or 14s. each, 6 copies of *Some Thoughts* and 6 copies of *Two Treatises of Government*, both lots at £1. 1s. 0d. or 3s. 6d. a copy, and copies of other Locke works.[3]

(d) The Fifth Edition (1705)

Title in double rules: SOME THOUGHTS CONCERNING Education. [Four lines of verse from Horace]. Hor. *L.* IV. *Od.* 4. *By Mr.* JOHN LOCKE. The Fifth Edition Enlarged. *LONDON*, Printed for *A.* and *J. Churchill*, at the *Black Swan* in *Pater-noster-row*, 1705. 8° (laid paper 181 × 112 mm cut) A⁴ B–2B⁸ 2C⁴; *i* title, *iii–vii* dedication, 1–390 text, *391–2* contents.

Published in the same year as the fifth edition of the *Essay concerning Human Understanding*, this edition is a posthumous one, though all

---

[1] *Corr.* vi, p. vii.

[2] *Corr.* 2482 (vi. 459–61) dated 18 Aug. 1698 NS, from Limborch, is the letter of introduction.

[3] We are indebted to Edwin Wolf 2nd, for bringing this information to our attention. Full details of this transaction are given in Wolf's article, 'A Parcel of Books for the Province in 1700', *The Pennsylvania Magazine of History and Biography*, 89 (1965), 428–46.

SOME

THOUGHTS

CONCERNING

Education.

Doctrina vires promovet insitas,
Rectique cultus pectora roborant :
Utcunque defecere mores,
Dedecorant bene nata culpæ.

Hor. *L.* IV. *Od.* 4.

By *Mr.* JOHN LOCKE.

𝕿𝖍𝖊 𝕱𝖎𝖋𝖙𝖍 𝕰𝖉𝖎𝖙𝖎𝖔𝖓 𝕰𝖓𝖑𝖆𝖗𝖌𝖊𝖉.

LONDON,

Printed for *A.* and *J. Churchill,* at the
Black Swan in *Pater-noster-row,* 1705.

4. Title-page of fifth edition

substantial changes and expansions in the text must have been made by Locke.

There are several minor changes: a sentence added to § 7, a marginal note in § 69, the first sentence of § 93 rephrased, and two sentences added at the end of § 167. Two other sections have received major additions. In § 143, on 'breeding' five and a half printed pages have been added concerning 'roughness', 'contempt', 'censoriness', 'raillery', 'contradiction', and 'captiousness'. Unfortunately, unlike the first and third editions, none of this material is foreshadowed in his surviving correspondence.

The other large addition is the insertion in § 195 of a long quotation from La Bruyère's *Les Caractères, ou Mœurs de ce siècle*, appended to *Les Caractères de Théophraste* (1696 edition). Presumably this is Locke's own translation, broken off half-way, by two paragraphs of commentary, before concluding the quotation.

The text of the fifth edition, even with some egregious errors (such as 'unreasonable' for 'unseasonable'), has been the model for all later English editions, whether issued separately or in a collected 'works'. Since each eighteenth-century (and later) edition uses as copy-text that immediately preceding it, even where errors have crept in, each new error appears in the next edition, until nineteenth-century editions often do not reflect what Locke wrote.

(e) Translations

Within Locke's lifetime, *Some Thoughts* was translated into French and published in 1695, and a Dutch translation appeared in 1698. The French translation by Pierre Coste is of especial interest, since he can be presumed to have revised it when staying with Locke at Lady Masham's. A German translation appeared in 1708, a Swedish in 1709, and an Italian translation of the French translation in 1735.

Title: 'DE | L'EDUCATION | DES ENFANS. | Traduit de l'Anglois. | Par P** C**** | [printer's emblem, with scroll: 'QVÆRENDO'] | A AMSTER-DAM, | Chez Antoine Schelte, Marchand Li-|braire près de la Bourfe. | M. DC. XCV.' Small 8° (on paper 143 × 85 mm cut) *⁸ **⁴ A–2B⁸ 2C⁶; pp. *i* title, *iii–vi* dedication to Mlle Anne Wolfgang (Coste's cousin), *vii–xxiii* translator's preface, *xxiv* errata, 1–412 text.

This first French translation by Pierre Coste appearing in 1695 was based on the 1693 English editions, and was published anonymously in respect of author and translator. A second French edition, with the title *Nouvelles Instructions pour l'Education des Enfans*, appeared in 1699. Long considered a piracy because only the bookseller's name, Jacques Menassion, at Amsterdam, appears on the title-page, without a street address, it was in fact printed in Geneva. In a letter to Locke dated 29 June 1699, Pierre Coste reports he has learned from a friend, who had been informed by Pierre Desmaizeaux, that 'on avoit rimprimé à Geneve votre Livre de l'Education des Enfans avec les additions. Le Traducteur est, dit-on, un homme de peu de jugement, comme il paroit par ces deux beveuës: Dans l'endroit où vous conseillez de faire lire aux Enfans *Raynard the Fox*, il a mis à la marge on peut donner aux Enfans les Fables et les *Contes* de la Fontaine. C'est l'entendre. Dans un autre endroit où vous conseillez de donner aux Enfans quelque Catechisme où les principes de la Religion Chrétienne soient proposez dans les propres termes de l'Ecriture, il indique en marge le *Catechisme de Drelincourt* qui est tout rempli de méchante controverse. D'ailleurs ce beau faiseur de Notes écrit fort mal. Il s'est hazardé de faire une Préface qui n'est, dit-on, qu'un continuel galimathias.'[1] It is indeed a curious composition, in a sense based on the third English edition; as the translator explains in his preface, it has been 'fort enrichie' over the first French edition 'par de nouvelles pensées, qui remplissent souvent les douze et les quinze pages tout de suite', implying that these additions are from the third English edition. He includes in his preface an abridgement of Locke's dedication to Clarke, and reveals John Locke to be the author, further stating that he feels free to reveal that information, since it has already been made public by an article in the *Histoire des ouvrages des sçavans*, issue for November 1693. Of course the fact was stated in the preface of the third edition he is claiming to use. The text of his translation is Coste's translation, expanded by his own translations of those sections (e.g., 37, 62, 93–4, 98) by which Locke himself improved the third edition.

When we arrive at Coste's revised and improved second edition in 1708, a textual comparison shows us that just those sections the 'pirate' himself added to his edition bear a completely different turn of phrase from those Coste supplies. The pirated edition exhibits 216 sections (making up for the lack of § 213 by renumbering the final sections); Coste's 1708 edition, as we shall see, runs to 223 sections, but is based on the last edition Locke is known to have revised, the fifth edition of 1705. It was also sold, like the first French edition, by the Schelte firm in Amsterdam.

[1] *Corr.* 2601 (vi. 649–50).

Since Pierre Coste had come to England by 1698, as tutor to Francis Cudworth Masham and to translate the *Essay concerning Human Understanding* under Locke's supervision, it is a fair assumption that the many minor improvements in phraseology that occur in the French edition of 1708 were the result of the close contacts between author and translator. The title-page stated it was 'revue, corrigée et augmentée de plus d'un tiers par l'auteur'. The November 1708 issue of the *Journal de Trévoux* mentions it as having already appeared, 'mais M. Coste l'a retouchee: & pour la rendre conforme à la derniere Edition de son original, il a éte obligé de la refondre presque entierement' (pp. 1971–2).

The 1708 edition and all subsequent French ones revert to the 1695 title, *De l'Education des Enfans*. Apart from improvements in phraseology, the 'recasting' encompasses dividing the text into twenty-eight chapters and a resultant expansion of the 216 English sections into 223 French. After the introductory § 1 and the first two sentences of § 2, the text is given a chapter-heading, and the rest of § 2 becomes § 3. Other later sections are also split and given new numbering so as to make discrete chapters. Ch. I, 'De la santé, précautions nécessaires pour la conserver aux enfans', covers §§ 2–30 English, numbered 3–31. Ch. II, 'Du soin qu'on doit prendre de l'âme des enfans', covers English §§ 31–42, numbered 32–43 in the French translation. Ch. XXVII, 'Pourquoi et en quel temps on doit faire voyager les jeunes gens', contains § 219–22, corresponding to the English §§ 212–16. The final chapter, XXVIII, 'Conclusion de tout l'ouvrage', is numbered § 223, corresponding to § 217 of the last English edition. This pattern of sections and chapters is followed in all subsequent French editions.

III. Other Educational Writings

Among the many letters, notebooks, account-books, and journals Locke left behind (now mostly in the Lovelace Collection in the Bodleian Library, Oxford), there are three manuscripts on educational matters. The first is a long essay marked 'Study' in his journal for 1677, beginning after his entry for Friday, 26 March NS. The journal is an appendage of many leaves bound after the printed *Grand Almanach journalier* for 1677 (Lyon: Par Jean Malpech). The text begins: 'The end of Study is Knowledg & the end of Knowledg practise or communication.' The text, 'Study', occupies many leaves in whole or in part (MS Locke f. 2, fos. 87–141), being frequently broken off for daily notes of the temperature, towns visited in France, expenses, books ordered, etc. It ends before the journal entry for Sunday, 9 May 1677 NS, with the words: 'And soe much concerning study. JL.'

Since this essay forms part of a complete edition of Locke's journals being edited—and in many places deciphered from Locke's version of Jeremiah Rich's shorthand—by Professor H. A. S. Schankula for this Clarendon Edition, it would be a repetition to reprint it here.

A second piece among his many manuscripts is that with a docket title: 'Education 97 To the Countesse of Peterborow'. Cary Fraser married Charles Mordaunt, the third Earl of Peterborough, in about 1676. She presumably met Locke through Benjamin Furly, while the earl, a general, was serving in the United Provinces. Locke's recommendations to her were sent in September or October 1697. They are a brief two-leaved manuscript (Bodleian Library, MS Locke c. 24, fos. 196–7) and have been transcribed in the *Correspondence* by de Beer (no. 2320, vi. 212–16).

The third item has always been thought to be Locke's, though it is in the large, not too neat handwriting of Samuel Bold. Bold had guessed at the authorship of *The Reasonableness of Christianity*, and had defended it in some five printed tracts. Locke also befriended him, and it was to him that Locke dictated 'Some Thoughts concerning Reading and Study for a Gentleman'.[1] The manuscript was first published under that title in Pierre Desmaizeaux's *Collection of Several Pieces of Mr. John Locke* (1720). The original occurs in a volume of mixed papers belonging to Bold in the British Library (MS Sloane 4290, fos. 11–14), with the heading 'Mr Locke's Extemporè Advice &c.' The transcription given below (Appendix III, pp. 319–27) is from this manuscript, with substantive variants from the first published edition given in notes.

IV. The Copy-Text

Ideally the aim of a copy-text editor is to work from an early printed edition, usually the first, though 'a surviving manuscript will of course be of great value to the editor . . . for it will serve as a check upon the accuracy of the printed version.'[2] No manuscript copy used for the first printed edition survives; the Harvard College Library and the British Library drafts described above serve as checks on the accuracy

---

[1] Cf. *Corr.* 2232 (vi. 66).
[2] P. Gaskell, *A New Introduction to Bibliography* (Oxford, 1972), p. 340.

of some passages. We suspect the original manuscript the Churchills used was in the handwriting of Sylvester Brounower, since Locke was trying to keep his authorship a secret and the Churchills would have been familiar with Locke's handwriting. The aim of the editor is to establish a text printed, so far as is possible, as the author wanted it to be, bibliographically speaking to 'establish authorial intention'. As we have noted, the third edition contained many large additions, as well as corrections to the first edition, and very few misprints. The fourth edition was poorly printed, and with slight expansions, except for the material added in § 167. The fifth edition, though published after Locke's death, has some additions in § 143 (on 'breeding') and the insertion of a large quotation from La Bruyère in § 195.

The changes in both the fourth and fifth editions are otherwise more in the nature of retouching than of substantial rewriting, whereas the third edition is a considerable reworking of the 1693 editions. The fourth and fifth editions contain increasing error and corruption at the hands of the compositors, as well as authorial additions.

We have therefore chosen the third edition as copy-text. So far as substantive variants are concerned, they have been incorporated from the later editions where they are what Locke wrote or rewrote as improvements of the third edition. The text has also been purged so far as possible of deliberate but unauthorized alterations. We have not modernized the spelling or the punctuation, but notes have been added where an unfamiliar word or the earlier spelling of a modern word might puzzle readers. Leaving the words as Locke is presumed to have written them, even if this gives rise to ambiguities, also preserves the literary quality the text has from its own period of conception.

The notes to the text which follow are of five kinds:

*	Locke's own notes to his text
[section-number]	Uncued sidenotes within the section
[line-number]	Substantive variants
[a], [b], etc.	Comparable passages, including variants, from the Harvard College Library and the British Library manuscripts, and from the *Correspondence*
[1], [2], etc.	Editors' notes

Line-numbers and phrases at the bottom of the page following Locke's own notes signal substantive variations in the text from the two 1693, the fourth, and the fifth editions. Formal, or accidental variants are contained in Appendix I (pp. 269 ff.).

The editors are grateful for the inspiration and early guidance of the late Peter Nidditch. Without the model for precision, the encyclopædic knowledge gently imparted, and the monumental editorial labours of Esmond de Beer in his edition of Locke's correspondence, this edition of Locke's *Education* would have been infinitely more difficult to complete. Members of the Editorial Board for the Clarendon Edition of the Works of John Locke have been extremely helpful, as have the staff of the Oxford University Press, especially Leofranc Holford-Strevens, whose immense scholarship and meticulous attention to detail have preserved us from many an error. We are also grateful to Marilynn Phillips for her verification of details of French translations; and to Stephanie Welch Edwards, whose wide knowledge of classical literature assisted us in pinpointing the various Latin quotations peppered throughout this work. To all these the editors are indeed indebted.

John W. Yolton
Jean S. Yolton

Oxford
June 1986

C. COMPARATIVE TABLES

The table on pp. 72–5 shows the relationship between the two manuscript drafts (those at Harvard College and at the British Library) and
the first five published editions. Since the textual variants between
NN and NA are few, they are treated as one edition.

It is difficult in a table to indicate the correspondence of sections in
Locke's letters to the Clarkes with the published editions. The exact
correspondence is shown in footnotes to the text. We therefore indicate below in summary form, in the order they occur in the letters, what
sections of the third edition (and text of this edition) the letters correspond to. Square brackets indicate only partial or incomplete relev-
ance.

Letters (*Corr.* no.) Published sections

782	1–5, 7
799	23–8
803	[40], [95]
807	150–1, 153–4, [100]
822	110, 150–1, 153–4
829	118–21, 141–5, 116, 156–7
844	111–14, 156–9, [162–3], 165–7, 170, 169, 171–5, 186, [181], 210–11, [161], 197–9, 187–8, [190], 193, 200, 95–7
845	122, 92, [156]
929	45–53, 61, 63, 72–4, 76, 103–10, 116, 88–9, [162–3], [180], 160
999	201, [203], 204, 206–8, [209], 214–15, 129, 202
1098	81–2
1370	[123], 124–7

Corr. 809, dated 7 February 1685 NS (ii. 686–9) concerns bringing
up girls, and was not included in the published *Some Thoughts*.
Another letter, no. 1376, though part of the 'education' series, has 'no
general reproduction' in *Some Thoughts* (ibid. iv. 239n.)

In this table, dashes indicate the lack of existing material in the
drafts or in the published editions.

Concordance of Sections in MSS and Editions

H	K	1	3	4	5
1, 2[a]	1	1	1	1	1
2[b]	2	2	2	2	2
3	3	3	3	3	3
4–5	4–5	4[c]	4	4	4
6	6	5	5[d]	5	5
—	—	6	6	6	6
7	7	7[c]	7[d]	7[d]	7[d]
—	—	8	8[d]	8	8
8	8	9[c]	9	9	9
—	—	10	10[g]	10	10
9	9	11	11	11	11
10	10	12	12	12	12
	11	13	13[d]	13	13
	12–13	14	14[d]	14	14
11	16	15	15[d]	15	15
	14	16, 17[e]	16–17	16–17	16–17
	15	18	18	18	18
12–13	17–18	19–20	19–20	19–20	19–20
14	19–20	21–2	21[c], 22[h]	21–2	21–2
—	21	23	23	23	23
—	22–6	24	24	24	24
—	27–9	25, 26[g], 27[c]	25–7	25–7	25–7
—	30	28[c]	28[h]	28	28
15	31	29	29[h]	29	29
16	32[a]	30	30	30	30
17	32[b]	31	31	31	31
18–19	33–4	32–3	32–3	32–3	32–3
20[a]	35	34–5	34, 35[h]	34–5	34–5
20[b]	36–7	36	36	36	36
—	—	—	37[f]	37	37
21–2	38–9	37[h], 38[h]	38–9	38–9	38–9
23	40–1	39–40	40–1	40–1	40–1
24–5	42–3	41[h], 42	42–3	42–3	42–3
26	44				
27	45–6	43–51, 52[c]	44–7, 48[h], 49–53	44–53	44–53
28	47				
29	48				

H	K	1	3	4	5
30, 31	49	53, 54	54–5	54–5	54–5
32–3	50–1	55	56	56	56
34–6	52–4	56, 57[d], 58	57–8, 59[h]	57–9	57–9
39[b]	57	59	60[d]	60	60
—	—	60	61	61	61
40	58	—	—	—	—
—	—	—	62[f]	62	62
—	—	61–2	63–4	63–4	63–4
37	55[a]	—	—	—	—
38	55[b]	—	—	—	—
39[a]	56	63	65	65	65
—	—	64	66[d]	66	66
41	59	65[h]	67[d]	67	67
42	60	66–7	68–9	68–9	68, 69[g]
43	61	68	70[d]	70	70
44	62	69	71[h]	71	71
—	—	70–2	72[c], 73, 74[d]	72–4	72–4
—	—	73–4	75[gh], 76[h]	75–6	75–6
—	—	75	77[i]	77	77
—	—	76–7	78[i]	78	78
—	—	78–9	79, 80[d]	79–80	79–80
—	—	80–6	81–3, 84[h], 85–7	81–7	81–7
—	—	87	88[c], 89	88–9	88–9
45–6	63–4	88–9	90, 91[h]	90–1	90–1
—	—	90	92	92	92[h]
—	—	—	93–4	93, 94[d]	93[h], 94
—	—	91–3	95, 96[h], 97	95–7	95–7
—	—	—	98	98	98[h]
—	—	94–100	99–105	99–105	99–105
—	—	101–2	106[hi], 107[c]	106–7	106–7
—	—	103–4	108[d], 109[h]	108–9	108–9
—	—	105	110[d]	110	110
—	—	106–9	111[h]–114[h]	111–14	111–14
—	—	—	115	115	115
—	—	110	116[c]	116	116

H	K	1	3	4	5
—	—	—	117	117	117
—	—	111	118[h]	118	118
—	—	112–17	119, 120[h], 121, 122[h], 123, 124[h]	119–24	119–24
—	—	118–19	125[g], 126[h]	125–6	125–6
—	—	120–2	127–9	127–9	127–9
—	—	123	130[d]	130	130
—	—	124–5	131–2	131–2	131–2
47–8	65–6	126–7	133–4	133–4	133–4
49	67	128–9	135, 136[hi]	135–6	135–6
50[a]	68	130, 131[a]	137, 138[a]	137–8[a]	137–8[a]
50[b]	69[a]	131[b]	138[b]	138[b]	138[b]
51	69[b]	132[a]	139[a]	139[a]	139[a]
52	70	132[b]	139[b]	139[b]	139[b]
53	71	133	140	140	140
54[e]	72[e]	134[d]	141	141	141
—	—	135–7	142–4	142–4	142, 143[d], 144
54[a]	72[a]	138	145[d]	145	145
55	73	139	146[h]	146	146
56	74–5	140	147	147	147
57–8	76	141–2	148–9	148–9	148–9
59–60	77	143	150–1[a]	150–1[a]	150–1[a]
—	—	—	151[b]	151[b]	151[b]
61	78	144	152	152	152
62, 63[a]	79	145–6	153–4	153–4	153–4
63[b]	80	147	155	155	155
—	—	148–50	156–8	156–8	156–8
—	—	151–3	159[i], 160, 161[a]	159–61	159–61
—	—	154–5	162–3	162–3	162–3
64	81	156	164	164	164
65	82	157	165, 166[d]	165–6	165–6
—	—	158	167	167[d]	167[i]
—	—	159	168[h]	168	168[d]
—	—	160–6	169[i], 170–1, 172[h], 173–5	169–75	169–75

H	K	1	3	4	5
—	—	—	176	176	176
—	—	167–9	177–9	177–9	177–9
—	—	170–2	180^d, 181^i, 182	180–2	180–2
—	—	172*bis*	183	183	183
—	—	173–6	184–5, 186^i, 187	184–7	184–7
—	—	177^a	188, 189^d	188–9	188–9
—	—	177^b	190^h	190	190
—	—	179^k	191	191	191
—	—	180	192^h	192^g	192
—	—	181–2	193–4	193^h, 194	193–4
—	—	183	195^d	195	195^d
—	—	184–92	196–8, 199^h, 200, 201^h–2^h	196–204	196–204
—	—	—	205	205	205^g
—	—	193–5	206, 207^{cd}, 208^h	206–8	206–8
—	—	196–9	209–11, 212^k	209–12	209–12
—	—	200	214–15	214–15	214–15
—	—	201–2	216–17	216–17	216–17

[a] first part of section   [b] latter part of section
[c] recast   [d] enlarged
[e] first sentence only   [f] added
[g] sentence omitted   [h] slightly recast
[i] slightly expanded   [j] marginal note added
[k] §§ 178, 213 omitted in numbering

SOME
THOUGHTS
CONCERNING
EDUCATION

TO
Edward Clarke
Of *CHIPLEY*, Esq;.

SIR;

T*HESE* Thoughts concerning Education, *which now come abroad into* 5
the World, do of right belong to You, being written several Years since for your
sake, and are no other than what you have already by you in my Letters. I have so
little varied any thing, but only the Order of what was sent you at different Times,
and on several Occasions, that the Reader will easily find, in the Familiarity and
Fashion of the Style, that they were rather the private Conversation of two 10
Friends, than a Discourse designed for publick view.

The Importunity of Friends is the common Apology for Publications Men are
afraid to own themselves forward to. But you know I can truly say, That if some,
who having heard of these Papers of mine, had not pressed to see them, and after-
wards to have them printed, they had lain dormant still in that privacy they were 15
designed for. But those whose Judgment I defer[1] *much to, telling me, That they*
were persuaded, that this rough Draught of mine might be of some use, if made
more publick, touch'd upon what will always be very prevalent with me. For I
think it every Man's indispensible Duty, to do all the Service he can to his Coun-
try: And I see not what difference he puts between himself and his Cattel, who 20
lives without that Thought. This Subject is of so great Concernment, and a right
way of Education is of so general Advantage, that did I find my Abilities answer
my Wishes, I should not have needed Exhortations or Importunities from others.
However, the Meanness of these Papers, and my just Distrust of them, shall not
keep me, by the shame of doing so little, from contributing my Mite, when there is 25
no more required of me, than my throwing it into the publick Receptacle. And if
there be any more of their Size and Notions, who liked them so well, that they
thought them worth printing, I may flatter my self, they will not be lost Labour to
every body.

I my self have been consulted of late by so many, who profess themselves at a loss 30
how to breed their Children; and the early corruption of Youth, is now become so
general a Complaint, that he cannot be thought wholly impertinent, who brings

---

[1] **NN** has *deferr*; see p. 52 n. 1.

the Consideration of this Matter on the Stage, and offers something, if it be but to excite others, or afford matter of correction. For Errours in Education should be less indulged than any: These, like Faults in the first Concoction, that are never mended in the second or third, carry their afterwards-incorrigible Taint
5 *with them, through all the parts and stations of Life.*

I am so far from being conceited of any thing I have here offered, that I should not be sorry, even for your sake, if some one abler and fitter for such a Task, would in a just Treatise of Education, suited to our English *Gentry, rectifie the Mistakes I have made in this; it being much more desirable to me, that*
10 *young Gentlemen should be put into (that which every one ought to be sollicitous about) the best way of being formed and instructed, than that my Opinion should be received concerning it. You will however, in the mean time bear me Witness, that the Method here propos'd has had no ordinary Effects upon a Gentleman's Son, it was not designed for. I will not say the good Temper of the*
15 *Child did not very much contribute to it, but this I think, you and the Parents are satisfied of, that a contrary usage according to the ordinary disciplining of Children, would not have mended that Temper, nor have brought him to be in love with his Book, to take a pleasure in Learning, and to desire as he does to be taught more, than those about him think fit always to teach him.*

20 *But my Business is not to recommend this Treatise to you, whose Opinion of it I know already; nor it to the World, either by your Opinion or Patronage.*[2] *The well Educating of their Children is so much the Duty and Concern of Parents, and the Welfare and Prosperity of the Nation so much depends on it, that I would have every one lay it seriously to Heart; and after having well*
25 *examined and distinguished what Fancy, Custom or Reason advises in the Case, set his helping hand to promote every where that Way of training up Youth, with regard to their several Conditions, which is the easiest, shortest, and likeliest to produce vertuous, useful, and able Men in their distinct Callings: Though that most to be taken Care of, is the Gentleman's Calling. For if those of*
30 *that Rank are by their Education once set right, they will quickly bring all the rest into Order.*

I know not whether I have done more than shewn my good Wishes towards it in this short Discourse; such as it is the World now has it, and if there be any thing in it worth their acceptance, they owe their thanks to you for it. My Affec-
35 *tion to you gave the first rise to it, and I am pleased, that I can leave to Posterity this Mark of the Friendship has been between us. For I know no greater Pleasure in this Life, nor a better remembrance to be left behind one, than a long*

26–7 set . . . Conditions,] *help to promote that way in the several degrees of Men,* 1

[2] **NN** has *Patronnge*; see p. 52.

continued Friendship, with an honest, useful, and worthy Man, and lover of his Country. I am,

SIR,

Your most humble and

7 March. 1692.   5

most faithful Servant,

JOHN LOCKE.

5 *Date om.* **1**   1692] 1690 **5**   6–7 Servant, *JOHN LOCKE.*] Servant. **1**

SOME

THOUGHTS

CONCERNING

EDUCATION

§. 1. ᵃ⁻A Sound Mind in a sound Body,[1] is a short, but full Descrip-   5
tion of a Happy State in this World: He that has these Two, has little
more to wish for; and he that wants either of them, will be but little the
better for any thing else. Mens Happiness or Misery is most part of
their own making. He, whose Mind directs not wisely, will never take
the right Way; and he, whose Body is crazy and feeble, will never be   10
able to advanceᵇ in it. I ᶜconfess, there are some Mens Constitutions of
Body and Mind so vigorous, and well framed by Nature, that they
need not much Assistance from others, but by the strength of their
natural Genius, they are from their Cradles carried towards what is
Excellent; and by the Privilegeᵈ of their happy Constitutions, are able   15
to do Wonders: But Examples of this Kind are but few, and I think I
may say, that of all the Men we meet with, Nine Parts of Ten are what
they are, Good or Evil, useful or not, by their Education. 'Tis that
which makes the great Difference in Mankind: The little, and almost
insensible Impressions on our tender Infancies, have very important   20
and lasting Consequences: And there 'tis, as in the Fountains of some
Rivers, where a gentle Application of the Hand turns the flexible
Waters into Chanels, that make them take quite contrary Courses, and
by this little Direction given them at first in the Source, they receive
different Tendencies, and arrive at last, ᵉ⁻at very remote and distant   25
Places.⁻ᵉ

§. 2. ᶠI imagine the Minds of Children as easily turned this or that

7 will be] is **1**   16 this Kind] these **1**

ᵃ⁻ᵃ **Corr.** 782 (ii. 626–7) **HK** §§ 1–3   ᵇ march **Corr.HK**   ᶜ §2 *begins* **H**
ᵈ *vigor* **HK**   ᵉ⁻ᵉ at places quite distant and opposite. **Corr.HK**   ᶠ § 2
begins **K**

[1] Juvenal, *Satires* 10. 356: 'mens sana in corpore sano', left untranslated in **Corr.HK.**

83

way, as Water it self; and though this be the principal Part, and our main Care should be about the inside, yet the Clay Cottage is not to be neglected. I shall therefore begin with the Case, and consider first the *Health* of the Body, as that, which perhaps you may rather expect from that Study, I have been thought more peculiarly to have applied my self to; and that also which will be soonest dispatched, as lying, if I guess not amiss, in a very little Compass.

§. 3. How necessary *Health* is to our Business and Happiness; And how requisite a strong Constitution, able to endure Hardships and Fatigue, is to one that will make any Figure in the World, is too obvious to need any Proof.⁻ᵃ

§. 4. ᵍ⁻The Consideration, I shall here have of *Health*, shall be, not what a Physician ought to do with a sick or crazy Child; but what the Parents, without the Help of Physick, should do for the *Preservation and Improvement of an healthy*, or at least, *not sickly Constitution* in their Children: And this perhaps might be all dispatched, in this one short Rule, *viz.* That Gentlemen should use their Children, as the honest Farmers and substantial Yeomen do theirs. But because the Mothers possibly may think this a little too hard, and the Fathers too short, I shall explain my self more particularly; only laying down this as a general and certain Observation for the Women to consider, *viz.* That most Children's Constitutions are either spoiled, or at least harmed, by *Cockering* and *Tenderness.*⁻ᵍ

§. 5. ʰ⁻The first Thing to be taken care of, is, That Children be not too *warmly Clad or Covered*, Winter or Summer. The Face, when we are Born, is no less tender than any other part of the Body: 'Tis use alone hardens it, and makes it more able to endure the Cold. And therefore the *Scythian*² Philosopher gave a very significant Answer to the

---

§ 3 *Health.*   § 4 *Health.   Tenderness.*   § 5 *Warmth.*

---

15 *not*] *nor* **NN** (*all copies seen exc. Univ. Toronto Lib., cf. pp.* 54–5)   16 *be . . . in*] *be* dispatched, all in **1**   22 *at least*] *add.* **3**

ᵍ⁻ᵍ *Revision of* **Corr.** ii. 627; **HK** §§ 4–5, *rewritten to remove personal references*
ʰ⁻ʰ *Revision of* **HK** § 6, *which add at end* Tis time now to leave off his cap and never to put it on ag⟨ai⟩n night nor day, unless about 20 yeares hence it be thought fit to put on a thinne holland one for fashons sake to please the young Lady when he goes a wooing. *Similar content* **Corr.** ii. 627–8, *where final sent.* I think it therefore time now, if we have not before done so, to leave off his cap, and perhaps no more ⟨to put it on⟩ again, unless about twenty years hence, if it be thought fit, ⟨to put on⟩ a thin holland one for fashion's sake to please the young lady when he goes a-wooing.

² Nomadic people with pastoral way of life on lower reaches of the River Dnieper. For the story see Aelian, *Varia Historia* 7. 6, where, however, the Scythian is the king, not a philosopher.

Athenian, who wonder'd how he could go Naked in Frost and Snow: How, said the *Scythian*, can you endure your Face exposed to the sharp Winter-Air? My Face is used to it, said the *Athenian*. Think me all Face, replied the *Scythian*. Our Bodies will endure any thing, that from the beginning they are accustomed to.$^{-h}$ 5

An Eminent Instance of this, though in the contrary Excess of Heat, being to our present purpose, to shew what Use can do, I shall set down in the Author's words, as I meet with it in a late ingenious Voyage*. 'The Heats, says he, are more violent in *Malta*, than in any 'part of *Europe*; they exceed those of *Rome* it self, and are perfectly   10 'Stifling; and so much the more, because there are seldom any cooling 'Breezes here. This makes the common People as black as Gypsies: 'But yet the Peasants defie the Sun; they work on in the hottest part of 'the Day, without intermission, or sheltering themselves from his 'scorching Rays. This has convinced me that Nature can bring it self   15 'to many things, which seem impossible, provided we accustom our 'selves from our Infancy. The *Malteses* do so, who harden the Bodies of 'their Children, and reconcile them to the Heat, by making them go 'stark Naked, without Shirt, Drawers, or any thing on their Heads, 'from their Cradles till they are ten Years old.'   20

Give me leave therefore to advise you, not to fence too carefully against the Cold of this our Climate. There are those in *England* who wear the same Clothes Winter and Summer, and that without any inconvenience, or more sense of Cold than others find. But if the Mother will needs have an Allowance for Frost and Snow, for fear of   25 Harm; and the Father, for fear of Censure; be sure let not his Winter-

---

* *Nouveau Voiage du Levant*: $\frac{150}{175}$ 3

6–86.1 An Eminent . . . warm: And] *add.* 3

3 *Nouveau voyage du Levant, par le sieur D. M.* [Jean Du Mont, baron de Carlscroon]. *Contenant ce qu'il a vû de plus remarquable en Allemagne, France, Italie, Malthe, et Turquie* (The Hague, E. Foulque, 1694). 475 [not 175] pp. Locke's reference is to pp. 150–1 in that edition. His own copy (LL 2028) is now in the Bodleian Library. The original text is as follows: 'Les chaleurs sont ici plus excessives qu'en lieu de l'Europe, elles passent celles de Rome, c'est un étoufement d'autant plus insuportable, que rarement on est rafraichi du vent, & que la coline de la montagne, est justement exposée au midi; aussi tout [*sic*] les Païsans sont noirs comme des Egiptiens, au reste ils ne se soucient nullement du Soleil, la plus brûlante chaleur n'étant pas capable de les faire rentrer dans leur maison, ni de leur faire cesser le travail; ce qui m'a fait connoître que la nature se peut faire à bien des choses qui paroissent impossibles, pourveu qu'on si [= s'y] habituë dés l'enfance, & c'est ce que font les Malthois, qui endurcissent le corps de leurs enfans à la chaleur, en les faisant aller nuds comme la main, sans chemise, ni calçons, ni bonnet, depuis la mammelle, jusques a l'age de dix ans; de sorte que leur peau devient comme du cuir.'

Clothing be too warm: And amongst other things remember, That
when Nature has so well covered his Head with Hair, and strengthen'd it with a Year or two's Age, that he can run about, by Day, without a Cap, it is best that, by Night, a Child should also lie without one;
5   there being nothing that more exposes to Head-ach, Colds, Catarrhs,
Coughs, and several other Diseases, than keeping the *Head warm.*

   §. 6. ⁱ⁻I have said *He* here, because the principal aim of my Discourse is, how a young Gentleman should be brought up from his
Infancy, which, in all things, will not so perfectly suit the Education of
10 *Daughters*; though where the difference of Sex requires different treatment, 'twill be no hard matter to distinguish.⁻ⁱ

   §. 7. ʲ⁻I would also advise his *Feet to be washed* every Day in cold
Water; and to have his *Shooes* so thin, that they might leak and *let in
Water*, when ever he comes near it. Here, I fear, I shall have the
15   Mistriss and Maids too against me. One will think it too filthy; and the
other, perhaps, too much pains to make clean his Stockings. But yet
truth will have it, that his Health is much more worth than all such
Considerations, and ten-times as much more. And he that considers
how Mischievous and Mortal a thing, taking *Wet in the Feet* is to those,
20   who have been bred nicely, will wish he had, with the poor People's
Children, gone *Bare-foot*; who, by that means, come to be so reconciled, by Custom, to Wet in their Feet, that they take no more Cold or
Harm by it, than if they were wet in their Hands. And what is it, I pray,
that makes this great difference between the Hands and the Feet in
25   others, but only Custom? I doubt not, but if a Man from his Cradle had
been always used to go bare-foot, whilst his Hands were constantly
wrapped up in warm Mittins, and covered with *Hand-shooes*, as the
Dutch call *Gloves*; I doubt not, I say, but such a Custom would make
taking Wet in his Hands as dangerous to him, as now taking Wet in
30   their Feet is to a great many others. The way to prevent this, is, to have
his Shooes made so, as to leak Water; and his Feet washed constantly
every ᵏ⁻Day in cold Water.⁻ᵏ It is recommendable for its cleanliness: But

§ 7 *Feet. Alterations.*

1 amongst . . . That] therefore, amongst other things I think, [**NN**; think **NA**] that
when **1**   12 Day] Night **1 3**   31 constantly] *add.* **4**   32 Day . . . Water.
4] Night in cold Water, both for Health and Cleanliness sake. **1 3**   32–87.15 It is
. . . Consideration.] *add.* **4**

ⁱ⁻ⁱ *Cf.* **Corr.** 801 (ii. 697)   ʲ⁻ʲ *Varied from* **Corr.** 782 (ii. 628) **HK** § 7; *cf.* **Corr.** 809
(ii. 687). **HK** *add at end* And if you have any convenient place neare you since you can
swim soe well your self have him often into the water with you whereby he will have
other advantages besides learning to swim.   ᵏ⁻ᵏ **Corr.** *as* **1**; night in cold water. **HK**

that which I aim at in it is Health. And therefore I limit it not precisely to any time of the Day. I have known it used every Night, with very good Success, and that all the Winter, without the omitting it so much as one Night in extream cold Weather, when thick Ice cover'd the Water, the Child bath'd his Legs and Feet in it; Though he was of an 5 Age not big enough to rub and wipe them himself, and when he began this Custom, was puleing and very tender. But the great End being to harden those Parts by a frequent and familiar use of cold Water, and thereby to prevent the Mischiefs that usually attend accidental taking Wet in the Feet in those who are Bred otherwise; I think it may be left 10 to the Prudence and Convenience of the Parents, to choose either Night or Morning. The Time I deem indifferent, so the thing be effectually done. The Health and Hardiness procured by it, would be a good Purchase at a much dearer rate. To which, if I add the preventing of Corns, that to some Men would be a very valuable Consideration. 15 But begin first in the Spring, with luke-warm, and so colder and colder every Night, till, in a few days, you come to perfectly cold Water, and then continue it so Winter and Summer. For it is to be observed in this, as in all other *Alterations* from our ordinary way of Living, the Changes must be made by gentle and insensible Degrees; and so we 20 may bring our Bodies to any thing, without pain, and without danger.⁻ʲ

How fond Mothers are like to receive this Doctrine, is not hard to foresee. What can it be less than to Murder their tender Babes to use them thus? What! put their Feet in cold Water in Frost and Snow, when all one can do is little enough to keep them warm? A little to 25 remove their Fears by Examples, without which the plainest Reason is seldom hearken'd to; *Seneca* tells us of himself, *Ep.* 53. and 83.[4] that he used to Bathe himself in cold Spring Water in the midst of Winter. This, if he had not thought it not only tollerable, but healthy too, he would scarce have done; in an exuberant Fortune, that could well have 30 born the Expence of a warm Bath; and in an Age (for he was then Old) that would have excused greater Indulgence. If we think his Stoical Principles led him to this Severity; let it be so, that his Sect reconciled cold Water to his Sufferance: What made it agreeable to his Health? for that was not impair'd by this hard Usage. But what shall we say to 35

---

17 Night] time **4 5**   18 Winter and Summer] *add.* **3**   22–88.11 How fond ... it.] *add.* **3**

---

[4] Seneca, *Ep.* 53. 3: 'Memor artificii mei vetus frigidae cultor' (mindful of my skill as a veteran devotee of cold water); ibid. 83. 6: 'Panis deinde siccus et sine mensa prandium ...' (after my bath, dry bread for lunch without a table).

Horace,[5] who warm'd not himself with the Reputation of any Sect, and
least of all affected Stoical Austerities? yet he assures us, he was wont in
the Winter Season to bathe himself in cold Water. But perhaps *Italy* will
be thought much warmer than *England*, and the chilness of their Waters
5   not to come near ours in Winter. If the Rivers of *Italy* are warmer, those
of *Germany* and *Poland* are much colder, than any in this our Country;
And yet in these, the *Jews* both Men and Women, bathe all over, at all
Seasons of the Year, without any Prejudice to their Health. And every
one is not apt to believe it is Miracle, or any peculiar Virtue of St. *Wini-*
10 *fred's Well*,[6] that makes the cold Waters of that famous Spring do no
harm to the tender Bodies, that bathe in it. Every one is now full of the
Miracles done by cold Baths on decay'd and weak Constitutions for the
Recovery of Health and Strength, and therefore they cannot be impracticable or intollerable for the improving and hardening the Bodies of
15 those who are in better Circumstances.

   If these Examples of grown Men be not thought yet to reach the
Case of Children; but that they may be judg'd still to be too tender,
and unable to bear such Usage; let them examine what the *Germans* of
old, and the *Irish* now do to them; and they will find, that Infants too,
20 as tender as they are thought, may, without any Danger, endure
Bathing, not only of their Feet, but of their whole Bodies, in cold
Water: And there are at this day Ladies in the Highlands of *Scotland*,
who use this Discipline to their Children in the midst of Winter; and
find that cold Water does them no harm, even when there is Ice in it.
25   §. 8. I shall not need here to mention *Swiming*, when he is of an Age
able to learn, and has any one to teach him. 'Tis that saves many a
Man's life: and the *Romans* thought it so necessary, that they rank'd it
with Letters; and it was the common Phrase to mark one ill Educated
and good for Nothing; That he had neither learnt to Read nor to
30 Swim. *Nec literas didicit nec natare.*[7] But besides the gaining a Skill,
which may serve him at need; the Advantages to health, by often
bathing in cold Water, during the heat of Summer, are so many, that

   § 8 *Swiming.*

11–15 Every one ... Circumstances.] *add.* **5**   25 *Swiming*,] his learning to
Swim, **1**   26–32 'Tis ... are] The advantages (besides that of *Swiming*) to health,
by often *bathing* in the summer [**NN**; Summer **NA**] *in cold Water*, are **1**

   [5] Cf. *Epistles* i. 15. 4: '... gelida cum perluor unda per medium frigus' (now that in
midwinter I drench myself in cold water).
   [6] At Holywell, Flint. (now Clwyd), a place of pilgrimage in the Middle Ages and well
into the 18th c.
   [7] Erasmus, *Adagia*, i. 1. 13, from a Greek (not Roman) saying.

I think nothing need to be said to encourage it, provided this one caution be used, That he never go into the Water, when Exercise has at all
warm'd him, or left any Emotion in his Blood or Pulse.

§. 9. [1-]Another Thing that is of great Advantage to every One's Health,
but especially Children's, is, to be much in the *open Air*, and very little as
may be by the Fire, even in Winter. By this he will accustom himself also
to Heat and Cold, Shine and Rain; all which, if a Man's Body will not
endure, it will serve him to very little purpose in this World: And when
he is grown up, it is too late to begin to use him to it: It must be got early,
and by degrees. Thus the Body may be brought to bear almost any
Thing. If I should advise him to play in the *Wind and the Sun without a Hat*,
I doubt whether it could be born. There would a Thousand Objections
be made against it, which at last would amount to no more, in Truth,
than being Sunburnt. And if my young Master be to be kept always in the
Shade, and never exposed to the Sun and Wind, for fear of his Com-
plexion, it may be a good Way to make him a *Beau*, but not a Man of
Business. And although greater Regard be to be had to Beauty in the
Daughters, yet I will take the Liberty to say, that the more they are in the
Air, without prejudice to their Faces, the stronger and healthier they
will be; and the nearer they come to the Hardships of their Brothers in
their Education, the greater Advantage will they receive from it all the
remaining Part of their Lives.[-1]

§. 10. [m-]Playing in the *open Air* has but this one Danger in it, that

§ 9 *Air.*   § 10 *Air.*   *Habits.*

---

14 if] *om.* 5   18 take] take take 4

[1-1] *Varied from* **HK** § 8   m–m **H** fo. 10 *exhibits a MS draft in Locke's hand of* § 10
(*recto*) *and part of* § 66 (*verso*). *The transcription testifies to Locke's style of composition:* Playing
['and runing up and down'] in the open air has but this one danger in it that I know. and
that is that when he {h}is hot with runing up and down [in it] he shuld sit or lye down on
the cold or mojst earth. This and drinkeing cold drinke when 'they are' [people] are hot
with labour or exerceise [causes more feavers and diseases] brings more people to
the[ir] graves or to the brinke of [them,] 'it' by feavers and other diseases than any thing
that I know. [Ag⟨ains⟩t these you must use all the cautions you can.] These mischeifs are
easily enough prevented whilst he is litle being then seldome out of sight. And if dureing
his childhood he be constantly kept from sit⟨tin⟩g on the ground [w] or drinking any
cold liquor whilst he is hot [the custome of avoiding it whilst] the custom 'of forbearing'
grown into habit will help much to preserve him when he is noe longer under his maids
or tutors eye. This and repeated cautions of inculcated to him ag⟨ains⟩t soe dangerous
practises is all I thinke can be don in the case For as years increase liberty must come
with them and in a great many things he must be trusted to his owne conduct since there
cannot always be a guard upon him, [unlesse] 'except' what you have put into his owne
minde by good principles and instructions which is the best and surest and therefor
most [attenti] to be taken care of.

I know; and that is, That when he is hot with running up and down, he should sit or lie down on the cold or moist Earth. This, I grant, and drinking cold Drink, when they are hot with Labour or Exercise, brings more People to the Grave, or to the Brink of it, by Fevers, and other Dis-
5 eases, than any Thing I know. These Mischiefs are easily enough pre-
vented whilst he is little, being then seldom out of sight. And if, during his Childhood, he be constantly and rigorously kept from sitting on the Ground, or drinking any cold Liquor, whilst he is hot, the Custom of Forbearing grown into Habit, will help much to preserve him, when he
10 is no longer under his Maid's or Tutor's Eye. This is all I think can be done in the Case; for, as Years increase, Liberty must come with them; and in a great many Things he must be trusted to his own Conduct; since there cannot always be a Guard upon him, except what you have put into his own Mind by good Principles, and established Habits, which is the
15 best and surest, and therefore most to be taken care of.⁻ᵐ For, from repeated Cautions and Rules, never so often inculcated, you are not to expect any thing either in this, or any other case, farther than Practice has established them into Habits.

§. 11. ⁿ⁻One thing the Mention of the Girls brings into my Mind,
20 which must not be forgot; and that is, That your Sons *Cloths* be *never* made *strait*, especially about the Breast. Let Nature have Scope to fashion the Body as she thinks best. She works, of her self, a great deal better, and exacter, than we can direct her. And if Women were themselves to frame the Bodies of their Children in their Wombs, as they
25 often endeavour to mend their Shapes when they are out, we should as certainly have no perfect Children born, as we have few well-shaped that are *strait-laced*,[8] or much tamper'd with. This Consideration should, me thinks, keep busie People (I will not say ignorant Nurses and Bodice-makers) from medling in a Matter they understand not;
30 and they should be afraid to put Nature out of her Way in fashioning the Parts, when they know not how the least and meanest is made. And yet I have seen so many Instances of Children receiving great harm from *strait-lacing*, that I cannot but conclude there are other Creatures, as well as Munkeys, who, little wiser than they, destroy their young
35 Ones by sensless fondness, and too much embracing.⁻ⁿ

§§ 11–12. *Cloths.*

17 either . . . case,] *add.* **3**
ⁿ⁻ⁿ **HK** § 9
[8] 'Strait-laced': narrow or tight binding about the bodice or chest (*OED*).

§. 12. °⁻Narrow Breasts, short and stinking Breath, ill Lungs, and Crookedness, are the Natural and almost constant Effects of *hard Bodice*, and *Cloths that pinch*. That way of making slender Wastes and fine Shapes, serves but the more effectually to spoil them. Nor can there indeed but be disproportion in the Parts, when the nourishment 5 prepared in the several Offices of the Body, cannot be distributed as Nature designs: And therefore what wonder is it, if it being laid, where it can, on some part not so *braced*, it often makes a Shoulder or a Hip higher or bigger than its just proportion. 'Tis generally known, that the Women of *China* (imagining I know not what kind of Beauty in it) 10 by bracing and binding them hard from their Infancy, have very little Feet. I saw lately a pair of *China* Shooes, which I was told were for a grown Woman; they were so exceedingly disproportioned to the Feet of one of the same Age amongst us, that they would scarce have been big enough for one of our little Girls. Besides this, 'tis observed that 15 their Women are also very little, and short-lived; whereas the Men are of the ordinary Stature of other Men, and live to a proportionable Age. These Defects in the Female Sex, in that Country, are, by some, imputed to the unreasonable binding of their Feet; whereby the free Circulation of the Blood is hindred, and the Growth and Health of the 20 whole Body suffers. And how often do we see, that some small part of the Foot being injured by a Wrench or a Blow, the whole Leg and Thigh thereby lose their Strength and Nourishment, and dwindle away? How much greater Inconveniencies may we expect, when the *Thorax*, wherein is placed the Heart and Seat of Life, is unnaturally 25 *compressed*, and hindred from its due Expansion?⁻°

§. 13. ᴾ⁻As for his *Diet*, it ought to be very *plain* and simple; and, if I might advise, Flesh should be forborn as long as he was in Coats, or at least till he was two or three Years old. But whatever Advantage this may be to his present and future Health and Strength, I fear it will hardly be 30 consented to by Parents, mislead by the Custom of eating too much Flesh themselves, who will be apt to think their Children, as they do themselves, in danger to be Starved, if they have not Flesh at least twice

§§ 13–14 *Diet.*

12–13 lately . . . so] a pair of *China* Shooes lately, **1**   14–15 us . . . big] us; their Womens Shooes would scarce be big **1**   27–92.8 simple; . . . Beef,] simple. *Flesh once a Day, and of one Sort at a Meal, is enough. Beef,* **1**   28 was] is **5** 29 was] is **5**

°⁻° **HK** § 10   ᴾ⁻ᴾ §§ 13–18 *constitute* **H** § 11 *in a varying arrangement; in* **K** *the same material is rearranged as* §§11–13, 16, 14, *and* 15

a Day. This I am sure, Children would breed their Teeth with much less danger, be freer from Diseases whilst they were little, and lay the Foundations of an healthy and strong Constitution much surer, if they were not cram'd so much as they are by fond Mothers and foolish Ser-
5 vants, and were kept wholly from Flesh the first three or four Years of their Lives.

But if my young Master must needs have Flesh, let it be but once a Day, and of one Sort at a Meal. Plain Beef, Mutton, Veal, &c. without other Sawce than Hunger, is best; and great care should be used, that
10 he eat *Bread* plentifully, both alone and with every thing else. And whatever he eats that is solid, make him *chew* it well. We *English* are often negligent herein; from whence follow Indigestion, and other great Inconveniences.

§. 14. ꟐFor *Breakfast* and *Supper*, *Milk*, *Milk-Pottage*, *Water-Gruel*,
15 *Flummery*,[9] and twenty other Things, that we are wont to make in *England*, are very fit for Children: Only, in all these, let Care be taken, that they be plain, and without much Mixture, and very sparingly seasoned with *Sugar*, or rather none at all: Especially all *Spice*, and other Things, that may heat the Blood, are carefully to be avoided. Be
20 sparing also of *Salt* in the Seasoning of all his Victuals, and use him not to high-seasoned Meats. Our Palates grow into a relish and liking of the Seasoning and Cookery which by Custom they are set to, and an over-much Use of Salt, besides that it occasions Thirst, and over-much Drinking, has other ill Effects upon the Body. I should think
25 that a good Piece of well made, and well baked *Brown Bread*, sometimes with, and sometimes without *Butter* or *Cheese*, would be often the best Breakfast for my young Master. I am sure 'tis as wholsom, and will make him as strong a Man as greater Delicacies; And if he be used to it, it will be as pleasant to him.¬Ꟑ ꟑ If he at any Time calls for Vic-
30 tuals between Meals, use him to nothing but dry *Bread*. If he be hungry more than wanton, *Bread* alone will down; and if he be not hungry, 'tis not fit he should eat. By this you will obtain two good Effects; 1. That by Custom he will come to be in love with *Bread*; for, as I said, our Palates and Stomachs too are pleased with the Things we are used to.
35 Another Good, you will gain hereby, is, That you will not teach him to eat more, nor oftner than Nature requires. I do not think that all People's Appetites are alike: Some have naturally stronger, and some

21–2 grow ... Custom] like the Seasoning and Cookery 1   27 as wholsom]
wholsom 1   34 and Stomachs too] add. 3

Ꟑ–Ꟑ **K** § 12   ꟑ–ꟑ *First part of* **K** § 13

[9] Flummery is a sweet dish of eggs, flour, milk, etc. (*OED*).

weaker Stomachs. But this I think, that many are made *Gormands* and *Gluttons* by Custom, that were not so by Nature: And I see in some Countries Men as lusty and strong, that eat but two Meals a Day, as others that have set their Stomachs by a constant Usage, like Larms, to call on them for four or five.⁻ʳ The *Romans* usually fasted till Supper; the only set Meal, even of those who eat more than once a Day: And those who used Breakfasts, as some did at eight, some at ten, others at twelve of the Clock, and some later, neither eat Flesh, nor had any thing made ready for them. *Augustus*,[10] when the greatest Monarch on the Earth, tells us, he took a bit of dry Bread in his Chariot. And *Seneca* in his 83d. Epistle,[11] giving an account how he managed himself, even when he was Old, and his Age permitted Indulgence, says, That he used to eat a piece of dry Bread for his Dinner, without the Formality of sitting to it: Though his Estate would have as well paid for a better Meal (had health required it) as any Subject's in *England*, were it doubled. The Masters of the World were bred up with this spare Diet: And the young Gentlemen of *Rome* felt no want of Strength or Spirit, because they eat but once a Day. Or if it happen'd by Chance, that any one could not fast so long as till Supper, their only set Meal; he took nothing but a bit of dry Bread, or at most, a few Raisins, or some such slight thing with it, to stay his Stomach. This part of Temperance was found so necessary both for Health and Business, that the Custom of only one Meal a Day held out against that prevailing Luxury, which their Eastern Conquests and Spoils had brought in amongst them: And those who had given up their old frugal Eating, and made Feasts, yet began them not till the Evening. And more than one set Meal a Day was thought so monstrous, that it was a Reproach, as low down as *Cæsar*'s time, to make an Entertainment, or sit down to a full Table, till towards Sun-set. ˢ⁻And therefore, if it would not be thought too severe, I should judge it most convenient, that my Young Master should have nothing but *Bread* too for *Breakfast*. You cannot imagine of what Force Custom is: And I impute a great part of our Diseases in *England* to our eating too much *Flesh*, and too little *Bread*. ⁻ˢ

§. 15. ᵗ⁻As to his *Meals*, I should think it best, that, as much as it can

§ 15 *Meals.*

5–29 The *Romans* . . . Sun-set.] *add.* **3**   7 used] use **5**   29 would] should **1**
30 my Young Master] he **1**   34 as it] as **1**

ˢ⁻ˢ *Last part of* **K** § 13   ᵗ⁻ᵗ *Expanded and altered from* **K** § 16

[10] Suetonius, *Divus Augustus*, 76. 1–2.
[11] *Ep.* 83. 6; cf. n. 4.

be conveniently avoided, they should not be kept constantly to an Hour. For when Custom has fixed his Eating to certain stated Periods, his Stomach will expect Victuals at the usual Hour, and grow peevish if he passes it; either fretting it self into a troublesome Excess, or
5 flaging into a downright want of Appetite. Therefore I would have no time kept constantly to for his Breakfast, Dinner, and Supper, but rather varied almost every Day. And if betwixt these, which I call *Meals*, he will eat, let him have, as often as he calls for it, good dry Bread. If any one think this too hard and sparing a Diet for a Child, let
10 them know, that a Child will never starve, nor dwindle for want of Nourishment, who, besides Flesh at Dinner, and Spoon-meat,[12] or some such other thing at Supper, may have good Bread and Beer as often as he has a Stomach: For thus, upon second thoughts, I should judge it best for Children to be order'd. The Morning is generally
15 designed for Study, to which a full Stomach is but an ill Preparation. Dry Bread, though the best Nourishment, has the least Temptation: And nobody would have a Child cram'd at Breakfast, who has any regard to his Mind or Body, and would not have him dull and un-healthy. Nor let any One think this unsuitable to one of Estate and
20 Condition. A Gentleman, in any Age, ought to be so bred, as to be fitted to bear Arms, and be a Soldier. But he that, in this, breeds his Son so as if he designed him to sleep over his Life, in the Plenty and Ease of a full Fortune he intends to leave him, little considers the Examples he has seen, or the Age he lives in.⁻ᵗ

25 §. 16. ᵘ⁻His *Drink* should be only Small Beer;[13] and that too he should never be suffered to have between Meals, but after he had eat a Piece of Bread. The Reasons why I say this, are these:

§. 17. 1. More Fevers and Surfeits are got by People's Drinking when they are hot, than by any one Thing I know. Therefore, if by Play
30 he be hot and dry, Bread will ill go down; and so if he cannot have

§§ 16–17 *Drink.*

3–5 grow . . . Therefore] if he passes it, either grow indisposed, and as it were peev-ish, or lose its Appetite. In short, I think it best he should eat Flesh but once a Day, plain Flesh, and of one Sort at a time; and whilst young, Spoon-meat also once a Day; and if you please, once a Day Cheese or Butter with his Bread; but 1   6 for . . . Supper,] *add.* **3**   10 dwindle for want of] want 1   11–12 at Dinner . . . at Supper,] once a Day, and other Things once or twice more, 1   13–19 For thus . . . unhealthy.] *add.* **3**   24 or] nor 1

ᵘ⁻ᵘ **K** § 14

¹² Spoon-meat: soft or liquid food, espec. for invalids (*OED*).
¹³ Small beer, i.e. weak beer (*OED*).

94

Drink, but upon that Condition, he will be forced to forbear. For, if he be very hot, he should by no means *drink*. At least, a good piece of Bread first to be eaten, will gain Time to warm the Beer *Blood-hot*, which then he may drink safely. If he be very dry, it will go down so warm'd, and quench his Thirst better: And if he will not drink it so 5 warm'd, Abstaining will not hurt him. Besides, This will teach him to forbear, which is an Habit of greatest Use for Health of Body and Mind too.⁻ᵘ

§. 18. 2. ᵛ⁻Not being permitted to *drink* without eating, will prevent the Custom of having the Cup often at his Nose; a dangerous Begin- 10 ning, and Preparation to *Good-fellowship*. Men often bring Habitual Hunger and Thirst on themselves by Custom. And if you please to try, you may, though he be weaned from it, bring him, by Use, to such a Necessity again of *Drinking* in the Night, that he will not be able to sleep without it. It being the Lullaby used by Nurses, to still crying 15 Children, I believe Mothers generally find some Difficulty to wean their Children from *Drinking* in the Night, when they first take them home. Believe it, Custom prevails as much by Day as by Night; and you may, if you please, bring any One to be Thirsty every Hour.

I once lived in an House, where, to appease a froward Child, they 20 gave him *Drink* as often as he cried; so that he was constantly bibbing: And tho' he could not speak, yet he drunk more in Twenty four Hours than I did. Try it when you please, you may with Small, as well as with Strong Beer, drink your self into a Drought. The great Thing to be minded in Education is, what *Habits* you settle: And therefore in this, 25 as all other Things, do not begin to make any Thing *customary*, the Practice whereof you would not have continue, and increase. It is con- venient for Health and Sobriety, to *drink* no more than Natural Thirst requires: And he that eats not Salt Meats, nor drinks Strong Drink, will seldom thirst between Meals, unless he has been accustomed to 30 such unseasonable *Drinking*.⁻ᵛ

§. 19. ʷ⁻Above all, Take great Care that he seldom, if ever, taste any *Wine*, or *Strong Drink*. There is nothing so ordinarily given Children in *England*, and nothing so destructive to them. They ought *never* to drink any *Strong Liquor*, but when they need it as a Cordial, and the 35 Doctor prescribes it. And in this Case it is, that Servants are most

---

§ 18 *Drink.*   *Habits.*   § 19 *Strong Drink.*

15 It] And it **1**

ᵛ⁻ᵛ *Altered from* **K** § 15   ʷ⁻ʷ **H** § 12; **K** § 17

narrowly to be watched, and most severely to be reprehended, when they transgress. Those mean Sort of People, placing a great Part of their Happiness in *Strong Drink*, are always forward to make Court to my young Master, by offering him that, which they love best themselves: And finding themselves made merry by it, they foolishly think 'twill do the Child no Harm. This you are carefully to have your Eye upon, and restrain with all the Skill and Industry you can; There being nothing that lays a surer Foundation of Mischief, both to Body and Mind, than Children's being used to *Strong Drink*; especially, to drink in private, *with the Servants.* ⁻ʷ

§. 20. ˣ⁻*Fruit* makes one of the most difficult Chapters in the Government of Health, especially that of Children. Our first Parents ventur'd *Paradise* for it: And 'tis no Wonder our Children cannot stand the Temptation, though it cost them their Health. The Regulation of this cannot come under any one General Rule. For I am by no Means of their Mind, who would keep Children almost wholly from *Fruit*, as a Thing totally unwholsome for them: By which strict Way they make them but the more ravenous after it; and to eat Good and Bad, Ripe or Unripe, all that they can get, whenever they come at it. *Melons, Peaches*, most sorts of *Plumbs*, and all sorts of *Grapes* in *England*, I think Children should be *wholly kept from*, as having a very tempting Taste, in a very unwholsome Juice; so that, if it were possible, they should never so much as see them, or know there were any such Thing. But *Strawberries, Cherries, Goose-berries*, or *Currans*,ʸ when through ripe, I think may be very safely allowed them, and that with a pretty liberal Hand, if they be eaten with these Cautions. 1. Not after Meals, as we usually do, when the Stomach is already full of other Food. But I think they should be eaten rather before, or between Meals, and Children should have them for their Breakfasts. 2. Bread eaten with them. 3. Perfectly ripe. If they are thus eaten, I imagine them rather conducing, than hurtful to our Health. *Summer-Fruits*, being suited to the hot Season of the Year they come in, refresh our Stomachs, languishing and fainting under it: And therefore I should not be altogether so strict in this Point, as some are to their Children; who being kept so very short, instead of a moderate Quantity of well-chosen *Fruit*, which being allowed them would content them, when-ever they can get loose, or

§ 20. *Fruit.*

---

32 come in,] come in and 1

ˣ⁻ˣ **H** § 13; **K** § 18   ʸ Currans, Apples and peares **HK**

bribe a Servant to supply them, satisfie their Longing with any Trash they can get, and eat to a Surfeit.

ᶻ⁻*Apples* and *Pears* too, which are through ripe, and have been gathered some Time, I think may be safely eaten at any Time, and in pretty large Quantities; especially *Apples*, which never did any Body 5 hurt, that I have heard, after *October*. ⁻ᶻ

Fruits also *dried* without Sugar, I think very wholsome. But *Sweet-meats* of all Kinds are to be avoided; which, whether they do more Harm to the Maker, or Eater, is not easie to tell. This I am sure, It is one of the most inconvenient Ways of Expence, that Vanity hath yet 10 found out; and so I leave them to the Ladies.⁻ˣ

§. 21. ᵃ⁻Of all that looks soft and effeminate, nothing is more to be indulged Children than *Sleep*. In this alone they are to be permitted to have their full Satisfaction; nothing contributing more to the Growth and Health of Children than *Sleep*. All that is to be regulated in it is, in 15 what Part of the Twenty four Hours they should take it: Which will easily be resolved, by only saying, That it is of great Use to accustom them to rise early in the Morning. It is best so to do, for Health: And he that, from his Childhood, has, by a setled Custom, made *Rising betimes* easie and familiar to him, will not, when he is a Man, waste the best and 20 most useful Part of his Life in Drowziness, and Lying a-bed. If Children therefore are to be called up early in the Morning, it will follow of Course, that they must go to Bed betimes; whereby they will be accustomed to avoid the unhealthy and unsafe Hours of Debauchery, which are those of the Evenings: And they who keep good Hours, seldom are 25 guilty of any great Disorders. I do not say this, as if your Son, when grown up, should never be in Company past Eight, nor ever chat over a Glass of Wine till Midnight. You are now, by the Accustoming of his tender Years, to indispose him to those Inconveniences, as much as you can: And it will be no small Advantage, that Contrary Practice having 30 made Sitting up uneasie to him, it will make him often avoid, and very seldom propose Mid-night-Revels. But if it should not reach so far, but Fashion and Company should prevail, and make him live as others do about Twenty, 'tis worth the while to accustom him to *Early Rising*, and Early Going to Bed, between this and that; for the present Improvement 35 of his Health, and other Advantages.⁻ᵃ

§ 21 *Sleep.*

---

8 are] *add.* **3**   30 it] that **1**

ᶻ⁻ᶻ *Not in* **HK**; *cf. p.* 96.23–4   ᵃ⁻ᵃ **K** § 19; *combined with* § 22 *forms* **H** § 14

Though I have said a large Allowance of *Sleep*, even as much as they will take, should be made to Children when they are little, yet I do not mean, that it should always be continued to them in so large a Proportion, and they suffer'd to indulge a drowzy laziness in their Beds as
5 they grow up bigger. But whether they should begin to be restrain'd at Seven, or Ten Years old, or any other time, is impossible to be precisely determin'd. Their Tempers, Strength and Constitutions, must be consider'd. But some time between Seven and Fourteen, if they are too great lovers of their Beds, I think it may be seasonable to begin to
10 reduce them by degrees to about Eight Hours, which is generally rest enough for healthy grown People. If you have accustom'd him, as you should do, to rise constantly very early in the Morning, this Fault of being too long in Bed will easily be reformed; and most Children will be forward enough to shorten that time themselves, by coveting to sit
15 up with the Company at Night: though, if they be not look'd after, they will be apt to take it out in the Morning, which should by no means be permitted. They should constantly be call'd up, and made to rise at their early Hour: but great Care should be taken in waking them, that it be not done hastily, nor with a loud or shrill Voice, or any other
20 suddain violent Noise. This often affrights Children, and does them great harm. And sound *Sleep* thus broke off, with suddain Alarms, is apt enough to discompose any one. When Children are to be waken'd out of their *Sleep*, be sure[14] to begin with a low Call, and some gentle Motion, and so draw them out of it by degrees, and give them none but
25 kind words, and usage, till they are come perfectly to themselves, and being quite Dressed, you are sure they are throughly awake. The being forced from their *Sleep*, how gently soever you do it, is Pain enough to them: And Care should be taken not to add any other uneasiness to it, especially such that may terrifie them.

30 §. 22. [b-]Let his *Bed* be *hard*, and rather Quilts than Feathers. Hard Lodging strengthens the Parts; whereas being buried every Night in Feathers, melts and dissolves the Body, is often the Cause of Weakness, and the Fore-runner of an early Grave. And, besides the Stone, which has often its Rise from this warm Wrapping of the Reins;

§ 22 *Bed.*

1–29 Though . . . terrifie them.] *add.* **3**   23 be sure] besure **3 4 5**

[b-b] *Part of* **H** § 14; **K** § 20

[14] 'besure' perhaps correct, cf. 'beware'; used in 18th c. for 'you may be sure, certainly' (*OED*).

several other Indispositions, and that which is the Root of them all, a tender weakly Constitution, is very much owing to *Downe-Beds.* Besides, He that is used to hard Lodging at home, will not miss his Sleep (where he has most need of it) in his Travels abroad, for want of his soft Bed, and his Pillows laid in order. And therefore, I think it would not be amiss, to *make* his *Bed* after different Fashions, sometimes lay his Head higher, sometimes lower, that he may not feel every little Change he must be sure to meet with, who is not design'd to lie always in my young Master's Bed at home, and to have his Maid lay all Things in print, and tuck him in warm. The great Cordial of Nature is Sleep. He that misses that, will suffer by it: And he is very unfortunate, who can take his Cordial only in his Mother's fine Gilt Cup, and not in a Wooden Dish. He that can sleep soundly, takes the Cordial: And it matters not, whether it be on a soft *Bed*, or the hard Boards. 'Tis Sleep only that is the Thing necessary.⁻ᵇ

§. 23. ᶜ⁻One thing more there is, which has a great Influence upon the Health, and that is, *Going to Stool* regularly. People that are very *loose*, have seldom strong Thoughts, or strong Bodies. But the Cure of this, both by Diet and Medicine, being much more easie than the contrary Evil, there needs not much to be said about it: For if it come to threaten, either by its Violence, or Duration, it will soon enough, and sometimes too soon, make a Physician be sent for: And if it be moderate or short, it is commonly best to leave it to Nature. On the other Side, *Costiveness* has too its ill Effects, and is much harder to be dealt with by Physick; purging Medicines, which seem to give Relief, rather increasing than removing the Evil.

§. 24. ᵈ⁻It being an Indisposition, I had a particular Reason to enquire into; and not finding the Cure of it in Books; I set my Thoughts on work, believing that greater Changes than that might be made in our Bodies, if we took the right Course, and proceeded by Rational Steps.

1. Then I considered, that *Going to Stool*, was the effect of certain Motions of the Body, especially of the Peristaltick Motion of the Guts.

2. I considered, that several Motions, that were not perfectly voluntary, might yet by Use and constant Application, be brought to be

§ 23–8. *Costiveness.*

---

1 several other Indispositions,] *add.* **3**   27 It . . . Indisposition,] It having been an Inconvenience, **1**

ᶜ⁻ᶜ §§ 23–8 *not in* **H**; *shorter version in* **Corr.** 799 (ii. 667–8); **K** §§ 21–30   ᵈ⁻ᵈ **K** §§ 22–6

Habitual, if by an unintermitted Custom, they were at certain Seasons endeavoured to be constantly produced.

3. I had observed some Men, who, by taking after Supper a Pipe of *Tabaco*, never failed of a *Stool*; and began to doubt with my self, whether it were not more Custom, than the Tabaco, that gave them the benefit of Nature; or at least, if the Tabaco did it, it was rather by exciting a vigorous Motion in the Guts, than by any purging Quality; for then it would have had other Effects.

Having thus once got the Opinion, that it was possible to make it habitual; the next thing was to consider, what Way and Means was the likeliest to obtain it.⁻ᵈ

4. ᵉ⁻Then I guessed, that if a Man, after his first Eating in the Morning, would presently sollicite Nature, and try, whether he could strain himself so as to obtain a *Stool*, he might in time, by a constant Application, bring it to be Habitual.

§. 25. The Reasons that made me chuse this time, were,

1. Because the Stomach being then empty, if it received any thing grateful to it (for I would never, but in case of necessity, have any one eat, but what he likes, and when he has an Appetite) it was apt to imbrace it close by a strong Constriction of its Fibres; which Constriction, I supposed, might probably be continued on in the Guts, and so increase their peristaltick Motion; as we see in the *Ileus*, that an inverted Motion, being begun any where below, continues it self all the whole length, and makes even the Stomach obey that irregular Motion.

2. Because when Men eat, they usually relax their Thoughts, and the Spirits, then free from other Imployments, are more vigorously distributed into the lower Belly, which thereby contribute to the same effect.

3. Because, when ever Men have leisure to eat, they have leisure enough also to make so much court to Madam *Cloacina*,¹⁵ as would be necessary to our present purpose; but else, in the variety of Humane Affairs and Accidents, it was impossible to affix it to any hour certain; whereby the Custom would be interrupted. Whereas Men in health, seldom failing to eat once a Day, tho' the Hour changed, the Custom might still be preserved.⁻ᵉ

§. 26 ᶠ⁻Upon these Grounds, the Experiment began to be tried, and I

ᵉ⁻ᵉ **K** § 27   ᶠ⁻ᶠ *Revision of* **K** § 28, *which adds at end* and this I thinke any one else may doe that will at first but take constantly a litle pains with himself.

¹⁵ After Latin *cloaca*, 'sewer', thus taken as 'goddess of the lavatory' in 17th c., though in fact a cult-title of Venus.

have known none, who have been steady in the prosecution of it, and taken care to go constantly to the necessary House, after their first Eating, when ever that happen'd, whether they found themselves called on or no, and there endeavour'd to put Nature upon her Duty, but in a few Months they obtained the desired success, and brought themselves to so regular an habit, that they seldom ever failed of a *Stool*, after their first Eating, unless it were by their own neglect. For, whether they have any Motion or no, if they go to the Place, and do their part, they are sure to have Nature very obedient.⁻ᶠ

§. 27. ᵍ⁻I would therefore advise, that this Course should be taken with a Child every day, presently after he has eaten his Break-fast. Let him be set upon the Stool, as if disburthening were as much in his power, as filling his Belly; and let not him, or his Maid know any thing to the contrary, but that it is so: And if he be forced to endeavour, by being hindred from his play, or Eating again till he has been effectually at *Stool*, or at least done his utmost, I doubt not but in a little while it will become naturalʰ to him. For there is reason to suspect, that Children being usually intent on their Play, and very heedless of any thing else, often let pass those Motions of Nature, when she calls them but gently; and so they neglecting the seasonable Offers, do by degrees bring themselves into an Habitual Costiveness.⁻ᵍ That by this Method Costiveness may be prevented, I do more than guess; having known, by the constant Practice of it for some time, a Child brought to have a *Stool* regularly after his Break-fast every Morning.

§. 28. ⁱ⁻How far any grown People will think fit to make tryal of it, must be left to them, tho' I cannot but say, that considering the many Evils that come from that Defect, of a requisite easing of Nature, I scarce know any thing more conducing to the Preservation of Health than this is. Once in Four and Twenty hours, I think, is enough;⁻ⁱ and no body, I guess, will think it too much. And by this means it is to be obtained without Physick, which commonly proves very ineffectual, in the cure of a settled and habitual Costiveness.⁻ᶜ

§. 29. ʲ⁻This is all I have to trouble you with concerning his Management, in the ordinary Course of his Health. Perhaps it will be expected

§§ 29–30 *Physick.*

---

5 they] *add.* **3**   6 themselves] Nature **1**   21 this] his **NN**   26 must
... them,] I know not, **1**   33 29] 22 **NA**   34 Health. Perhaps] Health; and
perhaps **1**

ᵍ⁻ᵍ *Varied from* **K** § 29   ʰ habitual **K**   ⁱ⁻ⁱ *Varied from* **K** § 30   ʲ⁻ʲ **H** §
15; **K** § 31

from me, that I should give some Directions of *Physick*, to prevent Diseases: For which, I have only this one very sacredly to be observed; Never to give Children any *Physick* for prevention. [k]-The-[k] observation of what I have already advised, will, I suppose, do that better than
5   the Ladies Diet-drinks or Apothecarie's Medicines. Have a great care of tampering that way, least, instead of preventing, you draw on Diseases. Nor even upon every little Indisposition is *Physick* to be given, or the Physician to be called to Children; especially if he be a Busy-man, that will presently fill their Windows with Gally-pots,[16]
10 and their Stomachs with Drugs. It is safer to leave them wholly to Nature, than to put them into the hands of one, forward to tamper; or that thinks Children are to be cured in ordinary Distempers, by any thing but Diet, or by a Method very little distant from it. It seeming suitable both to my Reason and Experience, that the tender Constitu-
15 tions of Children should have as little done to them, as is possible, and as the absolute necessity of the Case requires. A little cold-still'd red *Poppy-water*,[17] which is the true Surfeit-water, with Ease, and Abstinence from Flesh, often puts an end to several Distempers in the beginning, which, by too forward Applications, might have been made lusty
20 Diseases. When such a gentle Treatment will not stop the growing Mischief, nor hinder it from turning into a form'd Disease, it will be time to seek the Advice of some sober and discreet Physician. In this part, I hope, I shall find an easy belief; and no body can have a pretence to doubt the Advice of one, who has spent some time in the Study
25 of Physick, when he counsels you, not to be too forward in making use of *Physick* and *Physicians.*-[j]

§. 30. [l]-And thus I have done with what concerns the Body and Health, which reduces it self to these few and easily observable Rules. Plenty of open *Air, Exercise* and *Sleep*; Plain *Diet*, no *Wine* or *Strong*
30 *Drink*, and very little or no *Physick*; not too Warm and straight *Clothing*, especially the *Head* and *Feet* kept cold, and the *Feet* often used to cold Water, and exposed to Wet.-[l]

§. 31. [m]-Due care being had to keep the Body in Strength and Vigor, §§ 31-3 *Mind*.

4–5 than . . . Medicines.] than Apothecarie's Drugs and Medicines. 1
20–1 stop . . . turning into] prevent the growing Mischief, but that it will turn into 1

[k–k] The rules I have already given **HK**   [l–l] **H** § 16; *first part of* **K** § 32
[m–m] **H** § 17; *latter part of* **K** § 32

[16] 'Gally-pots': gallipots, small glazed pots used for ointments, unguents (*OED*).
[17] '*Poppy-water*', a soporific drink made from poppies (*OED*).

so that it may be able to obey and execute the Orders of the *Mind*; The next and principal Business is, to set the *Mind* right, that on all Occasions it may be disposed to consent to nothing, but what may be suitable to the Dignity and Excellency of a rational Creature.⁻ᵐ

§. 32. ⁿ⁻If what I have said in the beginning of this Discourse be true, 5 as I do not doubt but it is, *viz.* That the difference to be found in the Manners and Abilities of Men, is owing more to their *Education* than to any thing else; we have reason to conclude, that great care is to be had of the forming Children's *Minds*, and giving them that seasoning early, which shall influence their Lives always after. For when they do 10 well or ill, the Praise or Blame will be laid there: And when any thing is done untowardly, the common Saying will pass upon them, That it is suitable to their *Breeding.* ⁻ⁿ

§. 33. ᵒ⁻As the Strength of the Body lies chiefly in being able to endure Hardships, so also does that of the Mind. And the great Prin- 15 ciple and Foundation of all Vertue and Worth, is placed in this, That a Man is able to *deny himself* his own Desires, cross his own Inclinations, and purely follow what Reason directs as best, tho' the appetite lean the other way.⁻ᵒ

§. 34. ᵖ⁻The great Mistake I have observed in People's breeding 20 their Children has been, that this has not been taken care enough of in its *due Season*; That the Mind has not been made obedient to Discipline,�q and pliant to Reason, when at first it was most tender, most easy to be bowed. Parents, being wisely ordain'd by Nature to love their Children, are very apt, if Reason watch not that natural 25 Affection very warily, are apt, I say, to let it run into fondness. They love their little ones, and 'tis their Duty: But they often, with them, cherish their Faults too. They must not be crossed, forsooth; they must be permitted to have their Wills in all things; and they being in their Infancies not capable of great Vices, their Parents think they may 30 safely enough indulge their little irregularities, and make themselves Sport with that pretty perverseness, which, they think, well enough becomes that innocent Age. But to a fond Parent, that would not have his Child corrected for a perverse Trick, but excused it, saying, It was

§§ 34–7 *Early.*

---

3 consent to] do **1**   12 untowardly,] outwardly, **4 5**   23 Discipline,]
Rules, **1**

ⁿ⁻ⁿ **H** § 18; **K** § 33   ᵒ⁻ᵒ **H** § 19; **K** § 34   ᵖ⁻ᵖ *First part of* **H** § 20; **K** § 35
q rules **HK**

a small matter; *Solon*[18] very well replied, Ay, but Custom is a great one.⁻ᵖ

§. 35. ʳ⁻The Fondling must be taught to strike, and call Names; must have what he Cries for, and do what he pleases. Thus Parents, by humoring and cockering them when *little*, corrupt the Principles of Nature in their Children, and wonder afterwards to taste the bitter Waters, when they themselves have poisoned the Fountain. For when their Children are grown up, and these ill Habits with them; when they are now too big to be dandled, and their Parents can no longer make use of them, as Play-things; then they complain, that the Brats are untoward and perverse; then they are offended to see them wilful, and are troubled with those ill Humours, which they themselves ˢ⁻infused and fomented⁻ˢ in them; And then, perhaps too late, would be glad to get out those Weeds, which their own hands have planted, and which now have taken too deep root to be easily extirpated. For he that has been used to have his Will in every thing, as long as he was in Coats, why should we think it strange, that he should desire it, and contend for it still, when he is in Breeches? Indeed, as he grows more towards a Man, Age shews his Faults the more, so that there be few Parents then so blind, as not to see them; few so insensible, as not to feel the ill Effects of their own Indulgence. He had the Will of his Maid before he could Speak or Go; he had the Mastery of his Parents ever since he could Prattle; and why, now he is grown up, is Stronger and Wiser than he was then, why now of a suddain must he be restrained and Curbed? Why must he at seven, fourteen, or twenty Years old, lose the Privilege which the Parent's indulgence, till then, so largely allowed him? Try it in a Dog or an Horse, or any other Creature, and see whether the ill and resty Tricks, they have learn'd when young, are easily to be mended when they are knit: And yet none of those Creatures are half so wilful and proud, or half so desirous to be Masters of themselves and others, as Man.⁻ʳ

§. 36. ᵗ⁻We are generally wise enough to begin with Them, when they are *very young*; and Discipline *betimes* those other Creatures we would make useful and good for somewhat. They are only our own Off-spring, that we neglect in this Point; and having made them ill

12–13 infused and fomented] inspired and cherished **1** (so **HK**)   17 should we] would we **NN** (**K** 'should we')   34 useful . . . somewhat.] usefull to us. **1**

ʳ⁻ʳ *Latter part of* **H** § 20; **K** § 36   ˢ⁻ˢ **HK** *as* **1**   ᵗ⁻ᵗ *Part of* **H** § 20; **K** § 37

[18] Athenian statesman: *c.* 600 BC; devised law-code, of which fragments survive. The story, however, is Locke's adaptation of Diogenes Laertius iii. 38, concerning Plato.

Children, we foolishly expect they should be good Men. For if the Child must have Grapes[u] or Sugar-plumbs, when he has a Mind to them, rather than make the poor Baby cry, or be out of Humour; why, when he is grown up, must he not be satisfied too, if his Desires carry him to Wine or Women? They are Objects as suitable to the longing of one of more Years, as what he cried for when little was to the inclinations of a Child. The having Desires accommodated to the Apprehensions and Relish of those several Ages is not the Fault; but the not having them subject to the Rules and Restraints of Reason: The Difference lies not in the having or not having Appetites, but in the Power to govern, and deny our selves in them. He that is not used to submit his Will to the Reason of others, *when* he is *young*, will scarce hearken or submit to his own Reason, when he is of an Age to make use of it. And what a kind of a Man such an one is like to prove, is easie to foresee.[-t]

§. 37. These are Over-sights usually committed, by those who seem to take the greatest Care of their Childrens Education. But if we look into the common Management of Children, we shall have reason to wonder, in the great Dissoluteness of Manners which the World complains of, that there are any Foot-steps at all left of Virtue. I desire to know what Vice can be named, which Parents, and those about Children, do not season them with, and drop into them the Seeds of, as soon as they are capable to receive them? I do not mean by the Examples they give, and the Patterns they set before them, which is Encouragement enough; But that which I would take notice of here, is the downright teaching them Vice, and actual putting them out of the way of Virtue. Before they can go, they Principle them with Violence, Revenge, and Cruelty. *Give me a blow that I may beat him*, is a Lesson, which most Children every Day hear: And it is thought nothing, because their Hands have not Strength to do any Mischief. But I ask, Does not this corrupt their Minds? Is not this the way of Force and Violence, that they are set in? And if they have been taught, when little, to strike and hurt others by Proxy, and incouraged to rejoyce in the harm they have brought upon them, and see them suffer, are they not prepar'd to do it, when they are strong enough to be felt themselves, and can strike to some purpose?

The Coverings of our Bodies, which are for Modesty, Warmth, and

7 accommodated] suitable **1**   11 He] And he, **1**   16–107.31 § 37 *add.* **3**

[u] wine **HK**

Defence; are, by the Folly or Vice of Parents, recommended to their Children for other Uses. They are made Matter of Vanity and Emulation. A Child is set a longing after a new Suit, for the finery of it: And when the little Girl is tricked up in her new Gown and Commode, how
5 can her Mother do less than teach her to Admire her self, by calling her *her little Queen* and *her Princess?* Thus the little ones are taught to be *Proud* of their Clothes, before they can put them on. And why should they not continue to value themselves for this out-side fashionableness of the Taylor or Tire-woman's[19] making, when their Parents have
10 so early instructed them to do so?

Lying and Equivocations, and Excuses little different from Lying, are put into the Mouths of Young People, and commended in Apprentices and Children, whilst they are for their Master's or Parent's Advantage. And can it be thought, that he, that finds the Straining of
15 Truth dispensed with, and incouraged, whilst it is for his Godly Master's turn, will not make use of that Privilege for himself, when it may be for his own Profit.

Those of the meaner Sort are hindred by the streightness of their Fortunes, from incouraging *Intemperance* in their Children, by the
20 temptation of their Diet, or Invitations to Eat or Drink more than enough: But their own ill Examples, whenever Plenty comes in their way, shew that 'tis not the dislike of Drunkenness and Gluttony that keeps them from Excess, but want of Materials. But if we look into the Houses of those, who are a little warmer in their Fortunes, there Eat-
25 ing and Drinking are made so much the great Business and Happiness of Life, that Children are thought neglected, if they have not their share of it. Sauces, and Raggousts, and Food disguised by all the Arts of Cookery, must tempt their Palates, when their Bellies are full: And then, for fear the Stomach should be over-charg'd, a Pretence is found
30 for t'other Glass of Wine to help Digestion, though it only serves to increase the Surfeit.

Is my young Master a little out of order; The first Question is, *What will my Dear eat? what shall I get for thee?* Eating and Drinking are instantly pressed: And every bodies invention is set on work to find
35 out something, luscious and delicate enough to prevail over that want of Appetite, which Nature has wifely order'd in the beginning of Distempers, as a defence against their increase; that being freed from the ordinary labour of digesting any new Load in the Stomach, she may be at leisure to correct, and master the peccant humours.

[19] 'Tire-woman', or attirewoman, i.e. dressmaker (*OED*).

And where Children are so happy in the Care of their Parents, as by their Prudence to be kept, from the excess of their Tables, to the Sobriety of a plain and simple Diet; yet there too they are scarce to be preserved from the Contagion, that Poisons the Mind. Though by a discreet Management, whilst they are under Tuition, their Healths perhaps may be pretty well secur'd; yet their Desires must needs yield to the Lessons, which every where will be read to them upon this part of Epicurism. The Commendation that *eating well* has every where, cannot fail to be a successful incentive to natural Appetite, and bring them quickly to the liking and expence of a fashionable Table. This shall have from every one, even the Reprovers of Vice, the title of *Living well.* And what shall sullen Reason dare to say against the Publick Testimony? Or can it hope to be heard, if it should call that *Luxury*, which is so much owned, and universally practised by those of the best Quality?

This is now so grown a Vice, and has so great Supports, that I know not whether it do not put in for the Name of Vertue; and whether it will not be thought Folly, or want of Knowledge of the World, to open ones Mouth against it. And truly I should suspect, that what I have here said of it might be censured as a little Satyr out of my way, did I not mention it with this view, that it might awaken the Care and Watchfulness of Parents in the Education of their Children; when they see how they are beset on every side, not only with Temptations, but Instructors to Vice, and that perhaps in those they thought Places of Security.

I shall not dwell any longer on this Subject; much less run over all the particulars, that would shew what Pains are used to corrupt Children, and instill Principles of Vice into them: But I desire Parents soberly to consider, what Irregularity or Vice there is, which Children are not visibly taught; and whether it be not their Duty and Wisdom to provide them other Instructions.

§. 38. ᵛ⁻It seems plain to me, that the Principle of all Vertue and Excellency lies in a power of denying our selves the satisfaction of our own Desires, where Reason does not authorize them. This Power is to be got and improved by Custom, made easy and familiar by an *early* Practice. If therefore I might be heard, I would advise, that, contrary to

§§ 38–9 *Craving.*

---

32 38] 37 **1**

ᵛ⁻ᵛ *Slightly revised from* **H** § 21, **K** § 38

the ordinary way, Children should be used to submit their Desires, and go without their Longings, even *from their very Cradles*. The first thing they should learn to know should be, that they were not to have any thing, because it pleased them, but because it was thought fit for them. If things suitable to their Wants were supplied to them, so that they were never suffered to have what they once cried for, they would learn to be content without it; would never with Bawling and Peevishness contend for Mastery; nor be half so uneasy to themselves and others as they are, because *from the first* beginning they are not thus handled. If they were never suffered to obtain their desire by the Impatience they expressed for it, they would no more cry for other Things, than they do for the Moon.⁻ᵛ

§. 39. ᵂ⁻I say not this, as if Children were not to be indulged in any Thing; or that I expected they should, in Hanging-Sleeves,²⁰ have the Reason and Conduct of Councellors. I consider them as Children, who must be tenderly used, who must play, and have Play-things. That which I mean is, That whenever they crav'd what was not fit for them to have or do, they should not be permitted it, because they were *little*, and desired it: Nay, ˣ⁻Whatever they were importunate for,⁻ˣ they should be sure, for that very Reason, to be denied. I have seen Children at a Table, who, whatever was there, never asked for any thing, but contentedly took what was given them: And at another Place I have seen others cry for every Thing they saw, must be served out of every Dish, and that first too. What made this vast Difference, but this; That one was accustomed to have what they called or cried for; the other to go without it? The *younger* they are, the less, I think, are their unruly and disorderly Appetites to be complied with; and the less Reason they have of their own, the more are they to be under the Absolute Power and Restraint of those, in whose Hands they are. From which, I confess, it will follow, That none but discreet People should be about them. If the World commonly does otherwise, I cannot help that. I am saying what I think should be; which, if it were already in Fashion, I should not need to ʸ⁻trouble the World with a Discourse on this Subject.⁻ʸ But yet I doubt not, but when it is considered, there will be Others of Opinion with me, That the *sooner* this Way is begun with Children, the easier it will be for them, and their

---

13 39] 38 **1**   15–16 Children, who] Children that **1**   17 crav'd] crave **1**

ᵂ⁻ᵂ *Slightly revised from* H § 22, **K** § 39   ˣ⁻ˣ what they once craved were importunate for or once cried for **HK**   ʸ⁻ʸ trouble you with such a discourse as this **HK**

²⁰ 'Hanging-Sleeves', *fig.* relying or depending on another's support (*OED*).

Governors too; And, that this ought to be observed as an inviolable
Maxim, That whatever once is denied them, they are certainly not to
obtain by Crying or Importunity, unless one has a Mind to teach them
to be impatient, and troublesome,ᶻ by rewarding them for it, when they
are so.⁻ʷ 5

§. 40. ᵃ⁻Those therefore that intend ever to govern their Children,
should begin it whilst they are *very little*; and look, that they perfectly
comply with the Will of their Parents. Would you have your Son
obedient to you when past a Child? Be sure then to establish the
Authority of a Father, *as soon* as he is capable of Submission, and can 10
understand in whose Power he is. If you would have him stand in awe
of you, imprint it *in his Infancy*; and, as he approaches more to a Man,
admit him nearer to your Familiarity: So shall you have him your
obedient Subject (as is fit) whilst he is a Child, and your affectionate
Friend when he is a Man. For, methinks, they mightily misplace the 15
Treatment due to their Children, who are indulgent and familiar,
when they are little, but severe to them, and keep them at a distance,
when they are grown up. For, Liberty and Indulgence can do no Good
to *Children*: Their Want of Judgment makes them stand in need of
Restraint and Discipline. And, on the contrary, Imperiousness and 20
Severity is but an ill Way of Treating Men, who have Reason of their
own to guide them, unless you have a Mind to make your Children,
when grown up, weary of you; and secretly to say within themselves,
When will you die, Father?⁻ᵃ

§. 41. ᵇ⁻I imagine every one will judge it reasonable, that their Chil- 25
dren, *when little*, should look upon their Parents as their Lords, their
Absolute Governors; and, as such, stand in awe of them: And that,
when they come to riper Years, they should look on them as their best,
as their only sure Friends; and as such, love and reverence them. The
Way I have mentioned, if I mistake not, is the only one to obtain this. 30
We must look upon our Children, when grown up, to be like our
selves; with the same Passions, the same Desires. We would be
thought Rational Creatures, and have our Freedom; we love not to be
uneasie, under constant Rebukes and Brow-beatings; nor can we bear
severe Humours, and great Distance in those we converse with. 35

§§ 40–2 *Early.*

---

6 40] 39 ɪ   25 41] 40 ɪ

ᶻ impatient importunate and troublesome **HK**   ᵃ⁻ᵃ *Similar to first part of* **H** § 23;
K § 40; **Corr.** 803 (ii. 677) *expresses some of the same ideas*   ᵇ⁻ᵇ *New para. in* **H** § 23; **K**
§ 41

Whoever has such Treatment when he is a Man, will look out other Company, other Friends, other Conversation, with whom he can be at Ease. If therefore a strict Hand be kept over Children *from the Beginning*, they will in that Age be tractable, and quietly submit to it, as never having known any other: And if, as they grow up to the Use of Reason, the Rigour of Government be, as they deserve it, gently relaxed, the Father's Brow more smooth'd to them, and the Distance by Degrees abated; his former Restraints will increase their Love, when they find it was only a Kindness to them, and a Care to make them capable to deserve the Favour of their Parents, and the Esteem of every Body else.⁻ᵇ

§. 42. ᶜ⁻Thus much for the Settling your Authority over your Children in general.ᵈ Fear and Awe ought to give you the first Power over their Minds, and Love and Friendship in riper Years to hold it: For the Time must come, when they will be past the Rod, and Correction; and then, if the Love of you make them not obedient and dutifull, if the Love of Vertue and Reputation keep them not in Laudable Courses, I ask, What Hold will you have upon them, to turn them to it? Indeed, Fear of having a scanty Portion if they displease you, may make them Slaves to your Estate, but they will be never the less ill and wicked in private; and that Restraint will not last always. Every Man must some Time or other be trusted to himself, and his own Conduct; and he that is a good, a vertuous andᵉ able Man, must be made so within. And therefore, what he is to receive from Education, what is to sway and influence his Life, must be something put into him betimes; Habits woven into the very Principles of his Nature; and not a counterfeit Carriage, and dissembled Out-side, put on by Fear, only to avoid the present Anger of a Father, who perhaps may dis-inherit him.⁻ᶜ

§. 43. ᶠ⁻This being laid down in general, asᵍ⁻ the Course ought to be taken, 'tis fit we now come to consider the Parts of the Discipline to be used, a little more particularly.⁻ᵍ I have spoken so much of Carrying a *strict Hand* over Children, that perhaps I shall be suspected of not

§ 43 *Punishments.*

---

7 smooth'd] smooth 1   12 42] 41 1   29 43] 42 1

ᶜ⁻ᶜ **H** § 24, **K** § 42, *but first sentence* Thus much for the method of your discipline in generall. ᵈ if you thinke a strict hand at all is to be held upon children I thinke it should be most soe when they are youngest from the time they are capable of understanding any thing. *add* **HK** ᵉ an **HK** ᶠ⁻ᶠ **H** § 25; **K** § 43 ᵍ⁻ᵍ the method ought to be taken, 'tis fit we now come to particulars. The first thing parents are to doe is to get an awe upon the mindes of their children and then by that and not by blowes to bring them to submit their will p⟨e⟩rfectly to theirs. **HK**

Considering enough, what is due to their tender Ages and Constitutions. But that Opinion will vanish, when you have heard me a little farther. For I am very apt to think that *great Severity* of Punishment does but very little Good; nay, great Harm in Education: And I believe it will be found, that, *Cæteris paribus*, those Children, who have been   5
most *chastised*, seldom make the best Men. All that I have hitherto contended for, is, That whatsoever *Rigour* is necessary, it is more to be used the younger Children are; and having, by a due Application, wrought its Effect, it is to be relaxed, and changed into a milder Sort of Government.^{-f}   10

§. 44. ^{h-}A Compliance, and Suppleness of their Wills, being by a steady Hand introduced by Parents, before Children have Memories to retain the Beginnings of it, will seem natural to them, and work afterwards in them, as if it were so; preventing all Occasions of Struling, or Repining. The only Care is, That it be begun early, and   15
inflexibly kept to, till *Awe* and *Respect* be grown familiar, and there appears not the least Reluctancy in the Submission and ready Obedience of their Minds. When this *Reverence* is once thus established, (which it must be early, or else it will cost Pains and Blows to recover it; and the more, the longer it is deferred,) 'tis by it, mixed still with as   20
much Indulgence as they make not an ill Use of, and not by *Beating, Chiding*, or other *Servile Punishments*, they are for the future to be governed, as they grow up to more Understanding.

§. 45. That this is so, will be easily allowed, when it is but considered, what is to be aimed at in an ingenuous Education; and upon   25
what it turns.

1. ⁱ⁻He that has not a Mastery over his Inclinations, he that knows not how to *resist* the importunity of *present Pleasure or Pain*, for the sake of what Reason tells him is fit to be done, wants the true Principle of Vertue and Industry; and is in danger never to be good for   30
any thing. This Temper therefore, so contrary to unguided Nature, is to be got betimes; and this Habit, as the true foundation of future Ability and Happiness, is to be wrought into the Mind, as early as may be, even from the first dawnings of any Knowledge, or Apprehension in Children; and so to be confirmed in them, by all the Care   35

---

§ 44 *Awe.*   § 45 *Self-denial.*

---

11 44] 43 I   24 45] 44 I

^{h-h} §§ 44–52 *are an extensive reworking of* **H** §§ 26–9, **K** §§ 44–8   ⁱ⁻ⁱ **Corr.** 929
(iii. 173–5) *with minor variants, corresponds to* §§ 45–52, *first four sentences*

and Ways imaginable, by those who have the over-sight of their Education.

§. 46. 2. On the other side, if the *Mind* be curbed, and *humbled* too
much in Children; if their *Spirits* be abased and *broken* much, by too
strict an hand over them, they lose all their Vigor and Industry, and are
in a worse State than the former. For extravagant young Fellows, that
have Liveliness and Spirit, come sometimes to be set right, and so
make Able and Great Men: But *dejected Minds*, timorous, and tame,
and *low Spirits*, are hardly ever to be raised, and very seldom attain to
any thing. To avoid the danger, that is on either hand, is the great Art;
and he that has found a way, how to keep up a Child's Spirit, easy,
active and free; and yet, at the same time, to restrain him from many
things he has a Mind to, and to draw him to things that are uneasy to
him; he, I say, that knows how to reconcile these seeming Contradic-
tions, has, in my Opinion, got the true Secret of Education.

§. 47. The usual lazy and short way by Chastisement, and the Rod,
which is the only Instrument of Government that Tutors generally
know, or ever think of, is the most unfit of any to be used in Education;
because it tends to both those Mischiefs; which, as we have shewn, are
the *Sylla*[21] and *Charybdis*, which on the one hand or the other, ruine all
that miscarry.

§. 48. 1. This kind of Punishment, contributes not at all to the
mastery of our Natural Propensity to indulge Corporal and present
Pleasure, and to avoid Pain at any rate; but rather encourages it; and
thereby strengthens that in us, which is the root from whence spring
all Vitious Actions, and the Irregularities of Life. For what other
Motive, but of sensual Pleasure and Pain, does a Child act by, who
drudges at his Book against his Inclination, or abstains from eating
unwholsome Fruit, that he takes pleasure in, only out of fear of
whiping? He in this only preferrs the greater *Corporal Pleasure*, or
avoids the greater *Corporal Pain.* And what is it, to govern his Actions,
and direct his Conduct by such Motives as these? What is it, I say, but
to cherish that Principle in him, which it is our Business to root out
and destroy? And therefore I cannot think any Correction usefull to a

§ 46 *Dejected.*   §§ 47–51 *Beating.*

---

3 46] 45 **1**   16 47] 46 **1**   20 the other] other **1**   22 48] 47 **1**
24–8 and thereby ... drudges] and so strengthens that in us, which is the root of all
vitious and wrong Actions. For what Motives, I pray, does a Child Act by, but of such
Pleasure and Pain, that drudges **1**

[21] Sc. Scylla, often thus misspelt by Locke.

Child, where the Shame of Suffering for having done Amiss, does not work more upon him, than the Pain.

§. 49. 2. This sort of Correction naturally breeds an Aversion to that, which 'tis the Tutor's Business to create a liking to. How obvious is it to observe, that Children come to hate things which were at first 5 acceptable to them, when they find themselves *whiped*, and *chid*, and *teased* about them? And it is not to be wonder'd at in them; when grown Men would not be able to be reconciled to any thing by such Ways. Who is there that would not be disgusted with any innocent Recreation, in it self indifferent to him, if he should with *blows*, or ill 10 Language be *haled* to it, when he had no Mind? Or be constantly so treated, for some Circumstance in his application to it? This is natural to be so. Offensive Circumstances ordinarily infect innocent things, which they are joined with: And the very sight of a Cup, wherein any one uses to take nauseous Physick, turns his Stomach; so that nothing 15 will relish well out of it, tho' the Cup be never so clean, and well shaped, and of the richest Materials.

§. 50. 3. Such a sort of *slavish Discipline* makes a *slavish Temper*. The Child submits, and dissembles Obedience, whilst the fear of the Rod hangs over him; but when that is removed, and by being out of sight, 20 he can promise himself impunity, he gives the greater scope to his natural Inclination; which by this way is not at all altered, but on the contrary heightned and increased in him; and after such restraint, breaks out usually with the more violence; or,

§. 51. 4. If *Severity* carried to the highest pitch does prevail, and 25 works a Cure upon the present unruly Distemper, it is often by bringing in the room of it, a worse and more dangerous Disease, by breaking the Mind, and then in the place of a disorderly young Fellow, you have a *low spirited, moap'd* Creature: Who, however with his unnatural Sobriety he may please silly People, who commend tame, unactive 30 Children, because they make no noise, nor give them any trouble; yet, at last, will probably prove as uncomfortable a thing to his Friends, as he will be, all his life, an useless thing to himself and others.

§. 52. Beating then, and all other Sorts of slavish and corporal Punishments, are not the Discipline fit to be used in the Education of 35 those we would have wise, good, and ingenuous Men; and therefore

§§ 52–5 *Rewards.*

2 work more] more work 1   3 49] 48 1   5–7 things . . . about] things liked at first, as soon as they come to be *whipped* or *chid*, and teased about 1 18 50] 49 1   25 51] 50 1   34 52] 51 1

very rarely to be applied, and that only in great Occasions, and Cases of Extremity. On the other side, to flatter Children by *Rewards* of things, that are pleasant to them, is as carefully to be avoided. He that will give his Son *Apples*, or *Sugar-plumbs*, or what else, of this kind, he is most delighted with, to make him learn his Book, does but authorize his love of pleasure, and cocker up that dangerous propensity, which he ought by all means to subdue and stifle in him. You can never hope to teach him to master it, whilst you compound for the Check you give his Inclination in one place, by the Satisfaction you propose to it in another.⁻ⁱ To make a good, a wise, and a vertuous Man, 'tis fit he should learn to cross his Appetite, and deny his Inclination to *riches*, *finery*, or *pleasing his Palate*, &c. when ever his Reason advises the contrary, and his Duty requires it. But when you draw him to do any thing that is fit, by the offer of *Money*; or reward the pains of learning his Book, by the pleasure of a luscious Morsel; When you promise him a *Lace-Crevat*, or a *fine new Suit*, upon the performance of some of his little Tasks; what do you by proposing these as *Rewards*, but allow them to be the good Things he should aim at, and thereby encourage his longing for them, and accustom him to place his happiness in them? Thus People, to prevail with Children to be industrious about their Grammar, Dancing, or some other such matter, of no great moment to the happiness or usefulness of their Lives, by misapplied *Rewards* and *Punishments* sacrifice their Vertue, invert the Order of their Education, and teach them Luxury, Pride, or Covetousness, *&c.* For in this way, flattering those wrong Inclinations, which they should restrain and suppress, they lay the Foundations of those future Vices, which cannot be avoided, but by curbing our Desires, and accustoming them early to submit to Reason.⁻ʰ

§. 53. ʲ⁻I say not this, that I would have Children kept from the Conveniences or Pleasures of Life, that are not injurious to their Health or Vertue. On the contrary, I would have their Lives made as pleasant, and as agreeable to them, as may be, in a plentiful enjoyment of whatsoever might innocently delight them: Provided it be with this Caution, that they have those Enjoyments, only as the Consequences of the State of Esteem and Acceptation they are in with their Parents and Governors; but they should *never* be offer'd or bestow'd on them, as the *Rewards of this or that particular Performance* that they shew an

29 53] 52 **1**   29–30 Conveniencies] Conveniences **NN**

ʲ⁻ʲ *More briefly stated in* **Corr.** 929 (iii. 175)

Aversion to, or to which they would not have applied themselves without that Temptation.⁻ʲ

§. 54. But, if you take away the Rod on one hand, and these little Encouragements, which they are taken with, on the other, ᵏ⁻How then (will you say) shall Children be govern'd? Remove Hope and Fear, and there is an end of all Discipline. I grant, that Good and Evil, *Reward* and *Punishment*, are the only Motives to a rational Creature; these are the Spur and Reins, whereby all Mankind are set on work, and guided, and therefore they are to be made use of to Children too. For I advise their Parents and Governors always to carry this in their Minds, that Children are to be treated as rational Creatures.⁻ᵏ

§. 55. ˡ⁻*Rewards*, I grant, and *Punishments* must be proposed to Children, if we intend to work upon them. The Mistake, I imagine, is, that those that are generally made use of, are *ill chosen*. The Pains and Pleasures of the Body are, I think, of ill consequence, when made the Rewards and Punishments, whereby Men would prevail on their Children: For, as I said before, they serve but to increase and strengthen those Inclinations which 'tis our business to subdue and master. What principle of Vertue do you lay in a Child, if you will redeem his Desires of one Pleasure, by the proposal of another? This is but to enlarge his Appetite, and instruct it to wander. If a Child cries for an unwholsome and dangerous Fruit, you purchase his quiet by giving him a less hurtful Sweet-meat. This perhaps may preserve his Health; but spoils his Mind, and sets that farther out of order. For here you only change the Object; but flatter still his *Appetite*, and allow that must be satisfied; Wherein, as I have shewed, lies the root of the Mischief: And till you bring him to be able to bear a denial of that Satisfaction, the Child may at present be quiet and orderly, but ᵐ⁻the Disease is not cured.⁻ᵐ By this way of proceeding you foment and cherish in him, that which is the Spring from whence all the Evil flows, which will be sure on the next occasion to break out again with more violence, give him stronger Longings, and you more trouble.⁻ˡ

§. 56. ⁿ⁻The *Rewards* and *Punishments* then, whereby we should keep Children in order, *are* quite of another kind; and of that force, that

§ 56–9 *Reputation.*

3 54] 53 **1**   these] those **NN**   11 Children] they **1**   12 55] 54 **1**
17 as . . . before,] *add.* **3**   18 Inclinations] Appetites, **1**   33 56] 55 **1**

ᵏ⁻ᵏ **H** § 30; *first part of* **K** § 49   ˡ⁻ˡ **H** § 31; *new para. in* **K** § 49   ᵐ⁻ᵐ the disease `continues' The mischief is not cured, **H** the disease the mischief is not curd **K**
ⁿ⁻ⁿ **H** § 32; **K** § 50

when we can get them once to work, the business, I think, is done, and the difficulty is over. *Esteem* and *Disgrace* are, of all others, the most powerful incentives ᵒ⁻to the Mind, when once it is brought to relish them.⁻ᵒ If you can once get into Children a love of Credit, and an apprehension of Shame and Disgrace, you have put into them the true Principle, which will constantly work, and incline them to the right. But it will be asked, how shall this be done?⁻ⁿ

ᵖ⁻I confess, it does not at first appearance want some difficulty; but yet I think it worth our while, to seek the ways (and practise them when found,) to attain this, which I look on as the great Secret of Education.⁻ᵖ

§. 57. q⁻*First*, Children (earlier perhaps than we think) are very sensible of *Praise* and Commendation. They find a Pleasure in being esteemed, and valued, especially by their Parents, and those whom they depend on. If therefore the Father *caress and commend them, when they do well*; *shew a cold and neglectful Countenance to them upon doing ill*; And this accompanied by a like Carriage of the Mother, and all others that are about them, it will in a little Time make them sensible of the Difference; and this if constantly observed, I doubt not but will of it self work more than Threats or Blows, which lose their Force, when once grown common, and are of no use when Shame does not attend them; and therefore are to be forborn, and never to be used, but in the Case hereafter mentioned, when it is brought to Extremity.⁻q

§. 58. r⁻But *Secondly*, To make the Sense of *Esteem* or *Disgrace* sink the deeper, and be of the more weight, other *agreeable or disagreeable Things should constantly accompany these different States*; not as particular Rewards and Punishments of this or that particular Action,ˢ but as necessarily belonging to, and constantly attending one, who by his Carriage has brought himself into a State of Disgrace or Commendation. By which Way of Treating them, Children may, as much as possible, be brought to conceive, that those that are commended, and in Esteem for doing well, will necessarily be beloved and cherished by every Body, and have all other good Things as a Consequence of it; and, on the other Side, when any one by Miscarriage falls into Disesteem, and ᵗ⁻cares not to preserve his Credit,⁻ᵗ he will unavoidably fall under Neglect and Contempt; and in that State, the Want of what

12 57] 56 1   24 58] 57 1

ᵒ⁻ᵒ to virtuous and generous mindes. **HK**   ᵖ⁻ᵖ H § 33; K § 51   q⁻q H § 34;
K § 52, *with slight variations*   r⁻r *Slightly rewritten from* H § 35, K § 53   ˢ fact
HK   ᵗ⁻ᵗ cares not what he is thought of, **HK**

ever might satisfie or delight him, will follow. ᵘ⁻In this way, the
Objects of their Desires are made assisting to Vertue; when a settled
Experience from the beginning teaches Children, that the Things they
delight in belong to, and are to be enjoyed by those only, who are in a
State of Reputation.⁻ᵘ If by these Means you can come once to shame ⁵
them out of their Faults, (for besides that, I would willingly have no
Punishment,) and make them in love with the Pleasure of being well
thought on, you may turn them as you please, and they will be in love
with all the ways of Vertue.⁻ʳ

§. 59. ᵛ⁻The great Difficulty here, is, I imagine, from the Folly and ₁₀
Perverseness of Servants, who are hardly to be hinder'd from
ʷ⁻crossing herein the Design of the Father and Mother.⁻ʷ Children,
discountenanced by their Parents for any Fault, find usually a Refuge
and Relief in the Caresses of those foolish Flatterers, who thereby
undo whatever the Parents endeavour to establish. When the Father ₁₅
or Mother looks sowre on the Child, every Body else should put on the
same Coldness to him, and no Body give him Countenance; till
Forgiveness asked, and a ˣ⁻Reformation of his Fault, has set him right
again, and restored him to his former Credit.⁻ˣ If this were constantly
observed, I guess there would be little need of Blows, or Chiding: ₂₀
Their own Ease and Satisfaction would quickly teach Children to
court Commendation, and avoid doing that which they found every
Body condemned, and they were sure to suffer for, without being chid
or beaten. This would teach them Modesty and Shame; and they
would quickly come to have a natural Abhorrence for that, which, they ₂₅
found, made them slighted and neglected by every Body. But how this
Inconvenience from Servants is to be remedied, I must leave to
Parents Care and Consideration. Only I think it of great Importance;
And that they are very happy, who can get discreet People about their
Children.⁻ᵛ ₃₀

§. 60. ʸ⁻Frequent *Beating* or *Chiding* is therefore carefully *to be*
§ 60 *Shame.*

10 59] 58 ɪ   13–14 Refuge and Relief] Remedy and Retreat ɪ   17 Cold-
ness] Carriage ɪ (so **HK**)   18–19 Reformation . . . Credit.] contrary Carriage restored him to his Esteem and former Credit again. ɪ   27 must] can only ɪ
29 that] *add.* **3**   31 60] 59 ɪ

ᵘ⁻ᵘ *Not in* **HK**   ᵛ⁻ᵛ **H** § 36; **K** § 54, *slightly revised*   ʷ⁻ʷ crossing herein
their Master and Mistris. **HK**   ˣ⁻ˣ **HK** *as* ɪ   ʸ⁻ʸ *Slightly rewritten from latter
part of* **H** § 39, **K** § 57; *both begin* 'Frequent punishm⟨en⟩t is'. *The following MS sections* (**H** §
40, **K** § 58) *are omitted from published editions:* I would therefore have noething but vice
absolutely forbidden and since there are very few vices that a child of your sons age is

avoided. Because this sort of Correction never produces any Good, farther than it serves to raise *Shame* and Abhorrence of the Miscarriage that brought it on them. And if the greatest part of the Trouble be not the Sense that they have done amiss, and the Apprehension
5 that they have drawn on themselves the just Displeasure of their best Friends, the Pain of Whipping will work but an imperfect Cure. It only patches up for the present, and skins it over, but reaches not to the Bottom of the Sore. Ingenuous *Shame*, and the Apprehension of Displeasure, are the only true Restraint: These alone ought to hold
10 the Reins, and keep the Child in order. But corporal Punishments must necessarily lose that Effect, and wear out the sense of *Shame*, where they frequently return. Shame in Children has the same Place that Modesty has in Women; which cannot be kept, and often transgressed against. And as to the Apprehension of *Displeasure in the*
15 *Parents*, that will come to be very insignificant, if the Marks of that Displeasure quickly cease, and a few Blows fully expiate. Parents should well consider, what Faults in their Children are weighty enough to deserve the Declaration of their Anger: But when their Displeasure is once declared, to a Degree that carries any Pun-
20 ishment with it, they ought not presently[22] to lay by the Severity of their Brows, but to restore their Children to their former Grace with some Difficulty; and delay a full reconciliation, till their Conformity, and more than ordinary Merit, make good their Amendment. If this be not so ordered, *Punishment* will, by Familiarity, become a mere
25 thing of Course, and lose all its influence: Offending, being chastised, and then forgiven, will be thought as natural and necessary as Noon, Night, and Morning following one another.⁻ʸ

1 *avoided ... Correction*] *avoided, because it* 1   8–12 Ingenuous ... return.] *Shame* then, and Apprehension of Displeasure, being that which ought alone to give a Check, and hold the Reins, 'tis impossible but Punishment should lose that Efficacy, when it often returns. 1   12 in Children has] has in Children 1   13 that Modesty has] as Modesty 1   16 cease ... Parents] cease. And therefore I think, Parents 1   22 a full reconciliation] *add.* 3   24–6 will, by ... necessary as] will be, by Familiarity, but a Thing of Course; and Offending, being punished, and then forgiven, be as natural and ordinary, as 1

capeable of I thinke there will not need many precepts to be given him Lying [and stubbornesse *add.* **K**] and some ill naturd tricks are all the vices I thinke children of that age can be guilty of but these are not neither to be forbid till he appeares guilty of them for feare least by forbidding you teach them for when he is first found in a lie or an ill naturd trick the first remedy should be to talke to him of it as of a strange monstrous thing that it could not be supposd he would have donne a thing to be wonderd at and soe shame him out of it.

²² 'presently': immediately (*OED*).

§. 61. ᶻ⁻Concerning Reputation, I shall only remark this one Thing more of it; That though it be not the true Principle and Measure of Vertue, (for that is the Knowledge of a Man's Duty, and the Satisfaction it is to obey his Maker, in following the Dictates of that Light God has given him, with the Hopes of Acceptation and Reward) yet it is 5 that, which comes nearest to it: And being the Testimony and Applause that other People's Reason, as it were by common Consent, gives to vertuous and well-ordered Actions, it is the proper Guide and Encouragement of Children, till they grow able to judge for themselves, and to find what is right, by their own Reason.⁻ᶻ 10

§. 62. This Consideration may direct Parents, how to manage themselves in reproving and commending their Children. The rebukes and chiding, which their Faults will sometimes make hardly to be avoided, should not only be in sober, grave, and unpassionate words, but also alone and in private: But the Commendations Children deserve, they 15 should receive before others. This doubles the Reward, by spreading their Praise; but the Backwardness Parents shew in divulging their Faults, will make them set a greater Value on their Credit themselves, and teach them to be the more careful to preserve the good opinion of others, whilst they think they have it: But when being expos'd to 20 Shame, by publishing their Miscarriages, they give it up for lost, that Check upon them is taken off; And they will be the less careful to preserve others good Thoughts of them, the more they suspect that their Reputation with them is already blemished.

§. 63. ᵃ⁻But if a right Course be taken with Children, there will not 25 be so much need of the Application of the common Rewards and Punishments as we imagine, and as the general Practice has established. For, All their innocent Folly, Playing, and *Childish Actions, are to be* left perfectly free and *unrestrained*, as far as they can consist with the Respect due to those that are present; and that with the greatest 30 Allowance. If these Faults of their Age, rather than of the Children themselves, were, as they should be, left only to Time and Imitation, and riper Years to cure, Children would escape a great deal of misapplied and useless Correction; which either fails to over-power the natural Disposition of their Childhood, and so, by an ineffectual 35

§§ 61–2 *Reputation.*　　§ 63 *Childishness.*

1 61] 60 **1**　　7 by] by a **4 5**　　8 it] *add.* **3**　　11–24 § 62 *add.* **3**
25 63] 61 **1**

ᶻ⁻ᶻ **Corr.** 929 (iii. 175–6)　　ᵃ⁻ᵃ **Corr.** 929 (iii. 176)

Familiarity, makes Correction in other necessary Cases of less use; or else, if it be of force to restrain the natural gaiety of that Age, it serves only to spoil the Temper both of Body and Mind. If the Noise and Bustle of their Play prove at any Time inconvenient, or unsuitable to the Place or Company they are in, (which can only be where their Parents are,) a Look or a Word from the Father or Mother, if they have established the Authority they should, will be enough either to remove, or quiet them for that Time. But this Gamesome Humour, which is wisely adapted by Nature to their Age and Temper, should rather be encouraged, to keep up their Spirits, and improve their Strength and Health, than curbed, or restrained: And the chief Art is, to make all that they have to do, Sport and Play too.⁻ᵃ

§. 64. And here give me Leave to take notice of one thing I think a Fault in the ordinary Method of Education; and that is, The Charging of Children's Memories, upon all Occasions, with *Rules* and Precepts, which they often do not understand, and constantly as soon forget as given. If it be some Action you would have done, or done otherwise; whenever they forget, or do it awkardly, make them do it over and over again, till they are perfect: Whereby you will get these two Advantages; *First*, To see whether it be an Action they can do, or is fit to be expected of them. For sometimes Children are bid to do Things, which, upon Trial, they are found not able to do; and had need be taught and exercised in, before they are required to do them. But it is much easier for a Tutor to command, than to teach. *Secondly*, Another Thing got by it will be this; That by repeating the same Action, till it be grown habitual in them, the Performance will not depend on Memory, or Reflection, the Concomitant of Prudence and Age, and not of Childhood; but will be natural in them. Thus bowing to a Gentleman when he salutes him, and looking in his Face when he speaks to him, is by constant use as natural to a well-bred Man, as breathing; it requires no Thought, no Reflection. Having this way cured in your Child any Fault, it is cured for ever: And thus one by one you may weed them out all, and plant what Habits you please.

§. 65. ᵇ⁻I have seen Parents so heap *Rules* on their Children, that it

§§ 64–5 *Rules.*

---

13 64] 62 **1**   34 65] 63 **1**

ᵇ⁻ᵇ **H** § 38; *latter part of* **K** § 55. **H** § 37 *and first part of* **K** § 55 *read* Haveing thus told you what rewards and punish⟨men⟩ts I would have made use of to children the next thing to `be´ considerd `is´ [to consider is **K**] what those things are that should be punishd in them and those are very few but every good action I would have rewarded i.e. com̄ended.

was impossible for the poor little ones to remember a Tenth part of them, much less to observe them. However they were either by Words or Blows corrected for the Breach of those multiplied and often very impertinent Precepts. Whence it naturally followed, that the Children minded not, what was said to them; when it was evident to them, that ⁵ no Attention, they were capable of, was sufficient to preserve them from Transgression, and the Rebukes which followed it.⁻ᵇ

ᶜ⁻Let therefore your *Rules*, to your Son, be as few as is possible, and rather fewer than more than seem absolutely necessary. For if you burden him with many *Rules*, one of these two things must necessarily ¹⁰ follow; that either he must be very often punished, which will be of ill consequence, by making Punishment too frequent and familiar; or else you must let the Transgressions of some of your Rules go un-punished, whereby they will of course grow contemptible, and your Authority become cheap to him. Make but few *Laws*, but see they be ¹⁵ well observed, when once made. Few Years require but few Laws, and as his Age increases, when one Rule is, by practice, well established, you may add another.⁻ᶜ

§. 66. ᵈ⁻But pray remember, Children are *not* to be *taught by Rules*, which will be always slipping out of their Memories. What you think ²⁰ necessary for them to do, settle in them by an indispensible practice, as often as the occasion returns; and if it be possible, make occasions. This will beget Habits in them, which, being once established, operate of themselves easily and naturally, without the assistance of the Memory. But here let me give two Cautions, 1. The one is, that you ²⁵ keep them to the practice, of what you would have grow into a Habit in them, by kind Words, and gentle Admonitions, rather as minding them of what they forget, than by harsh Rebukes and Chiding, as if

§ 66 *Habits.   Practice.   Affectation.*

19 66] 64 1

ᶜ⁻ᶜ *First part of* **H** § 39; **K** § 56 (*entire*)   ᵈ⁻ᵈ **H** fo. 10ᵛ *reads* Rules   Adde an other—but pray remember children are not to be taught by Rules which will always be sliping out of their memorys. what you thinke necessary for them to [practise] doe setle in them by an indispensible practise as often as the occasion returns   this will beget habits in them which being once establishd operate of them selves easily and naturally without the assistance of the memory. But here let me give you two cautions 1º The one is that you keep them to the practise of what you would have grow into a habit in them by kinde words and gentle admonitions rather as mindeing of what they forget than by harsh rebukes and chideing as if they was wilfully guilty 2º An other thing you are to take care is, not to endeavour to setle too many habits at once least by variety you confound them and soe perfect none when constant custome has made any one thing easy and naturall to them

they were wilfully guilty. 2dly, Another thing you are to take care of, is, not to endeavour to settle too many Habits at once, lest by variety you confound them, and so perfect none. When constant custom has made any one thing easy and natural to them,⁻ᵈ and they practice it without
5 Reflection, you may then go on to another.

This Method of teaching Children by a repeated Practice, and the same Action done over and over again, under the Eye and Direction of the Tutor, till they have got the habit of doing it well, and not by relying on *Rules* trusted to their Memories, has so many Advantages,
10 which way ever we consider it, that I cannot but wonder (if ill Customs could be wonder'd at in any thing) how it could possibly be so much neglected. I shall name one more that comes now in my way. By this Method we shall see, whether what is requir'd of him be adapted to his Capacity, and any way suited to the Child's natural Genius and Con-
15 stitution; for that too must be consider'd in a right Education. We must not hope wholly to change their Original Tempers, nor make the Gay Pensive and Grave, nor the Melancholy Sportive, without spoiling them. God has stampt certain Characters upon Mens Minds, which, like their Shapes, may perhaps be a little mended; but can
20 hardly be totally alter'd, and transform'd into the contrary.

He therefore, that is about Children, should well study their Natures and Aptitudes, and see, by often trials, what turn they easily take, and what becomes them; observe what their Native Stock is, how it may be improved, and what it is fit for: He should consider, what
25 they want; whether they be capable of having it wrought into them by Industry, and incorporated there by Practice; and whether it be worth while to endeavour it. For in many cases, all that we can do, or should aim at, is to make the best of what Nature has given; to prevent the Vices and Faults to which such a Constitution is most inclined, and
30 give it all the Advantages it is capable of. Every one's Natural Genius should be carried as far as it could, but to Attempt the putting another upon him, will be but Labour in vain: And what is so Plaister'd on, will at best sit but untowardly, and have always hanging to it the Ungracefulness of Constraint and Affectation.

35 *Affectation* is not, I confess, an early Fault of Childhood, or the Product of untaught Nature; it is of that sort of Weeds, which grow not in the wild uncultivated Wast, but in Garden-Plotts, under the Negligent Hand, or Unskilfull Care of a Gardner. Management, and

Instruction, and some sense of the Necessity of Breeding, are requisite to make any one capable of *Affectation*, which endeavours to correct Natural Defects, and has always the laudable aim of Pleasing, though it always misses it; and the more it labours to put on Gracefulness, the farther it is from it. For this Reason it is the more carefully to be watched, because it is the proper Fault of Education; a perverted Education indeed, but such as young People often fall into, either by their own Mistake, or the ill Conduct of those about them.

He that will examine, wherein that Gracefulness lies which always pleases, will find it arises from that natural coherence, which appears between the Thing done, and such a Temper of Mind as cannot but be approved of, as suitable to the Occasion. We cannot but be pleased with an Humane, Friendly, Civil Temper, where-ever we meet with it. A Mind free, and Master of it self and all its actions, not low and narrow, not haughty and insolent, not blemished with any great Defect, is what every one is taken with. The Actions, which naturally flow from such a well-formed Mind, please us also, as the genuine Marks of it; and being as it were natural Emanations from the Spirit and Disposition within, cannot but be easy and unconstrain'd. This seems to me to be that Beauty, which shines through some Mens Actions, sets off all that they do, and takes all they come near; when, by a constant Practice, they have fashion'd their Carriage, and made all those little Expressions of Civility and Respect, which Nature or Custom has established in Conversation, so easy to themselves, that they seem not Artificial or Studied, but naturally to flow from a sweetness of Mind, and a well turn'd Disposition.

On the other side, *Affectation* is an awkard and forced Imitation of what should be Genuine and Easie, wanting the Beauty that Accompanies what is Natural; because there is always a Disagreement between the outward Action and the Mind within, one of these two ways; 1. Either when a Man would outwardly put on a Disposition of Mind, which then he really has not, but endeavours by a forced Carriage to make shew of; yet so, that the Constraint he is under discovers it self: And thus Men affect sometimes to appear Sad, Merry, or Kind, when in truth they are not so.

2. The other is, when they do not endeavour to make shew of Dispositions of Mind, which they have not; but to express those they have by a Carriage not suited to them: And such in Conversation are all constrain'd Motions, Actions, Words, or Looks, which though designed to shew either their Respect or Civility to the Company, or

their Satisfaction and Easiness in it, are not yet Natural nor Genuine Marks of the one or the other; but rather of some Defect or Mistake within. Imitation of others, without discerning what is Graceful in them, or what is peculiar to their Characters, often makes a great part
5 of this. But *Affectation* of all kinds, whence soever it proceeds, is always Offensive: because we naturally hate whatever is Counterfeit; and contemn those, who have nothing better to recommend themselves by.

Plain and rough Nature, left to it self, is much better than an Artificial Ungracefulness, and such studied Ways of being ill fashion'd.
10 The want of an Accomplishment, or some Defect in our Behaviour, coming short of the utmost Gracefulness, often scapes Observation and Censure. But *Affectation* in any part of our Carriage, is lighting up a Candle to our Defects; and never fails to make us be taken notice of, either as wanting Sense, or wanting Sincerity. This Governors ought
15 the more diligently to look after; because, as I above observ'd, 'tis an acquired Ugliness, owing to Mistaken Education, few being Guilty of it, but those who pretend to Breeding, and would not be thought ignorant of what is fashionable, and becoming in Conversation: And, if I mistake not, it has often its rise, from the lazy Admonitions of those
20 who give Rules, and propose Examples, without joyning Practice with their Instructions, and making their Pupils repeat the Action in their Sight, that they may Correct what is indecent or constrain'd in it, till it be perfected into an habitual and becoming Easiness.

§. 67. ᵉ⁻*Manners*, as they call it, about which Children are so often
25 perplexed, and have so many goodly Exhortations made them, by their wise Maids and Governesses, I think, are rather to be learnt by Example than Rules; and then Children, if kept out of ill Company, will take a pride to behave themselves prettily, after the fashion of others, perceiving themselves esteemed and commended for it. But if
30 by a little negligence in this part, the Boy should not put off his Hat, nor make Leggs very gracefully,ᶠ a Dancing-master will cure that Defect, and wipe off all that plainness of Nature, which the A-la-mode People call Clownishness.ᵍ And since nothing appears to me to give Children so much becoming Confidence and Behaviour, and so to
35 raise them to the conversation of those above their Age, as *Dancing*;²³

§ 67 *Manners.   Dancing.*

24 67] 65 **1**   31 will] would **1**
ᵉ⁻ᵉ *First part of* **H** § 41, **K** § 59, *slightly revised*   ᶠ legs a la mode **HK**   ᵍ rusticity **HK**
²³ *Cf.* **Corr.** 809 (ii. 687–8): 'Girls should have a dancing master at home early . . .'.

I think they should be taught to Dance, as soon as they are capable of Learning it. For though this consist only in outward gracefulness[h] of Motion, yet, I know not how, it gives Children manly Thoughts, and Carriage more than any thing. But otherwise, I would not have little Children much tormented about Punctilio's, or Niceties of Breeding.⁻ᵉ 5

Never trouble your self about those Faults in them, which you know Age will cure. And therefore want of well-fashion'd Civility in the Carriage, whilst *Civility* is not wanting in the Mind (for there you must take care to plant it early) should be the Parent's least care, whilst they are young. If his tender Mind be fill'd with a Veneration for his 10 Parents and Teachers, which consists in Love and Esteem, and a fear to offend them; and with *Respect and good Will* to all People; that respect will of it self teach those ways of Expressing it, which he observes most acceptable. Be sure to keep up in him the Principles of good Nature and Kindness; make them as habitual as you can, by Credit and Com- 15 mendation, and the good Things accompanying that State: And when they have taken root in his Mind, and are settled there by a continued Practice, fear not, the Ornaments of Conversation, and the out-side of fashionable Manners, will come in their due time; If when they are removed out of their Maids Care, they are put into the Hands of a 20 well-bred Man to be their Governor. ⁱ⁻Whilst they are very young, any *carelessness* is to be born with in Children, that carries not with it the Marks of Pride or ill Nature: But those, when ever they appear in any Action, are to be Corrected immediately, by the ways above-mentioned.⁻ⁱ 25

What I have said concerning Manners, I would not have so under-stood, as if I meant that those, who have the Judgment to do it, should not gently fashion the Motions, and Carriage of Children, when they are very young. It would be of great Advantage, if they had People about them, from their being first able to go, that had the Skill, and 30 would take the right way to do it. That which I complain of, is the wrong course is usually taken in this matter. Children who were never taught any such thing as Behaviour, are often (especially when Strangers are present) Chid for having some way or other failed in

4 little] *add.* **3**   5–6 *run on* **1**   9 Parent's] Parent's and Tutor's **1**
19–21 If . . . Governor.] *add.* **3**   21 Whilst . . .] *new para.* **5**   very] *add.* **3**
23 ever] *add.* **3**   25–6 *run on* **5**   26–126.22 What . . . grow up,] and what else remains like Clownishness, or want of good [ofg ood **NN**] Breeding, time and observa-tion will of it self reform in them as they ripen in Years, **1**

ʰ decency **HK**   ⁱ⁻ⁱ *Rest of* **H** § 41, **K** § 59, *slightly revised, as in* **1**

good Manners, and have thereupon Reproofs and Precepts heaped upon them, concerning putting off their Hats, or making of Leggs, &c. Though in this, those concern'd, pretend to correct the Child, yet in truth, for the most part, it is but to cover their own Shame: And they
5 lay the blame on the poor little ones, sometimes passionately enough, to divert it from themselves, for fear the By-standers should impute to their want of Care or Skill the Child's ill Behaviour. For, as for the Children themselves, they are never one jot better'd by such occasional Lectures. They at other times should be shewn what to do, and
10 by reiterated Actions, be fashioned before-hand into the Practice of what is fit and becoming; and not told, and talk'd to upon the spot, of what they have never been accustomed, nor know how to do as they should. To hare and rate them thus at every turn, is not to teach them, but to vex and torment them to no purpose. They should be let alone,
15 rather than Chid for a Fault, which is none of theirs, nor is in their power to mend for speaking to. And it were much better their natural childish Negligence or Plainness should be left to the Care of riper Years, than that they should frequently have Rebukes misplaced upon them, which neither do, nor can, give them graceful Motions. If their
20 Minds are well disposed, and principled with inward Civility, a great part of the roughness, which sticks to the out-side for want of better teaching, Time and Observation will rub off, as they grow up, if they are bred in good Company; but if in ill, all the Rules in the World, all the Correction imaginable, will not be able to polish them. For you
25 must take this for a certain truth, that let them have what Instructions you will, and ever so learned Lectures of Breeding daily inculcated into them, that, which will most influence their Carriage, will be the Company they converse with, and the fashion of those about them. Children (nay, and Men too) do most by Example. We are all a sort of
30 Camelions, that still take a Tincture from things near us: Nor is it to be wonder'd at in Children, who better understand what they see, than what they hear.

§. 68. ʲ⁻I mentioned above, one great Mischief that came by Servants to Children, when by their Flatteries they take off the edge and force of

§§ 68–69 *Company.*

---

7 For,] *new para.* **5**   26–8 and . . . about them.] what Teachers soever you please, that, which will most influence their Actions, will be the Company they converse with; **1**   30 near] about **1**   33 68] 66 **1**

ʲ⁻ʲ **H** § 42; **K** § 60, *both ending* in love with their Company.

the Parents rebukes, and so lessen their Authority. And here is another great inconvenience which Children receive from the ill Examples, which they meet with amongst the meaner Servants. They are wholly, if possible, to be kept from such Conversation: For the contagion of these ill precedents, both in Civility and Vertue, horribly infects Chil- 5 dren, as often as they come within reach of it. They frequently learn from unbred or debauched Servants such Language, untowardly Tricks and Vices, as otherwise they possibly would be ignorant of all their Lives.

§. 69. 'Tis a hard matter wholly to prevent this Mischief. You will 10 have very good luck, if you never have a clownish or vitious Servant, and if from them your Children never get any infection. But yet as much must be done towards it, as can be; and the Children kept as much as may be* *in the Company of their Parents*, and those to whose care they are committed. To this purpose, their being in their 15 presence, should be made easy to them: They should be allowed the liberties and freedom suitable to their Ages, and not be held under unnecessary Restraints, when in their Parent's or Governor's sight. If it be a Prison to them, 'tis no wonder they should not like it. They must not be hindred from being Children, or from playing, or doing as Chil- 20 dren, but from doing ill: All other Liberty is to be allowed them. Next, to make them in love with the *company of their Parents*, they should receive all their good things there, and from their hands. The Servants should be hindred from making court to them, by giving them strong Drink, Wine, Fruit, Play-things, and other such matters, which may 25 make them in love with their conversation.⁻ʲ

§. 70. ᵏ⁻Having named *Company*, I am almost ready to throw away my Pen, and trouble you no farther on this Subject. For since that does, more than all Precepts, Rules and Instructions, methinks 'tis

* *How much the* Romans thought *the Education of their Children a business that properly belonged to the Parents themselves, see in* Suetonius *August.* §. 64. Plutarch *in vitâ Catonis Censoris.* Diodorus Siculus, *l.* 2, *cap.* 3.²⁴

§ 70 *Company. Vertue.*

3 They . . .] *new para.* **5**　　　10 69] 67 **1**　　　16 They should] They shall **NN**
* footnote *add.* **5**　　　27 70] 68 **1**

ᵏ⁻ᵏ **H** § 43, **K** § 61

²⁴ References are to Suetonius, *Divus Augustus*, 64–5; Plutarch, *Cato Maior*, 20. 5–12; Diodorus Siculus l. 80–1 (which speaks not of Roman children, but of those of Egyptian priests; Locke uses Poggio Bracciolini's translation of Diodorus' *Bibliotheca historica*, LL 968).

almost wholly in vain to make a long Discourse of other things, and to talk of that almost to no purpose. For you will be ready to say, What shall I do with my Son? If I keep him always at home, he will be in danger to be my young Master; and if I send him abroad, how is it pos-
5 sible to keep him from the contagion of Rudeness and Vice, which is so every where in fashion? In my house, he will perhaps be more inno-cent, but more ignorant too of the World: Wanting there change of Company, and being used constantly to the same Faces, he will, when he comes abroad, be a sheepish[1] or conceited Creature.

10 I confess, both sides have their Inconveniences.⁻ᵏ Being abroad, 'tis true, will make him bolder, and better able to bustle and shift amongst Boys of his own age; and the emulation of School-fellows, often puts Life and Industry into young Lads. But till you can find a School, wherein it is possible for the Master to look after the Manners of his
15 Scholars, and can shew as great Effects of his Care of forming their Minds to Virtue, and their Carriage to good Breeding, as of forming their Tongues to the learned Languages; you must confess, that you have a strange value for words, when preferring the Languages of the Ancient *Greeks* and *Romans*, to that which made them such brave
20 Men, you think it worth while, to hazard your Son's Innocence and Vertue, for a little Greek and Latin. For, as for that Boldness and Spirit, which Lads get amongst their Play-fellows at School, it has ordinarily such a mixture of Rudeness and an ill-turn'd Confidence, that those mis-becoming and dis-ingenuous Ways of shifting in the
25 World must be unlearnt, and all the tincture wash'd out again, to make way for better Principles, and such Manners, as make a truly worthy Man. He that considers how diametrically opposite the Skill of living well, and managing, as a Man should do, his Affairs in the World, is to that malapertness, tricking, or violence learnt amongst School-boys,
30 will think the Faults of a Privater Education infinitely to be preferr'd to such Improvements; and will take care to preserve his Child's

7–8 World: . . . will,] World, and being used constantly to the same Faces, and little Company, will, 1   9–10 *run on* 1   10 Inconveniences.] Inconveniencies, but whilst he is at home, use him as much to your company, and the company of Men, genteel and well-bred People, that come to your House, as you can; and keep him from the Taint of your Servants, and meaner People: And about his going abroad, or staying at home, it must be left to the Parents Conveniences [**NN**; Conveniencies **NA**] and Cir-cumstances. But this is certain, breeding at home in their own sight, under a good Governor [**NN**; Governour **NA**], is much the best, when it can be had, and is ordered, as it should be. 1   10–133.7 Being . . . other.] *add.* 3

[1] sleepish **K**

Innocence and Modesty at home, as being nearer of Kin, and more in the way of those qualities which make an Useful and Able Man. Nor does any one find, or so much as suspect, that that Retirement and Bashfulness, which their Daughters are brought up in, make them less knowing or less able Women. Conversation, when they come into the World, soon gives them a becoming assurance; and whatsoever, beyond that, there is of rough and boisterous, may in Men be very well spared too: For Courage and Steadiness, as I take it, lie not in Roughness and ill Breeding.

Vertue is harder to be got, than a Knowledge of the World; and if lost in a Young Man is seldom recovered. Sheepishness and ignorance of the World, the faults imputed to a private Education, are neither the necessary Consequents of being bred at home, nor if they were, are they incurable Evils. Vice is the more stubborn, as well as the more dangerous Evil of the two; and therefore, in the first place, to be fenced against. If that sheepish softness, which often enervates those who are bred like Fondlings at home, be carefully to be avoided, it is principally so for Vertue's sake: For fear lest such a yielding temper should be too susceptible of vitious Impressions, and expose the Novice too easily to be corrupted. A young Man, before he leaves the shelter of his Father's House and the guard of a Tutor, should be fortified with Resolution, and made acquainted with Men, to secure his Vertue; lest he should be led into some ruinous course, or fatal precipice, before he is sufficiently acquainted with the Dangers of Conversation, and has Steadiness enough not to yield to every Temptation. Were it not for this, a young Man's Bashfulness, and Ignorance of the World, would not so much need an early Care. Conversation would cure it in great measure; or if that will not do it early enough, it is only a stronger reason for a good Tutor at home. For if Pains be to be taken to give him a manly air and assurance betimes, it is chiefly as a fence to his Vertue when he goes into the World under his own Conduct.

It is preposterous therefore to sacrifice his Innocency to the attaining of Confidence, and some little Skill of bustling for himself amongst others, by his conversation with ill-bred and vitious Boys; when the chief use of that sturdiness, and standing upon his own Legs, is only for the Preservation of his Vertue. For if Confidence or Cunning come once to mix with Vice, and support his Miscarriages, he is only the surer lost: And you must undo again, and strip him of all that he has

27 of] in **4 5**

got from his Companions, or give him up to Ruin. Boys will unavoidably be taught assurance by Conversation with Men, when they are
brought into it; and that is time enough. Modesty and Submission, till
then, better fits them for Instruction: And therefore there needs not
5 any great Care to stock them with Confidence before-hand. That
which requires most time, pains, and assiduity, is to work into them
the Principles and Practice of Vertue, and good Breeding. This is the
Seasoning they should be prepar'd with, so as not easie to be got out
again. This they had need to be well provided with. For Conversation,
10 when they come into the World, will add to their knowledge and
assurance, but be too apt to take from their Vertue; which therefore
they ought to be plentifully stored with, and have that tincture sunk
deep into them.

How they should be fitted for Conversation, and entred into the
15 World, when they are ripe for it, we shall consider in another place.
But how any one's being put into a mixed Herd of unruly Boys, and
there learning to wrangle at Trap, or rook at Span-farthing,[25] fits him
for civil Conversation, or Business, I do not see. And what Qualities
are ordinarily to be got from such a Troop of Play-fellows as Schools
20 usually assemble together from Parents of all kinds, that a Father
should so much covet, is hard to divine. I am sure, he who is able to be
at the charge of a Tutor at home, may there give his Son a more genteel Carriage, more manly Thoughts, and a Sense of what is worthy
and becoming, with a greater Proficiency in Learning into the Bar-
25 gain, and ripen him up sooner into a Man, than any at School can do.
Not that I blame the School-Master in this, or think it to be laid to his
charge. The difference is great between two or three Pupils in the
same House, and three or fourscore Boys lodg'd up and down. For let
the Master's Industry and Skill be never so great, it is impossible he
30 should have 50. or 100. Scholars under his Eye, any longer than they
are in the School together: Nor can it be expected, that he should
instruct them Successfully in any thing, but their Books: The forming
of their Minds and Manners requiring a constant Attention, and particular Application to every single Boy, which is impossible in a numer-
35 ous Flock; And would be wholly in vain, (could he have time to Study
and Correct every one's particular Defects, and wrong Inclinations)

---

[25] 'Trap', a wooden instrument used to throw and catch a ball, in the game of trap-
ball; thus the game of trap-ball itself. 'Span-farthing', a game in which the object was to
throw a farthing near enough to the opponent's throw for the distance to be spanned by
a hand. Cf. *OED*.

when the Lad was to be left to himself, or the prevailing Infection of his Fellows, the greatest part of the Four and twenty Hours.

But Fathers observing, that Fortune is often most Successfully courted by bold and bustling Men, are glad to see their Sons pert and forward betimes; take it for an happy Omen, that they will be thriving Men; and look on the Tricks they play their School-fellows, or learn from them, as a Proficiency in the Art of Living, and making their Way through the World. But I must take the liberty to say, that he, that lays the Foundation of his Son's Fortune in Vertue, and good Breeding, takes the only sure and warrantable way. And 'tis not the Waggeries or Cheats practised amongst School-boys, 'tis not their Roughness one to another, nor the well-laid Plots of Robbing an Orchard together, that make an able Man; But the Principles of Justice, Generosity and Sobriety, joyn'd with Observation and Industry, Qualities, which I judge School-boys do not learn much of one another. And if a young Gentleman, bred at home, be not taught more of them than he could learn at School, his Father has made a very ill choice of a Tutor. Take a Boy from the top of a Grammar-School, and one of the same Age bred, as he should be, in his Father's Family, and bring them into good Company together, and then see which of the two will have the more manly Carriage, and address himself with the more becoming Assurance to Strangers. Here I imagine the School-boys Confidence will either fail or dis-credit him: And if it be such as fits him only for the Conversation of Boys, he were better be without it.

Vice, if we may believe the general Complaint, ripens so fast now a-days, and runs up to Seed so early in young People, that it is impossible to keep a Lad from the spreading Contagion; if you will venture him abroad in the Herd, and trust to Chance or his own Inclination for the choice of his Company at School. By what Fate Vice has so thriven amongst us these Years past, and by what hands it has been nurs'd up into so uncontroul'd a Dominion, I shall leave to others to enquire. I wish, that those, who complain of the great Decay of Christian Piety and Vertue every where, and of Learning and acquired Improvements, in the Gentry of this Generation, would consider how to retrieve them in the next. This I am sure, That if the Foundation of it be not laid in the Education and Principling of the Youth, all other Endeavours will be in vain. And if the Innocence, Sobriety, and Industry, of those who are coming up, be not taken care of and preserved, 'twill be ridiculous to expect, that those who are to succeed next on the Stage, should abound in that Vertue, Ability, and Learning, which has hitherto made

England considerable in the World. I was going to add Courage too, though it has been looked on as the Natural Inheritance of Englishmen. What has been talked of some late Actions at Sea, of a Kind unknown to our Ancestors,[26] gives me occasion to say, that Debauchery sinks the Courage of Men: And when Dissoluteness has eaten out the Sense of true Honour, Bravery seldom stays long after it. And I think it impossible to find an instance of any Nation, however renowned for their Valour, who ever kept their Credit in Arms, or made themselves redoubtable amongst their Neighbours, after Corruption had once broke through, and dissolv'd the restraint of Discipline; and Vice was grown to such an head, that it durst shew it self bare-faced, without being out of Countenance.

'Tis Vertue then, direct Vertue, which is the hard and valuable part to be aimed at in Education; and not a forward Pertness, or any little Arts of Shifting. All other Considerations and Accomplishments should give way and be postpon'd to this. This is the solid and substantial good, which Tutors should not only read Lectures, and talk of; But the Labour, and Art of Education should furnish the Mind with, and fasten there, and never cease till the young Man had a true relish of it, and placed his Strength, his Glory, and his Pleasure in it.

The more this Advances, the easier way will be made for all other Accomplishments, in their turns. For he that is brought to submit to Vertue, will not be refractory, or resty, in any thing, that becomes him. And therefore I cannot but preferr Breeding of a young Gentleman at home, in his Father's sight, under a good Governor as much the best and safest way to this great and main End of Education; when it can be had, and is order'd as it should be. Gentlemens Houses are seldom without Variety of Company: They should use their Sons to all the Strange Faces that come there, and ingage them in Conversation with Men of Parts and Breeding, as soon as they are capable of it. And why those who live in the Country should not take them with them, when they make Visits of Civility to their Neighbours, I know not. This I am sure, a Father that breeds his Son at home, has the Opportunity, to have him more in his own Company, and there give him what Encouragement he thinks fit; and can keep him better from the taint of Servants, and the meaner sort of People, than is possible to be done Abroad. But what shall be resolv'd in the case, must in great measure be left to the Parents, to be determin'd by their Circumstances and

---

[26] Perhaps a reference to the battle of Beachy Head in June 1690.

Conveniencies. Only I think it the worst sort of good Husbandry, for a Father not to strain himself a little for his Son's Breeding; which, let his Condition be what it will, is the best Portion he can leave him. But if, after all, it shall be thought by some, that the Breeding at Home has too little Company; and that at ordinary Schools, not such as it should be, for a young Gentleman; I think there might be ways found out to avoid the Inconveniencies on the one side and the other.

§. 71. ᵐ⁻Having under Consideration how great the Influence of *Company* is, and how prone we are all, especially Children, to Imitation; I must here take the liberty to ⁿ⁻mind Parents of this one Thing, *viz.* That he that will have his Son⁻ⁿ have a Respect for him, and his Orders, must himself have a great Reverence for his Son. *Maxima debetur pueris reverentia.*[27] You must do nothing before him, which you would not have him imitate. If any thing scape you, which you would have pass for a Fault in him, he will be sure to shelter himself under your Example; and shelter himself so as that it will not be easie to come at him, to correct it in him the right Way. If you punish him for what he sees you practise your self, he will not think that Severity to proceed from Kindness in you, careful to amend a Fault in him; but will be apt to interpret it, the Peevishness, and Arbitrary Imperiousness of a Father, who, without any Ground for it, would deny his Son the Liberty and Pleasures he takes himself. Or if you assume to your self the liberty you have taken, as a Privilege belonging to riper Years, to which a Child must not aspire, you do but add new force to your Example, and recommend the Action the more powerfully to him. For you must always remember, that Children affect to be Men earlier

§ 71 *Example.*

---

8 71] 69 1   16–19 and . . . him; but] And how then you will be able to come at him [NN; him, NA] to correct it in the right way [NN; Way, NA] I do not easily see: And if you will punish him for it, he cannot look on it as a Thing which Reason condemns, since you practise it; but he 1   21 who,] which, 1   22–5 assume . . . For] would have it thought, it is a Liberty belonging to riper Years, and not to a Child, you add but a new Temptation, since 1

ᵐ⁻ᵐ *Slight revision of* H § 44, K § 62. *Both add at end* And this leads me to another Consideration which is the haveing some body about them whose only businesse should be to forme their tendʳ years and manners.   ⁿ⁻ⁿ to set down one thing (though I doubt not but you need not be advised of it but if that were a reason for me passe it in silence I might very well be excused from writeing at all) That which I was goeing to say is this that if you will have your son **HK**

[27] Juvenal, *Satires*, 14. 47 'The greatest respect is due to boys', that is, everything done and said in the presence of youth should be weighed carefully. Original text has 'puero', singular.

than is thought: And they love Breeches, not for their Cut, or Ease, but because the having them is a Mark of a Step towards Manhood. What I say of the Father's Carriage before his Children, must extend it self to all those who have any Authority over them, or for whom he would
5 have them have any Respect.⁻ᵐ

§. 72. But to return to the Businesses of Rewards and Punishments. All the Actions of Childishness, and unfashionable Carriage, and whatever Time and Age will of it self be sure to reform, being, (as I have said) exempt from the Discipline of the Rod, there will not be so
10 much need of beating Children, as is generally made use of. ᵒ⁻To which if we add Learning to Read, Write, Dance, Foreign Languages, *&c.* as under the same Privilege, there will be but very rarely any Occasion for Blows or Force in an ingenuous Education. The right Way to teach them those Things is, to give them a Liking and Inclina-
15 tion to what you propose to them to be learn'd; and that will engage their Industry and Application. This I think no hard Matter to do, if Children be handled as they should be, and the Rewards and Punishments above-mentioned be carefully applied, and with them these few Rules observed in the Method of Instructing them.⁻ᵒ

20 §. 73. 1. ᵖ⁻None of the Things they are to learn should ever be made a Burthen to them, or imposed on them as a *Task.* Whatever is so proposed presently becomes irksome: The Mind takes an Aversion to it, though before it were a Thing of Delight or Indifferency. Let a Child be but ordered to whip his Top at a certain Time every Day, whether
25 he has, or has not a Mind to it; let this be but required of him as a Duty, wherein he must spend so many Hours Morning and Afternoon, and see whether he will not soon be weary of any Play at this Rate? Is it not so with grown Men? What they do chearfully of themselves; Do they not presently grow sick of, and can no more endure, as soon as
30 they find it is expected of them, as a Duty? Children have as much a Mind to shew that they are free, that their own good Actions come from themselves, that they are absolute and independent, as any of the proudest of you grown Men, think of them as you please.

§. 74. 2. As a Consequence of this, they should seldom be put about

§ 72 *Punishment.*   § 73 *Task.*   §§ 74–5 *Disposition.*

---

6 72] 70 **1**   6–9 But . . . said)] Thus all the Actions of Childishness, and unfashionable Carriage, and whatever Time and Age will of it self be sure to reform, being **1**
13 ingenuous] ingenious **5**   20 73] 71 **1**   33 you] your **NN**   34 74] 72 **1**

ᵒ⁻ᵒ *Expanded from* **Corr.** 929 (iii. 176)   ᵖ⁻ᵖ **Corr.** 929 (iii. 176–8) doing even those Things you have got an Inclination in them to, but when they have a Mind and *Disposition* to it. He that loves Reading, Writing, Musick, *&c.* finds yet in himself certain Seasons wherein those things have no Relish to him: And if at that time he forces himself to it, he only pothers[28] and wearies himself to no purpose. So it is with Children. This Change of Temper should be carefully observed in them, and the favourable *Seasons of Aptitude and Inclination* be heedfully laid hold of: And if they are not often enough forward of themselves, a good Disposition should be talk'd into them, before they be set upon any thing. This I think no hard matter for a discreet Tutor to do; who has studied his Pupil's temper, and will be at little pains to fill his Head with suitable Idea's, such as may make him in love with the present Business. By this Means a great Deal of Time and Tiring would be saved. For a Child will learn three times as much when he is *in tune*, as he will with double the Time and Pains, when he goes awkardly, or is drag'd unwillingly to it. If this were minded as it should, Children might be permitted to weary themselves with Play, and yet have Time enough to learn what is suited to the Capacity of each Age. But no such thing is considered in the ordinary Way of Education, nor can it well be. That rough Discipline of the Rod is built upon other Principles, has no Attraction in it, regards not what humour Children are in, nor looks after favourable Seasons of Inclination. And indeed it would be ridiculous, when Compulsion and Blows have raised an aversion in the Child to his Task, to expect he should freely of his own accord leave his Play, and with Pleasure court the Occasions of Learning. Whereas were Matters order'd right, Learning any thing, they should be taught, might be made as much a Recreation to their Play, as their Play is to their Learning. The Pains are equal on both Sides: Nor is it that which troubles them, for they love to be busie, and the Change and Variety is that which naturally delights them. The only Odds is, in that which we call Play, they act at liberty, and employ their Pains (whereof you may observe them never sparing) freely; but what they are to learn, is forced upon them: they are called, compelled, and driven to it. This is that, that at first Entrance balks and cools them; they want their Liberty: Get them but to ask their Tutor to teach them, as they do often their Play-fellows, instead of his

8–13 of: . . . Business.] of, to set them upon any Thing. **1**   16 awkardly, . . . to it.] awkardly and unwillingly to it. **1**   19–26 But no . . . Matters] And if Things were **1** 33–4 is forced . . . to it.] they are driven to it, called on, or compelled. **1**   36 his] this **1**

[28] 'pothers', disturbs, from 'pother' (also 'pudder', p. 222, l. 35), turmoil (*OED*).

Calling upon them to learn; and they being satisfied that they act as freely in this, as they do in other Things, they will go on with as much Pleasure in it, and it will not differ from their other Sports and Play. By these Ways, carefully pursued, a Child may be brought to desire to be
5 taught any Thing, you have a Mind he should learn. The hardest Part, I confess, is with the first, or eldest; but when once he is set right, it is easie by him to lead the rest whither⁹ one will.⁻ᵖ

§. 75. Though it be past doubt, that the fittest Time for Children to learn any Thing, is, when their *Minds* are *in tune, and well-disposed*
10 to it; when neither Flagging of Spirit, nor Intentness of Thought upon something else makes them awkard and averse; yet two Things are to be taken care of: 1. That these Seasons either not being warily observed, and laid hold on, as often as they return; or else, not returning as often as they should, the Improvement of the Child be
15 not thereby neglected, and so he be let grow into an habitual Idleness, and confirmed in this Indisposition. 2. That though other Things are ill learned when the Mind is either indisposed, or otherwise taken up, yet it is of great moment, and worth our Endeavours, to teach the Mind to get the Mastery over it self; and to be able,
20 upon Choice, to take it self off from the hot Pursuit of one Thing, and set it self upon another with Facility and Delight; or at any Time to shake off its Sluggishness, and vigorously employ it self about what Reason, or the Advice of another shall direct. This is to be done in Children, by trying them sometimes, when they are by
25 Laziness unbent, or by Avocation bent another Way, and endeavouring to make them buckle to the Thing proposed. If by this Means the Mind can get an habitual Dominion over it self, lay by *Idea's*, or Business, as Occasion requires, and betake it self to new and less acceptable Employments, without Reluctancy or Discomposure, it
30 will be an Advantage of more Consequence than Latin or Logick, or most of those Things Children are usually required to learn.

§. 76. ʳ⁻Children being more active and busie in that Age, than in any other Part of their Life, and being indifferent to any Thing they

§ 76 *Compulsion.*

---

4 pursued,] pursued, I guess, 1   7 whither] whether **NN**   8 75] 73 1
14 should,] should, (as always happens in the ordinary Method and Discipline of Education, when Blows and Compulsion have raised an Aversion in the Child to the Thing he is to learn,) 1   18 of great moment,] a great Matter, 1   32 76] 74 1
than in] than 1

⁹ **Corr.** 929 (iii. 178) *as* **NN**   ʳ⁻ʳ **Corr.** 929 (iii. 178–9)

can do, so they may be but doing, *Dancing* and *Scotch-hoppers*[29] would be the same thing to them, were the Encouragements and Discouragements equal. But to Things we would have them learn, the great and only Discouragement I can observe is, that they are called to it; 'tis *made their Business*; they are *teazed* and *chid* about it, and do it with Trembling 5 and Apprehension: or, when they come willingly to it, are kept too long at it, till they are quite tired: All which intrenches too much on that natural Freedom they extreamly affect. And 'tis that Liberty alone which gives the true Relish and Delight to their ordinary Play-Games. Turn the Tables, and you will find, they will soon change their Applica- 10 tion; especially if they see the Examples of others, whom they esteem and think above themselves. And if the Things which they observed others to do be ordered so that they insinuate themselves into them, as the Privilege of an Age or Condition above theirs, then Ambition, and the Desire still to get forward, and higher, and to be like those above 15 them, will set them on work and make them go on with Vigour and Pleasure: Pleasure in what they have begun by their own desire. In which way the enjoyment of their dearly beloved Freedom will be no small Encouragement to them. To all which, if there be added the Satis- faction of Credit and Reputation, I am apt to think, there will need no 20 other Spur to excite their Application and Assiduity, as much as is necessary. I confess, there needs Patience and Skill, Gentleness and Attention, and a prudent Conduct to attain this at first. But, why have you a Tutor, if there needed no pains? But when this is once established, all the rest will follow, more easily than in any more severe and imperi- 25 ous Discipline. And I think it no hard matter, to gain this Point; I am sure it will not be, where Children have no ill Examples set before them. The great danger therefore I apprehend, is only from Servants, and other ill-ordered Children, or such other vicious or foolish People, who spoil Children, both by the ill pattern they set before them in their own 30 ill manners, and by giving them together, the two things they should never have at once; I mean, vicious Pleasures and Commendation.⁻ʳ

§ 77. As Children should very seldom be corrected by Blows; so, I

§ 77 *Chiding.*

---

10 find,] see 1   12–13 which . . . do] they see others do 1   13 insinuate . . . them, as] are persuaded it is 1   16–19 will set . . . added] will give them an Incli- nation which will set them on work in a Way wherein they will go on with Vigour and Pleasure, enjoying in it their dearly beloved Freedom; which, if it brings with it also 1 33 77] 75 1

29 'Scotch-hoppers', obs. name for 'hopscotch' (*OED* s.v. Scotch *sb.*¹ 2).

think, frequent, and especially, passionate *Chiding*, of almost as ill consequence. It lessens the Authority of the Parents, and the Respect of the Child: For I bid you still remember, they distinguish early between Passion and Reason: And as they cannot but have a Rever-
5 ence for what comes from the latter, so they quickly grow into a contempt of the former; or if it causes a present Terrour, yet it soon wears off; and natural Inclination will easily learn to slight such Scarecrows, which make a noise, but are not animated by Reason. Children being to be restrained by the Parents only in vicious (which, in their
10 tender Years, are only a few) things, a Look or Nod only ought to correct them, when they do amiss: Or, if Words are sometimes to be used, they ought to be grave, kind and sober, representing the ill, or unbecomingness of the Fault, rather than a *hasty rating* of the Child for it, which makes him not sufficiently distinguish, whether your Dislike
15 be not more directed to him, than his Fault. Passionate chiding usually carries rough and ill Language with it; which has this further ill effect, that it teaches and justifies it in Children: And the Names that their Parents or Preceptors give them, they will not be asham'd, or backward to bestow on others, having so good Authority for the use of
20 them.

§. 78. I fore-see here it will be objected to me; What then, Will you have Children never Beaten nor Chid for any Fault? This will be to let loose the Reins to all kind of Disorder. Not so much, as is imagined, if a right Course has been taken in the first Seasoning of their Minds,
25 and implanting that Awe of their Parents above-mentioned. For Beating, by constant Observation, is found to do little good, where the Smart of it is all the Punishment is feared, or felt in it; for the influence of that quickly wears out, with the memory of it. But yet there is one, and but one Fault, for which, I think, Children should be Beaten; and
30 that is, *Obstinacy* or *Rebellion*. And in this too, I would have it ordered so, if it can be, that the shame of the Whipping, and not the Pain, should be the greatest part of the Punishment. Shame of doing amiss, and deserving Chastisement, is the only true Restraint belonging to Vertue. The Smart of the Rod, if Shame accompanies it not, soon
35 ceases, and is forgotten, and will quickly, by use, lose its Terrour. I have known the Children of a Person of Quality kept in awe, by the

§§ 78–80 *Obstinacy.*

---

2 It] For it **1**   4 between] betwixt **4 5**   15–20 Passionate ... of them.]
add. **3**   21 78] 76 **1**

fear of having their Shooes pulled off, as much, as others by apprehensions of a Rod hanging over them. Some such Punishment, I think, better than Beating; for, 'tis Shame of the Fault, and the Disgrace that attends it, that they should stand in fear of, rather than Pain, if you would have them have a Temper truly ingenuous. But *Stubbornness*, and an *obstinate Disobedience*, must be master'd with Force and Blows: For this there is no other Remedy. Whatever particular Action you bid him do, or forbear, you must be sure to see your self obey'd; no Quarter in this case, no resistance. For when once it comes to be a Trial of Skill, a Contest for Mastery betwixt you, as it is if you command, and he refuses, you must be sure to carry it, whatever Blows it costs, if a Nod or Words will not prevail; unless, for ever after, you intend to live in obedience to your Son. A prudent and kind Mother, of my Acquaintance, was, on such an occasion, forced to whip her little Daughter, at her first coming home from Nurse, eight times successively the same Morning, before she could master her *Stubbornness*, and obtain a compliance in a very easy and indifferent matter. If she had left off sooner, and stop'd at the seventh Whipping, she had spoiled the Child for ever; and, by her unprevailing Blows, only confirmed her *refractoriness*, very hardly afterwards to be cured: But wisely persisting, till she had bent her Mind, and suppled her Will, the only end of Correction and Chastisement, she established her Authority throughly in the very first occasion, and had ever after a very ready Compliance and Obedience in all things from her Daughter. For as this was the first time, so, I think, it was the last too she ever struck her.

The Pain of the Rod, *the first* occasion that requires it, continued and increased without leaving off till it has throughly prevailed, should first bend the Mind, and settle the Parents Authority: And then Gravity mixed with Kindness should for ever after keep it.

This, if well reflected on, would make People more wary in the use of the Rod and the Cudgel; and keep them from being so apt to think Beating the safe and universal Remedy, to be applied at random, on all occasions. This is certain however, if it does no good, it does great harm; if it reaches not the Mind, and makes not the Will supple, it hardens the Offender; and whatever pain he has suffered for it, it does but indear to him his beloved *stubbornness*, which has got him this time the victory, and prepares him to contest, and hope for it for the future. Thus, I doubt not, but by ill order'd Correction, many have been

26–9 The Pain ... keep it.] *add.* **3**   30 This, if ...] § 77 *begins* **1**   38 Thus,] This, **1**

taught to be *obstinate* and *refractory*, who otherwise would have been very pliant and tractable. For if you punish a Child so, as if it were only to revenge the past Fault, which has raised your Choler, What operation can this have upon his Mind, which is the part to be amended? If
5 there were no *sturdy humor*, or *wilfulness* mixed with his Fault, there was nothing in it, that required the severity of Blows. A kind, or grave Admonition is enough, to remedy the slips of frailty, forgetfullness, or inadvertency, and is as much as they will stand in need of. But if there were a *perverseness* in the Will, if it were a designed, resolved Dis
10 obedience, the Punishment is not to be measured by the greatness or smallness of the Matter, wherein it appeared, but by the opposition it carries, and stands in, to that Respect and Submission is due to the Father's Orders; which must always be rigorously exacted, and the Blows, by pauses laid on, till they reach the Mind, and you perceive
15 the Signs of a true Sorrow, Shame, and purpose of Obedience.

This, I confess, requires something more than setting Children a Task, and Whipping them without any more adoe, if it be not done, and done to our fancy. This requires Care, Attention, Observation, and a nice study of Children's Tempers, and weighing their Faults
20 well, before we come to this sort of Punishment. But is not that better, than always to have the Rod in hand, as the only Instrument of Government? And by frequent use of it on all Occasions, misapply and render inefficacious this last and useful Remedy, where there is need of it? For what else can be expected, when it is promiscuously used
25 upon every little slip? When a Mistake in *Concordance*, or a wrong *Position* in Verse, shall have the severity of the Lash, in a well-temper'd and industrious Lad, as surely as a wilfull Crime, in an obstinate and perverse Offender; How can such a way of Correction be expected to do good on the Mind, and set that right? Which is the only thing to be
30 looked after; and when set right, brings all the rest, that you can desire, along with it.

§. 79. ˢ⁻Where a *wrong bent of the Will* wants not Amendment, there can be no need of Blows. All other Faults, where the Mind is rightly disposed, and refuses not the Government and Authority of the Father
35 or Tutor, are but Mistakes, and may often be over-looked; or when

---

5 sturdy ... wilfulness] *sturdy wilfulness* of Mind 1   6 required] needed 1
7 is] would have been 1   slips] Faults 1   8 is as ... need of.] as much as they
needed. 1   13 which] and 1   15 purpose] resolution 1   15–16 *run on* 1
32 79] 78 1

ˢ⁻ˢ *Cf.* **Corr.** 1020 (iii. 386)

they are taken notice of, need no other but the gentler Remedies of
Advice, Direction and Reproof; till the repeated and wilfull neglect of
those, shews the Fault to be in the Mind, and that a manifest *perversness* of the Will lies at the root of their Disobedience. But when ever
obstinacy, which is an open defiance, appears, that cannot be winked 5
at, or neglected, but must in the first instance, be subdued and
master'd: Only care must be had, that we mistake not; and we must be
sure it is Obstinacy, and nothing else.⁻ˢ

§. 80. But since the Occasions of Punishment, especially Beating,
are as much to be avoided as may be, I think it should not be often 10
brought to this Point. If the Awe I spoke of be once got, a Look will be
sufficient in most Cases. Nor, indeed, should the same Carriage, Seriousness, or Application be expected from young Children, as from
those of riper Growth. They must be permitted, as I said, the foolish
and childish Actions suitable to their Years, without taking notice of 15
them. Inadvertency, Carelesness and Gayety is the Character of that
Age. I think the Severity I spoke of is not to extend it self to such
unseasonable Restraints. Nor is that hastily to be interpreted Obstinacy, or Wilfullness, which is the natural Product of their Age or
Temper. In such Miscarriages they are to be assisted, and help'd 20
towards an Amendment, as weak People under a natural Infirmity;
which though they are warned of, yet every Relapse must not be
counted a perfect Neglect, and they presently treated as obstinate.
Faults of frailty, as they should never be neglected, or let pass without
minding, so, unless the Will mix with them, they should never be 25
exaggerated, or very sharply reproved; but with a gentle Hand set
right, as Time and Age permit. By this means, Children will come to
see what 'tis in any Miscarriage, that is chiefly Offensive, and so learn
to avoid it. This will incourage them to keep their Wills right; which is
the great Business; when they find that it preserves them from any 30
great Displeasure; and that in all their other failings they meet with
the Kind concern and help, rather than the Anger and passionate
Reproaches of their Tutor and Parents. Keep them from Vice, and
vicious Dispositions, and such a kind of Behaviour in general will
come, with every Degree of their Age, as is suitable to that Age, and 35
the Company they ordinarily converse with: And as they grow in
Years, they will grow in Attention and Application. But that your
Words may always carry Weight and Authority with them, if it shall

9 80] 79 ı   18–33 Nor . . . Parents.] *add.* 3

happen, upon any Occasion, that you bid him leave off the Doing of any even Childish Thing, you must be sure to carry the Point, and not let him have the Mastery. But yet, I say, I would have the Father seldom interpose his Authority and Command in these Cases, or in any
5 other but such as have a Tendency to vicious Habits. I think there are better ways of prevailing with them: And a gentle Persuasion in Reasoning (when the first Point of Submission to your Will is got) will most Times do much better.

§. 81. It will perhaps be wondered that I mention *Reasoning* with
10 Children: And yet I cannot but think that the true Way of Dealing with them. They understand it as early as they do Language; and, if I misobserve not, they love to be treated as Rational Creatures sooner than is imagined. 'Tis a Pride should be cherished in them, and, as much as can be, made the great Instrument to turn them by.

15 But when I talk of *Reasoning*, I do not intend any other, but such as is suited to the Child's Capacity and Apprehension. No Body can think a Boy of Three, or Seven Years old, should be argued with, as a grown Man. ᵗ⁻Long Discourses, and Philosophical Reasonings, at best, amaze and confound, but do not instruct Children. When I say
20 therefore, that they must be *treated as Rational Creatures*, I mean, that you should make them sensible by the Mildness of your Carriage, and the Composure even in your Correction of them, that what you do is reasonable in you, and useful and necessary for them: And that it is not out of *Caprichio*, Passion, or Fancy, that you command or forbid them
25 any Thing. This they are capable of understanding; and there is no Vertue they should be excited to, nor Fault they should be kept from, which I do not think they may be convinced of; but it must be by such *Reasons* as their Age and Understanding are capable of, and those proposed always *in* very *few and plain Words.* The Foundations on which
30 several Duties are built, and the Fountains of Right and Wrong, from which they spring, are not perhaps easily to be let into the Minds of grown Men, not used to abstract their Thoughts from common received Opinions. Much less are Children capable of *Reasonings* from remote Principles. They cannot conceive the Force of long Deduc-
35 tions: The *Reasons* that move them must be *obvious*, and level to their Thoughts, and such as may (if I may so say) be felt, and touched. But

§ 81 *Reasoning.*

---

4 or in] or **1**   9 81] 80 **1**   14 great] greatest **5**
ᵗ⁻ᵗ *With* § 82, *slightly altered from* **Corr.** 1098 (iii. 535–6)

yet, if their Age, Temper, and Inclinations be considered, there will never want such Motives, as may be sufficient to convince them. If there be no other more particular, yet these will always be intelligible, and of force, to deterr them from any Fault, fit to be taken notice of in them, (*viz.*) That it will be a Discredit and Disgrace to them, and dis- 5 please you.

§. 82. But of all the Ways whereby Children are to be instructed, and their Manners formed, the plainest, easiest and most efficacious, is, to set before their Eyes the *Examples* of those Things you would have them do, or avoid. Which, when they are pointed out to them, in the 10 Practice of Persons within their Knowledge, with some Reflection on their Beauty or Unbecomingness, are of more force to draw or deterr their Imitation, than any Discourses which can be made to them. Vertues and Vices can by no Words be so plainly set before their Understandings, as the Actions of other Men will shew them, when 15 you direct their Observation, and bid them view this or that good or bad Quality in their Practice. And the Beauty or Uncomeliness of many Things, in good and ill Breeding, will be better learnt, and make deeper Impressions on them, in the *Examples* of others, than from any Rules or Instructions can be given about them. 20

This is a Method to be used, not only whilst they are young, but to be continued even as long as they shall be under another's Tuition or Conduct. Nay, I know not whether it be not the best Way to be used by a Father, as long as he shall think fit, on any Occasion, to reform any Thing he wishes mended in his Son: Nothing sinking so gently, and 25 so deep, into Men's Minds, as *Example*. And what Ill they either over-look, or indulge in them themselves, they cannot but dis-like, and be ashamed of, when it is set before them in another.⁻ᵗ

§. 83. It may be doubted concerning *Whipping*, when, as the last Remedy, it comes to be necessary; at what Time, and by whom it 30 should be done: Whether presently upon the Committing the Fault, whilst it is yet fresh and hot; And whether Parents themselves should beat their Children. As to the First, I think it should *not* be done *presently*, lest Passion mingle with it; and so, though it exceed the just Proportion, yet it lose of its due Weight: For even Children discern 35 when we do Things in Passion. But, as I said before, that has most

§ 82 *Examples.*   §§ 83–8 *Whipping.*

---

7 82] 81 **1**   11 Reflection] Reflections **5**   13 which] *add.* **3**   29 83]
82 **1**   35 of . . . Weight:] the Authority: **1**

143

Weight with them, that appears sedately to come from their Parents Reason; and they are not without this Distinction. Next, If you have any discreet Servant capable of it, and has the Place of governing your Child (for if you have a Tutor, there is no doubt) I think it is best the *Smart* should come more immediately *from another's Hand*, though by the Parents Order, who should see it done; whereby the Parent's Authority will be preserved, and the Child's Aversion for the Pain it suffers rather be turned on the Person that immediately inflicts it. For I would have a *Father seldom strike his Child*, but upon very urgent Necessity, and as the last Remedy: And then perhaps it will be fit to do it so, that the Child should not quickly forget it.

§. 84. But, as I said before, ᵘ⁻*Beating* is the worst, and therefore the last Means to be used in the Correction of Children; and that only in Cases of Extremity, after all gentler Ways have been tried, and proved unsuccessful: Which, if well observed, there will be very seldom any need of Blows. For, it not being to be imagined that a Child will often, if ever, dispute his Father's present Command, in any particular Instance; and the Father not interposing his absolute Authority in peremptory Rules, concerning either Childish or indifferent Actions, wherein his Son is to have his Liberty; or concerning his Learning or Improvement, wherein there is no Compulsion to be used; There remains only the Prohibition of some vicious Actions, wherein a Child is capable of *Obstinacy*, and consequently can deserve Beating: And so there will be but very few Occasions of that Discipline to be used by any one, who considers well, and orders his Child's Education as it should be. For the first Seven Years, What Vices can a Child be guilty of, but Lying, or some ill-natur'd Tricks; the repeated Commission whereof, after his Father's direct Command against it, shall bring him into the Condemnation of *Obstinacy*, and the Chastisement of the Rod? If any vicious Inclination in him be, in the first Appearance and Instances of it, treated as it should be, first with your Wonder, and then, if returning again a second Time, discountenanced with the severe Brow of the Father, Tutor, and all about him, and a Treatment suitable to the State of Discredit before-mentioned; and this contin-ued till he be made sensible, and ashamed of his Fault; I imagine there will be no need of any other Correction, nor ever any Occasion to

7 preserved] preferred 1   12 84] 83 1   18–19 interposing . . . either] rigor-ously interposing his Authority in positive Rules concerning 1   20 or concerning] nor concerning 1   31 be] *add.* 3

ᵘ⁻ᵘ *Cf.* **Corr.** 897 (iii. 108–9)

come to Blows.⁻ᵘ The Necessity of such Chastisement is usually the
Consequence only of former Indulgencies, or Neglects. If vicious
Inclinations were watched from the Beginning, and the first Irregularities which they caused, corrected by those gentler Ways, we should
seldom have to do with more than one Disorder at once; which would ₅
be easily set right without any Stir or Noise, and not require so harsh a
Discipline as Beating. Thus one by one, as they appear'd, they might
all be weeded out, without any Signs or Memory that ever they had
been there. But we letting their Faults (by Indulging and Humouring
our little Ones) grow up, till they are Sturdy and Numerous, and the ₁₀
Deformity of them makes us asham'd and uneasie, we are fain to come
to the Plough and the Harrow, the Spade and the Pick-ax, must go
deep to come at the Roots; and all the Force, Skill, and Diligence we
can use, is scarce enough to cleanse the vitiated Seed-Plat over-grown
with Weeds, and restore us the hopes of Fruits, to reward our Pains in ₁₅
its season.

§. 85. This Course, if observed, will spare both Father and Child the
trouble of repeated Injunctions, and multiplied Rules of Doing and
Forbearing. For I am of Opinion, that of those Actions, which tend to
vitious Habits (which are those alone that a Father should interpose ₂₀
his Authority and Commands in) none should be forbidden Children
till they are found Guilty of them. For such untimely Prohibitions, if
they do nothing worse, do at least so much towards teaching and
allowing them, that they suppose that Children may be guilty of them;
who would possibly be safer in the Ignorance of any such Faults. And ₂₅
the best Remedy to stop them, is, as I have said, to shew *Wonder and
Amazement* at any such Action, as hath a vitious Tendency, when it is
first taken Notice of in a Child. For Example, When he is first found
in a Lye, or any ill natur'd Trick; The first Remedy should be, to talk
to him of it as a *strange Monstrous Matter*, that it could not be imagin'd ₃₀
he would have done, and so shame him out of it.

§. 86. It will be ('tis like) objected, That whatever I fansie of the
Tractableness of Children, and the prevalency of those softer Ways of
Shame and Commendation, yet there are many, who will never apply
themselves to their Books, and to what they ought to Learn, unless ₃₅
they are scourged to it. This I fear is nothing but the Language of
ordinary Schools and Fashion, which have never suffered the other to
be tried, as it should be, in Places where it could be taken Notice of.

4 which] *add.* **3**   10 little **1 4 5**] littles **3**   17 85] 84 **1**   32 86] 85 **1**

Why, else, *does the Learning of Latin and Greek need the Rod, when French and Italian needs it not?* Children learn to Dance and Fence without Whipping; nay, Arithmetick, Drawing, *&c.* they apply themselves well enough to without beating: Which would make one suspect, that there is something strange, unnatural, and disagreeable to that Age, in the Things requir'd in Grammar-Schools, or in the Methods used there, that Children cannot be brought to, without the severity of the Lash, and hardly with that too; or else, that it is a mistake, that those Tongues could not be taught them without Beating.

§. 87. But let us suppose some so Negligent or Idle, that they will not be brought to learn by the gentler Ways proposed: For we must grant, that there will be Children found of all Tempers: Yet it does not thence follow, that the rough Discipline of the Cudgel is to be used to all. Nor can any one be concluded unmanageable by the *milder Methods* of Government, till they have been *throughly tried* upon him; And if they will not prevail with him to use his Endeavours, and do what is in his Power to do, we make no Excuses for the obstinate: Blows are the proper Remedies for those; but Blows laid on in a way different from the ordinary. He that wilfully neglects his Book, and stubbornly refuses any thing he can do, required of him by his Father, expressing himself in a positive serious Command, should not be Corrected with two or three angry Lashes, for not performing his Task, and the same Punishment repeated again and again upon every the like Default. But when it is brought to that pass, that wilfulness evidently shews it self, and makes Blows necessary; I think the Chastisement should be a little more Sedate and a little more Severe, and the Whipping (mingled with Admonitions between) so continued, till the Impressions of it on the Mind were found legible in the Face, Voice, and Submission of the Child, not so sensible of the Smart, as of the Fault he has been guilty of, and melting in true Sorrow under it. If such a Correction as this, tried some few times at fit Distances, and carried to the utmost Severity, with the visible Displeasure of the Father all the while, will not work the Effect, turn the Mind, and produce a future Compliance; What can be hoped from *Blows*, and to what purpose should they be any more used? *Beating*, when you can expect no good from it, will look more like the Fury of an enraged Enemy, than the good will of a compassionate Friend; and such Chastisement carries with it only Provocation without any prospect of

6 in the] in 1   10 87] 86 1   11 gentler] gentle 5   37-8 Chastisement] Chastisements **NN**

amendment. If it be any Father's Misfortune to have a Son thus perverse and untractable, I know not what more he can do, but pray for him. But, I imagine, if a right Course be taken with Children from the beginning, very few will be found to be such; And when there are any such Instances, they are not to be the Rule for the Education of those, who are better Natur'd, and may be managed with better Usage.

§. 88. ᵛ⁻If a *Tutor* can be got, that thinking himself in the Father's place, charged with his Care, and relishing these Things, will at the beginning apply himself to put them in practice, he will afterwards find his Work very easie: And you will, I guess, have your Son in a little time a greater Proficient in both Learning and Breeding, than perhaps you imagine. But let him by no means Beat him, at any time, without your Consent and Direction; at least till you have Experience of his Discretion and Temper. But yet to keep up his Authority with his Pupil, besides concealing that he has not the Power of the Rod, you must be sure to use him with great respect your self, and cause all your Family to do so too. For you cannot expect, your Son should have any regard for one, whom he sees you, or his Mother, or others slight. If you think him worthy of contempt, you have chosen amiss: And if you shew any contempt of him, he will hardly scape it from your Son: And whenever that happens, whatever worth he may have in himself, and Abilities for this Imployment, they are all lost to your Child, and can afterwards never be made useful to him.

§. 89. As the Father's Example must teach the Child respect for his Tutor, so the Tutor's Example must lead the Child into those Actions he would have him do. His Practice must by no means cross his Precepts, unless he intend to set him wrong. It will be to no purpose for the Tutor to talk of the Restraint of the Passions, whilst any of his own are let loose: And he will in vain indeavour to reform any Vice or indecency in his Pupil, which he allows in himself. Ill Patterns are sure to be follow'd more than good Rules: And therefore he must also carefully preserve him from the influence of ill Precedents, especially the most dangerous of all, the Examples of the Servants; from whose Company he is to be kept, not by Prohibitions, for that will but give him an Itch after it, but by other Ways I have mentioned.⁻ᵛ

§ 89 *Tutor.*

---

7 88] 87 **1** (*expanded in* **3** *to form* §§ 88–9)   *Tutor* **5** marg.   12 at any time,] at least, **1**   13–32 at least . . . carefully] He must be sure also to shew him the Example of the Things, he would have the Child practise, and carefully to **1**   33 the Examples] that **1**   35 after it] *add.* **3**

ᵛ⁻ᵛ *Expansion of* **Corr.** 929 (iii. 182–3)

§. 90. ᵂ⁻In all the whole Business of Education, there is nothing like to be less hearken'd to, or harder to be well observed, than what I am now going to say; and that is, that I would from their first beginning to talk, have some *Discreet*,ˣ *Sober*, nay, *Wise* Person about
5 Children, whose Care it should be to Fashion them aright, and keep them from all ill, especially the infection of bad Company. I think this Province requires great *Sobriety, Temperance*,ʸ *Tenderness, Diligence*, and *Discretion*; Qualities hardly to be found united in Persons, that are to be had for ordinary Salaries; nor easily to be found any
10 where. As to the Charge of it, I think it will be the Money best laid out, that can be, about our Children; and therefore though it may be Expensive more than is ordinary, yet it cannot be thought dear. He that at any Rate proceuresᶻ his Child a good Mind, well principled, temper'd to Vertue and Usefulness, and adorned with Civility and
15 good Breeding, makes a better purchase for him, than if he laid out the Money for an Addition of more Earth to his former Acres. Spare it in Toys and Play-Games, in Silk and Ribbons, Laces and other useless Expences, as much as you please; but be not sparing in so necessary a Part as this. 'Tis not good Husbandry to make his For-
20 tune rich, and his Mind poor. I have often with great Admiration seen People lavish it profusely in tricking up their Children in fine Clothes, Lodging and Feeding them Sumptuously, allowing them more than enough of useless Servants, and yet at the same time starve their Minds, and not take sufficient Care to cover that, which
25 is the most shameful Nakedness, *viz.* their natural wrong Inclinations and Ignorance. This I can look on as no other than a Sacrificing to their own Vanity; it shewing more their Pride, than true Care of the good of their Children. Whatsoever you imploy to the Advantage of your Son's Mind will shew your true Kindness, though it be
30 to the lessening of his Estate. A Wise and Good Man can hardly want either the Opinion or Reality of being Great and Happy. But he, that is Foolish or Vicious, can be neither Great nor Happy, what Estate soever you leave him: And I ask you, Whether there be not Men in the World, whom you had rather have your Son be with 500
35 *l. per Annum*, than some other you know with 5000 *l.*⁻ᵂ

§§ 90–1 *Governour.*

1 90] 88 **1**   3 I would] Children should **5**   5 Children] *om.* **5**
9 nor] or **1**

ᵂ⁻ᵂ *Slight revision of* **H** § 45, **K** § 63   ˣ describd **K**   ʸ temp⟨e⟩r **HK**
ᶻ purchases **HK**

§. 91. ᵃ⁻The Consideration of Charge ought not therefore to ᵇ⁻deterr those, who are able:⁻ᵇ The great Difficulty will be where to find a *proper Person*. For those of small Age, Parts, and Vertue, are unfit for this Imployment; and those that have greater, will hardly be got to undertake such a Charge. You must therefore look out early, and 5 enquire every where: For the World has People of all sorts. And I remember, *Montaigne* says in one of his Essays, That the Learned *Castalio*[30] was fain to make Trenchers at *Basle*ᶜ to keep himself from starving, when his Father would have given any Money for such a Tutor for his Son, and *Castalio* have willingly embraced such an 10 Imployment upon very reasonable Terms: But this was for want of Intelligence.⁻ᵃ

§. 92. ᵈ⁻If you find it difficult to meet with such a Tutor, as we desire, you are not to wonder. I can only say, Spare no Care nor Cost to get such an one. All things are to be had that way: And I dare 15 assure you, that if you get a good one, you will never repent the Charge; but will always have the Satisfaction to think it the Money of all other the best laid out. But be sure take no Body upon Friends or Charitable, no, nor bare great Commendations. Nay, if you will do as you ought, the Reputation of a Sober Man with a good Stock 20 of Learning (which is all usually required in a Tutor) will not be enough to serve your Turn. In this Choice be as Curious, as you would be in that of a Wife for him: For you must not think of Trial, or Changing afterwards: That will cause great Inconvenience to you, and greater to your Son. When I consider the Scruples and Cautions 25 I here lay in your way, methinks it looks, as if I advised you to something, which I would have offer'd at, but in Effect not done.⁻ᵈ But he that shall consider, how much the Business of a Tutor, rightly imployed, lies out of the Road; and how remote it is from the Thoughts of many, even of those who propose to themselves this 30

§§ 92–4 *Tutor.*

1 91] 89 1   13 92] 90 1   16 you get] you can get 5   19–22 Nay . . . turn. 5] Nor will the Reputation of a Sober Man with Learning enough (which is all usually that is required in a Tutor) serve the Turn. 1 3 4   23 would be] would 1

ᵃ⁻ᵃ *Slight revision of* H § 46, K § 64   ᵇ⁻ᵇ deterre you from thoughts like mine HK
ᶜ Geneva HK   ᵈ⁻ᵈ Corr. 845 (ii. 790–1)

[30] Sebastianus Castalio, in *Essais*, i. 35. Locke's memory of this passage is very confused: Montaigne indeed says that Castalio starved 'en Allemagne' for the want of the employment many would have gladly given him, but not that his father was in search of a tutor; he had wished to set up an office where buyers and sellers, masters and servants, could advertise their wants.

Imployment, will perhaps be of my Mind, that one fit to Educate and Form the Mind of a Young Gentleman is not every where to be found; and that more than ordinary Care is to be taken in the Choice of him, or else you may fail of your End.

§. 93. The Character of a Sober Man and a Scholar, is, as I have above observ'd, what every one expects in a Tutor. This generally is thought enough, and is all that Parents commonly look for. But when such an one has emptied out into his Pupil all the Latin, and Logick, he has brought from the University, will that Furniture make him a fine Gentleman? Or can it be expected, that he should be better Bred, better Skill'd in the World, better Principled in the Grounds and Foundations of true Vertue and Generosity, than his young *Tutor* is?

To form a young Gentleman as he should be, 'tis fit his *Governour* should himself be well bred, understand the Ways of Carriage, and Measures of Civility in all the Variety of Persons, Times and Places; and keep his Pupil, as much as his Age requires, constantly to the Observation of them. This is an Art not to be learnt, nor taught by Books. Nothing can give it but good Company, and Observation joyn'd together. The Taylor may make his Clothes Modish, and the Dancing-Master give fashion to his Motions; yet neither of these, though they set off well, make a well-bred Gentleman; No, though he have Learning to boot; which, if not well-managed, makes him but the more impertinent and intolerable in Conversation. Breeding is that, which sets a Gloss upon all his other good qualities, and renders them useful to him, in procuring him the Esteem and Good Will of all that he comes near. Without good Breeding his other Accomplishments make him pass but for Proud, Conceited, Vain, or Foolish.

Courage in an ill-bred Man, has the Air, and scapes not the Opinion of Brutality; Learning becomes Pedantry; Wit Buffoonry; Plainness Rusticity; Good Nature Fawning. And there can be not a good quality in him which want of Breeding will not warp, and disfigure to his Disadvantage. Nay, Vertue and Parts, though they are allowed their due Commendation, yet are not enough to procure a Man a good Reception, and make him Welcome wherever he comes. No body contents himself with rough Diamonds, and wears them so,

5-158.27 §§ 93-4 *add.* 3   5-6 The Character ... This 5] That a *Tutor* should have Latin and Learning, with the Reputation of Sobriety every one Expects. And this 3 4   7 that Parents commonly 5] Parents 3 4   23 but] *add.* 3   31 can be not] cannot be 5

who would appear with Advantage. When they are polish'd, and set, then they give a lustre. Good qualities are the Substantial Riches of the Mind, but 'tis good Breeding sets them off: And he that will be acceptable, must give Beauty as well as Strength to his Actions. Solidity, or even Usefulness, is not enough: A graceful Way and Fashion, in 5 every thing, is that which gives the Ornament and Liking. And in most cases the manner of doing is of more Consequence, than the thing done; And upon that depends the Satisfaction or Disgust wherewith it is received. This therefore, which lies not in the putting off the Hat, nor making of Complements; but in a due and free composure of Lan- 10 guage, Looks, Motion, Posture, Place, *&c.* suited to Persons and Occasions, and can be learn'd only by Habit and Use, though it be above the capacity of Children, and little ones should not be perplex'd about it, yet it ought to be begun, and in a good measure learn'd by a young Gentleman whilst he is under a Tutor, before he comes into the 15 World upon his own Legs: For then usually it is too late to hope to reform several habitual indecencies, which lie in little things. For the Carriage is not as it should be, till it is become Natural in every Part; falling, as Skillful Musicians Fingers do, into Harmonious Order without Care and without Thought. If in Conversation a Man's Mind 20 be taken up with a sollicitous watchfulness about any part of his Behaviour; instead of being mended by it, it will be constrain'd, uneasie and ungraceful.

Besides, this part is most necessary to be form'd by the Hands and Care of a *Governour:* Because, though the Errors committed in Breed- 25 ing are the first that are taken notice of by others, yet they are the last that any one is told of. Not, but that the Malice of the World is forward enough to tattle of them; but it is always out of his hearing, who should make Profit of their Judgment, and Reform himself by their Censure. And indeed, this is so nice a Point to be meddled with, that even those 30 who are Friends, and wish it were mended, scarce ever dare mention it, and tell those they love, that they are Guilty in such or such Cases of ill Breeding. Errors in other things, may often with Civility be shewn another; and 'tis no breach of good Manners or Friendship, to set him right in other Mistakes: But good Breeding it self allows not a Man to 35 touch upon this; or to insinuate to another, that he is guilty of want of Breeding. Such Information can come only from those, who have Authority over them: And from them too it comes very hardly and harshly to a grown Man; and however softned, goes but ill down with any one, who has lived ever so little in the World. Wherefore it is 40

necessary, that this Part should be the *Governour*'s principal Care; that an habitual Gracefulness, and Politeness in all his Carriage, may be settled in his Charge, as much as may be, before he goes out of his hands; And that he may not need Advice in this Point, when he has
5 neither Time, nor Disposition to receive it, nor has any body left to give it him. The *Tutor* therefore ought in the first place to be well Bred: And a young Gentleman, who gets this one Qualification from his *Governour*, sets out with great Advantage; and will find, that this one Accomplishment, will more open his way to him, get him more
10 Friends, and carry him farther in the World, than all the hard Words, or real Knowledge he has got from the Liberal Arts, or his *Tutor*'s learned *Encyclopaidia*.[31] Not that those should be neglected, but by no means preferr'd, or suffer'd to thrust out the other.

§. 94. Besides being well Bred, the *Tutor* should know the World
15 well; The Ways, the Humors, the Follies, the Cheats, the Faults of the Age he is fallen into, and particularly of the Country he lives in. These he should be able to shew to his Pupil, as he finds him capable; teach him Skill in Men, and their Manners; pull off the Mask, which their several Callings, and Pretences cover them with; and make his Pupil
20 discern what lies at the bottom, under such appearances; That he may not, as unexperienced young Men are apt to do, if they are unwarn'd, take one thing for another, judge by the out-side, and give himself up to shew, and the insinuation of a fair Carriage, or an obliging Application; A Governour should teach his Scholar to guess at, and beware of
25 the Designs of Men he hath to do with, neither with too much Suspicion, nor too much Confidence; but as the young Man is by Nature most inclin'd to either side, rectifie him and bend him the other way. He should accustom him to make as much as is possible a true Judgment of Men by those Marks, which serve best to shew, what they are,
30 and give a Prospect into their inside; which often shews it self in little things, especially when they are not in Parade, and upon their Guard. He should acquaint him with the true State of the World, and dispose him to think no Man better or worse, wiser or foolisher, than really he is. Thus by safe and insensible degrees, he will pass from a Boy to a
35 Man; which is the most hazardous step in all the whole course of Life. This therefore should be carefully watch'd, and a young Man

24 A . . . Scholar **5**] Teach him **3 4**   27–8 way. He should accustom **5**] way; Accustom **3 4**

[31] Learned compilation of information, from the circle of the arts and sciences the Greeks considered essential to a liberal education (cf. *OED*).

with great Diligence handed over it; and not, as now usually is done, be taken from a *Governour*'s Conduct, and all at once thrown into the World under his own, not without manifest Danger of immediate Spoiling; there being nothing more frequent, than Instances of the great Loosness, Extravagancy and Debauchery, which young Men have run into as soon as they have been let loose from a severe and strict Education: Which I think may be chiefly imputed to their wrong way of Breeding, especially in this Part: For having been Bred up in a great Ignorance of what the World truly is, and finding it a quite other thing, when they come into it, than what they were taught it should be, and so imagin'd it was, are easily perswaded, by other kind of Tutors, which they are sure to meet with, that the Discipline they were kept under, and the Lectures were read to them, were but the Formalities of Education, and the Restraints of Childhood; that the Freedom belonging to Men, is to take their Swing in a full Enjoyment of what was before forbidden them. They shew the young Novice the World full of fashionable and glittering Examples of this every where, and he is presently dazled with them. My young Master failing not to be willing to shew himself a Man, as much as any of the Sparks of his Years, lets himself loose to all the Irregularities he finds in the most Debauch'd; and thus courts Credit and Manliness, in the casting off the Modesty, and Sobriety, he has till then been kept in; and thinks it Brave, at his first setting out, to signalize himself in running counter to all the Rules of Vertue, which have been Preach'd to him by his Tutor.

The shewing him the World, as really it is, before he comes wholly into it, is one of the best means, I think, to prevent this Mischief. He should by degrees be inform'd of the Vices in fashion, and warn'd of the Applications and Designs of those, who will make it their business to corrupt him. He should be told the Arts they use, and the Trains[32] they lay; and now and then have set before him the Tragical or Ridiculous Examples of those, who are Ruining, or Ruin'd this way. The Age is not like to want Instances of this Kind, which should be made Landmarks to him; that by the Disgraces, Diseases, Beggary, and Shame of Hopeful young Men thus brought to Ruin, he may be precaution'd, and be made see, how those joyn in the Contempt and Neglect of them that are Undone, who by Pretences of Friendship and Respect lead them into it, and help to prey upon them whilst they were Undoing; That he may see, before he buys it by a too dear Experience, that

---

[32] 'Trains', traps, snares (*OED*).

those, who perswade him not to follow the Sober Advices he has received from his *Governours*, and the Counsel of his own Reason, which they call being govern'd by others, do it only, that they may have the government of him themselves; and make him believe, he goes like
5 a Man of himself, by his own Conduct, and for his own Pleasure; when, in truth, he is wholly as a Child led by them into those Vices, which best serve their Purposes. This is a Knowledge which, upon all Occasions, a *Tutor* should endeavour to instill, and by all Methods try to make him comprehend, and throughly relish.

10   I know it is often said, That to discover to a young Man the Vices of the Age, is to teach them him. That I confess is a good deal so, according as it is done; and therefore requires a discreet Man of Parts, who knows the World, and can judge of the Temper, Inclination and weak side of his Pupil. This farther is to be remembred, that it is not pos-
15 sible now (as perhaps formerly it was) to keep a young Gentleman from Vice, by a total Ignorance of it; unless you will all his Life mue[33] him up in a Closet, and never let him go into Company. The longer he is kept thus hood-wink'd, the less he will see, when he comes abroad into open Day-light, and be the more expos'd to be a prey to himself,
20 and others. And an old Boy at his first appearance, with all the gravity of his Ivy-bush[34] about him, is sure to draw on him the Eyes and Chirping of the whole Town Volery;[35] Amongst which, there will not be wanting some Birds of Prey, that will presently be on the Wing for him.

25   The only Fence against the World is, a through Knowledge of it; into which a young Gentleman should be enter'd by degrees, as he can bear it; and the earlier the better, so he be in safe and skillful hands to guide him. The Scene should be gently open'd, and his Entrance made step by step, and the Dangers pointed out that attend him, from
30 the several Degrees, Tempers, Designs, and Clubs of Men. He should be prepared to be shock'd by some, and caress'd by others; warn'd who are like to oppose, who to mislead, who to undermine him, and who to serve him. He should be instructed how to know, and distinguish them; where he should let them see, and when dissemble the
35 Knowledge of them, and their aims and workings. And if he be too forward to venture upon his own Strength and Skill, the Perplexity and Trouble of a Mis-adventure now and then, that reaches not his

---

[33] 'mue', obs. for 'mew', coop or shut in (*OED*).
[34] 'Ivy-bush', *fig.* a display or sign (*OED*).
[35] 'Volery', obs. for Volary, the birds kept in an aviary, here *fig.* (*OED*).

Innocence, his Health, or his Reputation, may not be an ill way to teach him more Caution.

This, I confess, containing one great part of Wisdom, is not the product of some Superficial Thoughts, or much Reading; but the effect of Experience and Observation in a Man, who has lived in the World with his Eyes open, and conversed with Men of all sorts. And therefore I think it of most value to be instill'd into a young Man, upon all Occasions, which offer themselves, that when he comes to lanch into the Deep himself, he may not be like one at Sea without a Line, Compass, or Sea-Cart;[36] but may have some notice beforehand of the Rocks and Shoals, the Currents and Quick-sands, and know a little how to Steer, that he Sink not, before he get Experience. He that thinks not this of more moment to his Son, and for which he more needs a Governour, than the Languages and Learned Sciences, forgets of how much more use it is to judge right of Men, and manage his Affairs wisely with them, than to speak Greek and Latin, or argue in Mood and Figure; or to have his Head fill'd with the abstruse Speculations of Natural Philosophy, and Metaphysicks; nay, than to be well-versed in the Greek and Roman Writers, though that be much better for a Gentleman, than to be a good Peripatetick or Cartesian: Because those ancient Authors observed and painted Mankind well, and give the best light into that kind of Knowledge. He that goes into the Eastern Parts of *Asia*, will find able and acceptable Men without any of these: But without Vertue, Knowledge of the World, and Civility, an accomplished, and valuable Man can be found no where.

A great part of the Learning now in fashion in the Schools of *Europe*, and that goes ordinarily into the round of Education, a Gentleman may in a good measure be unfurnish'd with, without any great Disparagement to himself, or Prejudice to his Affairs. But Prudence and good Breeding are in all the Stations and Occurrences of Life necessary; and most young Men suffer in the want of them; and come Rawer and more Awkard into the World, than they should, for this very reason; because these Qualities, which are of all other the most Necessary to be Taught, and stand most in need of the Assistance and Help of a Teacher, are generally neglected, and thought but a slight, or no part of a *Tutor*'s Business. Latin and Learning make all the noise: And the main stress is laid upon his Proficiency in Things, a

---

1 his Reputation] Reputation **5**   19 the] *om.* **5**

[36] 'Sea-Cart', i.e. sea-card, obs. chart of the sea (*OED*).

great part whereof belong not to a Gentleman's Calling; which is to have the Knowledge of a Man of Business, a Carriage suitable to his Rank, and to be Eminent and Useful in his Country according to his Station. Whenever either spare Hours from that, or an Inclination to perfect himself in some parts of Knowledge, which his *Tutor* did but just enter him in, sets him upon any Study; the first Rudiments of it, which he learn'd before, will open the way enough for his own Industry to carry him as far, as his Fancy will prompt, or his Parts inable him to go. Or, if he thinks it may save his Time and Pains, to be help'd over some Difficulties, by the Hand of a Master, he may then take a Man that is perfectly well skill'd in it, or choose such an one as he thinks fittest for his purpose. But to initiate his Pupil in any part of Learning, as far as is necessary for a young Man in the ordinary course of his Studies, an ordinary Skill in the *Governour* is enough. Nor is it requisite, that he should be a through Scholar, or possess in Perfection all those Sciences, which 'tis convenient a young Gentleman should have a taste of in some general View, or short System. A Gentleman, that would penetrate deeper, must do it by his own Genius and Industry afterwards: For no body ever went far in Knowledge, or became Eminent in any of the Sciences by the Discipline, and Constraint of a Master.

The great Work of a *Governour* is to fashion the Carriage, and form the Mind; to settle in his Pupil good Habits, and the Principles of Vertue and Wisdom; to give him by little and little a view of Mankind; and work him into a love and imitation of what is Excellent and Praise-worthy; and in the Prosecution of it to give him Vigour, Activity, and Industry. The Studies which he sets him upon, are but as it were the Exercises of his Faculties, and Imployment of his Time, to keep him from Sauntering and Idleness, to teach him Application, and accustom him to take Pains, and to give him some little taste of what his own Industry must perfect. For who expects, that under a *Tutor* a young Gentleman should be an accomplished Critick, Orator, or Logician? Go to the bottom of Metaphysicks, Natural Philosophy or Mathematicks? Or be a Master in History or Chronology? Though something of each of these is to be taught him: But it is only to open the Door, that he may look in, and as it were begin an Acquaintance, but not to dwell there: And a *Governour* would be much blam'd, that should keep his Pupil too long, and lead him too far in most of them. But of good Breeding, Knowledge of the World, Vertue, Industry, and a love of Reputation, he cannot have

39 a love **4 5**] alove **3**

too much: And if he have these, he will not long want what he needs, or desires of the other.

And since it cannot be hoped, he should have Time and Strength to learn all Things, most Pains should be taken about that, which is most necessary; and that principally look'd after, which will be of most and 5
frequentest use to him in the World.

Seneca complains of the contrary Practice in his time: And yet the *Burgersdicius's* and the *Scheiblers*[37] did not swarm in those Days, as they do now in these. What would he have thought, if he had lived now, when the *Tutors* think it their great Business to fill the Studies and 10
Heads of their Pupils with such Authors as these? He would have had more reason to say, as he does, *Non vitæ sed Scholæ discimus*,[38] we learn not to Live, but to Dispute; and our Education fits us rather for the University, than the World. But 'tis no wonder if those who make the fashion suit it to what they have, and not to what their Pupils want. 15
The fashion being once establish'd, who can think it strange, that in this, as well as in all other things it should prevail, and that the greatest part of those, who find their account in an easie submission to it, should be ready to cry out *Heresie*, when any one departs from it? 'Tis never the less Matter of Astonishment, that Men of Quality, and Parts, 20
should suffer themselves to be so far misled by Custom and Implicite Faith. Reason, if consulted with, would advise, that their Childrens time should be spent in acquiring, what might be useful to them when they come to be Men; rather than to have their Heads stuff'd with a deal of trash, a great part whereof they usually never do ('tis certain 25
they never need to) think on again as long as they live; and so much of it as does stick by them, they are only the worse for. This is so well known, that I appeal to Parents themselves, who have been at Cost to have their young Heirs taught it, whether it be not Ridiculous for their Sons to have any tincture of that Sort of Learning, when they come 30
abroad into the World; whether any appearance of it would not lessen and disgrace them in Company. And that certainly must be an admirable Acquisition, and deserves well to make a part in Education, which Men are asham'd of where they are most concern'd to shew their Parts and Breeding. 35

8 *Burgersdicius*'s **5**] *Burgusdiscius*'s **3 4**   12 more] much more **4 5**
14–35 But 'tis . . . Breeding.] *add.* **4**

[37] Christoph Scheibler, author of an early logic work, *Epitome logica* (1624) and others. Franco Petri Burgersdijck, author of *Idea philosophiae moralis* (1623), *Institutionum logicarum libri duo* (1637), and other works.

[38] Seneca, *Ep.* 106. 12: 'We learn not for life but for the school.'

There is yet another Reason, why Politeness of Manners, and Knowledge of the World should principally be look'd after in a *Tutor:* And that is, because a Man of Parts, and Years, may enter a Lad far enough in any of those Sciences which he has no deep insight into 5 himself. Books in these will be able to furnish him, and give him Light, and Precedency enough, to go before a young follower: But he will never be able to set another right in the Knowledge of the World, and above all in Breeding, who is a Novice in them himself.

This is a Knowledge he must have about him, worn into him by 10 Use, and Conversation, and a long forming himself by what he has observed to be practised and allowed in the best Company. This, if he has it not of his own, is no where to be borrowed, for the use of his Pupil: Or if he could find pertinent Treatises of it in Books, that would reach all the particulars of an English Gentleman's Behaviour; his 15 own ill-fashion'd Example, if he be not well-bred himself, would spoil all his Lectures; it being impossible, that any one should come forth well-fashion'd, out of unpolish'd ill-bred, Company.

I say this, not that I think such a *Tutor* is every Day to be met with, or to be had at the ordinary Rates. But that those, who are able, may 20 not be sparing of Enquiry or Cost in what is of so great moment; And that other Parents, whose Estates will not reach to greater Salaries, may yet remember, what they should principally have an Eye to in the choice of one to whom they would commit the Education of their Children; and what part they should chiefly look after themselves, 25 whilst they are under their Care, and as often as they come within their Observation; and not think, that all lies in Latin and French, or some dry Systems of Logick and Philosophy.

§. 95. But to return to our Method again. Though I have mentioned the Severity of the Father's Brow, and the Awe setled thereby in the 30 Mind of Children when young, as one main Instrument, whereby their Education is to be managed; yet I am far from being of an Opinion, that it should be continued all along to them, whilst they are under the Discipline and Government of Pupilage. I think it should be relaxed, as fast as their Age, Discretion, and Good-Behaviour could allow it; 35 even to that degree, that a ᵉ⁻Father will do well, as his Son grows up,

§§ 95–8 *Familiarity.*

----

28 95] 91 **1**   30 Instrument] Foundation **1** (*some copies* **NN** *have* 'Founation', *cf. pp.* 54–5)

ᵉ⁻ᵉ **Corr.** 844 (ii. 786, l. 9–788 l. 9); *similar ideas expressed in* § 40 *and* **Corr.** 803 (ii. 677)

and is capable of it, to *talk familiarly* with him; nay, *ask his Advice, and Consult* with him, about those things wherein he has any knowledge, or understanding. By this, the Father will gain two things, both of great moment. The one is, That it will put serious Considerations into his Son's Thoughts, better than any Rules or Advices he can give him.   5
The sooner you *treat him as a Man*, the sooner he will begin to be one: And if you admit him into serious Discourses sometimes with you, you will insensibly raise his Mind above the usual Amusements of Youth, and those trifling Occupations which it is commonly wasted in. For it is easie to observe, that many young Men continue longer in the   10
Thoughts and Conversation of School-Boys, than otherwise they would; because their Parents keep them at that distance, and in that low Rank, by all their Carriage to them.

§. 96. Another thing of greater consequence, which you will obtain by such a way of treating him, will be *his Friendship*. Many Fathers,   15
though they proportion to their Sons liberal Allowances, according to their Age and Condition; yet they keep the knowledge of their Estates, and Concerns from them, with as much reservedness, as if they were guarding a secret of State from a Spy, or an Enemy. This, if it looks not like Jealousie, yet it wants those Marks of Kindness and Intimacy,   20
which a Father should shew to his Son; and, no doubt, often hinders, or abates, that Cheerfulness and Satisfaction, wherewith a Son should address himself to, and rely upon his Father. And I cannot but often wonder to see Fathers, who love their Sons very well, yet so order the matter by a constant Stiffness, and a mien of Authority and distance to   25
them all their Lives, as if they were never to enjoy, or have any comfort from those they love best in the World, till they had lost them, by being removed into another. Nothing cements and establishes Friendship and Good-will, so much as *confident Communication* of Concernments and Affairs. Other Kindnesses without this, leave still some Doubts: 30
But when your Son sees you open your Mind to him, when he finds that you interest him in your Affairs, as Things you are willing should in their turn come into his Hands, he will be concerned for them, as for his own; wait his Season with Patience, and Love you in the mean time, who keep him not at the distance of a Stranger. This will also   35
make him see, that the Enjoyment you have is not without Care; which the more he is sensible of, the less will he envy you the Possession, and

9 which] *add.* 3   14 96] 92 1   17–19 the . . . Enemy.] them as much un-
acquainted with their Estates, and all other such Concernments, as if they were
Strangers. 1   31 when he finds] *add.* 3

the more think himself Happy under the Management[f] of so favourable a Friend, and so careful a Father. There is scarce any Young Man
of so little Thought, or so void of Sense, that would not be glad of a
sure Friend, that he might have recourse to, and freely Consult on occa-
5 sion. The Reservedness and Distance, that Fathers keep, often
deprive their Sons of that refuge, which would be of more Advantage to
them, than an hundred more Rebukes and Chidings. Would your Son
engage in some Frolick, or take a Vagary, were it not much better he
should do it with, than without your Knowledge? For since Allowances
10 for such things must be made to Young Men, the more you know of his
Intrigues and Designs, the better will you be able to prevent great Mischiefs; and by letting him see what is like to follow, take the right way of
prevailing with him to avoid less Inconveniencies. Would you have him
open his Heart to you, and ask your Advice? You must begin to do so
15 with him first, and by your Carriage beget that Confidence.

§. 97. But whatever he Consults you about, unless it lead to some
fatal and irremediable Mischief, be sure you advise only as a Friend of
more Experience; but with your Advice mingle nothing of Command
or Authority, no more than you would to your Equal, or a Stranger.
20 That would be to drive him for ever from any farther demanding, or
receiving Advantage from your Counsel. You must consider, that he is
a Young Man, and has Pleasures and Fancies, which you are pass'd.
You must not expect his Inclinations should be just as yours, nor that
at Twenty he should have the same Thoughts you have at Fifty. All
25 that you can wish is, that since Youth must have some Liberty, some
Outleaps, they might be with the Ingenuity of a Son, and *under the Eye
of a Father*, and then no very great harm can come of it. The way to
obtain this, as I said before, is (according as you find him capable) to
talk with him about your Affairs, propose Matters to him *familiarly*,
30 and ask his Advice; and when he ever lights on the Right, follow it as
his; and if it succeeds well, let him have the Commendation. This will
not at all lessen your Authority, but increase his Love and Esteem of
you. Whilst you keep your Estate, the Staff will still be in your own
Hands; and your Authority the surer, the more it is strengthen'd with
35 *Confidence* and *Kindness*. For you have not that Power you ought to
have over him, till he comes to be more afraid of offending so good a
Friend, than of losing some part of his future Expectation.[-e]

6 deprive] deprives 1   16 97] 93 1   29 *familiarly*] *familiarity* **NN** (*Bodl. Lib.*
260 g. 512; *other copies have stop-press correction*)

[f] happy in the injoyment of soe favourable **Corr.** 844 (ii. 787, l. 8)

§. 98. Familiarity of Discourse, if it can become a Father to his Son, may much more be condescended to by a Tutor to his Pupil. All their time together should not be spent in Reading of Lectures, and magisterially dictating to him, what he is to observe and follow: Hearing him in his turn, and using him to reason about what is propos'd, makes the 5 Rules go down the easier, and sink the deeper, and gives him a liking to Study and Instruction: And he will then begin to value Knowledge when he sees, that it inables him to Discourse; and he finds the Pleasure, and Credit of bearing a Part in the Conversation, and to have his Reasons sometimes approved, and hearken'd to. Especially in 10 Morality, Prudence, and Breeding, Cases should be Put to him, and his Judgment asked. This opens the Understanding better than Maxims, how well soever explain'd, and settles the Rules better in the Memory for Practice. This way lets things into the Mind, which stick there, and retain their Evidence with them; whereas words at best are 15 faint Representations, being not so much as the true Shadows of Things, and are much sooner forgotten. He will better comprehend the Foundations, and Measures of Decency, and Justice; and have livelier, and more lasting Impressions, of what he ought to do, by giving his Opinion on Cases propos'd, and Reasoning with his Tutor 20 on fit Instances, than by giving a silent, negligent, sleepy Audience to his Tutor's Lectures; And much more than by captious Logical Disputes, or set Declarations of his own, upon any Question. The one sets the Thoughts upon Wit, and false Colours, and not upon Truth: The other teaches Fallacy, Wrangling and Opiniatrety: And they are 25 both of them Things, that spoil the Judgment, and put a Man out of the Way of right and fair Reasoning; And therefore carefully to be avoided, by one who would improve himself, and be acceptable to others.

§. 99. When, by making your Son sensible that he depends on you, 30 and is in your Power, you have establish'd your Authority; and by being inflexibly severe in your Carriage to him, when obstinately persisting in any ill natur'd Trick, which you have forbidden, especially Lying, you have imprinted on his Mind that awe, which is necessary; And on the other side, When, (by permitting him the full Liberty due 35

§ 99 *Reverence.*

1–29 § 98 *add.* 3   5 propos'd, makes] propos'd will make 5   6 gives] will
give 5   7–8 Study . . . it 5] Knowledge; when he sees, it 3 4   9–10 to have] of
having 5   10 Especially] Particularly 5   30 99] 94 1   33 which] *add.* 3

to his Age, and laying no restraint in your Presence to those childish Actions and gayety of Carriage, which, whilst he is very Young, is as necessary to him as Meat or Sleep) you have reconcil'd him to your Company, and made him sensible of your Care and Love of him, by
5 Indulgence and Tenderness, especially, Caressing him on all Occasions wherein he does any thing well, and being kind to him after a Thousand fashions suitable to his Age, which Nature teaches Parents better than I can; When, I say, by these Ways of Tenderness, and Affection, which Parents never want for their Children, you have also
10 planted in him a particular Affection for you, he is then in the State you could desire, and you have formed in his Mind that true *Reverence*, which is alway afterwards carefully to be continued, and maintained in both the Parts of it, *Love* and *Fear*, as the great Principle, whereby you will always have hold upon him, to turn his Mind to the Ways of
15 Vertue, and Honour.

§. 100. ᵍ⁻When this Foundation is once well laid, and you find this Reverence begin to work in him, the next thing to be done, is carefully to consider his *Temper*, and the particular Constitution of his Mind. Stubbornness, Lying, and ill natur'd Actions are not (as has been said)
20 to be permitted in him from the beginning, whatever his Temper be: Those Seeds of Vices are not to be suffered to take any root, but must be carefully weeded out, as soon as ever they begin to shew themselves in him; and your Authority is to take place and influence his Mind from the very dawning of any Knowledge in him, that it may operate as
25 a natural Principle, whereof he never perceived the beginning, never knew that it was, or could be otherwise.⁻ᵍ By this, if the *Reverence* he owes you be establish'd early, it will always be Sacred to him, and it will be as hard for him to resist it, as the Principles of his Nature.

§. 101. Having thus very early set up your Authority, and by the
30 gentler Applications of it, shamed him out of what leads towards any immoral Habit; as soon as you have observed it in him (for I would by no means have chiding used, much less Blows, till Obstinacy and Incorrigibleness make it absolutely necessary) it will be fit to consider which way the natural make of his *Mind inclines* him. Some Men by the
35 unalterable Frame of their Constitutions are *Stout*, others *Timorous*,

§§ 100–2 *Temper*.

12 continued] increased 1   13 both the] both 5   15 Vertue, and] Vertue of
NN   16 100] 95 1   22–3 carefully . . . him;] suppress'd in their appearance; 1
23 take . . . Mind] be establish'd 1   29 101] 96 1   set up] established 1

ᵍ⁻ᵍ *Similar ideas expressed* **Corr.** 808 (ii. 683)

some *Confident*, others *Modest, Tractable* or *Obstinate, Curious* or *Care-less, Quick* or *Slow.* There are not more Differences in Men's Faces, and the outward Lineaments of their Bodies, than there are in the Makes and Tempers of their Minds; Only there is this Difference, that the distinguishing Characters of the Face, and the Lineaments of the 5 Body grow more plain and visible with Time and Age, but the peculiar *Physiognomy of the Mind* is most discernable in Children, before Art and Cunning hath taught them to hide their Deformities, and conceal their ill Inclinations under a dissembled out-side.

§. 102. Begin therefore betimes nicely to observe your Son's *Temper*; 10 and that, when he is under least restraint, in his Play, and as he thinks out of your sight. See what are his *predominant Passions*, and *prevailing Inclinations*; whether he be Fierce or Mild, Bold or Bashful, Compassionate or Cruel, Open or Reserv'd, *&c.* For as these are different in him, so are your Methods to be different, and your Authority must 15 hence take measures to apply it self different ways to him. These *native Propensities*,[39] these prevalencies of Constitution, are not to be cured by Rules, or a direct Contest; especially those of them that are the humbler and meaner sort, which proceed from fear, and lowness of Spirit; though with Art they may be much mended, and turned to good 20 purposes. But this, be sure, after all is done, the Byass will always hang on that side, that Nature first placed it: And if you carefully observe the Characters of his Mind, now in the first Scenes of his Life, you will ever after be able to judge which way his Thoughts lean, and what he aims at, even hereafter, when, as he grows up, the Plot thickens, and he 25 puts on several Shapes to act it.

§. 103. [h-]I told you before, that Children love *Liberty*; and therefore

§§ 103–5 *Dominion.*

---

2 *Quick* or *Slow.*] *add.* **3**   10 102] 97 **1**   11–12 in his ... sight.] *add.* **3**
17 *Propensities*] *Propensions* **1**   19 which] that **1**   23 his Mind] this Mind **NN**
27 103] 98 **1**

[h-h] §§ 103–10 *first two sentences, expanded from* **Corr.** 929 (iii. 179–82)

[39] § 217 speaks of children as 'white Paper, or Wax, to be moulded and fashioned as one pleases'. The metaphor of 'white paper' recalls Book 2 of the *Essay*, and Locke's strong rejection of innate principles in Book 1. As §§ 101–2 make very clear, the white-paper metaphor must not be taken too literally; nor was talk of the tutor's moulding the child meant to deny the 'unalterable Frame of their Constitutions'. The innate principles Locke rejected were truths, and the ideas composing those truths, e.g. moral truths and logical truths. The *Essay* even speaks of an innate principle in all men to seek pleasure and avoid pain (1. 3. 3). The stereotype of Locke as believing the mind entirely empty at birth needs to be rejected and replaced by his recognition of traits, tempers, and tendencies, as well as of a large number of faculties.

they should be brought to do the things are fit for them, without feeling any restraint laid upon them. I now tell you, they love something more; and that is *Dominion:* And this is the first Original of most vicious Habits, that are ordinary and natural. This Love of *Power* and 5 Dominion shews it self very early, and that in these Two Things.

§. 104. 1. We see Children (as soon almost as they are born, I am sure long before they can speak) cry, grow peevish, sullen, and out of humour, for nothing but to have their *Wills*. They would have their Desires submitted to by others; they contend for a ready compliance 10 from all about them; especially from those that stand near, or beneath them in Age or Degree, as soon as they come to consider others with those distinctions.

§. 105. Another thing wherein they shew their love of Dominion, is their desire to have things to be theirs; they would have *Propriety* and 15 Possession, pleasing themselves with the Power which that seems to give, and the Right they thereby have, to dispose of them, as they please. He, that has not observed these two Humours working very betimes in Children, has taken little notice of their Actions: And he, who thinks that these two Roots of almost all the Injustice and Con-20 tention, that so disturb humane Life, are not early to be weeded out, and contrary Habits introduced, neglects the proper Season to lay the Foundations of a good and worthy Man. To do this, I imagine, these following things may somewhat conduce.

§. 106. 1. That a Child should never be suffered to have what he 25 *craves*, much less what he *cries for*, I had said, *or so much as speaks for*. But that being apt to be mis-understood, and interpreted as if I meant, a Child should never speak to his Parents for any thing; which will perhaps be thought to lay too great a Curb on the Minds of Children, to the prejudice of that Love and Affection which should be between 30 them and their Parents; I shall Explain my self a little more particularly. It is fit that they should have liberty to declare their Wants to their Parents, and that with all tenderness they should be hearken'd to, and supplied, at least whilst they are very little. But 'tis one thing to say, I am hungry; another to say, I would have Roast-Meat. Having 35 declared their Wants, their natural Wants, the pain they feel from

§§ 106–7 *Craving.*

---

6 104] 99 **1**   13 105] 100 **1**   15 which] *add.* **3**   19 who] that **1**
24 106] 101 **1**   25–32 less . . . and] and so much as *speaks for*, much less if he *cries for it*. What then, would you not have them declare their Wants? Yes, that is very fit; and 'tis as fit, **1**

Hunger, Thirst, Cold, or any other necessity of Nature; 'tis the Duty of their Parents, and those about them, to relieve them: But Children must leave it to the choice and ordering of their Parents, what they think properest for them, and how much; and must not be permitted to chuse for themselves, and say, I would have Wine, or White-bread; the 5
very naming of it should make them lose it.

§. 107. That which Parents should take care of here, is to distinguish between the Wants of Fancy, and those of Nature, which *Horace* has well taught them to do in this Verse.

Queis humana sibi doleat natura negatis. [40] 10

Those are truly Natural Wants, which Reason alone, without some other Help, is not able to fence against, nor keep from disturbing us. The Pains of Sickness and Hurts, Hunger, Thirst and Cold; want of Sleep, and Rest or Relaxation of the Part wearied with Labour, are what all Men feel, and the best dispos'd Minds cannot but be sensible 15
of their uneasiness: And therefore ought by fit Applications to seek their removal, though not with impatience, or over-great hast, upon the first approaches of them, where Delay does not threaten some irreparable harm. The Pains, that come from the Necessities of Nature, are Monitors to us, to beware of greater Mischiefs, which they 20
are the Forerunners of: And therefore they must not be wholly neglected, nor strain'd too far. But yet the more Children can be enur'd[41] to Hardships of this Kind, by a wise Care to make them Stronger in Body and Mind, the better it will be for them. I need not here give any Caution to keep within the Bounds of doing them good, and to take 25

7 107] 102 **1**   7–167.20 That ... rewarded] This is for natural Wants, which must be relieved: But for all *Wants of Fancy* and Affectation, they should *never*, if once *declar'd*, be hearken'd to, *or complied with*. By this means they will be brought to get a mastery over their Inclinations, and learn the Art of stifling their Desires, as soon as they rise up in them, and before they take vent, when they are easiest to be subdued, which will be of great use to them in the future course of their Lives. By this I do not mean, that they should not have the things, that one perceives would delight them: 'Twould be Inhumanity, and not Prudence, to treat them so. But they should not have the liberty to *carve*, or *crave* any thing to themselves; they should be exercised in keeping their Desires under, till they have got the habit of it, and it be grown easie; they should accustom themselves to be content in the want of what they wished for: And the more they practised Modesty and Temperance in this, the more should those about them study to reward them **1**

40 *Sermones*, i. 1. 74–5: 'panis ematur, holus, vini sextareius, adde quis humana sibi doleat natura negatis'. (Let bread be bought, vegetables, a pint of wine, and with them things at whose denial human nature would grieve.)
41 'enur'd', inured (*OED*).

Care, that what Children are made to suffer, should neither break their Spirits, nor injure their Health; Parents being but too apt of themselves to incline, more than they should, to the softer Side.

But whatever Compliance the Necessities of Nature may require, the Wants of Fancy Children should never be gratified in, nor suffer'd to *mention*. The very *speaking* for any such thing, should make them lose it. Cloaths, when they need, they must have; but if they *speak* for this Stuff, or that Colour, they should be sure to go without it. Nor that I would have Parents purposely cross the Desires of their Children in matters of indifferency: On the contrary, where their Carriage deserves it, and one is sure it will not corrupt, or effeminate their Minds, and make them fond of Trifles, I think all things should be contrived, as much as could be, to their Satisfaction, that they might find the ease and pleasure of doing well. The best for Children is, that they should not place any pleasure in such things at all: Nor regulate their Delight by their Fancies; but be indifferent to all, that Nature has made so. This is what their Parents and Teachers should chiefly aim at; but till this be obtain'd, all that I oppose here, is the liberty of *asking*; which in these things of Conceit ought to be restrain'd by a constant forfeiture annex'd to it.

This may perhaps be thought a little too severe by the natural Indulgence of tender Parents: But yet it is no more than necessary. For since the Method, I propose, is to banish the Rod; this Restraint of their Tongues will be of great use to settle that awe, we have elsewhere spoken of, and to keep up in them the respect and reverence due to their Parents. Next, it will teach them to keep in, and so master their Inclinations. By this means they will be brought to learn the Art of stifling their Desires as soon as they rise up in them, when they are easiest to be subdued. For giving vent, gives Life and Strength to our Appetites; and he that has the confidence to turn his Wishes into Demands, will be but a little way from thinking he ought to obtain them. This, I am sure, every one can more easily bear a denial from himself, than from any body else. They should therefore be accustomed betimes to consult, and make use of their Reason, before they give allowance to their Inclinations. 'Tis a great Step towards the mastery of our Desires, to give this stop to them, and shut them up in Silence. This habit, got by Children, of staying the forwardness of their Fancies, and deliberating whether it be fit or no, before they *speak*, will be of no small Advantage to them in Matters of greater Consequence, in the future course of their Lives. For that which I cannot too often inculcate, is, that whatever the matter be, about which it is conversant, whether great or small, the main (I had almost said only) thing to be consider'd, in every action of a Child, is, what influence it will have upon his Mind; what habit it tends to, and is like to settle in him; How it will become him when he is bigger; and if it be encouraged, whither it will lead him, when he is grown up.

My meaning therefore is not, that Children should purposely be made uneasie: This would relish too much of Inhumanity, and ill Nature; and be apt to infect them with it. They should be brought to deny their Appetites; and their Minds as well as Bodies, be made vigorous, easie, and strong, by the Custom of having their Inclinations in Subjection, and their Bodies exercised with Hardships: But all this, without giving them any mark or apprehension of ill-will towards them. The constant loss of what they *craved* or *carv'd*[42] to themselves should teach them Modesty, Submission, and a Power to forbear: But the rewarding their Modesty, and Silence, by giving them, what they liked, should also assure them of the love of those, who rigorously exacted this Obedience. The contenting themselves now in the want of what they wish'd for is a Vertue, that another time should be rewarded with what is suited and acceptable to them; which should be bestowed on them, as if it were a natural consequence of their Good-Behaviour, and not a Bargain about it. But you will lose your Labour, and what is more, their Love and Reverence too, if they can receive from others, what you deny them. This is to be kept very stanch,[43] and carefully to be watched. And here the Servants come again in my way.

§. 108. If this be begun betimes, and they accustom themselves early to silence their Desires, this useful habit will settle in them; and as they come to grow up in Age and Discretion, they may be allowed greater liberty; when Reason comes to speak in them, and not Passion. For when ever Reason would speak, it should be hearken'd to. But as they should never be heard, when they speak for any particular thing they would *have*, unless it be first proposed to them; so they should always be heard, and fairly and kindly answered, when they ask after any thing they would *know*, and desire to be inform'd about. *Curiosity* should be as carefully *cherished* in Children, as other Appetites suppressed.

§ 108 *Curiosity.*　　*Recreation.*

---

26 108] 103 **1**　　　31 particular] *add.* **3**

[42] '*carv'd*', helped or served themselves at their own discretion (*OED*).
[43] See *OED* s.v. staunch, 4b.

However strict an hand is to be kept upon all desires of Fancy, yet there is one case wherein Fancy must be permitted to speak, and be hearken'd to also. *Recreation* is as necessary, as Labour, or Food. But because there can be no *Recreation* without Delight, which depends
5 not alway on Reason, but oftener on Fancy, it must be permitted Children not only to divert themselves, but to do it after their own fashion; provided it be innocently and without prejudice to their Health: And therefore in this case they should not be deni'd, if they propos'd any particular kind of *Recreation.* Though, I think, in a well-order'd Edu-
10 cation, they will seldom be brought to the necessity of asking any such liberty. Care should be taken, that what is of Advantage to them, they should always do with delight; and before they are wearied with one, they should be timely *diverted* to some other useful Imployment. But if they are not yet brought to that degree of Perfection, that one way of
15 Improvement can be made a *Recreation* to another, they must be let loose to the childish Play they fansie; which they should be weaned from, by being made Surfeit of it: But from things of use, that they are imploy'd in, they should always be sent away with an Appetite; at least be dismissed, before they are tired, and grow quite sick of it; that so
20 they may return to it again, as to a Pleasure that diverts them. For you must never think them set right, till they can find Delight in the Practice of laudable Things; and the useful Exercises of the Body and Mind, taking their turns, make their Lives and Improvement pleasant in a continued train of *Recreations*, wherein the wearied part is con-
25 stantly relieved, and refresh'd. Whether this can be done in every Temper, or whether Tutors and Parents will be at the Pains, and have the Discretion, and Patience to bring them to this, I know not; but that it may be done in most Children, if a right course be taken to raise in them the desire of Credit, Esteem, and Reputation, I do not at all doubt. And
30 when they have so much true Life put into them, they may freely be talked with about what most *delights* them, and be directed, or let loose to it; so that they may perceive that they are belov'd and cherish'd, and that those under whose Tuition they are, are not Enemies to their Satisfaction. Such a Management will make them in love with the Hand that
35 directs them, and the Vertue they are directed to.

This farther Advantage may be made by a free liberty permitted them in their *Recreations*, That it will discover their Natural Tempers, shew their Inclinations, and Aptitudes; and thereby direct wise

1–169.4 However . . . Children.] *add.* **3**   15 another,] them, **4 5**

Parents in the choice, both of the course of Life, and Imployment they shall design them for, and of fit Remedies in the mean time to be applied to whatever bent of Nature, they may observe most likely to mislead any of their Children.

§. 109. 2. Children who live together often strive for mastery, whose Wills shall carry it over the rest: Whoever begins the *Contest*, should be sure to be crossed in it. But not only that, but they should be taught to have all the *Deference, Complaisance*, and *Civility* one for another imaginable. This, when they see it procures them respect, love and esteem, and that they lose no Superiority by it, they will take more pleasure in, than in insolent Domineering; for so plainly is the other.

The Accusations of Children one against another, which usually are but the Clamors of Anger and Revenge desiring Aid, should not be favourably received, nor hearken'd to. It weakens and effeminates their Minds to suffer them to *Complain:* And if they endure sometimes crossing, or pain from others, without being permitted to think it strange or intolerable, it will do them no harm to learn Sufferance, and harden[44] them early. But though you give no countenance to the *Complaints* of the *Querulous*, yet take care to curb the Insolence and Ill-nature of the Injurious. When you observe it your self, reprove it before the injured Party: But if the *Complaint* be of something really worthy your notice, and prevention another time, then reprove the Offender by himself alone, out of sight of him that complained, and make him go and ask pardon, and make reparation. Which coming thus, as it were, from himself, will be the more cheerfully performed, and more kindly received, the Love strengthned between them, and a custom of Civility grow familiar amongst your Children.

§. 110. 3. [i-]As to the having and possessing of Things, teach them to part with what they have easily and freely to their Friends; and let them find by Experience, that the most *liberal* has always most plenty, with Esteem and Commendation to boot, and they will quickly learn

§ 109 *Complaints.*   § 110 *Liberality.*   *Justice.*

---

5 109] 104 **1**   6 Wills] Will **NN**   9–10 love and esteem,] *add.* **3**
10 it, they] it; but on the Contrary [**NN**; contrary **NA**], they grow into love, and esteem with every body, they **1**   12 Accusations] *Complaints* **1**   12–13 usually . . . Aid,] is usually but the desiring the assistance of another to revenge them, **1**
19–20 curb . . . Injurious.] suppress all Insolence and Ill-nature. **1**   28 110] 105 **1**

[i-i] *Expanded from* **Corr.** 822 (ii. 720)

44 'harden' is found in some **NN** copies spelt 'hearden'; others show the stop-press correction.

to practise it. This I imagine will make Brothers and Sisters kinder and civiller to one another, and consequently to others, than twenty Rules about good Manners, with which Children are ordinarily perplexed and cumbred.⁻ʰ Covetousness, and the desire of having in our
5 possession, and under our Dominion, more than we have need of, being the root of all Evil, should be early and carefully weeded out, and the contrary Quality of a readiness to impart to others, implanted. This should be encouraged by great Commendation and Credit, and constantly taking care, that he loses nothing by his *Liberality.* Let all
10 the Instances he gives of such freeness, be always repaid, and with interest; and let him sensibly perceive, that the Kindness he shews to others is no ill husbandry for himself; but that it brings a return of Kindness both from those that receive it, and those who look on. Make this a Contest among Children, who shall out-do one another this way:
15 And by this means, by a constant practice, Children having made it easie to themselves to part with what they have, good Nature may be setled in them into an habit, and they may take pleasure, and pique themselves in being *kind, liberal*, and *civil* to others.⁻ⁱ

If Liberality ought to be incourag'd, certainly great Care is to be
20 taken, that Children transgress not the Rules of *Justice*: And whenever they do, they should be set right, and if there be occasion for it, severely rebuk'd.

Our first Actions being guided more by Self-love, than Reason or Reflection, 'tis no wonder, that in Children they should be very apt to
25 deviate from the just measures of Right and Wrong; which are in the Mind the result of improved Reason and serious Meditation. This the more they are apt to mistake, the more careful Guard ought to be kept over them; and every the least slip in this great Social Vertue taken notice of and rectified; and that in Things of the least weight and
30 moment; both to instruct their Ignorance, and prevent ill Habits, which from small Beginnings in Pins and Cherry-stones, will, if let alone, grow up to higher Frauds, and be in danger to end at last in a down-right harden'd dishonesty. The first Tendency to any *Injustice*, that appears, must be supprest with a shew of Wonder and Abhor-
35 rency in the Parents and Governours. But because Children cannot well comprehend what *Injustice* is, till they understand Property, and how particular Persons come by it, the safest way to secure Honesty, is to lay the Foundations of it early in Liberality, and an Easiness to part

19–171.23 If . . . obey'd.] *add.* **3**   32 in a] in **5**

with to others whatever they have or like themselves. This may be taught them early, before they have Language and Understanding enough to form distinct Notions of Property, and to know what is theirs by a peculiar Right exclusive of others. And since Children seldom have any thing but by gift, and that for the most part from their Parents, they may be at 5 first taught not to take, or keep any thing, but what is given them by those, whom they take to have a Power over it. And as their Capacities enlarge, other Rules, and Cases of *Justice*, and Rights concerning *meum* and *tuum*, may be propos'd and inculcated. If any act of *Injustice* in them appears to proceed, not from mistake, but a perversness in their wills, 10 when a gentle rebuke and shame will not reform this irregular and covetous Inclination, rougher Remedies must be applied: And 'tis but for the Father or Tutor to take, and keep from them something, that they value, and think their own; or order somebody else to do it; and by such Instances make them sensible, what little Advantage they are like to 15 make, by possessing themselves *unjustly* of what is another's, whilst there are in the World stronger and more Men than they. But if an ingenuous Detestation of this shameful Vice be but carefully and early instill'd into them, as I think it may, that is the true and genuine Method to obviate this Crime; and will be a better Guard against *Dishonesty*, than 20 any Considerations drawn from interest; habits working more constantly and with greater facility, than reason: Which, when we have most need of it, is seldom fairly consulted, and more rarely obey'd.

§. 111. ʲ⁻*Crying* is a fault, that should not be tolerated in Children; not only for the unpleasant and unbecoming Noise it fills the House 25 with, but for more considerable Reasons, in reference to the Children themselves; which is to be our aim in Education.

Their *Crying* is of two sorts; either *stubborn* and *domineering*, or *querulous* and *whining*.

1. Their *Crying* is very often a striving for Mastery, and an open 30 declaration of their Insolence, or Obstinacy: When they have not the power to obtain their Desire, they will by their *Clamour* and *Sobbing*, maintain their Title and Right to it. This is an avowed continuing of their Claim, and a sort of Remonstrance against the Oppression and Injustice of those who deny them, what they have a mind to. 35

§§ 111–14 *Crying.*

24 111] 106 **1**   30 striving] contention **1**   33–4 avowed . . . Claim,] open justifying themselves, **1**   34–5 against . . . deny] of the unjustness of the Oppression, which denies **1**

ʲ⁻ʲ §§ 111–14 *in* **Corr.** 943 (iii. 220–2); *cf.* 844 (ii. 771)

§. 112. 2. Sometimes their *Crying* is the effect of Pain, or true Sorrow, and a *bemoaning* themselves under it.

These Two, if carefully observed, may, by the Mien, Looks and Actions, and particularly by the Tone of their Crying, be easily distin-
5 guished; but neither of them must be suffer'd, much less incourag'd.

1. The obstinate or *stomachful crying* should by no means be per-mitted; because it is but another way of flattering their Desires, and incouraging those Passions, which 'tis our main Business to subdue: And if it be, as often it is, upon the receiving any Correction, it quite
10 defeats all the good Effects of it. For any Chastisement, which leaves them in this declar'd Opposition, only serves to make them worse. The Restraints and Punishments laid on Children are all misapplied and lost, as far as they do not prevail over their Wills, teach them to submit their Passions, and make their Minds supple and pliant, to
15 what their Parents Reason advises them now, and so prepare them to obey, what their own Reason shall advise hereafter. But if, in any thing, wherein they are crossed, they may be suffer'd to go away *crying*, they confirm themselves in their Desires, and cherish the ill Humour, with a Declaration of their Right, and a Resolution to satisfy their
20 Inclination the first Opportunity. This therefore is another Argument against the frequent use of Blows: For, whenever you come to that extremity, 'tis not enough to Whip, or Beat them, you must do it, till you find, you have subdued their Minds; till with Submission and Patience they yield to the Correction; which you shall best discover by
25 their *crying*, and their ceasing from it upon your bidding. Without this, the beating of Children is but a passionate Tyranny over them; and it is mere Cruelty, and not Correction to put their Bodies in Pain, with-out doing their Minds any good. As this gives us a Reason why Chil-dren should seldom be corrected, so it also prevents their being so.
30 For if, when-ever they are chastised, it were done thus without Pas-sion, soberly and yet effectually too, laying on the Blows and Smart, not furiously and all at once, but slowly, with Reasoning between, and with Observation how it wrought, stopping when it had made them pliant, penitent, and yielding; they would seldom need the like Pun-
35 ishment again, being made careful to avoid the Fault, that deserved it. Besides, by this means, as the Punishment would not be lost for being too little and not effectual, so it would be kept from being too much; if

1 112] 107 1   10 any Chastisement,] a Punishment, 1   16 Reason]
Reasons **NN**   20–1 Argument . . . Blows:] Reason why you should seldom Chas-
tise your Children, 1   32 furiously and] *add.* 3

we gave off, as soon as we perceived that it reach'd the Mind, and that was better'd. For since the Chiding or Beating of Children should be always the least, that possibly may be; that which is laid on in the heat of Anger, seldom observes that measure; but is commonly more than it should be, though it prove less than enough.

§. 113. 2. Many Children are apt to *Cry*, upon any little Pain they suffer; and the least Harm that befalls them puts them into *Complaints* and *Bawling*. This few Children avoid: For it being the first and natural Way to declare their Sufferings or Wants, before they can speak, the Compassion that is thought due to that tender Age, fool- ishly incourages, and continues it in them long after they can speak. 'Tis the Duty, I confess, of those about Children to compassionate them, when-ever they suffer any hurt; but not to shew it in pitying them. Help and ease them the best you can, but by no means bemoan them. This softens their Minds, and makes them yield to the little harms, that happen to them; whereby they sink deeper into that part, which alone feels, and make larger Wounds there, than otherwise they would. They should be harden'd against all Sufferings, especially of the Body, and have no tenderness but what rises from an ingenuous Shame, and a quick sence of Reputation. The many Inconveniencies this Life is exposed to, require we should not be too sensible of every little hurt. What our Minds yield not to, makes but a slight impression, and does us but very little harm: 'Tis the suffering of our Spirits that gives and continues the Pain. This brawniness and insensibility of Mind is the best Armour we can have, against the common Evils and Accidents of Life; and being a Temper that is to be got by Exercise and Custom, more than any other way, the practice of it should be begun betimes, and happy is he that is taught it early. That effeminacy of Spirit, which is to be prevented or cured, as nothing, that I know, so much increases in Children as *Crying*; so nothing, on the other side, so much checks and restrains, as their being hindred from that sort of *Complaining*. In the little harms they suffer from Knocks and Falls, they should not be pitied for falling, but bid do so again; which besides that it stops their *Crying*, is a better way to cure their heedlesness, and prevent their tumbling another time, than either chiding or bemoan- ing them. But let the hurts they receive, be what they will, stop their

5

10

15

20

25

30

35

3 possibly] possible 1   6 113] 108 1   15–16 them yield . . . deeper] the little harms, that happen to them, sink deep 1   19–20 no . . . sence of] a tender- ness only of Shame and for 1   33–4 besides . . . *Crying*,] *add.* 3   34–5 heed- lesness . . . time,] falling, 1

Crying, and that will give them more quiet and ease at present, and harden them for the future.

§. 114. The former sort of *Crying* requires severity to silence it, and where a Look or a positive Command will not do it, Blows must. For it proceeding from Pride, Obstinacy, and Stomach, the Will, where the Fault lies, must be bent, and made to comply, by a Rigour sufficient to Master it. But this latter, being ordinarily from softness of Mind, a quite contrary Cause, ought to be treated with a gentler Hand. Persuasion, or diverting the Thoughts another way, or laughing at their *Whining*, may perhaps be at first the proper Method. But for this the Circumstances of the Thing, and the particular Temper of the Child must be considered: No certain unvariable Rules can be given about it, but it must be left to the Prudence of the Parents or Tutor. But this I think I may say in general, that there should be a constant discountenancing of this sort of *Crying* also; and that the Father, by his Authority, should always stop it; mixing a greater Degree of roughness in his Looks or Words, proportionably as the Child is of a greater Age, or a sturdier Temper: But always let it be enough to silence their *whimpering*, and put an end to the Disorder.⁻ʲ

§. 115. *Cowardice* and *Courage* are so nearly related to the forementioned Tempers, that it may not be amiss here to take notice of them. Fear is a Passion, that, if rightly govern'd, has its use. And though Self-love seldom fails to keep it watchful and high enough in us, yet there may be an Excess on the daring side; *Fool-hardiness* and insensibility of Danger being as little reasonable, as trembling and shrinking at the approach of every little evil. Fear was given us as a Monitor to quicken our Industry, and keep us upon our Guard against the approaches of Evil: And therefore to have no apprehension of Mischief at hand; not to make a just Estimate of the Danger; but heedlesly to run into it, be the hazard what it will, without considering of what use or consequence it may be, is not the resolution of a rational Creature, but brutish Fury. Those, who have Children of this Temper, have nothing to do, but a little to awaken their Reason, which Self-preservation will quickly dispose them to hearken to; Unless (which is usually the Case) some other Passion hurries them on Head-long,

---

§ 115. *Fool-hardiness.*   *Courage.*   *Cowardice.*   *Timorousness.*   *Hardiness.*

---

3 114] 109 **1**   5 Stomach] Wilfullness **NN** Wilfulness **NA**   7 Master] subdue **1**   15 Authority,] Looks, Words [**NN**; Words, **NA**] and Authority, **1** 18–19 silence . . . end to] Master **1**   20–180.11 § 115 *add.* **3**

without Sense, and without Consideration. A dislike of Evil is so natural to Mankind, that no body, I think, can be without fear of it; Fear being nothing but an Uneasiness under the Apprehension of that coming upon us which we dislike. And therefore when ever any one runs into Danger, we may say, 'tis under the Conduct of Ignorance, or 5 the Command of some more imperious Passion; No body being so much an Enemy to himself, as to come within the reach of Evil out of free choice, and court Danger for Danger's sake. If it be therefore Pride, Vain-glory, or Rage, that silences a Child's fear, or makes him not hearken to its Advice, those are by fit means to be abated; that a 10 little Consideration may allay his heat, and make him bethink himself whether this Attempt be worth the Venture. But this being a Fault, that Children are not so often guilty of, I shall not be more particular in its Cure. Weakness of Spirit is the more common Defect, and therefore will require the greater Care. 15

Fortitude is the Guard and Support of the other Virtues; and without Courage a Man will scarce keep steady to his Duty, and fill up the Character of a truly worthy Man.

Courage, that makes us bear up against Dangers that we fear, and Evils that we feel, is of great Use in an Estate, as ours is in this Life, 20 expos'd to Assaults on all hands: And therefore it is very advisable to get Children into this Armour as early as we can. Natural Temper, I confess, does here a great deal: But even where that is defective, and the heart is in it self weak and timorous, it may, by a right management, be brought to a better resolution. What is to be done to prevent 25 breaking Childrens Spirits by frightful Apprehensions instill'd into them when Young, or bemoaning themselves under every little Suffering, I have already taken notice. How to harden their Tempers, and raise their *Courage*, if we find them too much subject to fear, is farther to be consider'd. 30

True Fortitude, I take to be the quiet Possession of a Man's self, and an undisturb'd doing his Duty, whatever Evil besets, or Danger lies in his way. This there are so few Men attain to, that we are not to expect it from Children. But yet something may be done: And a wise Conduct by insensible degrees, may carry them farther than one 35 expects.

The neglect of this great Care of them, whilst they are young, is the reason perhaps, why there are so few that have this Vertue in its full Latitude, when they are Men. I should not say this in a Nation so naturally Brave, as ours is, did I think, that true Fortitude required 40

nothing but Courage in the Field, and a Contempt of Life in the face of an Enemy. This, I confess, is not the least part of it, nor can be denied the Laurels and Honours always justly due to the Valour of those who venture their Lives for their Country. But yet this is not all. Dangers
5 attack us in other places, besides the Fields of Battle; and though Death be the King of Terrors, yet Pain, Disgrace, and Poverty have frightful looks, able to discompose most Men, whom they seem ready to seize on: And there are those who contemn some of these, and yet are heartily frighted with the other. True Fortitude is prepar'd for
10 Dangers of all kinds, and unmoved whatsoever Evil it be, that threatens. I do not mean unmoved with any Fear at all. Where Danger shews it self, Apprehension cannot, without Stupidity, be wanting. Where Danger is, Sense of Danger should be; and so much Fear as should keep us awake, and excite our Attention, Industry, and Vigour;
15 but not disturb the calm use of our Reason, nor hinder the execution of what that Dictates.

The first Step to get this noble, and manly steadiness, is, what I have above mentioned, carefully to keep Children from frights of all kinds; when they are young. Let not any fearful Apprehensions be
20 talked into them, nor terrible Objects surprize them. This often so shatters, and discomposes the Spirits; that they never recover it again; but during their whole Life, upon the first suggestion, or appearance of any terrifying Idea, are scatter'd and confounded; the Body is enervated, and the Mind disturb'd, and the Man scarce himself, or capable
25 of any composed or rational action. Whether this be from an habitual Motion of the Animal Spirits, introduced by the first strong Impression, or from the alteration of the Constitution by some more unaccountable way; this is certain, that so it is. Instances of such who in a weak timorous Mind have born, all their whole lives through, the
30 effects of a Fright when they were young, are every-where to be seen; and therefore as much as may be to be prevented.

The next Thing is by gentle degrees, to accustom Children to those things, they are too much afraid of. But here great Caution is to be used, that you do not make too much haste, nor attempt this Cure too
35 early, for fear lest you increase the Mischief instead of remedying it. Little ones in Arms may be easily kept out of the way of terrifying Objects, and till they can talk and understand what is said to them, are scarce capable of that Reasoning and Discourse, which should be used, to let them know there is no harm in those frightful Objects,
40 which we would make them familiar with, and do, to that purpose, by

gentle degrees bring nearer and nearer to them. And therefore 'tis seldom, there is need of any Application to them of this kind; till after they can run about, and talk. But yet, if it should happen, that Infants should have taken offence at any thing which cannot be easily kept out of their way; and that they shew marks of terror as often as it comes in sight; all the allays of fright, by diverting their Thoughts, or mixing pleasant and agreeable appearances with it, must be used, till it be grown familiar and inoffensive to them.

I think we may observe, That, when Children are first Born, all Objects of sight, that do not hurt the Eyes, are indifferent to them; and they are no more afraid of a Blackmore, or a Lion, than of their Nurse, or a Cat. What is it then, that afterwards, in certain mixtures of shape and colour, comes to affright them? Nothing but the apprehensions of harm, that accompanies those things. Did a Child suck every Day a new Nurse, I make account it would be no more affrighted, with the change of Faces at Six Months old than at Sixty. The reason then, why it will not come to a Stranger, is, because having been accustomed to receive its Food and Kind Usage only from one or two, that are about it, the Child apprehends, by coming into the Arms of a Stranger, the being taken from what delights and feeds it, and every moment supplies its Wants, which it often feels, and therefore fears when the Nurse is away.

The only thing, we naturally are afraid of, is Pain, or loss of Pleasure. And because these are not annex'd to any shape, colour, or size of visible Objects, we are frighted with none of them, till either we have felt Pain from them, or have Notions put into us, that they will do us harm. The pleasant brightness, and lustre of flame, and fire, so delights Children, that at first they always desire to be handling of it: But when constant Experience has convinced them, by the exquisite Pain it has put them to, how cruel and unmerciful it is, they are afraid to touch it, and carefully avoid it. This being the ground of Fear, 'tis not hard to find whence it arises, and how it is to be cured in all mistaken Objects of Terror. And when the Mind is confirm'd against them, and has got a mastery over it self, and its usual Fears, in lighter Occasions; it is in a good preparation to meet more real Dangers. Your Child shrieks, and runs away at the sight of a Frog; Let another catch it, and lay it down at a good distance from him: At first accustom him to look upon it; When he can do that, then to come nearer to it, and see it leap without Emotion; then to touch it lightly when it is held fast in another's hand; and so on, till he can come to handle it as confidently

as a Butter-fly, or a Sparrow. By the same way any other vain Terrors may be remov'd; if Care be taken, that you go not too fast, and push not the Child on to a new degree of assurance, till he be throughly confirm'd in the former. And thus the young Souldier is to be train'd
5 on to the Warfare of Life; wherein Care is to be taken, that more things be not represented as dangerous, than really are so; and then, that whatever you observe him to be more frighted at than he should, you be sure to tole[45] him on to by insensible degrees, till he at last, quitting his Fears, masters the Difficulty, and comes off with Applause. Suc-
10 cesses of this Kind often repeated, will make him find, that Evils are not always so certain, or so great, as our Fears represent them; and that the way to avoid them is not to run away, or be discompos'd, dejected, and deterr'd by Fear, where either our Credit, or Duty requires us to go on.
15 But since the great Foundation of Fear in Children is Pain, the way to harden, and fortifie Children against Fear and Danger, is to accustom them to suffer Pain. This 'tis possible will be thought, by kind Parents, a very unnatural thing towards their Children; And by most, unreasonable, to endeavour to reconcile any one to the sense of Pain,
20 by bringing it upon him. 'Twill be said, it may perhaps give the Child an aversion for him that makes him suffer; but can never recommend to him suffering it self. This is a strange Method. You will not have Children whipp'd and punish'd for their Faults, but you would have them tormented for doing well, or for Tormenting's sake. I doubt not
25 but such Objections as these will be made, and I shall be thought inconsistent with my self, or phantastical, in proposing it. I confess, it is a thing to be managed with great Discretion, and therefore it falls not out amiss, that it will not be received or relish'd, but by those who consider well, and look into the Reason of Things. I would not have
30 Children much beaten for their Faults, because I would not have them think bodily Pain the greatest Punishment: And I would have them, when they do well, be sometimes put in Pain; for the same Reason; that they might be accustom'd to bear it without looking on it as the greatest Evil. How much Education may reconcile young People to
35 Pain, and Sufferance, the Example of *Sparta* does sufficiently shew: And they who have once brought themselves not to think bodily Pain the greatest of Evils, or that which they ought to stand most in fear of,

35 *Sparta* 5] *Sport* 3 4

45 'tole': entice, incite (*OED* s.v. toll, tole, *v.*¹).

have made no small advance towards Vertue. But I am not so foolish to propose the Lacedæmonian[46] Discipline in our Age, or Constitution: But yet I do say, that enuring Children gently to suffer some degrees of Pain without shrinking, is a way to gain firmness to their Minds, and lay a Foundation for Courage and Resolution, in the future parts of their Lives.

Not to bemoan them, or permit them to bemoan themselves, on every little Pain, they suffer, is the first Step to be made. But of this I have spoken elsewhere.

The next thing is sometimes designedly to put them in Pain: But care must be taken, that this be done, when the Child is in good humour, and satisfied of the good Will and Kindness of him that hurts him, at the time that he does it. There must no marks of Anger, or Displeasure, on the one side; nor Compassion, or Repenting, on the other, go along with it: And it must be sure to be no more than the Child can bear, without repining or taking it amiss, or for a Punishment. Managed by these degrees, and with such Circumstances, I have seen a Child run away laughing, with good smart Blows of a Wand on his Back, who would have cried for an unkind Word, and have been very sensible of the Chastisement of a cold Look, from the same Person. Satisfie a Child by a constant course of your Care, and Kindness, that you perfectly love him; and he may by degrees be accustom'd to bear very painful, and rough usage from you, without flinching or complaining: And this we see Children do every Day, in play one with another. The softer you find your Child is, the more you are to seek Occasions, at fit times, thus to harden him. The great Art in this is to begin with what is but very little painful, and to proceed by insensible degrees, when you are playing, and in good humour with him; and speaking well of him; And when you have once got him, to think himself made amends for his Suffering, by the Praise is given him for his Courage; when he can take a Pride in giving such marks of his Manliness; and can preferr the Reputation of being Brave and Stout, to the avoiding a little Pain, or the Shrinking under it; you need not despair in time, and by the assistance of his growing Reason, to master his timorousness, and mend the weakness of his Constitution. As he grows bigger, he is to be set upon bolder Attempts, than his natural Temper carries him to; and whenever he is observ'd to flinch, from what one has reason to think he would come off well in, if

---

[46] 'Lacedæmonian', of Lacedæmon, the normal ancient name of Sparta, where boys were whipped to fortify them against pain.

he had but Courage to Undertake; That he should be assisted in at first, and by degrees shamed to, till at last Practice has given more Assurance, and with it a mastery; which must be rewarded with great Praise, and the good Opinion of others, for his Performance. When by
5 these Steps he has got Resolution enough not to be deterr'd, from what he ought to do, by the apprehension of Danger; when Fear does not, in suddain or hazardous Occurrences, discompose his Mind, set his Body a trembling, and make him unfit for Action, or run away from it, he has then the Courage of a rational Creature: And such an Hardi-
10 ness we should endeavour by Custom and Use to bring Children to, as proper Occasions come in our way.

§. 116. ᵏ⁻One thing I have frequently observed in Children, that when they have got possession of any poor Creature, they are apt to use it ill: They often *torment*, and treat very roughly young Birds, But-
15 terflies, and such other poor Animals, which fall into their Hands, and that with a seeming kind of Pleasure. This I think should be watched in them, and if they incline to any such *Cruelty*, they should be taught the contrary Usage. For the custom of tormenting and killing of Beasts will, by degrees, harden their Minds even towards Men; and they who
20 delight in the suffering and destruction of inferiour Creatures, will not be apt to be very compassionate or benigne to those of their own kind. ˡ⁻Our Practice⁻ˡ takes notice of this in the exclusion of *Butchers* from Juries of Life and Death. Children should from the beginning be bred up in an abhorrence of *killing*, or tormenting any living Creature; and
25 be taught not to *spoil* or destroy any thing, unless it be for the preservation or advantage of some other, that is Nobler. And truly, if the preservation of all Mankind, as much as in him lies, were every one's persuasion, as indeed it is every one's Duty, and the true Principle to regulate our Religion, Politicks and Morality by, the World would be
30 much quieter, and better natur'd than it is. But to return to our present Business; I cannot but commend both the Kindness and Prudence of a Mother I knew, who was wont always to indulge her Daughters, when any of them desired Dogs, Squirils, Birds, or any such things, as young Girls use to be delighted with: But then, when they had them, they

§§ 116–17 *Cruelty.*

---

12 116] 110 ɪ

ᵏ⁻ᵏ **Corr.** 829 (ii. 733). *Cf.* 929 (iii. 182): 'There is another ill disposition commonly to be observed in children, which I, who perhaps have noe more reve⟨rend op⟩inion of my two legged Companions, then others, cannot yet beleive to come from nature ...'.
ˡ⁻ˡ Our law **Corr.** 829 (ii. 733)

must be sure to keep them well and look diligently after them, that they wanted nothing, or were not ill used. For if they were negligent in their Care of them, it was counted a great Fault; which often forfeited their Possession, or at least they fail'd not to be rebuked for it; whereby they were early taught Diligence and good Nature. And indeed, I think People should be accustomed, from their Cradles, to be tender to all sensible Creatures, and to spoil or *waste* nothing at all.$^{-k}$

$^{m-}$This delight they take in *doing of Mischief*, whereby I mean spoiling of any thing to no purpose; but more especially the Pleasure they take to put any thing in Pain, that is capable of it, I cannot persuade my self to be any other than a foreign and introduced Disposition, an habit borrowed from Custom and Conversation. People teach Children to strike, and laugh, when they hurt, or see harm come to others: And they have the Examples of most about them, to confirm them in it. All the Entertainment and talk of History is of nothing almost but Fighting and Killing: And the Honour and Renown, that is bestowed on Conquerours (who for the most part are but the great Butchers of Mankind) farther mislead growing Youth, who by this means come to think Slaughter the laudable Business of Mankind, and the most Heroick of Vertues. By these Steps unnatural Cruelty is planted in us; and what Humanity abhorrs, Custom reconciles and recommends to us, by laying it in the way to Honour. Thus, by Fashion and Opinion, that comes to be a Pleasure, which in it self neither is, nor can be any. This ought carefully to be watched, and early remedied, so as to settle and cherish the contrary, and more natural Temper of Benignity and *Compassion* in the room of it: But still by the same gentle Methods, which are to be applied to the other two Faults before mentioned. It may not perhaps be unseasonable here to add this farther Caution, *viz.* That the Mischiefs, or Harms, that come by Play, Inadvertency, or Ignorance, and were not known to be Harms, or designed for Mischief's sake, though they may perhaps be sometimes of considerable damage, yet are not at all, or but very gently, to be taken notice of.$^{-m}$ For this, I think, I cannot too often inculcate, That whatever miscarriage a Child is guilty of, and whatever be the consequence of it, the thing to be regarded in taking notice of it, is only what root it springs

5

10

15

20

25

30

35

7–8 *run on* **1**   15 Entertainment] Entertainments **1**   18 mislead] misleads **1**
20–2 of Vertues . . . laying it] Vertue. This Custom plants unnatural Appetites, and
reconciles us to that, which it has laid **1**   22 way to] way of **NN**   27–9 It may
. . . That] But pray remember, that **1**   34 is] be **1**

$^{m-m}$ **Corr.** 929 (iii. 182)

from, and what habit it is like to establish; And to that the Correction ought to be directed, and the Child not to suffer any punishment, for any harm which may have come by his play or inadvertency. The Faults to be amended lie in the Mind; and if they are such, as either
5 Age will cure, or no ill habits will follow from; The present Action, whatever displeasing Circumstances it may have, is to be passed by without any Animadversion.

§. 117. Another way to instill Sentiments of Humanity, and to keep them lively in young folks, will be, to accustom them to Civility in their
10 Language, and Deportment, towards their Inferiours and the meaner sort of People, particularly Servants. It is not unusual to observe the Children in Gentlemens Families, treat the Servants of the House with domineering Words, Names of Contempt, and an imperious Carriage; as if they were of another Race, and Species beneath them.
15 Whether ill Example, the Advantage of Fortune, or their natural Vanity inspire this Haughtiness, it should be prevented, or weeded out; and a gentle, courteous, affable Carriage towards the lower Ranks of Men, placed in the room of it. No part of their Superiority will be hereby lost; but the distinction increased, and their authority streng-
20 then'd; when Love in Inferiours is joyn'd to outward Respect; and an esteem of the Person has a share in their Submission: And Domesticks will pay a more ready and cheerful Service, when they find themselves not spurn'd, because Fortune has laid them below the level of others, at their Masters feet. Children should not be suffer'd to lose the Con-
25 sideration of Humane Nature, in the shufflings of outward Conditions. The more they have, the better humour'd they should be taught to be; and the more compassionate, and gentle to those of their Brethren, who are placed lower, and have scantier Portions. If they are suffer'd from their Cradles to treat Men ill and rudely, because, by
30 their Father's Title, they think they have a little Power over them, at best it is ill bred, and if Care be not taken, will, by degrees, nurse up their natural Pride into an habitual Contempt of those beneath them. And where will that probably end; But in Oppression and Cruelty?

§. 118. [n-]Curiosity in Children (which I had occasion just to mention
35 §. 108.) is but an appetite after Knowledge; and therefore ought to be encouraged in them, not only as a good sign, but as the great Instru-

§§ 118–22 *Curiosity.*

---

3 which] *add.* **3**   8–33 § 117 *add.* **3**   34 118] 111 **1**   35 108 *ed.*] 103 **1** (*recte*), **3 4 5**
[n-n] §§ 118–21 *slightly varied from* **Corr.** 829 (ii. 729–32); *cf.* 822 (ii. 720)

ment Nature has provided, to remove that Ignorance, they were born with; and which, without this busie *Inquisitiveness*, will make them dull and useless Creatures. The ways to encourage it, and keep it active and busie, are, I suppose, these following:

1. Not to check or discountenance any *Enquiries* he shall make, nor suffer them to be laugh'd at; but to *answer* all his *Questions*, and *explain* the Matters, he desires to know, so as to make them as much intelligible to him, as suits the capacity of his Age and Knowledge. But confound not his Understanding with Explications or Notions, that are above it; or with the variety or number of Things, that are not to his present purpose. Mark what 'tis his Mind aims at in the *Question*, and not what Words he expresses it in: And when you have informed and satisfied him in that, you shall see how his Thoughts will enlarge themselves, and how by fit Answers he may be led on farther than perhaps you could imagine. For Knowledge is grateful to the Understanding, as Light to the Eyes: Children are pleased and delighted with it exceedingly, especially if they see, that their *Enquiries* are regarded, and that their desire of Knowing is encouraged and commended. And I doubt not, but one great reason, why many Children abandon themselves wholly to silly Sports, and trifle away all their time insipidly, is, because they have found their *Curiosity* bauk'd, and their *Enquiries* neglected. But had they been treated with more Kindness and Respect, and their *Questions* answered, as they should, to their satisfaction; I doubt not but they would have taken more pleasure, in learning and improving their Knowledge, wherein there would be still newness and variety, which is what they are delighted with, than in returning over and over to the same Play and Play-things.

§. 119. 2. To this serious answering their *Questions*, and informing their Understandings, in what they desire, as if it were a matter that needed it, should be added some peculiar ways of *Commendation*. Let others whom they esteem, be told before their faces of the knowledge, they have in such and such things; and since we are all, even from our Cradles, vain and proud Creatures, let their Vanity be flattered with Things, that will do them good; and let their Pride set them on work on something which may turn to their advantage. Upon this ground you shall find, that there cannot be a greater spur to the attaining what

---

4 busie] vigorous 1   13–14 enlarge . . . he] proceed on to other things, and how by fit Answers to his Enquiries, he 1   15–16 is . . . Understanding,] to the Understanding is acceptable, 1   16 Children] and Children 1   20–1 Sports . . . insipidly,] play, and spend all their time in trifling, 1   28 119] 112 1

you would have the eldest learn, and know himself, than to set him upon *teaching* it *his younger Brothers* and Sisters.

§. 120. 3. As Children's *Enquiries* are not to be slighted; so also great care is to be taken, that they *never* receive *Deceitful* and *Eluding*
5 *Answers.* They easily perceive when they are slighted, or deceived; and quickly learn the trick of Neglect, Dissimulation, and Falshood, which they observe others to make use of. We are not to intrench upon Truth in any Conversation, but least of all with Children; since if we play false with them, we not only deceive their Expectation, and
10 hinder their Knowledge, but corrupt their Innocence, and teach them the worst of Vices. They are Travellers newly arrived in a strange Country, of which they know nothing: We should therefore make Conscience not to mis-lead them. And though their *Questions* seem sometimes not very material, yet they should be seriously answer'd:
15 For however they may appear to us (to whom they are long since known) *Enquiries* not worth the making; they are of moment to those, who are wholly ignorant. Children are strangers to all we are acquainted with; and all the things they meet with, are at first unknown to them, as they once were to us: And happy are they who
20 meet with civil People, that will comply with their Ignorance, and help them to get out of it.

If you or I now should be set down in *Japan*, with all our Prudence and Knowledge about us, a Conceit whereof makes us perhaps so apt to slight the Thoughts and *Enquiries* of Children; should we, I say, be
25 set down in *Japan*, we should, no doubt (if we would inform our selves of what is there to be known) ask a thousand Questions, which to a supercilious or inconsiderate° *Japaner*, would seem very idle and impertinent; though to us they would be very material and of importance to be resolved; and we should be glad to find a Man so com-
30 plaisant and courteous, as to satisfie our Demands, and instruct our Ignorance.

When any new thing comes in their way, Children usually ask, the common *Question* of a Stranger: *What is it?* Whereby they ordinarily mean nothing but the Name; and therefore to tell them how it is call'd,
35 is usually the proper Answer to that Demand. The next Question

3 120] 113 **1**   slighted] slight **NN** slightd **NA**   21–2 *run on* **1**   27 inconsiderate] inconsiderable **1**   28–9 though . . . and we] and yet to us would be natural: And we **1**   29–30 complaisant . . . Demands,] kind and humane, as to answer them, **1**   31–2 *run on* **1**

° **Corr.** 829 (ii. 731) *as* **1**

usually is: *What is it for?* And to this it should be answered truly and directly: The use of the thing should be told, and the way explained, how it serves to such a Purpose, as far as their Capacities can comprehend it. And so of any other Circumstances they shall ask about it; not turning them going, till you have given them all the satisfaction they are capable of; and so leading them by your Answers into farther Questions. And perhaps to a grown Man, such Conversation will not be altogether so idle and insignificant, as we are apt to imagine. The native and untaught Suggestions of inquisitive Children, do often offer things, that may set a considering Man's Thoughts on work. And I think there is frequently more to be learn'd from the unexpected Questions of a Child, than the Discourses of Men, who talk in a road, according to the Notions they have borrowed, and the Prejudices of their Education.

§. 121. 4. Perhaps it may not sometimes be amiss to excite their Curiosity, by bringing strange and new things in their way, on purpose to engage their Enquiry, and give them occasion to inform themselves about them: And if by chance their Curiosity leads them to ask, what they should not know; it is a great deal better to tell them plainly, That it is a thing that belongs not to them to know, than to pop them off with a Falshood, or a frivolous Answer.⁻ⁿ

§. 122. ᵖ⁻*Pertness*, that appears sometimes so early, proceeds from a Principle, that seldom accompanies a strong Constitution of Body, or ripens into a strong Judgment of Mind. If it were desirable to have a Child a more brisk Talker, I believe there might be ways found to make him so: But, I suppose a wise Father had rather that his Son should be able and useful, when a Man, than pretty Company, and a Diversion to others, whilst a Child: Though if that too were to be consider'd, I think I may say, there is not so much pleasure to have a Child prattle agreeably, as to reason well. Encourage therefore his *Inquisitiveness* all you can, by satisfying his Demands, and informing his Judgment, as far as it is capable. When his Reasons are any way tolerable, let him find the Credit and Commendation of it; And when they are quite out of the way, let him, without being laugh'd at for his Mistake, be gently put into the right; And if he shew a forwardness to be reasoning about things that come in his way, take care as much as you can, that no body check this

15 121] 114 **1**   22 122] 115 **1**   35–6 if . . . way,] *add.* **3**   36–186.2 no body . . . him.] in this Inclination, he shews to reasoning about every thing, no body bauk, or impose [Inpose **NN**] upon him. **1**

ᵖ⁻ᵖ *Earlier version in* **Corr.** 845 (ii. 789–90)

Inclination in him, or mislead it by captious or fallacious ways of talking with him. For when all is done, this, as the highest and most important Faculty of our Minds, deserves the greatest Care and Attention in cultivating it; The right improvement, and exercise of our
5 Reason, being the highest Perfection, that a Man can attain to in this Life.⁻ᴾ

§. 123. ᑫ⁻Contrary to this busie inquisitive Temper there is sometimes observable in Children, a *listless carelesness*, a want of regard to any thing, and a sort of *trifling* even at their Business. This *Sauntring*⁴⁷
10 Humour I look on, as one of the worst Qualities can appear in a Child, as well as one of the hardest to be cured, where it is natural. But it being liable to be mistaken in some Cases, care must be taken to make a right Judgment concerning that *trifling* at their Books or Business, which may sometimes be complained of in a Child. Upon the first
15 suspicion a Father has, that his Son is of a *Sauntring* Temper, he must carefully observe him, whether he be *listless* and *indifferent* in all his Actions, or whether in some things alone he be slow and sluggish, but in others vigorous and eager. For though he find that he does loyter at his Book, and let a good deal of the time, he spends in his Chamber or
20 Study, run idly away; he must not presently conclude, that this is from a *sauntring* Humour in his Temper. It may be childishness, and a preferring something to his Study, which his Thoughts run on: And he dislikes his Book, as is natural, because it is forced upon him as a Task. To know this perfectly, you must watch him at play, when he is
25 out of his Place and time of Study, following his own Inclinations; and see there, whether he be stirring and active; whether he designs any thing, and with labour and eagerness pursues it, till he has accomplished what he aimed at; or whether he *lazily* and *listlesly dreams away his time*. If this sloth be only, when he is about his Book, I think it may
30 be easily cured. If it be in his Temper, it will require a little more Pains and Attention to remedy it.

§. 124. If you are satisfied by his earnestness at play, or any thing else he sets his Mind on, in the intervals between his Hours of Business, that he is not of himself inclin'd to *laziness*, but that only want of relish
35 of his Book makes him negligent, and *sluggish* in his application to it.

§ 123–7 *Sauntring.*

7 123] 116 **1**   26 stirring] vigorous **1**   32 124] 117 **1**   34 but that] but **1**

ᑫ⁻ᑫ §§ 123–7 *rewritten from* **Corr.** 1370 (iv. 222–5)

⁴⁷ '*Sauntring*', sauntering, dawdling, loitering (*OED*).

The first step is to try by talking to him kindly of the folly and inconvenience of it, whereby he loses a good part of his time, which he
might have for his diversion: But be sure to talk calmly and kindly, and
not much at first, but only these plain Reasons in short. If this prevails,
you have gain'd the point in the most desireable way, which is that of 5
Reason and Kindness. If this softer application prevails not, try to
shame him out of it, by laughing at him for it, asking every day, when
he comes to Table, if there be no Strangers there, how long he was that
Day about his Business; And if he has not done it, in the time he might
be well supposed to have dispatch'd it, expose and turn him into ridi- 10
cule for it; but mix no chiding; only put on a pretty cold Brow towards
him, and keep it till he reform; and let his Mother, Tutor, and all
about him do so too. If this work not the effect you desire, then tell
him, he shall be no longer troubled with a Tutor, to take care of his
Education, you will not be at the Charge to have him spend his time 15
idly with him; But since he preferrs this or that [whatever Play he
delights in] to his Book, that only he shall do; and so in earnest set him
on work on his beloved Play, and keep him steadily and in earnest to it
Morning and Afternoon, till he be fully surfeited, and would at any
rate change it for some hours at his Book again. But when you thus set 20
him a Task of his Play, you must be sure to look after him your self, or
set some-body else to do it, that may constantly see him imploy'd in it,
and that he be not permitted to be idle at that too. I say, your self look
after him; for it is worth the Father's while, whatever Business he has,
to bestow Two or Three Days upon his Son, to cure so great a Mis- 25
chief, as is *Sauntring* at his Business.

§. 125. This is what I propose, if it be *Idleness*, not from his general
Temper, but a peculiar or acquir'd aversion to Learning, which you
must be careful to examine, and distinguish. But though you have your
Eyes upon him, to watch what he does with the time which he has at 30
his own disposal, yet you must not let him perceive, that you, or any
body else do so. For that may hinder him from following his own Inclination, which he being full of, and not daring for fear of you, to

5 in the . . . way,] by the most desirable [**NN**; desireable **NA**] Remedy, 1   that of]
add. 3   6 this softer application] it 1   7–8 when . . . Strangers there,] if there
be no Strangers there, when he comes to Table, 1   27 125] 118 1   29 distinguish.] distinguish; which you shall certainly know by the way above propos'd. 1
32 hinder] restrain 1   33–188.9 which . . . his own] and that being the thing his
Head or Heart is upon, and not daring to prosecute it for fear of you, he may forbear doing
other things, and so seem to be idle and negligent; when in truth it is nothing, but being
intent on that, which the fear of your Eye or Knowledge keeps him from executing. You
must therefore, when you would try him, give full Liberty: But let some body, whom you

prosecute what his Head and Heart are set upon, he may neglect all other things, which then he rellishes not, and so may seem to be idle and listless, when in truth it is nothing, but being intent on that, which the fear of your Eye or Knowledge keeps him from executing. To be
5 clear in this Point, the Observation must be made, when you are out of the way, and he not so much as under the restraint of a Suspicion, that any body has an Eye upon him. In those Seasons of perfect Freedom, let somebody, you can trust, mark how he spends his time; whether he unactively loiters it away, when without any check he is left to his own
10 Inclination. Thus by his imploying of such times of Liberty, you will easily discern whether it be *listlesness* in his Temper, or aversion to his Book, that makes him *saunter* away his time of Study.

    §. 126. If some defect in his Constitution has cast a damp on his Mind, and he be naturally listless and dreaming, this unpromising disposition
15 is none of the easiest to be dealt with; because generally, carrying with it an unconcernedness for the future, it wants the two great Springs of Action *Foresight* and *Desire*; which how to plant and increase, where Nature has given a cold and contrary temper, will be the question. As soon as you are satisfied that this is the case, you must carefully enquire,
20 whether there be nothing he delights in: Inform your self, what it is he is most pleased with; And if you can find any particular Tendency his Mind hath, increase it all you can, and make use of that to set him on work, and to excite his Industry. If he loves Praise, or Play, or fine Cloths, *&c.* or, on the other side, dreads Pain, Disgrace, or your Dis-
25 pleasure; *&c.* whatever it be that he loves most, except it be Sloth (for that will never set him on work) let that be made use of to quicken him, and make him bestir himself. For in this *listless Temper*, you are not to fear an excess of Appetite (as in all other cases) by cherishing it. 'Tis that which you want, and therefore must labour to raise and increase. For
30 where there is no Desire, there will be no Industry.

can trust, observe what he does, and it will be best he should have his Play-day of Liberty, when you, and all, that he may suspect to have an Eye upon him, are abroad, that so he may without any check follow his natural 1   13 126] 119 1   13–23 If some . . . Industry.] If *listlesness* and dreaming be his natural Disposition. This unpromising Temper is one of the hardest to be dealt with, because it generally carrying with it an indifferency for future things, may be attributed to want of fore-sight and want of desire: and how to plant or increase either of these, where Nature has given a cold or contrary Temper, is not I think very easie. As soon as it is perceived, the first thing to be done, is to find out his most predominate Passion, and carefully examine, what it is, to which the greatest bent of his Mind has the most steady and earnest Tendency: And when you have found that, you must set that on work to excite his Industry to any thing else. 1 24 Pain . . . or] Shame and Disgrace, 1   26–7 quicken . . . himself.] excite him to activity. 1   29 raise] stir up 1

§. 127. If you have not hold enough upon him this way, to stir up Vigor and Activity in him, you must imploy him in some constant bodily Labour, whereby he may get an habit of doing something. The keeping him hard to some Study were the better way to get him an habit of exercising and applying his Mind. But because this is an invisible Attention, and no body can tell when he is, or is not idle at it, you must find bodily imployments for him, which he must be constantly busied in, and kept to: And if they have some little hardship and shame in them, it may not be the worse; that they may the sooner weary him, and make him desire to return to his Book. But be sure, when you exchange his Book for his other Labour, set him such a Task, to be done in such a time, as may allow him no opportunity to be idle. Only after you have by this way brought him to be Attentive and Industrious at his Book, you may, upon his dispatching his Study within the time set him, give him, as a Reward, some respit from his other Labour; which you may diminish,[r] as you find him grow more and more steddy in his Application, and at last wholly take off, when his *sauntering* at his Book is cured.[-q]

§. 128. [s-]We formerly observed, that Variety and Freedom was that that delighted Children, and recommended their Plays to them: And that therefore their Book, or any thing we would have them learn, should not be enjoined them *as Business*. This their Parents, Tutors, and Teachers, are apt to forget; And their impatience, to have them busied in what is fit for them to do, suffers them not to deceive them into it: But by the repeated Injunctions they meet with, Children quickly distinguish between what is required of them, and what not. When this Mistake has once made his Book uneasie to him, the Cure is to be applied at the other end. And since it will be then too late to endeavour to make it a play to him, you must take the contrary course; observe what Play he is most delighted with; enjoin that, and make him play so many Hours every Day, not as a punishment for playing, but as if it were the business required of him. This, if I mistake not, will, in a few Days, make him so weary of his most beloved Sport, that he will preferr his Book, or any thing to it; Especially if it may redeem him from any part of the task of play is set him, and he may be suffered

§§ 128–9 *Compulsion.*

---

1 127] 120 **1**   9 that they may] to make them **1**   10 make him] *add.* **3**
19 128] 121 **1**

[r] increase **Corr.** 1370 (iv. 225)   [s-s] **Corr.** 943 (iii. 224–5)

to imploy some part of the time destined to his *Task of Play*, in his Book, or such other Exercise as is really useful to him. This I at least think a better Cure, than that Forbidding, (which usually increases the Desire) or any other Punishment, should be made use of to remedy it.

5 For when you have once glutted his Appetite (which may safely be done in all things but eating and drinking) and made him surfeit of what you would have him avoid, you have put into him a Principle of Aversion, and you need not so much fear afterwards his longing for the same thing again.⁻ˢ

10 §. 129. ᵗ⁻This I think is sufficiently evident. That Children generally hate to be idle. All the care then is, that their busie Humour should be constantly imploy'd in something of use to them; which if you will attain, you must make, what you would have them do, a Recreation to them, and not a *Business*. The way to do this, so that they may not per-

15 ceive you have any hand in it, is this proposed here; *viz*. To make them weary of that which you would not have them do, by enjoyning, and making them, under some pretence or other, do it, till they are surfeited. For example: Does your Son play at Top, and scourge⁴⁸ too much? Enjoin him to play so many Hours every Day, and look that he

20 do it; and you shall see he will quickly be sick of it, and willing to leave it. By this means making the Recreations you dislike *a Business* to him, he will of himself with delight betake himself to those things, you would have him do; especially if they be proposed as Rewards for having performed his *Task* in that Play is commanded him. For if he

25 be ordered every Day to whip his Top, so long as to make him suffi-ciently weary, do you not think he will apply himself with eagerness to his Book, and wish for it, if you promise it him as a Reward of having whipped his Top lustily, quite out all the time that is set him? Chil-dren, in the things they do, if they comport with their Age, find little

30 difference so they may be doing: The esteem they have for one thing above another, they borrow from others: So that what those about them make to be a Reward to them, will really be so. By this Art it is in their Governour's choice, whether *Scotch-hoppers* shall reward their *Dancing*, or *Dancing* their *Scotch-hoppers*; whether Peg-top, or Read-

35 ing; playing at Trap, or studying the Globes, shall be more acceptable and pleasing to them; All that they desire being to be busie, and busie, as they imagine, in things of their own choice, and which they receive

10 129] 122 1

ᵗ⁻ᵗ **Corr.** 999 (iii. 348–50)

⁴⁸ 'scourge', whip a top, cf. 'Scourge-top', a spinning-top (*OED*).

as Favours from their Parents, or others for whom they have respect, and with whom they would be in credit. A Sett of Children thus ordered, and kept from the ill example of others, would all of them, I suppose, with as much earnestness and delight, learn to read, write, and what else one would have them, as others do their ordinary Plays: And the eldest being thus entered, and this made the fashion of the Place, it would be as impossible to hinder them from learning the one, as it is ordinarily to keep them from the other.⁻ᵗ

§. 130. ᵘ⁻Play-things I think Children should have, and of diverse sorts; but still to be in the custody of their Tutors, or some body else, whereof the Child should have in his power but one at once, and should not be suffered to have another, but when he restor'd that. This teaches them betimes to be careful of not losing, or spoiling the things they have: Whereas plenty and variety in their own keeping, makes them wanton and careless, and teaches them from the beginning to be Squanderers and Wasters. These, I confess, are little things, and such as will seem beneath the Care of a Governour: But nothing, that may form Children's Minds, is to be over-look'd and neglected, and what-soever introduces Habits, and settles Customs in them, deserves the Care and Attention of their Governours, and is not a small thing in its Consequences.⁻ᵘ

One thing more about Childrens Play-things may be worth their Parents care. Though it be agreed, they should have of several sorts, yet, I think, they should have none bought for them. This will hinder that great variety they are often over-charg'd with, which serves only to teach the Mind to wander after change, and superfluity; to be unquiet, and perpetually stretching it self after something more still, though it knows not what; and never to be satisfied with what it hath. The Court, that is made to People of condition, in such kind of presents to their Children, does the little ones great harm. By it they are taught Pride, Vanity, and Covetousness, almost before they can speak: And I have known a young Child so distracted with the number, and Variety of his Play-games, that he tired his Maid every day to look them over; and was so accustomed to abundance, that he never thought he had enough, but was always asking, What more? what

---

§ 130 *Play-Games.*

---

9 130] 123 **1**   diverse] all **1**   10 custody] keeping **1**   22–193.2 One . . . neglected.] *add.* **3**   30 ones] one **4 5**

ᵘ⁻ᵘ **Corr.** 943 (iii. 224–5)

more? what new Thing shall I have? A good Introduction to Moderate Desires, and the ready way to make a contented happy Man!

How then shall they have the Play-Games you allow them, if none must be bought for them? I answer, They should make them themselves, or at least endeavour it; and set themselves about it: Till then they should have none; and till then they will want none of any great artifice. A smooth Peble, a piece of Paper, the Mothers Bunch of Keys, or any thing they cannot hurt themselves with, serves as much to divert little Children, as those more chargeable[49] and curious Toys from the Shops, which are presently put out of order, and broken. Children are never dull or out of humour for want of such Play-things, unless they have been used to them. When they are little, whatever occurs serves the turn; and as they grow bigger, if they are not stored by the expensive Folly of others, they will make them themselves. Indeed, when they once begin to set themselves to work about any of their Inventions, they should be taught, and assisted: But should have nothing, whilst they lazily sit still, expecting to be furnish'd from others hands, without imploying their own. And if you help them where they are at a stand, it will more endear you to them, than any chargeable Toys you shall buy for them. Play-things which are above their Skill to make; as Tops, Gigs,[50] Battledors,[51] and the like, which are to be used with labour, should indeed be procur'd them: These 'tis convenient they should have, not for Variety, but Exercise. But these too should be given them as bare as might be. If they had a Top, the Scourge-stick[52] and Leather-strap should be left to their own making and fitting. If they sit gaping to have such things drop into their mouths, they should go without them. This will accustom them to seek for what they want, in themselves, and in their own indeavours: whereby they will be taught Moderation in their Desires, Application, Industry, Thought, Contrivance, and Good Husbandry; Qualities that will be useful to them when they are Men, and therefore cannot be learnt too soon, nor fixed too deep. All the Plays and Diversions of Children should be directed towards good and useful Habits, or else they will introduce ill ones. Whatever they do leaves some impression on that tender

18 others] other **5**

[49] 'chargeable', costly (*OED*).

[50] 'Gig', obs. spinning-, or whip-top (*OED*).

[51] 'Battledors', small rackets used in playing with a shuttlecock (*OED*).

[52] 'Scourge-stick', stick to whip a spinning-top (*OED*). Modern children use a piece of string instead of a 'Leather-strap'.

Age, and from thence they receive a Tendency to Good or Evil: And whatever hath such an influence ought not to be neglected.

§. 131. *Lying* is so ready and cheap a Cover for any Miscarriage, and so much in fashion amongst all sorts of People, that a Child can hardly avoid observing the use is made of it on all occasions; and so can scarce be kept, without great care, from getting into it. But it is so ill a Quality, and the mother of so many ill ones that spawn from it, and take shelter under it, that a Child should be brought up in the greatest abhorrence of it imaginable. It should be always (when occasionally it comes to be mentioned) spoke of before him with the utmost detestation, as a Quality so wholly inconsistent with the Name and Character of a Gentleman, that no body of any Credit can bear the imputation of a Lye; A mark that it is judg'd the utmost disgrace, which debases a Man to the lowest degree of a shameful meanness, and ranks him with the most contemptible part of Mankind, and the abhorred Rascality; and is not to be endured in any one, who would converse with People of Condition, or have any Esteem or Reputation in the World. The first time he is found in a *Lye*, it should rather be wondered at as a monstrous Thing in him, than reproved as an ordinary Fault. If that keeps him not from relapsing, the next time he must be sharply rebuked, and fall into the state of great Displeasure of his Father and Mother, and all about him, who take notice of it. And if this way work not the Cure, you must come to blows. For after he has been thus warned, a premeditated *Lye* must always be looked upon as obstinacy, and never be permitted to 'scape unpunished.

§. 132. Children, afraid to have their Faults seen in their naked Colours, will, like the rest of the Sons of *Adam*, be apt to make *Excuses*. This is a Fault usually bordering upon, and leading to untruth, and is not to be indulged in them: But yet it ought to be cured rather with shame than roughness. If therefore when a Child is questioned for any thing,[53] his first Answer be an *Excuse*, warn him soberly to tell the truth; And then if he persists to shuffle it off with a *Falshood*, he must be chastised. But if he directly confess, you must commend his Ingenuity, and pardon the Fault, be it what it will; And pardon it so,

§ 131 *Lying.*   §§ 132–5 *Excuses.*

---

3 131] 124 1   10 spoke] be spoke **NA**   11–12 inconsistent ... of a] incompetent with a 1   13–16 A mark ... endured] that is proper only to beggar-Boys [**NN**; Beggar-Boys **NA**], and the abhorr'd Rascality, and not tolerable 1 17 The] And the 1   26 132] 125 1

53 'th ing' **NN**: a stop-press correction. See Introd. , pp. 54–5.

that you never so much as reproach him with it, or mention it to him again. For if you would have him in love with Ingenuity, and by a constant practice make it habitual to him, you must take care, that it never procure him the least inconvenience; But on the contrary, his own
5 Confession bringing always with it perfect Impunity, should be besides incouraged by some Marks of Approbation. If his *Excuse* be such at any time, that you cannot prove it to have any Falshood in it, let it pass for True, and be sure not to shew any Suspicion of it. Let him keep up his Reputation with you as high as is possible: For when
10 once he finds he has lost that, you have lost a great and your best hold upon him. Therefore let him not think he has the Character of a Liar with you, as long as you can avoid it without flattering him in it. Thus some slips in Truth may be over-looked. But after he has once been corrected for a *Lye*, you must be sure never after to pardon it in him,
15 when ever you find, and take notice to him, that he is guilty of it. For it being a Fault, which he has been forbid, and may, unless he be wilful, avoid, the repeating of it is perfect perversness, and must have the Chastisement due to that Offence.

§. 133. ᵛ⁻This is what I have thought concerning the general Method
20 of Educating a young Gentleman; Which though I am apt to suppose may have some influence on the whole course of his Education, yet I am far from imagining it contains all those particulars, which his growing Years, or peculiar Temper may require.⁻ᵛ But this being premised in general, we shall in the next place descend to a more par-
25 ticular Consideration of the several parts of his Education.

§. 134. ʷ⁻That which every Gentleman (that takes any care of his Education) desires for his Son, besides the Estate he leaves him, is contain'd (I suppose) in these four Things; *Virtue, Wisdom, Breeding*, and *Learning*. I will not trouble my self, whether these names do not
30 some of them sometimes stand for the same thing, or really include one another. It serves my turn here to follow the popular use of these Words; which, I presume, is clear enough to make me be understood, and I hope there will be no difficulty to comprehend my Meaning.⁻ʷ

19 133] 126 **1**   26 134] 127 **1**   29 names] words **1**

ᵛ⁻ᵛ *First part of* **H** § 47, **K** § 65. *Both conclude* Nay haveing writ these general part⟨s⟩ in the warmth of my running thoughts there may I suppose be many things I have overseen which if hereafter they shall offer them selves to my thoughts in any of the returns of my minde to its usuall and most acceptable imploym⟨en⟩t of thinking on you and yours I shall take the liberty to mention them to you   ʷ⁻ʷ **H** § 48, **K** § 66, *both preceded by separate para.* In the meane time haveing promised this in generall we will now descend to a more particular consideration of what in the Education of your Son I suppose may be aimed at [**H**; . . . consideration of your Sons Education **K**]

§. 135. ˣ⁻I place *Vertue* as the first and most necessary of those Endowments, that belong to a Man or a Gentleman; as absolutely requisite to make him valued and beloved by others, acceptable or tolerable to himself. Without that, I think, he will be happy neither in this, nor the other World.

§. 136. As the Foundation of this, there ought very early to be imprinted on his Mind a true Notion of *God*, as of the independent Supreme Being, Author and Maker of all Things, from whom we receive all our Good, who loves us, and gives us all Things. And consequent to this, instill into him a Love and Reverence of this Supreme Being. This is enough to begin with, without going to explain this matter any farther; for fear, least, by talking too early to him of Spirits, and being unseasonably forward to make him understand the incomprehensible Nature of that infinite Being, his Head be either fill'd with false, or perplexed with unintelligible Notions of him. Let him only be told upon occasion, that *God* made and governs all Things, hears and sees every Thing, and does all manner of Good to those that love and obey him. You will find that being told of such a *God*, other Thoughts will be apt to rise up fast enough in his Mind about him; which, as you observe them to have any mistakes, you must set right. And I think it would be better if Men generally rested in such an Idea of *God*, without being too Curious in their Notions about a Being, which all must acknowledge incomprehensible; whereby many, who have not strength and clearness of Thought, to distinguish between what they can and what they cannot know, run themselves into Superstition or Atheism, making *God* like themselves, or (because they cannot comprehend any thing else) none at all.⁻ˣ And I am apt to think, the keeping Children constantly Morning and Evening to acts of Devotion to God, as to their Maker, Preserver and Benefactor, in some plain and short Form of Prayer, suitable to their Age and Capacity, will be of much more use to them in Religion, Knowledge and Vertue, than to distract their Thoughts with curious Enquiries into his inscrutable Essence and Being.

§. 137. ʸ⁻Having by gentle degrees, as you find him capable of it,

§ 136 *God.*   § 137 *Spirits.*

---

1 135] 128 **1**   4 be happy neither] neither be happy **1**   6 136] 129 **1**
9 who] that **1**   10–11 to this . . . Being.] to it a Love and Reverence of him. **1**
16 occasion, that *God*] occasion of *God*, that **1**   27–33 And . . . Being.] *add.* **3**
34 137] 130 **1**

ˣ⁻ˣ **H** § 49; **K** § 67   ʸ⁻ʸ *Revision of first part of* **H** § 50; *of* **K** § 68 *entire*

setled such an Idea of God in his Mind, ᶻ⁻and taught him to *pray* to
him,⁻ᶻ and *praise* him, as the Author of his Being, and of all the good he
does or can enjoy; forbear any Discourse of other *Spirits*, till the mention of them coming in his way, upon occasion hereafter to be set
5 down, and his reading the Scripture-History, put him upon that
enquiry.

§. 138. But even then, and always whilst he is Young, be sure to
preserve his tender Mind from all Impressions and Notions of *Sprites*
and *Goblins*, or any fearful Apprehensions in the dark. This he will be
10 in danger of from the indiscretion of Servants, whose usual Method it
is to awe Children, and keep them in subjection, by telling them of
Raw-Head and *Bloody Bones*, and such other Names, as carry with
them the Idea's of some thing terrible and hurtful, which they have
reason to be afraid of, when alone, especially in the dark. This must be
15 carefully prevented. For though by this foolish way, they may keep
them from little Faults, yet the Remedy is much worse than the
Disease; and there is stamped upon their Imaginations Idea's, that follow them with Terror and Affrightment. Such *Bug-bear* Thoughts
once got into the tender Minds of Children, and being set on with a
20 strong impression, from the Dread that accompanies such Apprehensions, sink deep, and fasten themselves so as not easily, if ever, to be
got out again; and whilst they are there, frequently haunt them with
strange Visions, making Children dastards⁵⁴ when alone, and afraid of
their Shadows and Darkness all their Lives after. I have had those
25 complain to me, when Men, who had been thus used when young; that
though their Reason corrected the wrong Idea's they had then taken
in, and they were satisfied, that there was no cause to fear invisible
Beings more in the Dark, than in the Light, yet that these Notions
were apt still upon any occasion to start up first in their prepossess'd
30 Fancies, and not to be removed without some Pains. And to let you

§ 138 *Goblins.*

1–3 and . . . enjoy;] *add.* **3**   7 138] 131 **1**   8 *Sprites*] *Spirits* **5**   9–
11 This . . . it is] It being the usual Method of Servants **1**   13–14 thing . . . dark.]
hurtful terrible Things, inhabiting darkness. **1**   17 Imaginations] Minds **1**
18 Such] For such **1**   19–20 and . . . Apprehensions,] *add.* **3**   21 deep,] deep
there, **1**   24 after.] after. For it is to be taken notice, that the first Impressions sink
deepest into the Minds of Children, and the Notions, they are possess'd with when
young, are scarce by any Industry or Art ever after quite wiped out. **1**   26 then]
om. **5**   27 and] and though **1**

ᶻ⁻ᶻ *Add.* **K**

⁵⁴ 'dastards', despicable cowards (*OED*).

see, how lasting frightful Images are, that take place in the Mind early, I shall here tell you a pretty remarkable but true Story. There was in a Town in the West, a Man of a disturb'd Brain, whom the Boys used to teaze, when he came in their way: This Fellow one Day seeing in the Street one of those Lads, that used to vex him, step'd into a *Cutler's* 5 Shop he was near; and there seizing on a naked Sword, made after the Boy; who seeing him coming so armed, betook himself to his Feet, and ran for his Life; and by good luck, had Strength and Heels enough to reach his Father's House, before the Mad-man could get up to him. The Door was only latch'd; And when he had the Latch in his Hand, he 10 turn'd about his Head to see how near his pursuer was, who was at the entrance of the Porch with his Sword up, ready to strike, and he had just time to get in and clap to the Door to avoid the Blow, which though his Body escaped, his Mind did not. This frightning Idea made so deep an Impression there,[55] that it lasted many Years, if not all his Life after. For, 15 telling this Story when he was a Man, he said, That after that time till then, he never went in at that Door (that he could remember) at any time, without looking back, whatever Business he had in his Head, or how little soever, before he came thither, he thought of this Mad-man.*-y*

*a-*If Children were let alone, they would be no more afraid in the 20 Dark, than in broad Sun-shine: They would in their turns as much welcome the one for Sleep, as the other to Play in. There should be no distinction made to them, by any Discourse, of more danger or *terrible Things* in the one than the other: But if the folly of any one about them should do them this Harm, and make them think, there is any differ- 25 ence between being in the dark and winking, you must get it out of their Minds as soon as you can; and let them know, That God, who made all Things good for them, made the Night that they might sleep the better and the quieter; and that they being under his Protection, there is nothing in the dark to hurt them. What is to be known more of 30 God and Good Spirits, is to be deferr'd till the time we shall hereafter mention; and of Evil Spirits,*b* 'twill be well if you can keep him from wrong Fancies about them, till he is ripe for that sort of Knowledge.*-a*

21 than in] than of the 1   22 There] and there 1   25 and] to 1

a-a *Latter part of* **H** § 50; *first part of* **K** § 69   *b* **HK** *continue* they will doe what you can come to have notice of and phansys about early enough and sooner then would [**H**; could **K**] be desird

[55] Locke gives more examples of the effects of early frightening or disturbing experiences upon the adult, in the chapter on 'the association of ideas', added to the fourth edition of the *Essay* (2. 33).

§. 139. ᶜ⁻Having laid the Foundations of Vertue in a true Notion of a God, such as the Creed wisely teaches, as far as his Age is capable, and by accustoming him to pray to him; The next thing to be taken Care of, is to keep him exactly to speaking of *Truth*, and by all the ways imagin-
5 able inclining him to be *good natur'd*. Let him know that Twenty Faults are sooner to be forgiven, than the *straining of Truth*, to cover any one *by an Excuse*. And to teach him betimes to love, and be *good natur'd* to others, is to lay early the true Foundation of an honest Man:ᵈ All Injustice generally springing from too great Love of our selves, and too
10 little of others.⁻ᶜ

ᵉ⁻This is all I shall say of this Matter in general, and is enough for laying the first Foundations of Vertue in a Child. As he grows up, the Tendency of his natural Inclination must be observed; which, as it inclines him, more than is convenient, on one or t'other side, from the
15 right Path of Vertue, ought to have proper Remedies applied. For few of *Adam*'s Children are so happy, as not to be born with some Byass in their natural Temper, which it is the Business of Education either to take off, or counter-balance: But to enter into the Particulars of this, would be beyond the Design of this short Treatise of Education.⁻ᵉ I
20 intend not a Discourse of all the Vertues and Vices, and how each Vertue is to be attained, and every particular Vice by its peculiar Remedies cured. Though I have mentioned some of the most ordinary Faults, and the ways to be used in correcting them.

§. 140. ᶠ⁻*Wisdom* I take, in the popular acceptation, for a Man's
25 managing his Business ably, and with fore-sight in this World. This is the product of a good natural Temper, application of Mind, and Experience together, and so above the reach of Children. The greatest Thing that in them can be done towards it, is to hinder them, as much as may be, from being *Cunning*; which, being the Ape of *Wisdom*, is the
30 most distant from it that can be: And as an Ape, for the likeness it has to a Man, wanting what really should make him so, is by so much the uglier. *Cunning* is only the want of Understanding; which, because it

---

§ 139 *Truth.*   *Good nature.*   § 140 *Wisdom.*

---

1 139] 123 (*misprint for* 132) **1**   18 the] *om.* **5**   24 140] 133 **1**   27 and
... of] not to be taught **1**

ᶜ⁻ᶜ **H** § 51; *latter part of* **K** § 69   ᵈ Foundation for justice. **HK**   ᵉ⁻ᵉ *Revision of* **H** § 52, **K** § 70   ᶠ⁻ᶠ *Slight revision of* **H** § 53, **K** § 71, *which continue* I doe not suspect that your son is like to be of a coverd wily temp⟨e⟩r when I consider his make and from what stock he comes I am apt to thinke he will be quite of another strain and therefore I will not trouble you or myself any farther concerning this matt⟨e⟩r

cannot compass its ends[g] by direct ways, would do it by a Trick and
Circumvention; and the Mischief of it is, a *cunning* Trick helps but
once, but hinders ever after. No cover was ever made either so big, or
so fine as to hide its self. No Body was ever so *cunning* as to conceal
their being so: And when they are once discovered, every Body is shie, 5
every Body distrustful of *crafty* Men; and all the World forwardly joyn
to oppose and defeat them: Whilst the open, fair, *wise* Man has every
Body to make way for him, and goes directly to his Business.[-f] To
accustom a Child to have true Notions of things, and not to be satisfied till he has them; To raise his Mind to great and worthy Thoughts; 10
and to keep him at a distance from Falshood, and Cunning, which has
always a broad mixture of Falshood in it; is the fittest preparation of a
Child for *Wisdom*. The rest, which is to be learn'd from Time, Experience, and Observation, and an Acquaintance with Men, their Tempers, and Designs, is not to be expected in the ignorance and 15
inadvertency of Childhood, or the inconsiderate heats and unwariness
of Youth: All that can be done towards it, during this unripe Age, is, as
I have said, to accustom them to Truth and Sincerity; to a submission
to Reason; and, as much as may be, to reflection on their own Actions.

§. 141. [h-]The next good Quality belonging to a Gentleman, is *good* 20
Breeding. [-h] There are Two Sorts of *ill Breeding:* The one a *sheepish*
Bashfulness: And the other a *mis-becoming Negligence and Disrespect* in our
Carriage; Both which are avoided by duly observing this one Rule, *Not*
to think meanly of our selves, and not to think meanly of others.

§. 142. The first Part of this Rule must not be understood in opposi- 25
tion to Humility, but to Assurance. We ought not to think so well of
our selves, as to stand upon our own Value; and assume to our selves a
Preference before others, because of any Advantage, we may imagine,
we have over them; but Modestly to take what is offered, when it is our
due. But yet we ought to think so well of our selves, as to perform those 30
Actions which are incumbent on, and expected of us, without discomposure, or disorder; in whose presence soever we are; keeping that
respect and distance, which is due to every one's Rank and Quality.

§§ 141–2 *Breeding.*

---

13 *Wisdom* . . . is] *Wisdom*, which being 1   15 is] are 1   18 Truth . . . to a]
Truth, and 1   20 141] 134 1   25 142] 135 1   27–8 and . . . before] or
assume a Preference to 1

[g] businesse **HK**   [h-h] *Parallels the opening of* **H** § 54, **K** § 72: 'The next good
quality belonging to a gent⟨leman⟩ is good breeding and civility . . .'; *for the remainder, see*
§ 145. *This section, together with* §§ 142–5, *is anticipated in* **Corr.** 829 (ii. 732–3)

There is often in People, especially Children, a clownish shame-fac'dness before Strangers, or those above them: They are confounded in their Thoughts, Words, and Looks; and so lose themselves in that confusion, as not to be able to do any thing, or at least not do with that
5 freedom and gracefulness, which pleases, and makes them acceptable. The only cure for this, as for any other Miscarriage, is by use to intro-duce the contrary Habit. But since we cannot accustom our selves to converse with Strangers, and Persons of Quality, without being in their company, nothing can cure this part of *Ill-breeding*, but change
10 and variety of Company, and that of Persons above us.

  §. 143. As the before-mentioned consist in too great a concern, how to behave our selves towards others; so the other part of *Ill-breeding*, lies in the appearance of too *little care* of pleasing, or *shewing respect* to those we have to do with. To avoid this these two things are requisite:
15 First, a disposition of the Mind not to offend others; and, secondly, the most acceptable, and agreeable way of expressing that Disposi-tion. From the one, Men are called *Civil*; from the other *Well-fashion'd*. The latter of these is that decency and gracefulness of Looks, Voice, Words, Motions, Gestures, and of all the whole outward
20 Demeanour, which takes in Company, and makes those with whom we converse, easie and well pleased. This is, as it were, the Language whereby that internal Civility of the Mind is expressed; which, as other Languages are, being very much governed by the Fashion and Custom of every Country, must, in the Rules and Practice of it, be
25 learn'd chiefly from Observation, and the Carriage of those, who are allow'd to be exactly *well-bred*. The other part, which lies in the Mind, is that general Good-will and Regard for all People, which makes any one have a care not to shew, in his Carriage, any contempt, disrespect, or neglect of them; but to express, according to the Fashion and Way
30 of that Country, a respect and value for them, according to their Rank and Condition. It is a disposition of the mind that shews it self in the carriage whereby a Man avoids making any one uneasie in Conver-sation.

  § 143. *Breeding. Roughness. Contempt. Censoriness. Railery. Contradic-tion. Captiousness.*

---

  4 not do] not to do it **NN** not do it **NA**   11 143] 136 **1**   14 this these] these,
1   20 takes] pleases **1**   20–1 with . . . pleased.] easie and delighted, whom
we Converse [**NN**; converse **NA**] with. **1**   22–3 which . . . are,] and **1**
24 Country,] Country, as other Languages are, **1**   26 in the Mind,] deeper than
the out side, **5**   29 or neglect of] of neglect o **NN**   30 for] far **NN**   31–
203.12 It is . . . Young people.] *add.* **5**

I shall take notice of four qualities that are most directly opposite to this first, and most taking of all the Social Virtues. And from some one of these four it is that Incivility commonly has its rise. I shall set them down, that Children may be preserv'd or recover'd from their ill influence.

1. The First is, a Natural *Roughness* which makes a Man uncomplaisant to others, so that he has no deference for their inclinations, tempers, or conditions. 'Tis the sure badge of a Clown not to mind what pleases or displeases those he is with: and yet one may often find a Man in fashionable cloaths give an unbounded swing to his own humour and suffer it to justle or over-run any one that stands in its way, with a perfect indifferency how they take it. This is a Brutality that every one sees and abhors, and no body can be easy with: And therefore this finds no place in any one who would be thought to have the least tincture of *Good-breeding*. For the very end and business of *Good-breeding* is to supple the natural stifness and so soften Mens Tempers that they may bend to a compliance and accommodate themselves to those they have to do with.

2. Contempt or want of due respect discovered either in looks, words, or gesture: This from whome soever it comes, brings alway uneasiness with it. For no body can contentedly bear being slighted.

3. *Censoriousness* and finding fault with others has a direct opposition to *Civilty*. Men, whatever they are or are not guilty of would not have their faults displaid, and set in open view and broad day light before their own or other Peoples Eyes. Blemishes affixed to any one always carry shame with them: And the discovery or even bare imputation of any defect is not born without some uneasiness. *Railery* is the most refined way of exposing the faults of others. But because it is usually done with wit and good Language, and gives entertainment to the company, People are lead into a mistake, that where it keeps within fair bounds there is no incivility in it. And so the pleasantry of this sort of Conversation often introduces it amongst People of the better rank; and such Talkers are favourably heard and generally applauded by the laughter of the By-standers on their side. But they ought to consider, that the entertainment of the rest of the Company is at the cost of that one who is set out in their burlesque colours, who therefore is not without uneasiness, unless the subject for which he is rallied,[56] be really in it

30 where *ed.*] were 5

[56] 'rallied', treated or assailed with banter (*OED*).

self matter of commendation. For then the pleasant images and representations, which make the *Railery*, carrying praise as well as sport with them, the rallied Person also finds his account, and takes part in the diversion. But because the right management of so nice and
5 tickle[57] a business, wherein a little slip may spoil all, is not every Bodys talent, I think those who would secure themselves from provoking others, especially all young People, should carefully abstain from *Railery*, which by a small mistake or any wrong turn may leave upon the Mind of those who are made uneasy by it the lasting memory of
10 having been picquantly, though wittily taunted for some thing censurable in them.

Besides Railery, *Contradiction* is a sort of Censoriousness wherein ill breeding often shews it self. Complaisance does not require that we should always admit all the reasonings or relations that the company is
15 entertain'd with, no nor silently to let pass all that is vented in our hearing. The opposing the opinions, and rectifying the mistakes of others, is what truth and charity sometimes requires of us, and civility does not oppose, if it be done with due caution and care of circumstances. But there are some People that one may observe, possessed as
20 it were with the spirit of Contradiction, that steadily and without regard to right or wrong oppose some one, or perhaps every one of the Company whatever they say. This is so visible and outrageous a way of *Censuring* that no body can avoid thinking himself injur'd by it. All opposition to what another Man has said is so apt to be suspected of
25 *Censoriousness*, and is so seldom received without some sort of humiliation that it ought to be made in the gentlest manner, and softest words can be found; and such as with the whole Deportment may express no forwardness to contradict. All marks of respect and good will ought to accompany it, that whilst we gain the argument we may
30 not lose the esteem of those that hear us.

4. *Captiousness* is another fault opposite to *Civility*, not only because it often produces misbecoming and provoking Expressions, and Carriage; but because it is a tacit accusation and reproach of some incivility taken notice of in those whom we are angry with. Such a
35 suspicion or intimation cannot be born by any one without uneasiness. Besides one angry body discomposes the whole Company, and the harmony ceases upon any such jarring.

The happiness that all Men so steadily pursue, Consisting in

---

[57] 'tickle', ticklish, nicely poised, delicate (*OED*).

pleasure, it is easie to see why the *Civil*, are more acceptable than the useful. The Ability, Sincerity, and good Intention, of a Man of weight and worth, or a real friend seldom atones for the uneasiness that is produced by his grave and solid Representations. Power and Riches, nay Vertue it self, are valued only as Conducing to our Happiness. 5 And therefore he recommends himself ill to another as aiming at his Happiness, who in the services he does him, makes him uneasie in the manner of doing them. He that knows how to make those he converses with easie without debasing himself to low and servile flattery, has found the true art of living in the World, and being both welcome and 10 valued every where. *Civility* therefore is what in the first place should with great care be made habitual to Children and Young people.

§. 144. There is another fault in good Manners, and that is *excess of Ceremony*, and an obstinate persisting to force upon another, what is not his due, and what he cannot take without folly or shame. This 15 seems rather a design to expose than oblige: Or at least looks like a contest for mastery, and at best is but troublesome, and so can be no part of *Good-Breeding*, which has no other use or end, but to make People easie and satisfied in their conversation with us. This is a fault few young People are apt to fall into; but yet if they are ever guilty of it, 20 or are suspected to encline that way, they should be told of it, and warned of this *mistaken Civility.* The thing they should endeavour and aim at in Conversation, should be to shew Respect, Esteem, and Good-will, by paying to every one that common Ceremony and Regard which is in civility due to them. To do this, without a suspicion 25 of Flattery, Dissimulation, or Meanness, is a great Skill, which good Sense, Reason, and good Company can only teach; but is of so much use in civil Life, that it is well worth the studying.

§. 145. ⁱ⁻Though the managing our selves well, in this part of our Behaviour, has the Name of *Good-Breeding*, as if peculiarly the effect of 30 Education; yet, as I have said, young Children should not be much perplexed about it; I mean about putting off their Hats, and making Legs modishly. Teach them Humility, and to be good-natur'd, if you can, and this sort of Manners will not be wanting: *Civility* being, in truth, nothing but a care not to shew any slighting, or contempt, of any 35 one in Conversation. What are the most allow'd and esteem'd ways of

§ 144 *Breeding.*   § 145 *Breeding.   Interruption.   Dispute.*

13 144] 137 **1**   21 and] or **1**   29 145] 138 **1**

ⁱ⁻ⁱ *Slight revision of rest of* **H** § 54, **K** § 72; *see p.* 199 n. ʰ⁻ʰ.

expressing this, we have above observed. It is as peculiar and different, in several Countries of the World, as their Languages; and therefore if it be rightly considered, Rules and Discourses, made to Children about it, are as useless and impertinent, as it would be now and then to give a Rule or two of the *Spanish*[j] Tongue, to one that converses only with *English*-men. Be as busie as you please with Discourses of *Civility* to your Son, such as is his Company, such will be his Manners. A Plough-man of your Neighbourhood, that has never been out of his Parish, read what Lectures you please to him, will be as soon in his Language, as his Carriage, a Courtier; that is, in neither, will be more polite than those he uses to converse with: And therefore of this, no other care can be taken till he be of an Age to have a Tutor put to him, who must not fail to be a well-bred Man. And, in good earnest, if I were to speak my Mind freely, so Children do nothing out of Obstinacy, Pride, and Ill-nature, 'tis no great matter how they put off their Hats, or make Legs.[k] If you can teach them to love and respect other People, they will, as their Age requires it, find ways to express it acceptably to every one, according to the Fashions they have been used to: And as to their Motions and Carriage of their Bodies, a Dancing-Master, as has been said, when it is fit, will teach them what is most becoming. In the mean time, when they are young, People expect not that Children should be over-mindful of these Ceremonies; Carelesness is allow'd to that Age, and becomes them as well as Complements do grown People: Or at least, if some [l-]very nice People[-l] will think it a fault, I am sure it is a fault, that should be over-look'd, and left to Time, a Tutor and Conversation to cure. And therefore I think it not worth your while to have your Son (as I often see Children are) molested or chid about it: But where there is *Pride* or *Ill-nature* appearing in his Carriage, there he must be persuaded or shamed out of it.[-i]

Though Children, when little, should not be much perplexed with the Rules and ceremonious parts of *Breeding*, yet there is a sort of Unmannerliness very apt to grow up with young People, if not early restrain'd, and that is a Forwardness to *interrupt* others that are speaking, and to stop them with some *Contradiction*. Whether the Custom of

---

10 in neither,] neither **1**   11 those] of those **1**   12–13 till . . . Man.] *add.* **3**
26 Time . . . Conversation] Time and Conversation only **1**   31–206.31 Though . . .
Habit.] *add.* **3**   32 the] *om.* **5**

[j] Japan **HK**   [k] make Legs or do it at all **HK**   [l-l] very nice and not very
wise People **HK**

Disputing, and the Reputation of Parts and Learning usually given to it, as if it were the only Standard and Evidence of Knowledge, make young Men so forward to watch Occasions, to correct others in their Discourse; and not to slip any Opportunity of shewing their Talents; So it is, That I have found Scholars most blam'd in this Point. There cannot be a greater Rudeness, than to *interrupt* another in the current of his Discourse; for if there be not impertinent Folly in answering a Man before we know what he will say, yet it is a plain Declaration, that we are weary to hear him talk any longer: And, have a Disesteem of what he says, which we judging not fit to entertain the Company, desire them to give Audience to us, who have something to produce worth their Attention. This shews a very great Disrespect, and cannot but be offensive: And yet, this is what almost all *Interruption* constantly carries with it. To which, if there be added, as is usual, a *correcting* of any Mistake, or a *contradicting* of what has been said, 'tis a Mark of yet greater Pride and Self-conceitedness, when we thus intrude our selves for Teachers; and take upon us, either to set another right in his Story, or shew the Mistakes of his Judgment.

I do not say this, That I think there should be no Difference of Opinions in Conversation, nor Opposition in Mens Discourses: This would be to take away the greatest Advantage of Society, and the Improvements are to be made by ingenious Company; where the light is to be got from the opposite Arguings of Men of Parts, shewing the different Sides of things, and their various Aspects, and Probabilities, would be quite lost, if every one were obliged to assent to, and say after the first Speaker. 'Tis not the owning ones Dissent from another, that I speak against, but the manner of doing it. Young Men should be taught not to be forward to *interpose* their Opinions, unless asked, or when others have done and are silent; and then only by way of Enquiry, not Instruction. The positive asserting, and the Magisterial Air should be avoided; and when a general Pause of the whole Company affords an Opportunity, they may modestly put in their Question as Learners.

This becoming Decency will not cloud their Parts, nor weaken the Strength of their Reason; but bespeak the more favourable Attention, and give what they say the greater Advantage. An ill Argument, or ordinary Observation thus introduced, with some civil Preface of Deference and Respect to the Opinions of others, will procure them

15 *contradicting*] contradiction **5**

more Credit, and Esteem, than the sharpest Wit, or profoundest Science, with a rough, insolent, or noisy Management, which always shocks the Hearers, and leaves an ill Opinion of the Man, though he get the better of it in the Argument.

5　This therefore should be carefully watched in young People, stopp'd in the Beginning, and the contrary Habit introduced in all their Conversation. And the rather, because Forwardness to talk, frequent *Interruptions* in arguing and loud *wrangling*, are too often observable amongst grown People, even of Rank amongst us. The

10　*Indians*, whom we call Barbarous, observe much more Decency and Civility in their Discourses and Conversation, giving one another a fair silent Hearing, till they have quite done; and then answering them calmly, and without Noise or Passion. And if it be not so in this civilized Part of the World, we must impute it to a Neglect in Education,

15　which has not yet reform'd this ancient Piece of Barbarity amongst us. Was it not, think you, an entertaining Spectacle, to see two Ladies of Quality accidentally seated on the opposite Sides of a Room, set round with Company, fall into a Dispute, and grow so eager in it, that in the Heat of their Controversie, edging by Degrees their Chairs forwards,

20　they were in a little time got up close to one another in the middle of the Room; where they for a good while managed the Dispute as fiercely as two Game-Cocks in the Pit, without minding, or taking any Notice of the Circle, which could not all the while forbear smiling? This I was told by a Person of Quality, who was present at the Combat,

25　and did not omit to reflect upon the Indecencies, that warmth in *Dispute* often runs People into; which since Custom makes too frequent, Education should take the more Care of. There is no Body but condemns this in others, though they over-look it in themselves: And many, who are sensible of it in themselves, and resolve against it, can-

30　not yet get rid of an ill Custom, which Neglect in their Education, has suffered to settle into an Habit.

§. 146. ᵐ⁻What has been above-said concerning *Company*, would perhaps, if it were well reflected on, give us a larger Prospect, and let us see how much farther its Influence reaches. 'Tis not the Modes of

§ 146 *Company.*

_____

29 of it in **4 5**] of in it **3**　　32 146] 139 **1**　　32–4 What . . . reaches.] This that I have said here, if it were well reflected on, would, perhaps, lead us a little farther, and let us see of what influence *Company* is. **1**

ᵐ⁻ᵐ *Slight revision of* **H** § 55, **K** § 73

Civility alone, that are imprinted by *Conversation:* The tincture[n] of Company sinks deeper than the out-side; and possibly, if a true estimate were made of the Morality, and Religions of the World, we should find, that the far greater part of Mankind received even those Opinions and Ceremonies they would die for, rather from the Fashions of their Countries, and the constant Practice of those about them, than from any conviction of their Reasons. I mention this only to let you see of what moment, I think, *Company* is to your Son, in all the parts of his Life, and therefore how much that one part is to be weighed, and provided for; it being of greater force to work upon him, than all you can do besides.[-m]

§. 147. [o-]You will wonder, perhaps, that I put *Learning* last, especially if I tell you I think it the least part. This may seem strange in [p-]the mouth of a bookish Man;[-p] and this making usually the chief, if not only bustle and stir about Children; this being almost that alone, which is thought on, when People talk of Education, makes it the greater Paradox. When I consider what a-do is made about a little *Latin* and *Greek*, how many Years are spent in it, and what a noise and business it makes to no purpose, I can hardly forbear thinking, that the Parents of Children still live in fear of the School-masters Rod, [q-]which they look on as the only Instrument of Education; as a Language or two to be its whole Business.[-q] How else is it possible that a Child should be chain'd to the Oar, Seven, Eight, or Ten of the best Years of his Life,[r] to get a Language or Two, which I think, might be had at a great deal cheaper rate of Pains and Time, and be learn'd almost in playing?[-o]

[s-]Forgive me therefore, if I say, I cannot with Patience think, that a young Gentleman should be put into the Herd, and be driven with a Whip and Scourge, as if he were to run the Gantlet through the several Classes, *ad capiendum ingenii cultum.* [58] What then, say you, would you not have him Write and Read? Shall he be more ignorant than the Clerk of our Parish, who takes *Hopkins* and *Sternhold*[59] for the best

§ 147 *Learning.*

6 Countries] Country 1   12 147] 140 1

[n] influence **HK**   [o-o] *Slightly revised from first part of* **H** § 56, **K** § 74 *entire*
[p-p] the mouth (though not of a Learned yet) of a bookish man **HK**   [q-q] and therefor sacrifice their children to this Moloch to appease his ang⟨e⟩r **HK**   [r] **HK** *insert* to get fee fa fum bonus bona bonum   [s-s] *Slight revision of latter part of* **H** § 56, **K** § 75 *entire*

[58] 'In order to receive the cultivation of the mind' (Gellius, *Noctes Atticae*, 1. 2. 1).

[59] John Hopkins, with Thomas Sternhold and others, made a famous metrical translation of the Book of Psalms (1549), which went through many editions, more than 600 up to 1828.

Poets in the World, whom yet he makes worse, than they are, by his ill Reading? Not so, not so fast, I beseech you. Reading, and Writing, and *Learning*, I allow to be necessary, but yet not the chief Business. I imagine you would think him a very foolish Fellow, that should not
5 value a Vertuous, or a Wise Man, infinitely before a great Scholar. Not but that I think *Learning* a great help to both in well dispos'd Minds; but yet it must be confess'd also, that in others not so dispos'd, it helps them only to be the more foolish, or worse Men.ᵗ I say this, that when you consider of the Breeding of your Son, and are looking out for a School-
10 Master, or a Tutor, you would not have (as is usual) *Latin* and *Logick* only in your Thoughts. *Learning* must be had, but in the second place, as subservient only to greaterᵘ Qualities. Seek out some-body, that may know how discreetly to frame his Manners: Place him in Hands, where you may, as much as possible, secure his Innocence, cherish and nurse
15 up the Good, and gently correct, and weed out any Bad Inclinations, ᵛ⁻and settle in him good Habits.⁻ᵛ This is the main Point, and this being provided for, *Learning* may be had in to the Bargain, and that, as I think, at a very easie rate, by Methods that may be thought on.⁻ˢ

§. 148. ʷ⁻When he can talk, 'tis time he should begin to *learn to read*.
20 But as to this, give me leave here to inculcate again, what is very apt to be forgotten, *viz.* That a great Care is to be taken, that it be never made as a Business to him, nor he look on it as a Task. We naturally, as I said, even from our Cradles, love Liberty, and have therefore an aversion to many Things, for no other Reason, but because they are
25 injoyn'd us. I have always had a Fancy, that *Learning* might be made a Play and Recreation to Children; and that they might be brought to desire to be taught, if it were propos'd to them as a thing of Honour, Credit, Delight and Recreation, or as a Reward for doing something else; and if they were never chid or corrected for the neglect of it. That
30 which confirms me in this Opinion, is, that amongst the *Portugueses*, 'tis so much a Fashion, and Emulation, amongst their Children, to *learn* to *Read*, and Write, that they cannot hinder them from it: They will learn it one from another, and are as intent on it, as if it were forbidden them. I remember that being at a Friend's House, whose
35 younger Son, a Child in Coats, was not easily *brought* to his Book

§§ 148–59 *Reading.*

---

19 148] 141 ɪ

ᵗ or more wicked Men **HK**   ᵘ greater and more necessary **HK**   ᵛ⁻ᵛ *Not in* **HK**   ʷ⁻ʷ *Slight revision of* **H** § 57, *first part of* **K** § 76

208

(being taught *to Read* at home by his Mother) I advised to try another way, than requiring it of him as his Duty; we therefore, in a Discourse on purpose amongst our selves, in his hearing, but without taking any notice of him, declared, That it was the Privilege and Advantage of Heirs and Elder Brothers, to be Scholars; that this made them fine 5 Gentlemen, and beloved by every body: And that for Younger Brothers, 'twas a Favour to admit them ˣ⁻to Breeding; to be taught⁻ˣ to *Read* and Write, was more than came to their share; they might be ignorant Bumpkins and Clowns, if they pleased. This so wrought upon the Child, that afterwards he desired to be taught; would come himself to 10 his Mother to *learn*, and would not let his Maid be quiet till she heard him his Lesson. I doubt not but some way like this might be taken with other Children; and when their Tempers are found, some Thoughts be instilled into them, that might set them upon desiring of *Learning* themselves, and make them seek it, as another sort of Play or Recre- 15 ation. But then, as I said before, it must never be imposed as a Task, nor made a trouble to them. There may be Dice and Play-things, with the Letters on them, to teach Children the *Alphabet* by playing; and twenty other ways may be found, suitable to their particular Tempers, to make this kind of *Learning a Sport* to them.⁻ʷ 20

§. 149. ʸ⁻Thus Children may be cozen'd into a Knowledge of the Letters; be *taught to read*, without perceiving it to be any thing but a Sport, and play themselves into that which others are whipp'd for. Children should not have any thing like Work, or serious, laid on them; neither their Minds, nor Bodies will bear it. It injures their 25 Healths; and their being forced and tied down to their Books, in an Age at enmity with all such restraint, has, I doubt not, been the reason, why a great many have hated Books and Learning, all their Lives after: 'Tis like a Surfeit, that leaves an Aversion behind not to be removed.⁻ʸ

§. 150. ᶻ⁻I have therefore thought, that if *Play-things* were fitted to 30 this purpose, as they are usually to none, Contrivances might be made *to teach Children to Read*, whilst they thought they were only Playing.⁻ᶻ ᵃ⁻For example, what if an *Ivory-Ball* were made like that of the Royal-Oak Lottery,⁶⁰ with Thirty two sides, or one rather of Twenty four, or

21 149] 142 1   23 which] *add.* **3**   30 150] 143 1

ˣ⁻ˣ to that breeding, to be taught **HK**   ʸ⁻ʸ **H** § 58; *part of* **K** § 76   ᶻ⁻ᶻ **H** § 59; *first part of* **K** § 77   ᵃ⁻ᵃ *Altered and expanded from* **Corr.** 807 (ii. 682); *cf.* 822 (ii. 720); **H** § 60; *latter part of* **K** § 77

⁶⁰ A lottery held in the late 17th c. for the benefit of the Royal Fisheries Company; prizes were usually in the form of terminal or perpetual annuities. After 1698 all other lotteries were prohibited as a public nuisance. *Encyc. Brit.* 11th edn., xvii. 21.

Twenty five sides; and upon several of those sides pasted on an A, upon several others B, on others C, and on others D. I would have you begin with but these four Letters, or perhaps only two at first; and when he is perfect in them, then add another; and so on till each side having one Letter, there be on it the whole Alphabet. This I would have others play with before him, it being as good a sort of Play to lay a Stake, who shall first throw an A or B, as who upon Dice shall throw Six or Seven. This being a Play amongst you, tempt him not to it, lest you make it Business; for I would not have him understand 'tis any thing but a Play of older People, and I doubt not but he will take to it of himself. And that he may have the more reason to think it is a Play, that he is sometimes in favour admitted to, when the Play is done, the Ball should be laid up safe out of his reach, that so it may not, by his having it in his keeping at any time, grow stale to him.

§. 151. To keep up his eagerness to it, let him think it a Game belonging to those above him: And when by this means he knows the Letters, by changing them into Syllables, he may *learn to Read*, without knowing how he did so, and never have any chiding or trouble about it; nor fall out with Books, because of the hard usage and vexation they have caused him. Children, if you observe them, take abundance of Pains to learn several Games, which, if they should be enjoined them, they would abhorr as a Task and Business.⁻ᵃ I know a Person of great Quality (more yet to be honoured for his Learning and Vertue, than for his Rank and high Place) who by pasting on the six Vowels (for in our Language Y is one) on the six sides of a Die, and the remaining eighteen Consonants on the sides of three other Dice, has made this a Play for his Children, that he shall win, who at one cast throws most Words on these four Dice; whereby his eldest Son, yet in Coats, has *play'd* himself *into Spelling* with great eagerness, and without once having been chid for it, or forced to it.

§. 152. ᵇ⁻I have seen little Girls exercise whole Hours together, and take abundance of pains to be expert at *Dibstones*,⁶¹ as they call it: Whilst I have been looking on, I have thought, it wanted only some good Contrivance, to make them employ all that Industry about something that might be more useful to them; and methinks 'tis only the fault and negligence of elder People, that it is not so. Children are

13 should] shall **1**   15 To keep . . .] *run on within § 143* **1**   31 152] 144 **1**

ᵇ⁻ᵇ **H** § 61; **K** § 78

⁶¹ '*Dibstones*', dibs, dabstones, or dabbers, game played with small round flintstones (*OED*).

much less apt to be idle, than Men; and Men are to be blamed, if some part of that busie Humour be not turned to useful Things; which might be made usually as delightful to them, as those they are employed in, if Men would be but half so forward to lead the way, as these little Apes would be to follow. I imagine some wise *Portuguese* heretofore began this Fashion amongst the Children of his Country, where, I have been told, as I said, it is impossible to hinder the Children from *learning to Read* and Write: And in some parts of *France* they teach one another to Sing and Dance from the Cradle.⁻ᵇ

§. 153. ᶜ⁻The *Letters* pasted upon the sides of the Dice, or Polygon, were best to be of the size of those of the Folio Bible to begin with, and none of them Capital Letters: when once he can read what is printed in such Letters, he will not long be ignorant of the great ones: And in the beginning, he should not be perplexed with variety; with this Die, also, you might have a Play just like the Royal-Oak, which would be another variety, and play for Cherries or Apples, *&c.*⁻ᶜ

§. 154. ᵈ⁻Besides these, Twenty other Plays might be invented, depending on *Letters*, which those, who like this way, may easily contrive and get made to this use if they will. But the Four Dice above-mentioned, I think so easy, and useful, that it will be hard to find any better, and there will be scarce need of any other.⁻ᵈ

§. 155. ᵉ⁻Thus much for *learning to read*, which let him never be driven to, nor chid for: cheat him into it if you can, but make it not a Business for him. 'Tis better it be a Year later *before he can read*, than that he should this way get an aversion to Learning. If you have any Contests with him, let it be in Matters of Moment, of Truth, and good Nature; but lay no Task on him about A B C. Use your Skill to make his Will supple and pliant to Reason: Teach him to love Credit and Commendation; to abhorr being thought ill or meanly of, especially by You and his Mother, and then the rest will come all easily. But I think, if you will do that, you must not shackle and tie him up with Rules about indifferent Matters, nor rebuke him for every little Fault, or perhaps some, that to others would seem great ones: But of this I have said enough already.⁻ᵉ

§. 156. ᶠ⁻When by these gentle ways he begins to be able to *read*, some easy pleasant Book suited to his Capacity, should be put into his

---

10 153] 145 ɪ   17 154] 146 ɪ   22 155] 147 ɪ   35 156] 148 ɪ

ᶜ⁻ᶜ **H** § 62; *first part of* **K** § 79; *both conclude* for farthings or pins.   ᵈ⁻ᵈ *First part of*
H § 63; *latter part of* **K** § 79   ᵉ⁻ᵉ *Latter part of* **H** § 63; **K** § 80 *entire*
ᶠ⁻ᶠ *Expanded from* **Corr.** 829 (ii. 733–4); *cf.* 844 (ii. 773), 845 (ii. 790)

Hands, wherein the entertainment, that he finds, might draw him on, and reward his Pains in Reading, and yet not such as should fill his Head with perfectly useless trumpery, or lay the principles of Vice and Folly. To this purpose, I think *Æsop*'s *Fables* the best, which being
5 Stories apt to delight and entertain a Child, may yet afford useful Reflections to a grown Man. And if his Memory retain them all his life after, he will not repent to find them there, amongst his manly Thoughts, and serious Business. If his *Æsop has Pictures* in it, it will entertain him much the better, and encourage him to read, when it
10 carries the increase of Knowledge with it. For such visible Objects Children hear talked of in vain, and without any satisfaction, whilst they have no Idea's of them; those Idea's being not to be had from Sounds; but from the Things themselves, or their Pictures. And therefore I think, as soon as he begins to spell, as many Pictures of Animals
15 should be got him, as can be found, with the printed names to them, which at the same time will invite him to read, and afford him Matter of Enquiry and knowledge. *Reynard the Fox*,[62] is another Book, I think, may be made use of to the same purpose. And if those about him will talk to him often about the Stories he has read, and hear him tell them,
20 it will, besides other Advantages, add Incouragement, and delight *to* his *Reading*, when he finds there is some use and pleasure in it. These Baits seem wholly neglected in the ordinary Method: And 'tis usually long before Learners find any use or pleasure in Reading, which may tempt them to it, and so take Books only for fashionable amuzements,
25 or impertinent troubles good for nothing.⁻ᶠ

§. 157. ᵍ⁻The Lord's Prayer, the Creeds, and Ten Commandments, 'tis necessary he should learn perfectly by heart, but I think, not by reading them himself in his Primer, but by some-body's repeating them to him, even before he can read. But learning by heart, and *learn-*
30 *ing to read*, should not, I think, be mixed, and so one made to clog the other. But his *learning to read* should be made as little trouble or business to him, as might be.⁻ᵍ

ʰ⁻What other *Books* there are in *English* of the kind of those above-mentioned, fit *to engage* the liking of Children, and tempt them *to read*,
35 I do not know: But am apt to think that Children, being generally

13 from] either **1**   21–4 it. These ... to it,] it, which in the ordinary Method, I think Learners do not till late; **1**   26 157] 149 **1**

ᵍ⁻ᵍ *Expanded from* **Corr.** 829 (ii. 734)   ʰ⁻ʰ *Revision of* **Corr.** 844 (ii. 773, ll. 16–27)

⁶² 'Reynard' is the name of the fox in the Old French *Roman de Renart*; Caxton published a translation (from the Dutch), in which he used this spelling (*cf. OED*).

delivered over to the Method of Schools, where the fear of the Rod is to inforce, and not any pleasure of the Imployment to invite them to learn, this sort of useful Books amongst the number of silly ones, that are of all sorts, have yet had the fate to be neglected; and nothing that I know has been considered of this kind out of the ordinary Road of the 5 Horn-Book, Primer, Psalter, Testament, and Bible.⁻ʰ

§. 158. ⁱ⁻As for the *Bible*, which Children are usually imploy'd in, to exercise and improve their Talent *in Reading*, I think, the promiscuous reading of it through, by Chapters, as they lie in order, is so far from being of any Advantage to Children, either for the perfecting their 10 *Reading*, or principling their Religion, that perhaps a worse could not be found. For what Pleasure or Incouragement can it be to a Child to exercise himself in reading those Parts of a Book, where he under-stands nothing? And how little are the Law of *Moses*, the Song of *Solomon*, the Prophecies in the Old, and the Epistles and *Apocalypse* in 15 the New Testament, suited to a Child's Capacity? And though the History of the Evangelists, and the Acts, have something easier; yet taken altogether, it is very disproportionate to the understanding of Childhood. I grant, that the Principles of Religion are to be drawn from thence, and in the Words of the Scripture: yet none should be 20 propos'd to a Child, but such, as are suited to a Child's Capacity and Notions. But 'tis far from this to read through *the whole Bible*, and that for reading's sake. And what an odd jumble of Thoughts must a Child have in his Head, if he have any at all, such as he should have concern-ing Religion, who in his tender Age, reads all the Parts of the *Bible* 25 indifferently as the Word of God, without any other distinction. I am apt to think, that this in some Men has been the very Reason, why they never had clear and distinct Thoughts of it all their Life–time.⁻ⁱ

§. 159. ʲ⁻And now I am by chance fallen on this Subject, give me leave to say, that there are some Parts of the *Scripture*, which may be 30 proper to be put into the Hands of a Child, to ingage him to read; such as are the Story of *Joseph*, and his Brethren, of *David* and *Goliah*,⁶³ of *David* and *Jonathan*, &c. And others, that he should be made to read for his Instruction, as That, *What you would have others do unto you, do you the same unto them*; and such other easy and plain moral Rules, which 35 being fitly chosen, might often be made use of, both for Reading and Instruction together; and so often read till they are throughly fixed in

---

7 158] 150 **1**   29 159] 151 **1**   37–214.3 and so . . . Action.] *add.* **3**

ⁱ⁻ⁱ **Corr.** 844 (ii. 773, l. 28–774, l. 14)   ʲ⁻ʲ **Corr.** 844 (ii. 774, ll. 15–28)

⁶³ i.e. Goliath (from medieval *Golias*).

the Memory; and then afterwards, as he grows ripe for them may in their turns, on fit Occasions, be inculcated as the standing and sacred Rules of his Life and Action. But the Reading of the whole Scripture indifferently, is what I think very inconvenient for Children, till after having
5 been made acquainted with the plainest Fundamental Parts of it, they have got some kind of general view of what they ought principally to believe and practise,⁻ʲ which yet, I think, they ought to receive in the very Words of the Scripture, and not in such, as Men prepossess'd by Systems and Analogies, are apt in this case to make use of, and force
10 upon them. Dr. *Worthington*, to avoid this, has made a Catechism,⁶⁴ which has all its Answers in the precise Words of the Scripture, a thing of good Example, and such a sound Form of Words, as no Christian can except against, as not fit for his Child to learn; of this, as soon as he can say the Lord's Prayer, Creed, and Ten Commandments by heart, it may
15 be fit for him to learn a Question every Day, or every Week, as his Understanding is able to receive, and his Memory to retain them. And when he has this Catechism perfectly by heart, so as readily and roundly to answer to any Question in the whole Book, it may be convenient to lodge in his Mind the remaining Moral Rules scattered up and down in
20 the Bible, as the best *Exercise of his Memory*, and that which may be always a Rule to him, ready at hand in the whole Conduct of his Life.

§. 160. ᵏ⁻When he can read English well, it will be seasonable to enter him in *Writing*: And here the first thing should be taught him is, to *hold his Pen right*; and this he should be perfect in, before he should
25 be suffered to put it to Paper. For not only Children, but any body else, that would do any thing well, should never be put upon too much of it at once, or be set to perfect themselves in two parts of an Action at the same time, if they can possibly be separated. I think the *Italian* way of holding the Pen between the Thumb and the Fore-finger, alone, may
30 be best: But in this, you should consult some good Writing-Master, or any other Person who writes well, and quick. When he has learn'd to hold his Pen right, in the next place, he should learn how to *lay his*

§ 160 *Writing*.

19 remaining] *add.* **3** 22 160] 152 **1** 28–31 I think . . . quick.] *add.* **3**
33 right, . . . he] right (to hold it betwixt the Thumb and Fore-finger alone, I think best; but in this, you should Consult [**NN**; consult **NA**] some good Writing-master, or any other person [**NN**; Person **NA**] who writes well [**NN**; well, **NA**] and quick) then next he
1

ᵏ⁻ᵏ **Corr.** 929 (iii. 183–4); *cf.* 998, *letter to Benjamin Furly* (iii. 340–2)

⁶⁴ John Worthington's 'Ὑποτύπωσις ὑγιεινῶν τῶν λόγων, *A Form of Sound Words, or A Scripture Catechism* (London, 1673, and later edns.).

Paper, and place his Arm and Body to it. These Practices being got over, the way to teach him to Write, without much trouble, is to get a Plate graved, with the Characters of such an Hand as you like best: But you must remember to have them a pretty deal bigger than he should ordinarily write; for every one naturally comes by degrees to write a less 5 Hand, than he at first was taught, but never a bigger. Such a Plate being graved, let several Sheets of good Writing-Paper be printed off with Red Ink, which he has nothing to do, but to go over with a good Pen fill'd with Black Ink, which will quickly bring his Hand to the formation of those Characters, being at first shewed where to begin, and 10 how to form every Letter.⁻ᵏ And when he can do that well, he must then exercise on fair Paper; and so may easily be brought *to Write* the Hand you desire.

§. 161. ˡ⁻When he can Write well, and quick, I think it may be convenient, not only to continue the exercise of his Hand in Writing, but 15 also to improve the use of it farther in *Drawing*, a thing very useful to a Gentleman in several occasions; but especially if he travel, as that which helps a Man often to express, in a few Lines well put together, what a whole Sheet of Paper in Writing, would not be able to represent, and make intelligible. How many Buildings may a Man see, how many 20 Machines and Habits meet with, the Idea's whereof would be easily retain'd and communicated, by a little Skill in *Drawing*; which being committed to Words, are in danger to be lost, or at best but ill retained in the most exact Descriptions? I do not mean, that I would have your Son a *perfect Painter*; to be that to any tolerable degree, will require more 25 time, than a young Gentleman can spare from his other Improvements of greater Moment. But so much insight into *Perspective*, and skill in *Drawing*, as will enable him to represent tolerably on Paper any thing he sees, except Faces, may, I think, be got in a little time, especially if he have a Genius to it: But where that is wanting, unless it be in things abso- 30 lutely necessary, it is better to let him pass them by quietly, than to vex him about them to no purpose: And therefore in this, as in all other things not absolutely necessary, the Rule holds, *Nihil invitâ Minervâ.* ⁻ˡ ⁶⁵

§ 161 *Drawing.   Short-hand.*

---

14 161] 153 **1**   27 Moment.] importance: **1**   31 by] *add.* **3**   33 *invitâ*
Minervâ] *invita Minerva* **NN**

ˡ⁻ **Corr.** 844 (ii. 781, l. 33–782, l. 22)

⁶⁵ From Horace, *De arte poetica*, 385: 'Tu nihil invita dices faciesve Minerva' (You will say nothing and do nothing against the will of Minerva, that is, against your natural talent); cf. Erasmus, *Adagia*, i. 1. 42.

¶ 1. *Short-hand*, an Art, as I have been told, known only in *England*, may perhaps, be thought worth the Learning, both for Dispatch in what Men write for their own Memory, and Concealment of what they would not have lie open to every Eye. For he that has once learn'd any
5   Sort of Character may easily vary it to his own private use or phansy, and with more Contraction suited to the Business he would Imploy it in. Mr. *Rich*'s,[66] the best contriv'd of any I have seen, may, as I think, by one who knows and considers Grammar well, be made much easier and shorter. But for the learning this compendious way of Writing, there
10   will be no need hastily to look out a Master: It will be early enough when any convenient Opportunity offers it self at any time after his Hand is well setled in fair and quick Writing. For Boys have but little use of *Short-hand*; And should by no means practise it, till they write perfectly well; and have throughly fixed the Habit of doing so.

15   §. 162. As soon as he can speak *English*, 'tis time for him to learn some other Language: This no body doubts of, when *French* is proposed.[67] And the Reason is, because People are accustomed to the right way of teaching that Language, which is by talking it into Children in constant Conversation, and not by Grammatical Rules. The
20   *Latin* Tongue ᵐ⁻would easily be taught the same way if his Tutor, being constantly with him, would talk nothing else to him, and make him answer still in the same Language. But because *French* is a living Language, and to be used more in speaking, that should be first learn'd, that the yet pliant Organs of Speech might be accustomed to a
25   due formation of those Sounds, and he get the habit of pronouncing *French* well, which is the harder to be done the longer it is delay'd.

§. 163. When he can speak and read *French* well, which in this Method is usually in a Year or two, he should proceed to *Latin*, which 'tis a wonder Parents, when they have had the experiment in *French*,
30   should not think ought to be learn'd the same way, by talking and reading. Only Care is to be taken whilst he is learning these Foreign Languages, by speaking and reading nothing else with his Tutor, that

§ 162 *French.*   §§ 163–7 *Latin.*

1–14 ¶. 1. *Short-hand* . . . doing so.] *add.* **3**   15 162] 154 **1**   27 163] 155 **1**
ᵐ⁻ᵐ *Rewritten from* **Corr.** 929 (iii. 183)

[66] Dr Jeremiah Rich wrote a *Semography* (1642) on a shorthand system invented by his uncle, William Cartwright. Later editions were entitled *The Pens Dexterity Compleated*. Locke admired this system and adapted it for his own use, chiefly in his journals.
[67] **Corr.** 844 (ii. 774 ll. 29–30) took it for granted that Latin should follow English. Cf. 897 (iii. 107–9).

he do not forget to read *English*, which may be preserved by his Mother, or some-body else, hearing him read some chosen Parts of the Scripture, or other *English* Book every Day.⁻ᵐ

§. 164. ⁿ⁻*Latin*, I look upon as absolutely necessary to a Gentleman; and indeed, Custom, which prevails over every thing, has made it so much a Part of Education, that even those Children are whipp'd to it, and made spend many Hours of their precious time uneasily in *Latin*, who, after they are once gone from School, are never to have more to do with it, as long as they live. Can there be any thing more ridiculous, than that a Father should waste his own Money, and his Son's time, in setting him to learn the *Roman Language*, when at the same time he designs him for a Trade, wherein he having no use of *Latin*, fails not to forget that little, which he brought from School, and which 'tis Ten to One he abhorrs, for the ill usage it procur'd him? Could it be believ'd, unless we had everywhere amongst us Examples of it, that a Child should be forced to learn the Rudiments of a Language, which he is never to use in the Course of Life, that he is designed to; and neglect all the while the writing a good Hand, and casting Account, which are of great Advantage in all Conditions of Life, and to most Trades indispensibly necessary? But though these Qualifications, requisite to

4 164] 156 1   17 that] *add.* 3

ⁿ⁻ⁿ *For* §§164-5, **HK** *have*

[**H** § 64, **K** § 81] I would also have him learne Latin now and not be whipt for it at Schoole hereafter where [if *add* **K**] possibly all the improvem⟨en⟩t he shall get of his tongue shall not to a tenth part contervaile the depravation of his manners. That it is possible to learne Latin now I thinke is past doubt if you consider that it is noe more uncouth or incomprehensible to an English child of his age then French is and that you see litle girles will in a yeare or two p⟨e⟩rfectly learne. If some body were about him that constantly spoke Latin to him and nothing else he would as certainly speake it as Tully did who learned it noe other way If you could finde a sober d[i]escreet man fit for this province and that would und⟨e⟩rtake it, within a yeare or two [and] I could easily tell how he might improve even in that age the young gent⟨le⟩mans time to more then p⟨e⟩rhaps you would thinke him capeable of.

But if you have thoughts 'of' this way pray still take care that it be a man who will thinke Latin and language the least part and would take the greatest care of formeing his minde and disposeing of that aright and therefor must have something more in him then Latin. He must have good sense and good humor and a skill to cary himself with ease gravity and kindenesse in a constant conv⟨e⟩rsation with your Son.

[**H** § 65, **K** § 82] I have met with soe very few that have not either thought this way inpracticable because it is quite out of the road or else that did not decline it for some other difficultys they imagind accompanied it that tis with some kinde of diffidence I propose it to you· nor have I explaind myself soe fully about it as I would if I knew you were inclined effectually to put it in use· when I know that I shall be more particular in the point or if you make choise of the ordinary way I will tell you the best I can how to contrive it [[best I can how to contrive it] **H**] to the best advantage and avoid as much as may be the ordinary inconveniencys.

Trade and Commerce and the Business of the World, are seldom or never to be had at Grammar-Schools, yet thither, not only Gentlemen send their younger Sons, intended for Trades; but even Tradesmen and Farmers fail not to send their Children, though they have neither
5   Intention nor Ability to make them Scholars. If you ask them why they do this, they think it as strange a Question, as if you should ask them, why they go to Church. Custom serves for Reason, and has, to those who take it for Reason, so consecrated this Method, that it is almost Religiously observed by them, and they stick to it, as if their Children had
10   scarce an Orthodox Education, unless they learn'd *Lily*'s Grammar.[68]

§. 165. °⁻But how necessary soever *Latin* be to some, and is thought to be to others, to whom it is of no manner of Use or Service; yet the ordinary way of Learning it in a Grammar-School is that which having had thoughts about, I cannot be forward to incourage. The Reasons against
15   it are so evident, and cogent, that they have prevailed with some intelligent Persons, to quit the ordinary Road, not without success, though the Method made use of, was not exactly that, which I imagine the easiest, and in short is this. To trouble the Child with no *Grammar* at all, but to have *Latin*, as *English* has been, without the perplexity of Rules, talked
20   into him; for if you will consider it, *Latin* is no more unknown to a Child, when he comes into the World, than *English:* And yet he learns *English* without Master, Rule, or Grammar; and so might he *Latin* too, as *Tully*[69] did, if he had some-body always to talk to him in this Language. And when we so often see a *French*-Woman teach an *English*-Girl to
25   speak and read *French* perfectly in a Year or Two, without any Rule of Grammar, or any thing else but pratling to her, I cannot but wonder, how Gentlemen have over-seen this way for their Sons, and thought them more dull or incapable than their Daughters.⁻ⁿ

§. 166. If therefore a Man could be got, who himself speaking good
30   *Latin*, would always be about your Son, talk constantly to him, and suffer him to speak or read nothing else, this would be the true and

11 165] 157 **1**   24 *English*-Girl] young Girl **1**   29 If therefore . . .] *run on within* § 157 **1**   29–30 speaking . . . *Latin*,] speaks good *Latin*, who **1** 30 talk] and talk **1**   31–219.5 suffer . . . boot] make him read *Latin*, that would be the true Genuine, and easy way of teaching him *Latin*, and that that I could wish, since besides teaching him a Language, without Pains or Chiding (which Children are wont to be whipp'd for at School Six or Seven Years together) he might at the same time, not only form his Mind and Manners, but instruct him also **1**

°⁻° **Corr.** 844 (ii. 774, l. 29–776, l. 3)

[68] William Lily's grammar became the national Latin grammar by appointment under Edward VI (*DNB*).

[69] Marcus Tullius Cicero.

genuine way, and that which I would propose, not only as the easiest and best, wherein a Child might without Pains or Chiding, get a Language, which others are wont to be whip'd for at School six or seven Years together; But also as that, wherein at the same time he might have his Mind and Manners formed, and he be instructed to boot in several Sciences, such as are a good Part of *Geography, Astronomy, Chronology, Anatomy*, besides some Parts of *History*, and all other Parts of Knowledge of Things, that fall under the Senses, and require little more than Memory. For there, if we would take the true way, our Knowledge should begin, and in those Things be laid the Foundation; and not in the abstract Notions of *Logick* and *Metaphysicks*, which are fitter to amuze, than inform the Understanding, in its first setting out towards Knowledge. When young Men have had their Heads imploy'd a while in those abstract Speculations without finding the Success and Improvement, or that Use of them, which they expected, they are apt to have mean Thoughts, either of Learning or themselves; they are tempted to quit their Studies, and throw away their Books, as containing nothing but hard Words, and empty Sounds; or else, to conclude, that if there be any real Knowledge in them, they themselves have not Understandings capable of it. That this is so, perhaps I could assure you upon my own Experience. Amongst other Things to be learn'd by a young Man in this Method, whilst others of his Age are wholly taken up with *Latin* and Languages, I may also set down *Geometry* for one, having known a young Gentleman, bred something after this way, able to demonstrate several Propositions in *Euclid*, before he was Thirteen.⁻ᵒ

§. 167. ᵖ⁻But if such a Man cannot be got, who speaks good *Latin*, and being able to instruct your Son in all these Parts of Knowledge, will undertake it by this Method; the next best is to have him taught as near this way as may be, which is by taking some easy and pleasant Book, such as *Æsop's Fables*, and writing the *English* Translation (made as literal as it can be) in one Line, and the *Latin* Words which answer each of them, just over it in another. These let him read every Day over and over again, till he perfectly understands the

13–14 When . . . Speculations] In which abstract Speculations when young Men have had their Heads imploy'd a while **1**   15 Improvement] *so* **Corr.** 844 (ii. 775); Imployment **NN** (cf. p. 54).   that . . . them,] Use of it **1**   17 they are tempted] *add.* **4**   18–19 else, to conclude,] else concluding, **1**   20 it. That] it; and that **1**   22 Man] Gentleman **5**   27 167] 158 **1**

ᵖ⁻ᵖ *Revision of* **Corr.** 844 (ii. 776, ll. 4–13)

Latin; and then go on to another Fable, till he be also perfect in that, not omitting what he is already perfect in, but sometimes reviewing that, to keep it in his Memory. And when he comes to write, let these be set him for Copies, which with the exercise of his Hand, will also

5 advance him in *Latin*. This being a more imperfect way than by *talking Latin* unto him; the formation of the Verbs first, and afterwards the declensions of the Nouns and Pronouns perfectly learn'd by heart, may facilitate his acquaintance with the genius and manner of the *Latin Tongue*, which varies the signification of Verbs, and Nouns, not

10 as the Modern Languages do by Particles prefixt, but by changing the last Syllables. More than this of Grammar, I think he need not have till he can read himself *Sanctii Minerva* with *Scioppius* and *Perizonius's*[70] Notes.⁻ᴾ

In teaching of Children this too, I think, is to be observed, that in

15 most Cases, where they stick, they are not to be farther puzzled, by putting them upon finding it out themselves; as by asking such Questions as these, (*viz.*) Which is the Nominative Case, in the Sentence they are to construe; or demanding, what *aufero* signifies, to lead them to the Knowledge what *abstulere* signifies, *&c.* when they cannot

20 readily tell. This wastes time only in disturbing them: for whilst they are Learning, and apply themselves with Attention, they are to be kept in good Humour, and every thing made easy to them, and as pleasant as possible. Therefore wherever they are at a stand, and are willing to go forwards, help them presently over the Difficulty, without any

25 Rebuke or Chiding, remembring, that where harsher Ways are taken, they are the effect only of Pride or Peevishness in the Teacher, who expects Children should instantly be Masters of as much, as he knows: whereas he should rather consider, that his Business is to settle in them habits, not angrily to inculcate Rules, which serve for little in the

30 Conduct of our Lives; at least are of no use to Children, who forget them as soon as given. In Sciences where their Reason is to be Exercised, I will not deny, but this Method may sometimes be varied, and Difficulties propos'd on purpose to excite Industry, and accustom

---

1 *Latin*,] *Latin*. (But have a Care still, whatever you are teaching him, of cloging him with too much at once; [**NN**; once: **NA**] Or making any thing his Business but downright Vertue; or reproving him for any Thing but Vice) 1   12 *Scioppius* and *Perizonius's*] *Scioppius's* 1   14–223.36 In teaching ... Learning.] *add.* 4

70 Francisco Sánchez de las Brozas wrote *Minerva, seu de causis linguae Latinae* (Salamanca, 1587); it was published with notes by Gaspar Scioppius (Kaspar Schoppe) in 1664, with Scioppius' and Jacobus Perizonius' notes at Frankfurt in 1693. It was a Latin grammar (LL 2543–4).

the Mind to imploy its own Strength and Sagacity in Reasoning. But yet, I guess, this is not to be done to Children, whilst very young; nor at their entrance upon any sort of Knowledge: Then every thing of it self is difficult, and the great Use and Skill of a Teacher is to make all as easy as he can. But particularly in learning of Languages there is least 5 occasion for poseing of Children. For Languages, being to be learn'd by Roate, Custom, and Memory, are then spoken in greatest Perfection, when all Rules of Grammar are utterly forgotten. I grant the Grammar of a Language is some times very carefully to be studied; but it is only to be studied by a grown Man, when he applies himself to the 10 Understanding of any Language critically, which is seldom the Business of any but profess'd Scholars. This I think will be agreed to, that if a Gentleman be to study any Language, it ought to be that of his own Country, that he may understand the Language, which he has constant use of, with the utmost Accuracy. 15

There is yet a farther reason why Masters and Teachers should raise no Difficulties to their Scholars; but on the contrary should smooth their way, and readily help them forwards, where they find them stop. Childrens Minds are narrow, and weak, and usually susceptible but of one Thought at once. Whatever is in a Child's Head 20 fills it for the time, especially if set on with any Passion. It should therefore be the skill and art of the Teacher to clear their Heads of all other Thoughts, whilst they are learning of any thing, the better to make room for what he would instill into them, that it may be received with Attention and Application, without which it leaves no Impres- 25 sion. The Natural Temper of Children disposes their Minds to wander. Novelty alone takes them; whatever that presents, they are presently eager to have a Taste of, and are as soon satiated with it. They quickly grow weary of the same thing, and so have almost their whole delight in change and variety. It is a contradiction to the 30 Natural state of Childhood for them to fix their fleeting Thoughts. Whether this be owing to the temper of their Brains, or the quickness or instability of their Animal Spirits, over which the Mind has not yet got a full Command; this is visible, that it is a Pain to Children to keep their Thoughts steady to any thing. A lasting continued Attention is 35 one of the hardest Tasks can be imposed on them: and therefore, he that requires their Application, should endeavour to make what he proposes as grateful and agreeable as possible: at least, he ought to

8–15 I grant . . . Accuracy.] *add.* 5

take care not to joyn any displeasing or frightful Idea with it. If they come not to their Books with some kind of liking and relish, 'tis no wonder their Thoughts should be perpetually shifting from what disgusts them; and seek better Entertainment in more pleasing Objects, after which they will unavoidably be gadding.

'Tis, I know, the usual Method of Tutors, to endeavour to procure Attention in their Scholars, and to fix their Minds to the Business in hand, by Rebukes and Corrections, if they find them ever so little wandring. But such treatment is sure to produce the quite contrary effect. Passionate words or blows from the Tutor fill the Child's Mind with Terror and Affrightment, which immediately takes it wholly up, and leaves no room for other Impressions. I believe there is no body, that reads this, but may recollect what disorder, hasty or imperious words from his Parents or Teachers have caus'd in his Thoughts; how for the time it has turn'd his Brains, so that he scarce knew what was said by or to him. He presently lost the sight of what he was upon, his Mind was fill'd with Disorder and Confusion, and in that state was no longer capable of Attention to any thing else.

'Tis true, Parents and Governors ought to settle and establish their Authority by an Awe over the Minds of those, under their Tuition; and to rule them by that: But when they have got an Ascendant over them, they should use it with great Moderation, and not make themselves such Scare-crows, that their Scholars should always tremble in their sight. Such an austerity may make their Government easie to themselves, but of very little use to their Pupils. 'Tis impossible Children should learn any thing whilst their Thoughts are possessed and disturb'd with any Passion, especially Fear, which makes the strongest impression on their yet tender and weak Spirits. Keep the Mind in an easie calm temper, when you would have it receive your Instructions, or any increase of Knowledge. 'Tis as impossible to draw fair and regular Characters on a trembling Mind as on a shaking Paper.

The great Skill of a Teacher is to get and keep the Attention of his Scholar, whilst he has that, he is sure to advance as fast, as the Learners Abilities will carry him: and without that, all his bustle and pudder[71] will be to little or no purpose. To attain this, he should make the Child comprehend (as much as may be) the Usefulness of what he teaches him, and let him see, by what he has learnt, that he can do something, which he could not do before; something, which gives him

---

[71] See n. 28.

some Power and real Advantage above others, who are ignorant of it. To this he should add sweetness in all his Instructions; and by a certain Tenderness in his whole Carriage, make the Child sensible, that he loves him and designs nothing but his good, the only way to beget love in the Child, which will make him hearken to his Lessons, and 5 relish what he teaches him.

Nothing but obstinacy should meet with any imperiousness or rough usage. All other Faults should be corrected with a gentle hand, and kind encouraging words will work better and more effectually upon a willing Mind, and even prevent a good deal of that Pervers- 10 ness, which rough and imperious usage often produces in well disposed and generous Minds. 'Tis true, Obstinacy and wilful Neglects must be Master'd, even though it cost blows to do it: But I am apt to think Perverseness in the Pupils is often the effect of Frowardness in the *Tutor*; and that most Children would seldom have deserv'd blows, if 15 needless and misapplied roughness had not taught them ill Nature, and given them an Aversion for their Teacher, and all that comes from him.

Inadvertency, forgetfulness, unsteadiness, and wandring of Thought, are the natural Faults of Childhood: and therefore where they are not observ'd to be wilful, are to be mention'd softly, and 20 gain'd upon by time. If every slip of this kind produces Anger and Rateing, the occasions of Rebuke and Corrections will return so often, that the Tutor will be a constant terror and uneasiness to his Pupils. Which one thing is enough to hinder their profiting by his Lessons, and to defeat all his Methods of Instruction. 25

Let the Awe he has got upon their Minds be so tempered with the constant Marks of Tenderness and good Will, that Affection may spur them to their Duty, and make them find a Pleasure in complying with his Dictates. This will bring them with Satisfaction to their Tutor; make them hearken to him, as to one who is their Friend, that 30 cherishes them, and takes pains for their good: This will keep their Thoughts easie and free, whilst they are with him, the only temper wherein the Mind is capable of receiving new Informations, and of admitting into it self those Impressions, which if not taken and retain'd, all that they and their Teacher do together is lost labour: 35 there is much Uneasiness and little Learning.

§. 168. When by this way of interlining *Latin* and *English* one with

§ 168 *Latin.*   *Grammar.*

---

37 168] 159 1

another, he has got a moderate Knowledge of the *Latin Tongue*, he may then be advanc'd a little farther to the reading of some other easy *Latin* Book, such as *Justin* or *Eutropius*,[72] and to make the reading and understanding of it the less tedious and difficult to him, let him help

5 himself if he please with the *English* Translation. Nor let the Objection, that he will then know it only by roat, fright any one. This when well consider'd, is not of any moment against, but plainly for this way of learning a Language. For Languages are only to be learn'd by roat; and a Man who does not speak *English* or *Latin* perfectly by roat, so

10 that having thought of the thing he would speak of, his Tongue of course without thought of Rule or Grammar, falls into the proper Expression and Idiom of that Language, does not speak it well, nor is Master of it. And I would fain have any one name to me that Tongue, that any one can learn, or speak as he should do by the Rules of Gram-

15 mar. Languages were made not by Rules, or Art, but by Accident, and the common Use of the People. And he that will speak them well, has no other Rule but that; nor any thing to trust to, but his Memory, and the habit of speaking after the Fashion learn'd from those, that are allow'd to speak properly, which in other Words is only to speak by

20 roat.

It will possibly be asked here, Is *Grammar* then of no use? and have those who have taken so much pains in reducing several Languages to Rules and Observations; who have writ so much about *Declensions* and *Conjugations*, about *Concords* and *Syntaxes*, lost their Labour, and been

25 learned to no purpose? I say not so, *Grammar* has its place too. But this I think I may say, There is more Stir a great deal made with it than there needs, and those are tormented about it to whom it does not at all belong. I mean Children at the Age, wherein they are usually perplexed with it, in Grammar-Schools.

30 There is nothing more evident, than that Languages learnt by roat serve well enough for the common Affairs of Life and ordinary commerce. Nay Persons of Quality of the Softer Sex, and such of them, as have spent their Time, in Well-bred Company, shews us, that this plain Natural way, without the least Study or Knowledge of *Grammar*,

---

6 roat, fright] roat (which is not when well consider'd of any moment against, but plainly for this way of learning a Language) fright 1   6–8 This . . . Language.] *add.*
3   12 Expression] Expressions 1   21–227.24 It will . . . Grammar.] *add.* **5**

---

[72] Marcus Junianus Justinus made an abridgement of Pompeius Trogus' *Historiae Philippicae*; Locke owned the 1613 Geneva edn. (LL 1609). He also owned Flavius Eutropius's *Historiae Romanae breviarium* (Paris, 1683; LL 1077).

can carry them to a great Degree of Elegancy and Politeness in their Language: And there are Ladies who without Knowing what *Tenses* and *Participles, Adverbs* and *Prepositions* are, speak as properly and as correctly (they might take it for an ill Complement if I said as any Country School-Master) as most Gentlemen who have been Bred up 5 in the ordinary Methods of Grammar-Schools. Grammar therefore we see may be spared in some Cases. The question then will be, To whom should it be Taught, and when? To this I Answer,

1. Men learn Languages for the ordinary intercourse of Society and Communication of thoughts in common Life without any farther 10 design in their use of them. And for this purpose, the Original way of Learning a Language by Conversation, not only serves well enough, but is to be prefer'd as the most Expedite, Proper, and Natural. Therefore, to this use of Language one may Answer, That Grammar is not Necessary. This so many of my Readers must be forced to allow, as 15 understand what I here say; and who conversing with others understand them without having ever been Taught the Grammar of the English Tongue. Which I suppose is the Case of Incomparably the greatest part of English Men; of whom I have never yet known any one who learnt his Mother Tongue by Rules. 20

2. Others there are the greatest part of whose Business in this World, is to be done with their Tongues, and with their Pens, and to those it is convenient if not necessary that they should speak properly and correctly, whereby they may let their Thoughts into other Mens minds, the more easily and with the greater impression. Upon this 25 account it is, that any sort of Speaking, so as will make him be understood, is not thought enough for a Gentleman. He ought to Study Grammar amongst the other helps of Speaking well, but it must be the Grammar of his own Tongue, of the Language he uses, that he may understand his own Country speech nicely, and speak it properly 30 without shocking the ears of those it is addressed to with solicisms and offensive irregularities. And to this purpose Grammar is necessary. But it is the Grammar only of their own proper Tongues, and to those only who would take pains in cultivating their Language, and in perfecting their stiles. Whether all Gentlemen should not do this I leave 35 to be Considered, since the want of Propriety, and Grammatical Exactness, is thought very misbecoming one of that Rank, and usually draws on one guilty of such Faults, the censure of having had a Lower Breeding and worse Company, than suits with his quality. If this be so, (as I suppose it is) it will be matter of wonder why young Gentlemen 40

are forced to learn the Grammars of Foreign, and dead Languages, and are never once told of the Grammar of their own Tongues: They do not so much as know there is any such thing, much less is it made their Business to be instructed in it. Nor is their own Language ever
5 proposed to them as worthy their Care and Cultivating, though they have Dayly use of it, and are not seldom in the future course of their Lives Judg'd of by their handsome or awkward way of Expressing themselves in it. Whereas the Languages whose Grammars they have been so much imployed in, are such as probably they shall scarce ever
10 speak or Write; or if upon occasion this should happen, they shall be excused for the Mistakes and Faults they make in it. Would not a *Chinese*, who took notice of this way of Breeding, be apt to imagine that all our young Gentlemen were design'd to be Teachers and Professors of the Dead Languages of Foreign Countries, and not to be
15 Men of Business in their own?

3. There is a third sort of Men, who apply themselves to two or three Foreign, Dead, and (which amongst us are called the) learned Languages; make them their study, and pique themselves upon their skill in them. No doubt those who propose to themselves the learning
20 of any Language with this view, and would be Critically exact in it, ought carefully to Study the Grammar of it. I would not be mistaken here, as if this were to under-value Greek and Latin: I grant these are Languages of great use and Excellency, and a Man can have no place amongst the Learned in this part of the World who is a stranger to
25 them. But the Knowledge a Gentleman would ordinarily draw for his use out of the Roman and Greek writers, I think he may attain without studying the Grammars of those Tongues, and by bare Reading, may come to understand them sufficiently for all his purposes. How much farther he shall at any time be concerned to look into the Grammar,
30 and Critical niceties of either of these Tongues, he himself will be able to determine when he comes to propose to himself the study of any thing that shall require it. Which brings me to the other part of the enquiry, *viz.*

When Grammar should be taught.

35 To which upon the premised grounds the answer is obvious, *viz.*

That if Grammar ought to be taught at any time, it must be to one that can speak the Language already, how else can he be taught the Grammar of it. This at least is evident from the practice of the Wise and Learned Nations amongst the Antients. They made it a part of
40 Education to cultivate their own, not foreign tongues. The Greeks

counted all other Nations barbarous, and had a contempt for their Languages. And though the Greek learning grew in Credit amongst the *Romans*, towards the end of their Commonwealth, yet it was the *Roman* Tongue that was made the Study of their Youth: Their own Language they were to make use of, and therefore it was their own Language they were instructed and exercised in.[73]

But more particularly to determine the proper season for Grammar, I do not see how it can reasonably be made any ones study, but as an introduction to Rhetorick: when it is thought time to put any one upon the care of polishing his Tongue, and of speaking better than the illiterate, then is the time for him to be instructed in the Rules of Grammar and not before. For Grammar being to teach Men not to speak, but to speak correctly and according to the exact Rules of the Tongue, which is one part of Elegancy, there is little use of the one to him that has no need of the other: where Rhetorick is not necessary, Grammar may be spared. I know not why any one should wast his Time, and beat his Head, about the Latin Grammar who does not intend to be a Critick, or make speeches and write Dispatches in it. When any one finds in himself a necessity or disposition to study any Foreign Language to the bottom, and to be nicely exact in the knowledge of it, it will be time enough to take a Grammatical survey of it. If his use of it be only to understand some Books writ in it, without a Critical knowledge of the Tongue it self, reading alone, as I have said, will attain this end without charging the Mind with the multiplied Rules and intricacies of Grammar.

§. 169. For the exercise of his Writing, let him sometimes *translate Latin* into *English:* q‑But the learning of *Latin*, being nothing but the learning of Words, a very unpleasant Business both to young and old, join as much other real Knowledge with it as you can, beginning still with that which lies most obvious to the Senses, such as is the Knowledge of *Minerals, Plants,* and *Animals*; and particularly Timber and Fruit-Trees, their parts and ways of propagation: Wherein a great deal may be taught a Child, which will not be useless to the Man.‑q But more especially *Geography, Astronomy,* and *Anatomy.* But whatever you are teaching him, r‑have a care still, that you do not clog him with too

§§ 169–70 *Latin.*

---

25 169] 160 **1**   33–228.3 But . . . to it.] *add.* **3**

q‑q *Revision of* **Corr.** 844 (ii. 776, ll. 13–19)   r‑r **Corr.** 929 (iii. 183); *forms part of* § 158 *in* **1**

[73] Not all Romans approved. Cf. Quintilian 1. 1. 12.

much at once; or make any thing his Business, but downright Vertue, or reprove him for any thing but Vice, or some apparent Tendency to it.⁻ʳ

170. ˢ⁻But if, after all, his Fate be to go to School to get the *Latin Tongue*, 'twill be in vain to talk to you concerning the method I think best to be observed in Schools; you must submit to that you find there; nor expect to have it changed for your Son: But yet by all means obtain, if you can, that he be not employ'd in making *Latin Themes* and *Declamations*, and least of all *Verses* of any kind. You may insist on it, if it will do any good, that you have no design to make him either a *Latin* Orator, or a Poet; but barely would have him understand perfectly a *Latin* Author; and that you observe, that those, who teach any of the modern Languages, and that with success, never amuse their Scholars, to make Speeches, or Verses, either in *French* or *Italian*, their Business being *Language barely*, and not Invention.⁻ˢ

§. 171. ᵗ⁻But to tell you a little more fully, why I would not have him exercis'd in making of *Themes and Verses*. 1. As to *Themes*, they have, I confess, the pretence of something useful, which is to teach People to speak handsomly and well, on any Subject: Which, if it could be attained this way, I own, would be a great advantage; there being nothing more becoming a Gentleman, nor more useful in all Occurrences of Life, than to be able, on any occasion, to speak well, and to the purpose. But this I say, That the making of *Themes*, as is usual in Schools, helps not one jot toward it. For do but consider what 'tis, in making a *Theme*, that a young Lad is employ'd about: 'Tis to make a Speech on some *Latin* Saying; as *Omnia vincit Amor*;⁷⁴ or, *Non licet in Bello bis peccare*,⁷⁵ &c. And here the poor Lad, who wants knowledge of those things, he is to speak of, which is to be had only from

§§ 171–3 *Themes.*

---

4 170] 161 ɪ 5 'twill be] 'tis ɪ 9 least **4 5**] least least **3** 12 that those,] those, **5** 16 171] 162 ɪ 28 those] these ɪ

ˢ⁻ˢ **Corr.** 844 (ii. 776, ll. 20–34) ᵗ⁻ᵗ **Corr.** 844 (ii. 777, ll. 1–29)

⁷⁴ Virgil, *Ecl.* x. 69 reads: 'Omnia vincit Amor: et nos cedamus Amori' (Love conquers all; let us too yield to love).

⁷⁵ Erasmus' translation (*Adagia*, iii. 1. 31) of οὐκ ἔστιν ἐν πολέμῳ δὶς ἁμαρτεῖν (In war it is not permitted to err twice), attributed to the Athenian general Lamachus (Plutarch(?), *Regum et imperatorum apophthegmata* = *Moralis* 186 F). **Corr.** 844 reads instead: 'Dulces sunt fructus, radix virtutis amara' (Sweet are the fruits, but bitter the root, of virtue), 'perhaps from an educational book, a collection of themes' (de Beer iii. 777 n.), cf. J. Leibius, *Studentica, hoc est apophthegmata, symbola et proverbia* (Coburg, 1627), sig. X3ᵛ, no. CCCXLVII.

Time and Observation, must set his Invention on the Rack to say something, where he knows nothing; which is a sort of *Egyptian* Tyranny, to bid them make Bricks, who have not yet any of the Materials.[76] And therefore it is usual, in such cases, for the poor Children, to go to those of Higher Forms with this Petition, *Pray give me a little* 5 *Sense*; which whether it be more reasonable, or more ridiculous, is not easie to determine. Before a Man can be in any capacity to speak on any Subject, 'tis necessary he be acquainted with it: Or else 'tis as foolish to set him to discourse of it, as to set a blind Man to talk of Colours, or a deaf Man of Musick. And would you not think him a 10 little crack'd, who would require another to make an Argument on a Moot Point, who understands nothing of our Laws? And what, I pray, do School-Boys understand concerning those matters, which are used to be proposed to them in their *Themes*, as Subjects to discourse on, to whet and exercise their Fancies?⁻ᵗ 15

§. 172. ᵘ⁻In the next place consider the Language that their *Themes* are made in: 'Tis *Latin*, a Language foreign in their Country, and long since dead every-where: A Language, which your Son, 'tis a thousand to one, shall never have an occasion once to make a Speech in, as long as he lives, after he comes to be a Man; and a Language, wherein the 20 manner of expressing ones self is so far different from ours, that to be perfect in that, would very little improve the Purity and Facility of his *English* Style.⁻ᵘ Besides that, there is now so little room, or use, for set Speeches in our own Language, in any part of our *English* Business, that I can see no pretence for this sort of Exercise in our Schools, 25 unless it can be supposed, that the making of set *Latin* Speeches, should be the way, to teach Men to speak well in *English extempore*. The way to that, I should think rather to be this: That there should be propos'd to young Gentleman rational and useful Questions, suited to their Age and Capacities, and on Subjects not wholly unknown to 30 them nor out of their way: Such as these, when they are ripe for Exercises of this Nature, they should *extempore*, or after a little meditation upon the Spot, speak to, without penning of any thing. For, I ask, if we will examine the effects of this way of learning to speak well, who speak best in any Business, when occasion calls them to it, upon any 35

8 he] to ɪ   9 of it,] on it, ɪ   16 172] 163 ɪ   29–32 to young . . .
Nature,] some rational and material Question to young Gentlemen, when they are of a
fit age for such Exercise, which ɪ   33 upon the Spot,] in the place, ɪ

ᵘ⁻ᵘ **Corr.** 844 (ii. 777, ll. 30–7)

[76] Cf. Exod. 5: 6–9.

debate, either those who have accustomed themselves to compose and
write down before-hand, what they would say; Or those, who thinking
only of the matter, to understand that as well as they can, use themselves only to speak *extempore?* And he, that shall judge by this, will be
5   little apt to think, that the accustoming him to studied Speeches, and
set Compositions, is the way to fit a young Gentleman for Business.

§. 173. ᵛ⁻But, perhaps, we shall be told, 'Tis to improve and perfect
them in the *Latin* Tongue. 'Tis true, that is their proper Business at
School; but the making of *Themes* is not the way to it: That perplexes
10 their Brains about invention of things to be said, not about the signification of Words to be learn'd: And when they are making a *Theme*, 'tis
Thoughts they search and sweat for, and not Language. But the
Learning and Mastery of a Tongue, being uneasie and unpleasant
enough in it self, should not be cumbred with any other Difficulties, as
15 is done in this way of proceeding. In fine, if Boys Invention be to be
quicken'd by such Exercise, let them make *Themes* in *English*, where
they have facility, and a command of Words, and will better see what
kind of Thoughts they have, when put into their own Language: And if
the *Latin* Tongue be to be learn'd, let it be done the easiest way, with-
20 out toiling and disgusting the Mind, by so uneasie an imployment, as
that of making Speeches join'd to it.⁻ᵛ

§. 174. ʷ⁻If these may be any Reasons against Children's making
Latin Themes at School, I have much more to say, and of more weight,
against their making *Verses*; Verses of any sort. For if he has no *Genius*
25 to *Poetry*, 'tis the most unreasonable thing in the World, to torment a
Child, and waste his time about that, which can never succeed: And if
he have a Poetick Vein, 'tis to me the strangest thing in the World, that
the Father should desire, or suffer it to be cherished, or improved.
Methinks the Parents should labour to have it stifled, and suppressed,
30 as much as may be: And I know not what reason a Father can have, to
wish his Son a Poet, who does not desire to have him bid defiance to
all other Callings, and Business: which is not yet the worst of the case.
For if he proves a successful Rhymer, and get once the Reputation of a
Wit, I desire it may be considered, what Company and Places he is like
35 to spend his Time in, nay, and Estate too: For it is very seldom seen,
that any one discovers Mines of Gold or Silver in *Parnassus*. 'Tis a

§ 174 *Verses.*

7 173] 164 1   22 174] 165 1

ᵛ⁻ᵛ **Corr.** 844 (ii. 778, ll. 1–16)   ʷ⁻ʷ **Corr.** 844 (ii. 778, l. 17–779, l. 7)

pleasant Air, but a barren Soil; and there are very few instances of those, who have added to their Patrimony by any thing they have reaped from thence. Poetry and Gaming, which usually go together, are alike in this too, That they seldom bring any advantage, but to those who have nothing else to live on. Men of Estates almost con- 5 stantly go away losers; and 'tis well if they escape at a cheaper rate than their whole Estates, or the greatest part of them. If therefore you would not have your Son the Fiddle to every jovial Company, without whom the Sparks could not relish their Wine, nor know how to pass an Afternoon idly, if you would not have him waste his Time and Estate, 10 to divert others, and contemn the dirty Acres left him by his Ancestors, I do not think you will much care he should be a *Poet*, or that his School-master should enter him in Versifying.⁻ʷ But yet, if any one will think Poetry a desireable Quality in his Son, and that the study of it would raise his Fancy and Parts, he must needs yet confess, that to 15 that end reading the excellent *Greek* and *Roman* Poets is of more use, than making bad Verses of his own, in a Language that is not his own. And he, whose design it is to excell in *English* Poetry, would not, I guess, think the way to it were to make his first Essays in *Latin* Verses.

§. 175. ˣ⁻Another thing very ordinary in the vulgar Method of 20 Grammar-Schools there is, of which I see no use at all, unless it be to balk young Lads in the way to learning Languages, which, in my Opinion, should be made as easie and pleasant as may be; and that which was painful in it, as much as possible quite removed. That which I mean, and here complain of, is, their being forced to learn by 25 heart, great parcels of the Authors which are taught them; wherein I can discover no advantage at all, especially to the Business they are upon. Languages are to be learn'd only by reading, and talking, and not by scraps of Authors got by heart; which when a Man's Head is stuff'd with, he has got the just Furniture of a Pedant, and 'tis the ready 30 way to make him one; than which there is nothing less becoming a Gentleman. For what can be more ridiculous, than to mix the rich and handsome Thoughts and Sayings of others, with a deal of poor Stuff of his own; which is thereby the more exposed, and has no other grace in it, nor will otherwise recommend the Speaker, than a thread-bare 35 russet Coat would, that was set off with large Patches of Scarlet, and

§§ 175–6 *Memoriter.*

20 175] 166 **1**

ˣ⁻ˣ **Corr.** 844 (ii. 779, ll. 8–35)

glittering Brocard. Indeed, where a Passage comes in the way, whose matter is worth remembrance, and the expression of it very close and excellent (as there are many such in the ancient Authors) it may not be amiss to lodge it in the Mind of young Scholars, and with such admir-

5 able Stroaks of those great Masters, sometimes exercise the Memory of School-boys. But their learning of their Lessons by heart, as they happen to fall out in their Books, without choice or distinction, I know not what it serves for, but to mis-spend their Time and Pains, and give them a disgust and aversion to their Books, wherein they find nothing

10 but useless trouble.⁻ˣ

§. 176. I hear it's said, That Children should be imploy'd in getting things by heart, to exercise and improve their Memories. I could wish this were said with as much Authority of Reason, as it is with forward-ness of Assurance, and that this practice were established upon good

15 Observation, more than old Custom. For it is evident, that strength of Memory is owing to an happy Constitution, and not to any habitual Improvement got by Exercise. 'Tis true, what the Mind is intent upon, and, for fear of letting it slip, often imprints afresh on it self by frequent reflection, that it is apt to retain, but still according to its own

20 natural strength of retention. An impression made on Bees-wax or Lead will not last so long as on Brass or Steel. Indeed, if it be renew'd often, it may last the longer; but every new reflecting on it is a new impression, and 'tis from thence one is to reckon, if one would know how long the Mind reteins⁷⁷ it. But the learning Pages of *Latin* by

25 heart, no more fits the Memory for Retention of any thing else, than the graving of one Sentence in Lead makes it the more capable of retaining firmly any other Characters. If such a sort of Exercise of the Memory were able to give it Strength and improve our Parts, Players of all other People must needs have the best Memories, and be the

30 best Company. But whether the Scraps, they have got into their Head this way, makes them remember other things the better; and whether their Parts be improved proportionably to the Pains they have taken in getting by heart others Sayings, Experience will shew. Memory is so necessary to all Parts and Conditions of Life, and so little is to be done

35 without it, that we are not to fear it should grow dull, and useless for want of Exercise, if Exercise would make it grow stronger. But I fear this Faculty of the Mind is not capable of much help and amendment in general by any Exercise or Endeavour of ours, at least not by that

11–234.2 § 176 *add.* **3**

⁷⁷ Variant sp., 'retains'.

used upon this pretence in Grammar Schools. And if *Xerxes* was able to call every common Soldier by Name in his Army,[78] that consisted of no less than an Hundred thousand Men, I think it may be guessed, he got not this wonderful Ability by learning his Lessons by heart when he was a Boy. This method of exercising and improving the Memory by toilsom Repetitions without Book of what they read, is, I think, little used in the Education of Princes, which if it had that Advantage is talked of, should be as little neglected in them as in the meanest School-boys: Princes having as much need of good Memories as any Man living, and have generally an equal share in this Faculty with other Men; though it has never been taken care of this way. What the Mind is intent upon, and careful of, that it remembers best, and for the Reason above-mentioned: To which, if Method and Order be joyn'd, all is done, I think, that can be, for the help of a weak Memory; and he that will take any other way to do it, especially that of charging it with a train of other Peoples words, which he that learns cares not for, will, I guess, scarce find the Profit answer half the Time and Pains imploy'd in it.

I do not mean hereby, that there should be no Exercise given to Childrens Memories. I think their Memories should be imploy'd, but not in learning by roat whole Pages out of Books, which the Lesson being once said, and that Task over, are deliver'd up again to Oblivion and neglected for ever. This mends neither the Memory nor the Mind. What they should learn by heart out of Authors, I have above-mentioned: And such Wise and Useful Sentences being once given in charge to their Memories, they should never be suffer'd to forget again, but be often call'd to an account for them: whereby, besides the Use those Sayings may be to them in their future Life, as so many good Rules and Observations, they will be taught to reflect often, and bethink themselves what they have to remember, which is the only way to make the Memory quick and useful. The Custom of frequent Reflection will keep their Minds from running adrift, and call their Thoughts home from useless unattentive roving: And therefore, I think, it may do well, to give them something every day to remember; but something still, that is in it self worth the remembring, and what you would never have out of Mind, whenever you call, or they themselves search for it. This

---

[78] Xerxes is an error for Cyrus, said to know all his officers by name at Xenophon, *Cyrop.* 5. 3. 46–50, but in later writers (e.g. Valerius Maximus 8. 7. ext. 16) the whole army.

will oblige them often to turn their Thoughts inwards, than which you cannot wish them a better intellectual habit.

§. 177. But under whose Care soever a Child is put, to be taught, during the tender and flexible Years of his Life, this is certain, it should be one, who thinks *Latin* and *Language* the least part of Education; one who knowing how much Vertue, and a well-temper'd Soul is to be preferr'd to any sort of *Learning* or *Language*, makes it his chief Business to form the Mind of his Scholars, and give that a right disposition: which, if once got, though all the rest should be neglected, would, in due time, produce all the rest: and which if it be not got, and setled, so as to keep out ill and vicious Habits, *Languages* and *Sciences*, and all the other Accomplishments of Education will be to no purpose, but to make the worse, or more dangerous Man. And, indeed, whatever stir there is made about getting of *Latin*, as the great and difficult business, his Mother may teach it him her self, if she will but spend two or three hours in a day with him, and make him read the Evangelists in *Latin* to her: For she need but buy a *Latin* Testament, and having got somebody to mark the last Syllable but one, where it is long, in Words above two Syllables (which is enough to regulate her Pronunciation and Accenting the Words) read daily in the *Gospels*, and then let her avoid Understanding them in *Latin* if she can. And when she understands the Evangelists in *Latin*, let her, in the same manner, read *Æsop*'s *Fables*, and so proceed on to *Eutropius, Justin*, and other such Books. I do not mention this, as an Imagination of what I fansie may do, but as of a thing I have known done, and the *Latin* Tongue with ease got this way.

But to return to what I was saying: He that takes on him the charge of bringing up young Men, especially young Gentlemen, should have something more in him than *Latin*, more than even a Knowledge in the Liberal Sciences: He should be a Person of eminent Vertue and Prudence, and with good Sense, have good Humour, and the skill to carry himself with gravity, ease, and kindness, in a constant Conversation with his Pupils. But of this I have spoken at large in another place.

§. 178. ʸ⁻At the same time that he is learning *French* and *Latin*, a Child, as has been said, may also be enter'd in *Arithmetick, Geography, Chronology, History*, and *Geometry* too. For if these be taught him in

§ 177 *Latin.*   § 178 *Geography.*

---

3 177] 167 **1**   33 But . . . place.] *add.* **3**   34 178] 168 **1**

ʸ⁻ʸ *Expansion of* **Corr.** 943 (iii. 222-3)

French or *Latin*, when he begins once to understand either of these Tongues, he will get a knowledge in these Sciences, and the Language to boot.

Geography, I think, should be begun with: For the learning of the Figure of the *Globe*, the Situation and Boundaries of the Four Parts of the World, and that of particular Kingdoms and Countries, being only an exercise of the Eyes and Memory, a child with pleasure will learn and retain them:^{-y} And this is so certain, that I now live in the House with a Child, whom his Mother[79] has so well instructed this way in *Geography*, that he knew the Limits of the Four Parts of the World, could readily point, being asked, to any Country upon the Globe, or any County in the Map of *England*, knew all the great Rivers, Promontories, Straits, and Bays in the World, and could find the Longitude and Latitude of any Place, before he was six Years old. ^{z-}These things, that he will thus learn by sight, and have by roat in his Memory, is not all, I confess, that he is to learn upon the *Globes*. But yet it is a good step and preparation to it, and will make the remainder much easier, when his Judgment is grown ripe enough for it:^{-z} Besides, that it gets so much time now; and by the pleasure of knowing things, leads him on insensibly to the gaining of Languages.

§. 179. When he has the natural Parts of the Globe well fix'd in his Memory, it may then be time to begin *Arithmetick.* By the natural Parts of the Globe, I mean the several Positions of the Parts of the Earth, and Sea, under different Names and Distinctions of Countries, not coming yet to those Artificial and imaginary Lines, which have been invented, and are only suppos'd for the better improvement of that Science.

§. 180. *Arithmetick*, is the easiest, and consequently the first sort of abstract Reasoning, which the Mind commonly bears, or accustoms it self to: And is of so general use in all parts of Life and Business, that scarce any thing is to be done without it. This is certain, a Man cannot have too much of it, nor too perfectly: He should therefore begin to be exercis'd in *counting*, as soon, and as far, as he is capable of it; and do something in it every Day, till he is Master of the Art of *Numbers*.

---

§ 179 *Arithmetick.*   § 180 *Arithmetick.   Astronomy.*

---

11 Country] County **1**   12 County *ed.*] Country **1 3 4 5**   21 179] 169 **1**
22 the] *om.* **5**   28 180] 170 **1**

^{z-z} **Corr.** 943 (iii. 223, ll. 27–31)

[79] Lady Masham, whose son Francis Cudworth Masham was six years old in 1693.

When he understands *Addition* and *Substraction*, he may then be advanced farther in *Geography*, and after he is acquainted with the *Poles, Zones, parallel Circles*, and *Meridians*, be taught *Longitude* and *Latitude*, and by them be made to understand the use of Maps, and by

5 the Numbers placed on their Sides, to know the respective Situation of Countries, and how to find them out on the Terrestrial Globe. Which when he can readily do, he may then be entred in the Celestial; and there going over all the Circles again, with a more particular Observation of the Eclyptick, or Zodiack, to fix them all very clearly

10 and distinctly in his Mind, he may be taught the Figure and Position of the several Constellations, which may be shewed him first upon the Globe, and then in the Heavens.

When that is done, and he knows pretty well the Constellations of this our Hemisphere, it may be time to give him some Notion of this

15 our planetary World, and to that purpose it may not be amiss to make him a Draught of the *Copernican* System, and therein explain to him the Situation of the Planets, their respective Distances from the Sun, the Center of their Revolutions. This will prepare him to understand the Motion and Theory of the Planets, the most easy and natural Way.

20 For since Astronomers no longer doubt of the Motion of the Planets about the Sun, it is fit he should proceed upon that Hypothesis which is not only the simplest and least perplexed for a Learner, but also the likeliest to be true in it self. But in this as in all other parts of Instruction, great Care must be taken with Children, to begin with that, which

25 is plain and simple, and to teach them as little as can be at once, and settle that well in their Heads, before you proceed to the next, or any thing new in that Science. Give them first one simple Idea, and see that they take it right, and perfectly comprehend it before you go any farther, and then add some other simple Idea which lies next in your

30 way to what you aim at, and so proceeding by gentle and insensible steps, Children without Confusion and Amazement, will have their Understandings opened, and their Thoughts extended farther, than

4–10 by them . . . taught] the use of Maps, and by that time he is perfected in these Circles of the Globe, with the *Horizon* and the *Eclyptick*, he may be taught the same thing also on the *Celestial Globe*, with 1   13–23 When . . . it self.] *add.* 3 14 Notion] Notions 5   23 But in . . .] *run on after* 'Heavens', l. 12 1   27– 32 Science . . . opened,] Science, whereby Children 'scape being amazed and confounded; by which way of giving them first one simple Idea, and taking Care that they took it right and perfectly comprehended it before you went any farther, and then adding some other simple Idea (which lay next in your way to what you aim'd at) and no more to it, and so proceeding by gentle and insensible steps, Children have had early righter Apprehensions, 1   28 comprehend 4 5] comprehended 3

could have been expected. And when any one has learn'd any thing himself, there is no such way to fix it in his Memory, and to incourage him to go on, as to set him to teach it others.[a]

§. 181. [b]When he has once got such an acquaintance with the *Globes*, as is above-mentioned, he may be fit to be tried a little in *Geometry*; wherein I think the six first Books of *Euclid* enough for him to be taught. For I am in some doubt, whether more to a Man of Business be necessary or useful. At least if he have a Genius and Inclination to it, being enter'd so far by his Tutor, he will be able to go on of himself without a Teacher.[-b]

[c]The *Globes* therefore must be studied, and that diligently, and I think, may be begun betimes, if the Tutor will but be careful to distinguish, what the Child is capable of knowing, and what not; for which this may be a Rule, that perhaps will go a pretty way (*viz.*) that Children may be taught any thing, that falls under their Senses, especially their sight, as far as their Memories only are exercised: And thus a Child very young may learn, which is the *Æquator*, which the *Meridian*, &c. which *Europe* and which *England* upon the Globes, as soon almost as he knows the Rooms of the House he lives in, if Care be taken not to teah him too much at once, nor to set him upon a new Part, till that, which he is upon, be perfectly learn'd and fix'd in his Memory.[-c]

§. 182. With Geography, *Chronology* ought to go hand in hand. I mean the general part of it, [d]so that he may have in his Mind a view of the whole current of time, and the several considerable *Epochs* that are made use of in History. Without these two, History, which is the great Mistress of Prudence and Civil Knowledge; and ought to be the proper Study of a Gentleman, or Man of Business in the World; without Geography and *Chronology*, I say, History will be very ill retained, and very little useful; but be only a jumble of Matters of Fact, confusedly heaped together without Order or Instruction. 'Tis by these two, that the Actions of Mankind are ranked into their proper Places of Times and Countries, under which Circumstances, they are not only much easier kept in the Memory, but in that natural Order, are

§ 181 *Geometry.*　　　§§ 182–3 *Chronology.*

1 any one] he 1　　4 181] 171 1　　5 as is above-mentioned] *add.* 3
23 182] 172 1

[a] **Corr.** 929 (iii. 183, ll. 17–18) *mentions the child as teacher*　　[b-b] *Cf.* **Corr.** 844 (ii. 780, ll. 14–16)　　[c-c] **Corr.** 943 (iii. 223, ll. 15–26)　　[d-d] **Corr.** 943 (iii. 223, ll. 2–15)

only capable to afford those Observations, which make a Man the better and the abler for reading them.$^{-d}$

§. 183. $^{e-}$When I speak of *Chronology* as a Science he should be perfect in, I do not mean the little Controversies, that are in it. These are
5 endless, and most of them of so little Importance to a Gentleman, as not to deserve to be inquir'd into, were they capable of an easy Decision. And therefore all that learned Noise and Dust of the Chronologist is wholly to be avoided. The most useful Book I have seen in that part of Learning, is a small Treatise of *Strauchius*, which is printed in
10 Twelves, under the Title of *Breviarum Chronologium*,^{80} out of which may be selected all that is necessary to be taught a young Gentleman concerning *Chronology*; for all that is in that Treatise a learner need not be cumbred with. He has in him the most remarkable or usual *Epochs* reduced all to that of the *Julian Period*,^{81} which is the easiest and
15 plainest, and surest Method, that can be made use of in *Chronology*. $^{-e}$ To this Treatise of *Strauchius*, *Helvicus*'s Tables^{82} may be added as a Book to be turned to on all occasions.

§. 184. As nothing teaches, so nothing delights more than History. The first of these recommends it to the Study of Grown Men, the
20 latter makes me think it the fittest for a young Lad, who as soon as he is instructed in Chronology, and acquainted with the several *Epochs* in use in this part of the World, and can reduce them to the *Julian Period*, should then have some *Latin History* put into his Hand. The choice should be directed by the easiness of the Stile; for where-ever he
25 begins, Chronology will keep it from Confusion; and the pleasantness of the Subject inviting him to read, the Language will insensibly be got, without that terrible vexation and uneasiness, which Children suffer, where they are put into Books beyond their Capacity, such as are the *Roman* Orators and Poets, only to learn the *Roman* Language.
30 When he has by reading Master'd the easier, such perhaps as *Justin*,

§ 184 *History*.

---

3 183] 172 **1** (*cf. p.* 59)   18 184] 173 **1**

$^{e-e}$ **Corr.** 943 (iii. 223, l. 31–224, l. 9)

^{80} Aegidius Strauch's *Breviarium Chronologicum* was first published in Wittenberg in 1657; an English translation from the third edn. was published in 1699 (LL 2793, 2793a).
^{81} The Julian Period, named by its inventor Josephus Justus Scaliger in honour of his father Julius Caesar Scaliger, is an astronomical era starting from 1 Jan. 4713 BC.
^{82} Christoph Helwig's *Chronologia universalis ab origine mundi per quattuor summa imperia* (Giessen, 1618). An English translation, with title: *Historical and Chronological Theatre*, was published in London in 1687.

Eutropius, Quintus Curtius,[83] &c. the next degree to these, will give him no great Trouble: And thus by a gradual Progress from the plainest and easiest *Historians*, he may at last come to read the most difficult and sublime of the *Latin* Authors, such as are *Tully, Virgil*, and *Horace*.

§. 185. The Knowledge of *Vertue*, all along from the beginning, in all the Instances he is capable of, being taught him, more by Practice than Rules; and the love of Reputation instead of satisfying his Appetite, being made habitual in him, I know not whether he should read any other Discourses of Morality, but what he finds in the Bible; or have any System of *Ethicks* put into his Hand, till he can read *Tully's Offices*,[84] not as a School-Boy to learn *Latin*, but as one that would be informed in the Principles and Precepts of Vertue, for the Conduct of his Life.

§. 186. [f-]When he has pretty well digested *Tully's Offices*, and added to it *Puffendorf de Officio hominis & civis*, it may be seasonable to set him upon *Grotius de Jure Belli & Pacis*, or which perhaps is the better of the two, *Puffendorf de Jure naturali & Gentium;*[85] wherein he will be instructed in the natural Rights of Men, and the Original and Foundations of Society, and the Duties resulting from thence. This *general Part of Civil-Law* and History, are Studies which a Gentleman should not barely touch at, but constantly dwell upon, and never have done with. A Vertuous and well behaved young Man, that is well versed in the *general Part of the Civil-Law* (which concerns not the chicane of private Cases, but the Affairs and Intercourse of civilized Nations in general, grounded upon Principles of Reason) understands *Latin* well, and can write a good hand, one may turn loose into the World, with great assurance, that he will find Imployment and Esteem every where.[-f]

§. 187. [g-]It would be strange to suppose an *English* Gentleman should be ignorant of the *Law* of his Country. This, whatever station he is in, is so requisite, that from a Justice of the Peace, to a Minister of

§ 185   *Ethics.*   § 186   *Civil-Law.*   § 187   *Law.*

---

5 185] 174 **1**   13 186] 175 **1**   13–14 and . . . *civis*,] add. **3**   15 perhaps]
I think, **1**   28 187] 176 **1**

[f-f] *Revision of* **Corr.** 844 (ii. 780, ll. 1–12)   [g-g] *Revision and expansion of* **Corr.** 844 (ii. 784, ll. 17–27)

[83] Quintus Curtius Rufus, an historian in the early Roman empire, wrote about Alexander the Great.

[84] Cicero's *De officiis* (On Moral Duties).

[85] Hugo Grotius' *De jure belli ac pacis libri tres* (Paris, 1625) dealt with international law and relations, especially their legal aspects. Samuel von Pufendorf wrote *De jure naturae et gentium* (Lund, 1672) and *De officio hominis et civis* (Lund, 1673).

State, I know no Place he can well fill without it. I do not mean the chicane or wrangling and captious part of the *Law*; a Gentleman, whose Business it is to seek the true measures of Right and Wrong, and not the Arts how to avoid doing the one, and secure himself in
5 doing the other, ought to be as far from such a study of the *Law*, as he is concerned diligently to apply himself to that, wherein he may be serviceable to his Country. And to that purpose, I think the right way for a Gentleman to study *Our Law*, which he does not design for his Calling, is to take a view of our *English* Constitution and Government,
10 in the ancient Books of the *Common Law*; and some more modern Writers, who out of them have given an account of this Government. And having got a true Idea of that, then to read our History, and with it join in every King's Reign the *Laws* then made. This will give an insight into the reason of our *Statutes*, and shew the true ground upon
15 which they came to be made, and what weight they ought to have.⁻ᵍ

§. 188. ʰ⁻*Rhetorick* and *Logick* being the Arts, that in the ordinary method usually follow immediately after Grammar, it may perhaps be wondered that I have said so little of them. The reason is, because of the little advantage young People receive by them. For I have seldom
20 or never observed any one to get the Skill of reasoning well, or speaking handsomly by studying those Rules, which pretend to teach it: And therefore I would have a young Gentleman take a view of them in the shortest Systems could be found, without dwelling long on the contemplation and study of those Formalities. Right Reasoning is
25 founded on something else than the *Predicaments* and *Predicables*, and does not consist in talking in *Mode* and *Figure* it self. But 'tis besides my present Business to enlarge upon this Speculation. To come therefore to what we have in hand; if you would have your Son *Reason well*, let him read *Chillingworth*;ⁱ ⁸⁶ and if you would have him speak well, let
30 him be conversant in *Tully*, to give him the true *Idea* of *Eloquence*; and let him read those things that are well writ in *English*, to perfect his Style in the purity of our Language.⁻ʰ

§. 189. If the use and end of right Reasoning, be to have right

§ 188 *Rhetorick. Logick.*   § 189 *Rhetorick. Logick. Style. Letters. English.*

3 it] *om.* **4 5**   15 ought] out **NA**   16 188] 177 **1**   33 If the . . .] *run on within* § 177 **1**

ʰ⁻ʰ **Corr.** 844 (ii. 784, l. 28–785, l. 7)   ⁱ Bacon **Corr.** 844; *changed by Locke in* 849 (iii. 3)

⁸⁶ William Chillingworth wrote *The Religion of Protestants* (1638).

Notions, and a right Judgment of things; to distinguish betwixt Truth and Falshood, Right and Wrong; and to act accordingly: be sure not to let your Son be bred up in the Art and Formality of Disputing, either practising it himself, or admiring it in others: unless instead of an able Man, you desire to have him an insignificant Wrangler, Opiniater in Discourse, and priding himself in contradicting others; or, which is worse, questioning every thing, and thinking there is no such thing as truth to be sought, but only Victory in Disputing. There cannot be any thing so disingenuous, so mis-becoming a Gentleman, or any one who pretends to be a rational Creature, as not to yield to plain Reason, and the Conviction of clear Arguments. Is there any thing more inconsistent with civil Conversation, and the end of all Debate, than not to take an Answer, though never so full and satisfactory; but still to go on with the Dispute as long as equivocal Sounds can furnish [a *Medius terminus*] a Term to wrangle with on the one side, or a Distinction on the other? whether pertinent or impertinent, Sense or Nonsense, agreeing with or contrary to what he had said before, it matters not. For this in short, is the Way and Perfection of Logical Disputes, That the opponent never take any Answer, nor the respondent ever yield to any Argument. This neither of them must do, whatever becomes of Truth or Knowledge; unless he will pass for a poor baffl'd Wretch, and lie under the Disgrace of not being able to maintain whatever he has once affirm'd, which is the great Aim and Glory in Disputing. Truth is to be found and supported by a mature and due Consideration of Things themselves, and not by artificial Terms and Ways of Arguing: These lead not Men so much into the discovery of Truth, as into a captious and fallacious use of doubtful Words, which is the most useless and most offensive way of talking, and such as least suits a Gentleman or a lover of Truth of any thing in the World.[87]

There can scarce be a greater Defect in a Gentleman, than not to express himself well either in Writing or Speaking. But yet, I think, I may ask my Reader, whether he doth not know a great many, who live upon their Estates, and so, with the Name, should have the Qualities of Gentlemen, who cannot so much as tell a Story as they should; much less speak clearly and perswasively in any Business. This, I

8–23 There . . . Disputing.] *add.* 3   24 supported] maintained 1
25 These] which 1   28 most offensive] disingenuos **NN** disingenuous **NA**   and
such . . . suits] and most unbecoming 1   30–244.35 There . . . in it.] *add.* 3

[87] Formal logic, and the method of disputing using the rules of syllogistic reasoning, came under heavy and extended attack in the *Essay*. See 4. 7, 4. 17.

think not to be so much their Fault, as the Fault of their Education. For, I must without partiality do my Countrymen this right, That where they apply themselves, I see none of their Neighbours out-go them. They have been taught *Rhetorick*, but yet never taught how to express themselves handsomly with their Tongues or Pens in the Language they are always to use: As if the Names of the Figures, that embellish'd the Discourses of those who understood the Art of Speaking, were the very Art and Skill of Speaking well. This, as all other things of Practice, is to be learn'd, not by a few, or a great many Rules given; But by Exercise and Application according to good Rules, or rather Patterns, till Habits are got, and a facility of doing it well.

Agreeable hereunto, perhaps it might not be amiss, to make Children, as soon as they are capable of it, often to tell a Story of any thing, they know; and to correct at first the most remarkable Fault, they are guilty of in their way of putting it together. When that Fault is cured, then to shew them the next, and so on, till one after another all, at least the gross ones, are mended. When they can tell Tales pretty well, then it may be time to make them write them. The Fables of *Æsop*, the only Book almost that I know fit for Children, may afford them Matter for this Exercise of writing *English*, as well as for reading and translating to enter them in the *Latin* Tongue. When they are got past the Faults of Grammar, and can joyn in a continued coherent Discourse the several parts of a Story, without Bald and Unhandsom Forms of Transition (as is usual) often repeated, he that desires to perfect them yet farther in this, which is the first step to speaking well, and needs no invention, may have recourse to *Tully*, and by putting in Practice those Rules which that Master of Eloquence gives in his First Book *De Inventione*, §. 20.[88] make them know wherein the Skill and Graces of an handsom Narrative, according to the several Subjects and Designs of it, lie. Of each of which Rules fit Examples may be found out, and therein they may be shewn how others have practis'd them. The ancient Classick Authors afford plenty of such Examples, which they should be made not only to Translate, but have set before them as Patterns for their daily imitation.

When they understand how to write *English* with due Connexion, Propriety, and Order, and are pretty well Masters of a tolerable Narrative Stile, they may be advanced to writing of Letters. Wherein they should not be put upon any strains of Wit or Complement; but taught

---

[88] That section treats of the form of narrative used in arguing legal cases: it should be brief, clear, and plausible.

to express their own plain easie Sence, without any incoherence, confusion or roughness. And when they are perfect in this, they may, to raise their Thoughts, have set before them the Example of *Voitures*[89] for the Entertainment of their Friends at a distance with Letters of Complement, Mirth, Raylery or Diversion; and *Tully*'s *Epistles* as the best Pattern, whether for Business or Conversation.[90] The writing of Letters has so much to do in all the occurrences of Humane Life, that no Gentleman can avoid shewing himself in this kind of Writing. Occasions will daily force him to make this use of his Pen, which, besides the Consequences, that in his Affairs, his well or ill managing of it often draws after it, always lays him open to a severer Examination of his Breeding, Sense, and Abilities, than oral Discourses; whose transient Faults dying for the most part with the Sound, that gives them Life, and so not subject to a strict review, more easily scape Observation and Censure.

Had the Methods of Education been directed to their right Ends, one would have thought this so Necessary a Part could not have been neglected, whilst Themes and Verses in *Latin*, of no use at all, were so constantly every where pressed, to the racking of Childrens Inventions beyond their Strength; and hindering their chearful Progress in learning the Tongues, by unnatural Difficulties. But Custom has so ordain'd it, and who dares Disobey? And would it not be very unreasonable to require of a learned Country School-master (who has all the Tropes and Figures in *Farnaby*'s *Rhetorick*[91] at his Fingers ends) to teach his Scholar to express himself handsomly in *English*, when it appears to be so little his Business or Thought, that the Boy's Mother (despised, 'tis like, as illiterate for not having read a System of *Logick* and *Rhetorick*) out-does him in it?

To Write and Speak correctly gives a Grace, and gains a favourable Attention to what one has to say: And since 'tis *English*, that an *English* Gent. will have constant use of, that is the Language he should chiefly Cultivate, and wherein most care should be taken to polish and perfect his Stile. To speak or write better *Latin* than *English*, may make a Man be talk'd of, but he would find it more to his purpose to Express himself well in his own Tongue, that he uses every moment, than to have

[89] Vincent Voiture was known for his excellent letters to friends, published in 1654 as *Les Lettres de Mr de Voiture*.

[90] Cicero's *Epistulae* (*ad Familiares, ad Atticum, ad Quintum fratrem*), still regarded as classics of their kind.

[91] Thomas Farnaby wrote an *Index Rhetoricus* (London, 1625 and subsequent revisions).

the vain Commendation of others for a very insignificant quality. This I find universally neglected, and no care taken any where to improve Young Men in their own Language, that they may throughly under-stand and be Masters of it. If any one among us have a facility or purity
5 more than ordinary in his Mother Tongue, it is owing to Chance, or his Genius, or any thing, rather than to his Education or any care of his Teacher. To Mind what *English* his Pupil speaks or writes is below the Dignity of one bred up amongst *Greek* and *Latin*, though he have but little of them himself. These are the learned Languages fit only for
10 learned Men to meddle with and teach: *English* is the Language of the illiterate Vulgar. Though yet we see the Politie of some of our Neigh-bours hath not thought it beneath the Publick Care, to promote and reward the improvement of their own Language; polishing and inrich-ing their Tongue is no small Business amongst them, it hath Colleges
15 and Stipends appointed it, and there is raised amongst them a great Ambition and Æmulation of writing correctly; and we see what they are come to by it, and how far they have spread one of the worst Lan-guages possibly in this part of the World, if we look upon it as it was in some few Reigns backwards, whatever it be now. The great Men
20 amongst the *Romans* were daily exercising themselves in their own Language, and we find yet upon Record the Names of Orators, who taught some of their Emperors *Latin*, though it were their Mother Tongue.

'Tis plain, the *Greeks* were yet more nice in theirs, all other Speech
25 was barbarous to them, but their own, and no foreign Language appears to have been studied or valued amongst that learned and acute People; though it be past doubt, that they borrowed their Learn-ing and Philosophy from abroad.

I am not here speaking against *Greek* and *Latin:* I think they ought
30 to be studied, and the *Latin* at least understood well by every Gentle-man. But whatever foreign Languages a Young Man meddles with (and the more he knows the better) that which he should critically study, and labour to get a facility, clearness and elegancy to Express himself in, should be his own, and to this purpose he should daily be
35 exercised in it.

§. 190. *ʲ⁻Natural Philosophy*, as a speculative Science, I imagin we

§ 190–4 *Natural Philosophy.*

---

36 190] *unnumbered para.* 1 imagin] think 1
ʲ⁻ʲ **Corr.** 844 (ii. 785, ll. 8–12)

have none, and perhaps, I may think I have reason to say, we never shall be able to make a Science of it. The Works of Nature are contrived by a Wisdom, and operate by ways too far surpassing our Faculties to discover, or Capacities to conceive, for us ever to be able to reduce them into a Science.⁻ʲ *Natural Philosophy* being the Know- 5
ledge of the Principles, Properties, and Operations of Things, as they are in themselves, I imagine there are Two Parts of it, one comprehending Spirits with their Nature and Qualities; and the other *Bodies.* The first of these is usually referr'd to *Metaphysicks:* But under what Title soever the consideration of *Spirits* comes, I think it ought to go 10
before the study of Matter, and Body, not as a Science that can be methodized into a System, and treated of upon Principles of Knowledge; but as an enlargement of our Minds towards a truer and fuller comprehension of the intellectual World, to which we are led both by Reason and Revelation. And since the clearest and largest Discoveries 15
we have of other *Spirits*, besides God, and our own Souls, is imparted to us from Heaven, by Revelation; I think the Information, that at least young People should have of them, should be taken from that Revelation. To this purpose, I conclude, it would be well, if there were made a good History of the Bible, for young People to read: wherein if every 20
thing, that is fit to be put into it, were laid down in its due Order of Time, and several things omitted, which are suited only to riper Age, that Confusion, which is usually produced by promiscuous reading of the Scripture, as it lies now bound up in our Bibles, would be avoided. And also this other good obtained, that by reading of it constantly, 25
there would be instilled into the Minds of Children, a notion and belief of *Spirits*, they having so much to do in all the Transactions of that History, which will be a good Preparation to the study of *Bodies.* For without the notion and allowance of *Spirits*, our Philosophy will be lame and defective in one main Part of it, when it leaves out the 30
Contemplation of the most Excellent and Powerful Part of the Creation.

§. 191. Of this *History of the Bible*, I think too it would be well, if there were a short and plain Epitome made, containing the chief and most material Heads, for Children to be conversant in, as soon as they can 35
read. This, though it will lead them early into some Notion of *Spirits*, yet is not contrary to what I said above, That I would not have

2 be able ... it.] *add.* **3** 4 ever to] ever **5** 19 conclude] think **1**
20 if] *add.* **3** 21 were] being **1** 22 are] were **1** 29 *Spirits*] *Spirit* **5**
33 191] 179 **1**

Children troubled whilst young with Notions of *Spirits*, whereby my meaning was, that I think it inconvenient, that their yet tender Minds should receive early Impressions of *Goblins, Spectres*, and *Apparitions*, wherewith their Maids, and those about them, are apt to fright them
5 into a compliance with their Orders, which often proves a great inconvenience to them all their Lives after, by subjecting their Minds to Frights, fearful Apprehensions, Weakness, and Superstition; which, when coming abroad into the World, and Conversation, they grow weary and asham'd of, it not seldom happens, that to make as they
10 think, a through Cure, and ease themselves of a load, which has sate so heavy on them, they throw away the thoughts of all *Spirits* together, and so run into the other but worse extream.

§. 192. The Reason why I would have this premised to *the study of Bodies*; and the Doctrine of the Scriptures well imbibed, before young
15 Men be entered in *Natural Philosophy*, is, because Matter being a thing, that all our Senses are constantly conversant with, it is so apt to possess the Mind, and exclude all other Beings, but Matter, that prejudice, grounded on such Principles, often leaves no room for the admittance of Spirits, or the allowing any such things as *immaterial*
20 *Beings in rerum natura:* when yet it is evident, that by mere Matter and Motion, none of the great Phænomena of Nature can be resolved, to instance but in that common one of Gravity, which I think impossible to be explained by any natural Operation of Matter, or any other Law of Motion, but the positive Will of a Superiour Being, so ordering it.[92]
25 And therefore since the Deluge cannot be well explained without admitting something out of the ordinary course of Nature, I propose it to be considered whether God's altering the Center of gravity in the Earth for a time (a thing as intelligible as gravity it self, which, perhaps a little variation of Causes unknown to us would produce) will not
30 more easily account for *Noah*'s Flood, than any *Hypothesis* yet made use of to solve it. I hear the great Objection to this is, that it would

10 which] *add.* **3**   13 192] 180 **1**   31–247.7 I hear . . . explain it.] *add.* **3**

[92] The reference here to the inadequacy of 'mere Matter and Motion' to explain the phenomena of nature echoes important doctrines discussed in the *Essay* and in Locke's exchanges with Stillingfleet. One issue was whether matter, even with motion added, could initiate and cause any events. Locke sided with those, such as Samuel Clarke and Isaac Newton, who reserved genuine causal action to God (and perhaps to other spirits). Matter was considered to be passive and inert. The other issue concerns the cause of gravity and whether it was natural and essential to matter. These same writers traced gravity to God and to his positive will to add it to matter. See *Essay* 2. 23 and Locke's *Reply to the Right Reverend the Lord Bishop of Worcester's Answer to His Second Letter*.

produce but a partial Deluge. But the alteration of the Center of Gravity once allow'd, 'tis no hard matter to conceive that the Divine Power might make the Center of gravity placed at a due distance from the Center of the Earth, move round it in a convenient space of time, whereby the Floud would become Universal, and as I think, answer all the Phænomena of the Deluge as deliver'd by *Moses*, at an easier rate than those many hard Suppositions that are made use of to explain it. But this is not a place for that Argument which is here only mentioned by the bye, to shew the necessity of having recourse to something beyond bare Matter and its Motion, in the explication of Nature; to which the Notions of Spirits and their Power, as deliver'd in the Bible, where so much is attributed to their Operation, may be a fit Preparative, reserving to a fitter Opportunity, a fuller Explication of this *Hypothesis*, and the Application of it to all the Parts of the Deluge, and any Difficulties can be supposed in the History of the Flood, as recorded in the Scripture.

§. 193. ᵏ⁻But to return to the study of *Natural Philosophy*, though the World be full of Systems of it,⁹³ yet I cannot say, I know any one which can be taught a Young Man as a Science, wherein he may be sure to find Truth and Certainty, which is, what all Sciences give an expectation of. I do not hence conclude that none of them are to be read: It is necessary for a Gentleman in this learned Age to look into some of them, to fit himself for Conversation. But whether that of *Des Cartes* be put into his Hands, as that which is most in Fashion; or it be thought fit to give him a short view of that and several other also, I think the Systems of *Natural Philosophy*, that have obtained in this part of the World, are to be read, more to know the *Hypotheses*, and to understand the Terms and Ways of Talking of the several Sects, than with hopes to gain thereby a comprehensive, scientifical, and satisfactory Knowledge of the Works of Nature:⁻ᵏ Only this may be said, that the Modern *Corpuscularians* talk, in most Things, more intelligibly than the *Peripateticks*,⁹⁴ who possessed the Schools immediately before

---

1–2 But the . . . once 4] But that 3   7–8 But . . . mentioned] But this I mention 1
11–12 as . . . Operation,] to whose Operation so much is attributed in the Bible, 1
15 Scripture.] Bible. 1   16 193] 181 1

ᵏ⁻ᵏ *Greatly altered from* **Corr.** 844 (ii. 785, ll. 19–24)

⁹³ That is, Cartesian or Newtonian physics.

⁹⁴ '*Peripateticks*' is a loose reference to Aristotelians of different sorts, who, Locke believed, relied too much on the authority of Aristotle, rather than upon observation and experiment. In saying that a science of nature is not possible, Locke seems to have meant that *certainty* about the principles, causes, and inner workings of nature was beyond man's knowledge. He did not mean to discourage the practice of experimental

them. He that would look farther back, and acquaint himself with the
several Opinions of the Ancients, may consult Dr. *Cudworth*'s *Intellectual System*;[95] wherein that very learned Author hath with such
Accurateness and Judgment collected and explained the Opinions of
5   the Greek Philosophers, that what Principles they built on, and what
were the chief *Hypotheses*, that divided them, is better to be seen in him,
than any where else that I know. But I would not deterr any one from the
study of Nature, because all the Knowledge we have, or possibly can
have of it, cannot be brought into a Science. There are very many things
10   in it, that are convenient and necessary to be known to a Gentleman:
[1-]And a great many other, that will abundantly reward the Pains of the
Curious with Delight and Advantage. But these, I think, are rather to be
found amongst such Writers, as have imploy'd themselves in making
rational Experiments and Observations, than in starting barely specu-
15   lative Systems. Such Writings therefore, as many of Mr. *Boyle*'s are,
with others, that have writ of *Husbandry, Planting, Gardening*, and the
like, may be fit for a Gentleman,[-1] when he has a little acquainted himself with some of the Systems of the *Natural Philosophy* in Fashion.

§. 194. Though the Systems of *Physicks*, that I have met with, afford
20   little encouragement to look for Certainty or Science in any Treatise,
which shall pretend to give us a body of *Natural Philosophy* from the
first Principles of Bodies in general, yet the incomparable Mr. *Newton*, has shewn, how far Mathematicks, applied to some Parts of
Nature, may, upon Principles that Matter of Fact justifie, carry us in
25   the knowledge of some, as I may so call them, particular Provinces of
the Incomprehensible Universe. And if others could give us so good
and clear an account of other parts of *Nature*, as he has of this our
Planetary World, and the most considerable *Phænomena* observable in
it, in his admirable Book, *Philosophiæ naturalis principia Mathematica*,
30   we might in time hope to be furnished with more true and certain
Knowledge in several Parts of this stupendious Machin, than hitherto

13 Writers] *add.* **3**   14 starting] writing **1**   19 194] 182 **1**   *Physicks*,]
Physick, **1**

[1-1] *Revision of* **Corr.** 844 (ii. 785, ll. 12–19)

science. The *Essay* is in large measure a defence of proper experimental science, of
careful observations and descriptions of phenomena. Hypotheses are to be used sparingly, and only when based upon observation. The reference to 'Modern *Corpuscularians*' is probably a reference to scientists such as Locke's friend Robert Boyle. The
'corpuscularian hypothesis' viewed matter as composed of insensible particles whose
organization and structure, and hardness and motion, could account for observed
phenomena.

[95] Ralph Cudworth's *A True Intellectual System of the Universe* was published in 1678.

we could have expected. And though there are very few, that have Mathematicks enough to understand his Demonstrations, yet the most accurate Mathematicians, who have examin'd them, allowing them to be such, his Book will deserve to be read, and give no small light and pleasure to those, who willing to understand the Motions, Properties, and Operations of the great Masses of Matter, in this our Solar System, will but carefully mind his Conclusions, which may be depended on as Propositions well proved.

§. 195. This is, in short, what I have thought concerning a young Gentleman's Studies; wherein it will possibly be wondred, that I should omit *Greek*, since amongst the *Grecians* is to be found the Original as it were, and Foundation of all that Learning, which we have in this part of the World. I grant it so; and will add, That no Man can pass for a Scholar, that is ignorant of the *Greek* Tongue. But I am not here considering of the Education of a profess'd Scholar, but of a Gentleman, to whom *Latin* and *French*, as the World now goes, is by every one acknowledged to be necessary. When he comes to be a Man, if he has a mind to carry his Studies farther, and look into the *Greek* Learning, he will then easily get that Tongue himself: And if he has not that Inclination, his learning of it under a Tutor will be but lost Labour, and much of his Time and Pains spent in that, which will be neglected and thrown away, as soon as he is at liberty. For how many are there of an hundred, even amongst Scholars themselves, who retain the *Greek* they carried from School; or ever improved it to a familiar reading, and perfect understanding of *Greek* Authors?

To conclude this Part, which concerns a Young Gentleman's Studies, his Tutor should remember, that his Business is not so much to teach him all that is knowable, as to raise in him a love and esteem of Knowledge; and to put him in the right way of knowing, and improving himself, when he has a Mind to it.

The Thoughts of a Judicious Author on the subject of Languages, I shall here give the Reader, as near as I can, in his own way of expressing them. He says,* 'One can scarce burden Children too much with

* *La Bruyer Moeurs de ce siecle* p. $\frac{577}{662}$ [96]

---

§ 195 *Greek.*   *Method.*

9 195] 183 **1**   26–30 To conclude ... to it.] *add.* **3**   31–251.29 The Thoughts ... Learning.] *add.* **5**

[96] Jean de La Bruyère's *Les caractères de Théophraste, traduits du grec, avec Les caractères ou mœurs de ce siècle*, 'De quelques usages' §§ 71–2. Locke owned the ninth edition, with imprint: A Paris, Chez Etienne Michallet, 1696. This duodecimo edition of 662 pages is listed as LL 505. The translation is presumably Locke's own.

'the knowledge of Languages. They are useful to Men of all Con-
'ditions, and they equally open them the entrance, either to the most
'profound, or the more easy and entertaining parts of Learning. If this
'irksome study be put off to a little more advanced Age, Young-men
5 'either have not resolution enough to apply to it out of choice; or
'steadiness to carry it on. And if any one has the gift of perseverance, it
'is not without the inconvenience of spending that time upon Lan-
'guages, which is destined to other uses: And he confines to the study
'of Words that Age of his Life that is above it, and requires things; at
10 'least it is the loosing the best and beautifullest season of ones life.
'This large foundation of Languages cannot be well laid but when
'every thing makes an easy and deep impression on the Mind; when
'the Memory is fresh, ready, and tenacious; when the Head and Heart
'are as yet free from Cares, Passions, and Designs; and those on whom
15 'the Child depends have authority enough to keep him close to a long
'continued application. I am perswaded that the small number of truly
'Learned, and the multitude of superficial pretenders, is owing to the
'neglect of this.'

I think every body will agree with this observing Gentleman, that
20 Languages are the proper study of our first Years. But 'tis to be considered by the Parents and Tutors, what Tongues 'tis fit the Child
should learn. For it must be confessed, that it is fruitless Pains, and
loss of Time to learn a Language which in the course of Life that he is
designed to, he is never like to make use of, or which one may guess by
25 his Temper he will wholly neglect and lose again, as soon as an
approach to Manhood, setting him free from a Governor, shall put
him into the hands of his own Inclination, which is not likely to allot
any of his time to the cultivating the learned Tongues; or dispose him
to mind any other Language, but what daily use, or some particular
30 necessity shall force upon him.

But yet for the sake of those who are designed to be Scholars, I will
add what the same Author subjoyns to make good his foregoing
remark. It will deserve to be considered by all who desire to be truly
Learned, and therefore may be a fit rule for Tutors to inculcate, and
35 leave with their Pupils to guide their future Studies.

'The Study, *says he*, of the original text can never be sufficiently
'recommended. 'Tis the shortest, surest, and most agreeable way to all
'sorts of Learning. Draw from the spring head, and take not things at
'second hand. Let the Writings of the great Masters be never laid
40 'aside, dwell upon them, settle them in your Mind, and cite them upon

'occasion; make it your Business throughly to understand them in
'their full Extent, and all their Circumstances: Acquaint your self fully
'with the principles of Original Authors; bring them to a consistency,
'and then do you your self make your deductions. In this state were the
'first Commentators, and do not you rest till you bring your self to the   5
'same. Content not your self with those borrowed lights, nor guide
'your self by their views, but where your own fails you, and leaves you
'in the dark. Their Explications are not yours, and will give you the
'slip. On the contrary, your own Observations are the product of your
'own Mind, where they will abide, and be ready at hand upon all occa-   10
'sions in converse, consultation, and dispute. Lose not the pleasure it
'is to see that you were not stop'd in your reading, but by difficulties
'that are invincible; where the Commentators and Scholiasts them-
'selves are at a stand, and have nothing to say. Those copious Exposi-
'tors of other places, who with a vain and pompous overflow of Learn-   15
'ing power'd out on passages plain and easy in themselves are very free
'of their Words and Pains where there is no need. Convince your self
'fully by thus ordering your Studies that 'tis nothing but Mens laziness
'which hath encouraged pedantry to cram rather than enrich Lib-
'raries, and to bury good Authors under heaps of Notes and Commen-   20
'taries, and you will perceive that sloath herein hath acted against it
'self and its own interest, by multiplying reading, and enquiries, and
'encreasing the pains it endeavour'd to avoid.'

   This, tho' it may seem to concern none but direct Scholars, is of so
great moment for the right ordering of their Education and Studies,   25
that I hope I shall not be blamed for inserting of it here, especially if it
be considered that it may be of use to Gentlemen too when at any time
they have a mind to go deeper than the surface, and get to themselves a
solid satisfactory and masterly insight in any part of Learning.

   Order and Constancy are said to make the great difference between   30
one Man and another: This I am sure, nothing so much clears a
Learner's Way, helps him so much on in it, and makes him go so easie
and so far in any Enquiry, as a good *Method*. His Governor should take
pains to make him sensible of this, accustom him to order and teach
him *Method* in all the application of his Thoughts; shew him wherein   35
it lies, and the Advantages of it; acquaint him with the several Sorts of
it, either from general to Particulars, or from Particulars to what is
more general; exercise him in both of them; and make him see, in what

30–252.12 Order . . . Idea's.] *add.* 3

cases each different *Method* is most proper, and to what ends it best serves.

In History the Order of Time should govern, in Philosophical Enquiries that of Nature, which in all Progression is to go from the place one is then in, to that which joyns and lies next to it; and so it is in the Mind, from the knowledge it stands possessed of already, to that which lies next, and is coherent to it, and so on to what it aims at, by the simplest and most uncompounded parts it can divide the Matter into. To this purpose, it will be of great use to his Pupil to accustome him to distinguish well, that is, to have distinct Notions, where-ever the Mind can find any real difference, but as carefully to avoid distinctions in terms, where he has not distinct and different clear Idea's.

§. 196. Besides what is to be had from Study and Books, there are other *Accomplishments* necessary for a Gentleman, to be got by exercise, and to which time is to be allowed, and for which Masters must be had.

^m-*Dancing* being that which gives *graceful Motions* all the life, and above all things Manliness, and a becoming Confidence to young Children, I think it cannot be learn'd too early, after they are once of an Age and Strength capable of it. But you must be sure to have a good Master, that knows, and can teach, what is graceful and becoming, and what gives a freedom and easiness to all the Motions of the Body. One that teaches not this, is worse than none at all, Natural Unfashionableness being much better, than apish, affected Postures; and I think it much more passable to put off the Hat, and make a Leg, like an honest Country-Gentleman, than like an ill-fashion'd Dancing-Master. For as for the jigging part, and the Figures of Dances, I count that little, or nothing, farther, than as it tends to perfect *graceful Carriage.*^-m

§. 197. ^n-*Musick* is thought to have some affinity with Dancing, and a good Hand, upon some Instruments, is by many People mightily valued. But it wastes so much of a young Man's time, to gain but a moderate Skill in it; and engages often in such odd Company, that many think it much better spared: And I have, amongst Men of Parts and Business, so seldom heard any one commended, or esteemed, for having an Excellency in *Musick*, that amongst all those things, that

§ 196 *Dancing.*   § 197 *Musick.*

---

13 196] 184 1   29 197] 185 1

^m-m *Slightly varied from* **Corr.** 844 (ii. 783, ll. 9–22)   ^n-n *Varied from* **Corr.** 844 (ii. 782, l. 22–783, l. 9)

ever came into the List of Accomplishments, I think I may give it the last place. Our short Lives will not serve us for the attainment of all things; nor can our Minds be always intent on something to be learn'd. The weakness of our Constitutions, both of Mind and Body, requires, that we should be often unbent: And he, that will make a good use of 5 any part of his Life, must allow a large Portion of it to Recreation. At least this must not be denied to young People, unless whilst you, with too much haste, make them old, you have the displeasure to see them in their Graves, or a second Childhood, sooner than you could wish. And therefore, I think, that the Time and Pains allotted to serious 10 Improvements, should be employ'd about things of most use and consequence, and that too in the Methods the most easie and short, that could be at any rate obtained: And perhaps, as I have abovesaid, it would be none of the least Secrets in Education, to make the Exercises of the Body and the Mind, the *Recreation* one to another. I doubt not 15 but that something might be done in it, by a prudent Man, that would well consider the Temper and Inclination of his Pupil. For he that is wearied either with Study or Dancing, does not desire presently to go to sleep; but to do something else, which may divert and delight him. But this must be always remembred, that nothing can come into the 20 account of *Recreation*, that is not done with delight.⌐ⁿ

§. 198. ᵒ⌐*Fencing* and *Riding* the *Great Horse*,[97] are look'd upon as so necessary parts of Breeding, that it would be thought a great *omission* to neglect them: The latter of the two being for the most part to be learn'd only in great Towns, is one of the best Exercises for Health, 25 which is to be had in those Places of Ease and Luxury: And upon that account, makes a fit part of a young Gentleman's Employment during his abode there. And as far as it conduces to give a Man a firm and graceful Seat on Horseback, and to make him able to teach his Horse to stop and turn quick, and to rest on his Hanches, is of use to a 30 Gentleman both in Peace and War. But whether it be of moment enough to be made a Business of, and deserve to take up more of his time, than should barely for his Health be employed at due intervals in

§§ 198–9 *Fencing.*

---

8 see] set **4 5**   13 as . . . abovesaid] *add.* **3**   14 in] of **5**   15 of] in **5**
22 198] 186 **1**

ᵒ⁻ᵒ *Altered and expanded from* **Corr.** 844 (ii. 783, ll. 23–9)

[97] '*Great Horse*', horse or warhorse, used in battle or tournaments; learning to manage horses was needed for the science of arms (*OED*).

some such vigorous Exercise, I shall leave to the Discretion of Parents and Tutors, who will do well to remember, in all the parts of Education, that most time and application is to be bestowed on that, which is like to be of greatest consequence, and frequentest use, in the ordinary course and occurrences of that Life, the young Man is designed for.⁻ᵒ

§. 199. ᵖ⁻As for *Fencing*, it seems to me a good Exercise for Health, but dangerous to the Life. The confidence of their Skill being apt to engage in Quarrels, those, that think they have learn'd to use their Swords. This Presumption makes them often more touchy than needs, on Points of Honour, and slight or no provocations. Young Men in their warm Blood are forward to think, they have in vain learned to Fence, if they never shew their Skill and courage in a Duel: and they seem to have Reason. But how many sad Tragedies that Reason has been the Occasion of, the Tears of many a Mother can witness. A Man that cannot *Fence* will be more careful to keep out of Bullies and Gamesters Company, and will not be half so apt to stand upon Punctilio's, nor to give Affronts, or fiercely justifie them when given, which is that, which usually makes the Quarrel. And when a Man is in the Field, a moderate Skill in Fencing rather exposes him to the Sword of his Enemy, than secures him from it. And certainly a Man of Courage who cannot *Fence* at all, and therefore will put all upon one thrust, and not stand parrying, has the odds against a moderate Fencer, especially if he has Skill in *Wrestling*. And therefore, if any Provision be to be made against such Accidents, and a Man be to prepare his Son for Duels, I had much rather mine should be a good *Wrestler*, than an ordinary *Fencer*, which is the most a Gentleman can attain to in it, unless he will be constantly in the Fencing-School, and every Day exercising.⁻ᵖ But since Fencing and Riding the great Horse, are so generally looked upon as necessary Qualifications in the breeding of a Gentleman, it will be hard wholly to deny any one of that rank these Marks of Distinction. I shall leave it therefore to the Father, to consider, how far the Temper of his Son, and the Station he is like to be in, will allow, or incourage him to comply with Fashions, which having very little to do with civil Life, were yet formerly unknown to the most

---

6 199] 187 **1**   7 their Skill] it **1**   8–10 learn'd … provocations.] some Skill, and to make them more touchy than needs, on Points of Honour, and slight Occasions. **1**   15 more] the more **1**   28 Fencing] *Fencing* **NN**   Riding] *Riding* **NN**

ᵖ⁻ᵖ *Slight revision of* **Corr.** 844 (ii. 783, l. 30–784, l. 16)

Warlike Nations;[98] and seem to have added little of Force, or Courage to those, who have received them, unless we will think Martial Skill or Prowess, have been improved by *Duelling*, with which Fencing came into, and with which, I presume, it will go out of the World.

§. 200. q‑These are my present Thoughts concerning *Learning* and *Accomplishments*. The great Business of all is *Virtue* and *Wisdom*.

Nullum numen abest si sit prudentia. [99]

Teach him to get a Mastery over his Inclinations, and *submit his Appetite to Reason*. This being obtained, and by constant practice settled into Habit, the hardest part of the Task is over. To bring a young Man to this, I know nothing which so much contributes, as the love of Praise and Commendation, which should therefore be instilled into him by all Arts imaginable. Make his Mind as sensible of Credit and Shame as may be: And when you have done that, you have put a Principle into him, which will influence his Actions, when you are not by, to which the fear of a little smart of a Rod is not comparable,‑q and which will be the proper Stock, whereon afterwards to graft the true Principles of Morality and Religion.

§. 201. r‑I have one Thing more to add, which as soon as I mention, I shall run the danger of being suspected to have forgot what I am about, and what I have above written concerning Education, all tending towards a Gentleman's Calling, with which a *Trade* seems wholly to be inconsistent. And yet, I cannot forbear to say, I would have him *learn a Trade, a Manual Trade*; nay, two or three, but one more particularly.‑r

§. 202. s‑The busy Inclination of Children being always to be directed to some thing, that may be useful to them, the Advantages propos'd, from what they are set about may be considered of two Kinds; 1. Where the Skill it self, that is got by exercise, is worth the having. Thus Skill not only in Languages, and learned Sciences, but in

§§ 201–2 *Trade*.

5 200] 188 **1**   19 201] 189 **1**   20 of being] to be **1**   21 all tending] which has all tended **1**   25 202] 190 **1**   26–7 them, . . . about] them. The Advantage **1**

q‑q **Corr.** 844 (ii. 785, l. 25–786, l. 8)   r‑r *Rewritten from* **Corr.** 999 (iii. 343, l. 26–344, l. 5)   s‑s **Corr.** 999 (iii. 350, ll. 3–27)

[98] The duel as a mode of personal quarrel (as opposed to the single combat of champions in war) was completely unknown to the ancient Hebrews, Greeks, and Romans.

[99] 'No heavenly power is wanting if there be wisdom', the corrupt text, current in Locke's day, of Juvenal, *Satires*, x. 365, xiv. 314. The true reading is not *abest* but *habes*: 'Thou [Fortune] hast no godhead, were there but wisdom [to see it].'

Painting, Turning, Gardening, Tempering, and Working in Iron, and all other useful Arts is worth the having. 2. Where the Exercise it self, without any other Consideration is necessary, or useful for Health. Knowledge in some things is so necessary to be got by Children, 5 whilst they are young, that some part of their time is to be allotted to their improvement in them, though those Imployments contribute nothing at all to their health: Such are Reading, and Writing, and all other sedentary Studies, for the ᵗ⁻cultivating of the Mind, which unavoidably take up a great part of Gentlemens time,⁻ᵗ quite from 10 their Cradles. Other *Manual Arts*, which are both got, and exercised by Labour, do many of them, by that Exercise, not only increase our Dexterity and Skill, but contribute to our Health too, especially, such as imploy us in the open Air. In these, then, Health and Improvement may be joyn'd together, and of these should some fit ones be chosen, 15 to be made the Recreations of one, whose chief Business is with Books and Study. In this Choice, the Age and Inclination of the Person is to be considered, and Constraint always to be avoided in bringing him to it. For Command and Force may often create, but can never cure an Aversion: And whatever any one is brought to by compulsion, he will 20 leave as soon as he can, and be little profitted, and less recreated by, whilst he is at it.⁻ˢ

203. ᵘ⁻That which of all others would please me best, would be a *Painter*, were there not an Argument or two against it not easie to be answered. First, ill Painting is one of the worst things in the World; 25 and to attain a tolerable degree of Skill in it, requires too much of a Man's Time. If he has a natural Inclination to it, it will endanger the neglect of all other more useful Studies, to give way to that; and if he have no inclination to it, all the Time, Pains, and Money shall be employ'd in it, will be thrown away to no purpose.⁻ᵘ Another Reason 30 why I am not for *Painting* in a Gentleman, is, Because it is a sedentary Recreation, which more employs the Mind than the Body. A Gentleman's more serious Employment I look on to be Study; and when that demands relaxation and refreshment, it should be in some Exercise of the Body, which unbends the Thought, and confirms

§ 203 *Painting.*

---

3 other] *om.* 5   8–9 cultivating . . . time,] improvement of the Mind, and are the unavoidable Business of Gentlemen 1   11 that] their 1   11–12 not . . . but] *add.* 3   22 203] 191 1

ᵗ⁻ᵗ **Corr.** *as* 1   ᵘ⁻ᵘ **Corr.** 999 (iii. 344, ll. 6–13)

the Health and Strength. ^{v-} For these two Reasons I am not for *Paint-ing.* ^{-v}

§. 204. ^{w-}In the next place, for a Country-Gentleman, I should propose one, or rather both these; *viz. Gardening* or *Husbandry* in general, and working in Wood, as a *Carpenter, Joyner*, or *Turner*, these being fit and healthy Recreations for a Man of Study, or Business. For since the Mind endures not to be constantly employ'd in the same Thing, or Way; and sedentary or studious Men, should have some Exercise, that at the same time might divert their Minds, and employ their Bodies; I know none that could do it better for a Country-Gentleman, than these two, the one of them affording him Exercise, when the Weather or Season keeps him from the other. Besides, that by being skill'd in the one of them, he will be able to govern and teach his Gardener; by the other, contrive and make a great many Things both of delight and use: Though these I propose not as the chief end of his Labour, but as Temptations to it; Diversion from his other more serious Thoughts and Employments, by useful and healthy manual Exercise, being what I chiefly aim at in it.^{-w}

§. 205. The great Men among the Ancients, understood very well how to reconcile manual Labour with Affairs of State, and thought it no lessening to their Dignity to make the one the Recreation to the other. That indeed which seems most generally to have imploy'd and diverted their spare hours was Agriculture. *Gideon*[100] amongst the *Jews* was taken from Thrashing, as well as *Cincinnatus*[101] amongst the *Romans* from the Plough, to Command the Armies of their Countries against their Enemies, and 'tis plain their dexterous handling of the Flayl or the Plough, and being good Workmen with these Tools, did not hinder their Skill in Arms, nor make them less able in the Arts of War or Government. They were great Captains and Statesmen as well as Husbandmen. *Cato major*,[102] who had with great Reputation born all the great Offices of the Commonwealth, has left us an Evidence under his own Hand, how much he was versed in Country Affairs, and as I remember, *Cyrus* when possess'd of the *Persian* Throne, thought

§§ 204–5 *Gardning.*   *Joyner.*

---

3 204] 192 **1**   4–5 or … general,] *add.* **3**   5 these] as **1**   19–258.5
§ 205 *add.* **3**   24 *Cincinnatus ed.*] *Cincinnetus* **3 4 5**   33 when … Throne,] *om.* **5**

^{v-v} **Corr.** 999 (iii. 344, ll. 13–14)   ^{w-w} **Corr.** 999 (iii. 344, ll. 15–31)

[100] Judg. 6: 11 ff.   [101] Livy 3. 26. 8–9.
[102] Marcus Porcius Cato, known as Cato the Elder, or Cato the Censor, left a still extant work *De agri cultura.*

Gardening so little beneath the Dignity and Grandeur of a Throne,
that he shew'd *Xenophon*[103] a large Field of Fruit-trees all of his own
Planting. The Records of Antiquity both amongst *Jews* and *Gentiles*,
are full of Instances of this kind, if it were necessary to recommend
5 useful Recreations by Examples.

§. 206. ˣ⁻Nor let it be thought that I mistake, when I call these or the
like Exercises of Manual Arts, *Diversions* or *Recreations:* For *Recreation*
is not being Idle (as every one may observe) but easing the wearied
part by change of Business: And he that thinks *Diversion* may not lie in
10 hard and painful Labour, forgets the early rising, hard riding, heat,
cold and hunger of Huntsmen, which is yet known to be the constant
Recreation of Men of the greatest Condition. *Delving, Planting, Inocu-
lating*, or any the like profitable Employments, would be no less a
Diversion, than any of the idle Sports in fashion, if Men could be but
15 brought to delight in them, which Custom and Skill in a Trade will
quickly bring any one to do. And I doubt not, but there are to be found
those, who being frequently call'd to Cards, or any other Play, by those
they could not refuse, have been more tired with these *Recreations*,
than with any the most serious Employment of Life, though the Play
20 has been such, as they have naturally had no aversion to, and with
which they could willingly sometimes divert themselves.

§. 207. Play, wherein Persons of Condition, especially Ladies, wast
so much of their time, is a plain instance to me, that Men cannot be
perfectly idle; they must be doing something. For how else could they
25 sit so many hours toiling at that, which generally gives more Vexation
than Delight to People, whilst they are actually engag'd in it? 'Tis
certain, Gaming leaves no Satisfaction behind it to those who reflect
when it is over, and it no way profits either Body or Mind: As to their
Estates, if it strike so deep as to concern them, it is a *Trade* then, and
30 not a *Recreation*, wherein few, that have any thing else to live on, thrive:

§§ 206–7 *Recreation.*

6 206] 193 **1**   7 Exercises . . . Arts,] Trades, **1**   15 a Trade] any Trade **1**
16 bring . . . do.] make any one do. **1**   22 207] 194 **1**   22–259.4 Play . . . Calling.] Though when one reflects on these and other the like *Pastimes*, (as they are call'd)
one finds they leave little satisfaction behind them, when they are over; and most commonly give more vexation than delight to People, whilst they are actually engaged in
them, and neither profit the Mind, nor the Body. They are plain instances to me, that
Men cannot be perfectly idle; they must be doing something. **1**

ˣ⁻ˣ *Revision of* **Corr.** 999 (iii. 34, l. 32–346, l. 20)

103 Cf. Xenophon, *Oeconomicus*, iv. 20–5. The visitor to whom Cyrus (never king)
showed his garden was Lysander.

and at best, a thriving Gamester has but a poor Trade on't, who fills his Pockets at the price of his Reputation.

Recreation belongs not to People, who are Strangers to Business, and are not wasted and wearied with the Employment of their Calling. The Skill should be, so to order their time of Recreation, that it may relax and refresh the part, that has been exercised, and is tired, and yet do something, which besides the present Delight and Ease, may produce, what will afterwards be profitable. It has been nothing but the Vanity and Pride of Greatness and Riches, that has brought unprofitable and dangerous *Pastimes* (as they are call'd) into fashion, and persuaded People into a belief, that the learning or putting their hands to any thing, that was useful, could not be a *Diversion* fit for a Gentleman. This has been that, which has given *Cards, Dice*, and *Drinking* so much Credit in the World: And a great many throw away their spare Hours in them, through the prevalency of Custom, and want of some better Employment to fill up the Vacancy of Leisure, more than from any real delight is to be found in them. They cannot bear the dead weight of un-imploy'd time lying upon their hands, nor the uneasiness it is to do nothing at all: and having never learn'd any laudable manual Art wherewith to divert themselves, they have recourse to those foolish, or ill ways in use, to help off their Time, which a rational Man, till corrupted by Custom, could find very little pleasure in.

§. 208. I say not this, that I would never have a young Gentleman accommodate himself to the innocent *Diversions* in fashion, amongst those of his Age and Condition. I am so far from having him austere and morose to that degree, that I would persuade him to more than ordinary complaisance for all the Gaieties and *Diversions* of those he converses with, and be averse or resty in nothing, they should desire of him, that might become a Gentleman and an honest Man. Though as to *Cards* and *Dice*, I think the safest and best way is never to learn any Play upon them, and so to be incapacitated for those dangerous Temptations and incroaching Wasters of useful Time. But allowance being made for *idle and jovial Conversation*, and all fashionable becoming

§§ 208–9 *Trade.*

5 order] employ 1   10 (as ... call'd)] *add.* 3   16 fill ... Leisure,] pass their time, 1   17–21 them. ... recourse] them, only because it being very irksome and uneasie to do nothing at all, they had never learn'd any laudable manual Art wherewith to divert themselves; and so they betake themselves 1   24 208] 195 1   29 resty] testy 4 5   30–3 Though ... Time.] *add.* 3

Recreations; I say, a young Man will have time enough, from his
serious and main Business, to learn almost any *Trade*. 'Tis want of
application, and not of leisure, that Men are not skilful in more *Arts*
than one; and an Hour in a Day, constantly employ'd in such a way of
5   *Diversion*, will carry a Man, in a short time, a great deal farther, than
he can imagine: which if it were of no other use, but to drive the
common, vicious, useless, and dangerous Pastimes out of fashion; and
to shew there was no need of them, would deserve to be encouraged. If
Men from their youth were weaned from that sauntring Humour,
10   wherein some, out of Custom, let a good part of their Lives run use-
lesly away, without either Business or Recreation, they would find
time enough to acquire *dexterity and skill in hundreds of Things*; which
though remote from their proper Callings, would not at all interfere
with them. And therefore, I think, for this, as well as other Reasons
15   before-mentioned; a lazy, listless Humour, that idly dreams away
the days, is of all others the least to be indulged, or permitted in young
People. It is the proper state of one Sick, and out of order in his
Health, and is tolerable in no body else, of what Age or Condition
soever.⁻ˣ

20   §. 209. To the Arts above-mentioned, may be added *Perfuming,
Varnishing, Graving*, and several sorts of working in *Iron, Brass*, and
Silver: And if, as it happens to most young Gentlemen, that a considerable part of his Time be spent in a great Town, he may learn to cut,
pollish, and set *precious Stones*,ʸ or employ himself in grinding and pol-
25   lishing *Optical Glasses*. Amongst the great variety there is of ingenious
Manual Arts, 'twill be impossible that no one should be found to please
and delight him, unless he be either idle or debauch'd, which is not to
be supposed in a right way of Education. And since he cannot be
always employ'd in Study, Reading, and Conversation, there will be
30   many an Hour, besides what his Exercises will take up, which, if not
spent this way, will be spent worse. For, I conclude, a young Man will
seldom desire to sit perfectly still and idle; or if he does, 'tis a fault that
ought to be mended.

     §. 210. But if his mistaken Parents, frighted with the disgraceful
35   Names of *Mechanick* and *Trade*, shall have an aversion to any thing of

    §§ 210–11 *Merchants Accompts.*

---

    3 leisure,] time, **1**   16 days] time **1**   20 209] 196 **1**   25 ingenious]
ingenuous **1**   34 210] 197 **1**   frighted] frightned **5**

    ʸ *Cf.* **Corr.** 999 (iii. 346, ll. 20–3)

this kind in their Children; yet there is one thing relating to Trade, which when they consider, they will think absolutely necessary for their Sons to learn.

^{z-}*Merchants Accompts*, though a Science not likely to help a Gentleman to get an Estate, yet possibly there is not any thing of more use and efficacy, to make him preserve the Estate he has. 'Tis seldom observed, that he who keeps an Accompt of his Income and Expences, and thereby has constantly under view the course of his domestick Affairs, lets them run to ruine: And I doubt not but many a Man gets behind-hand, before he is aware, or runs further on, when he is once in, for want of this Care, or the Skill to do it. I would therefore advise all Gentlemen to learn perfectly *Merchants Accompts*, and not think it is a Skill, that belongs not to them, because it has received its Name, and has been chiefly practised by Men of Traffick.

§. 211. When my young Master has once got the Skill of *keeping Accounts* (which is a Business of Reason more than Arithmetick) perhaps it will not be amiss, that his Father from thenceforth, require him to do it in all his Concernments. Not that I would have him set down every Pint of Wine, or Play, that costs him Money; the general Name of Expences will serve for such things well enough: Nor would I have his Father look so narrowly into these Accounts, as to take occasion from thence to criticize on his Expences. He must remember that he himself was once a young Man, and not forget the Thoughts he had then, nor the Right his Son has to have the same, and to have allowance made for them. If therefore, I would have the young Gentleman obliged to keep an Account, it is not at all to have that way a check upon his Expences (for what the Father allows him, he ought to let him be fully Master of) but only, that he might be brought early into the Custom of doing it, and that that might be made familiar and habitual to him betimes, which will be so useful and necessary to be constantly practised the whole Course of his Life. A Noble *Venetian*, whose Son wallowed in the Plenty of his Father's Riches, finding his Son's Expences grow very high and extravagant, ordered by his Casheer to let him have for the future, no more Money, than what he should count, when he received it. This one would think no great restraint to a young Gentleman's Expences, who could freely have as much Money, as he would tell. But, yet this, to one who was used to nothing but the pursuit of his Pleasures, proved a very great

12 think] to think **5**   15 211] 198 **1**   33 by] *add.* **3**   37 Pleasures] Pleasure **NN**

^{z-z} §§ 210–11 *one para. in* **Corr.** 844 (ii. 780, l. 21–781, l. 32)

trouble, which at last ended in this sober and advantageous Reflection. If it be so much Pains to me barely to count the Money, I would
spend, What Labour and Pains did it cost my Ancestors, not only to
count, but get it? This rational Thought, suggested by this little Pains
5 impos'd upon him, wrought so effectually upon his Mind, that it made
him take up, and from that time forwards, prove a good Husband.
This at least every body must allow, that nothing is likelier to keep a
Man within compass, than the having constantly before his Eyes, the
state of his Affairs in a regular course of *Accounts.* ⁻ᶻ

10 §. 212. The last Part usually in Education is *Travel*, which is commonly thought to finish the Work, and compleat the Gentleman. I
confess *Travel* into Foreign Countries has great Advantages, but the
time usually chosen to send young Men abroad, is, I think, of all other,
that which renders them least capable of reaping those Advantages.
15 Those which are propos'd, as to the main of them, may be reduced to
these Two, first Language, secondly an Improvement in Wisdom and
Prudence, by seeing Men, and conversing with People of Tempers,
Customs, and Ways of living, different from one another, and especially from those of his Parish and Neighbourhood. But from Sixteen
20 to One and Twenty, which is the ordinary *time of Travel*, Men are of all
their Lives, the least suited to these Improvements. The first Season
to get Foreign Languages, and form the Tongue to their true Accents,
I should think, should be from Seven to Fourteen or Sixteen; and then
too a Tutor with them is useful and necessary, who may, with those
25 Languages, teach them other things. But to put them out of their
Parents view at a great distance, under a Governour, when they think
themselves too much Men to be governed by others, and yet have not
Prudence and Experience enough to govern themselves, what is it, but
to expose them to all the greatest Dangers of their whole Life, when
30 they have the least Fence and Guard against them? Till that boyling
boistrous part of Life comes in, it may be hoped, the Tutor may have
some Authority: Neither the stubbornness of Age, nor the Temptation
or Examples of others can take him from his Tutor's conduct, till Fif-
teen or Sixteen: But then, when he begins to consort himself with
35 Men, and think himself one; when he comes to relish, and pride himself in manly Vices, and thinks it a shame to be any longer under the

§§ 212–16 *Travel.*

---

9 *Accounts*] *Account* **5**   10 212] 199 **1**   22 form the] from their **NN** from
the **5**

Controul and Conduct of another, what can be hoped from even the most careful and discreet Governour, when neither he has Power to compel, nor his Pupil a disposition to be perswaded; but on the contrary, has the advice of warm Blood, and prevailing Fashion, to hearken to the Temptations of his Companions, just as Wise as himself, rather than to the perswasions of his Tutor, who is now looked on as the Enemy to his Freedom? And when is a Man so like to miscarry, as when at the same time he is both raw and unruly? This is the Season of all his Life, that most requires the Eye and Authority of his Parents, and Friends to govern it. The flexibleness of the former part of a Man's Age, not yet grown up to be head-strong, makes it more governable and safe; and in the after-part, Reason and Fore-sight begin a little to take place, and mind a Man of his Safety and Improvement. The time therefore I should think the fittest for a young Gentleman to be *sent abroad*, would be, either when he is younger, under a Tutor, whom he might be the better for; Or when he is some Years older, without a Governour; when he is of Age to govern himself, and make Observations of what he finds in other Countries worthy his Notice, and that might be of use to him after his return: And when too, being throughly acquainted with the Laws and Fashions, the natural and moral Advantages and Defects of his own Country, he has something to exchange, with those abroad, from whose Conversation he hoped to reap any Knowledge.

§. 214.[104] a-The ordering of *Travel* otherwise is that, I imagine, which makes so many young Gentlemen come back so little improved by it. And if they do bring home with them any Knowledge of the Places and People, they have seen, it is often an admiration of the worst and vainest Practices they met with abroad; retaining a relish and memory of those Things wherein their Liberty took its first swing, rather than of what should make them better and wiser after their return. And indeed how can it be otherwise, going abroad at the Age they do, under the care of another, who is to provide their Necessaries, and make their Observations for them? Thus under the Shelter and Pretence of a Governour, thinking themselves excused from standing upon their own Legs, or being accountable for their own Conduct, they very seldom trouble themselves with Enquiries, or making useful

17 is] was **1**   18 finds] found **1**   24 214] 200 **1**   28 Practices] Fashions **1**   32 the . . . another,] a Governour, **1**

a-a §§ 214-15 *greatly altered from* **Corr.** 999 (iii. 346, l. 24-347, l. 17)

[104] For 213; so misnumbered in **3 4 5** and most subsequent edns.

Observations of their own. Their Thoughts run after Play and Pleasure, wherein, they take it as a lessening, to be controul'd: but seldom trouble themselves to examine the Designs, observe the Address, and consider the Arts, Tempers, and Inclinations of Men, they meet with; that so they
5   may know how to comport themselves towards them. Here he that Travels with them, is to skreen them; get them out when they have run themselves into the Briars; and in all their Miscarriages be answerable for them.

§. 215. I confess, the Knowledge of Men is so great a Skill, that it is not
10 to be expected, a young Man should presently be perfect in it. But yet his *going abroad* is to little purpose, if *travel* does not somewhat open his Eyes, make him cautious and wary, and accustom him to look beyond the out-side, and, under the inoffensive Guard of a civil and obliging Carriage, keep himself free and safe in his Conversation with Strangers,
15 and all sorts of People, without forfeiting their good Opinion. ^{b-} He that is sent out to *travel* at the Age, and with the Thoughts of a Man designing to improve himself, may get into the Conversation and Acquaintance of Persons of Condition where he comes; which though a thing of most advantage to a Gentleman that travels, yet I ask amongst our young
20 Men, that go abroad under Tutors, what one is there of an hundred, that ever visits any Person of Quality? much less makes an Acquaintance with such, from whose Conversation he may learn, what is good Breeding in that Country, and what is worth observation in it: Though from such Persons it is, one may learn more in one Day, than in a Years
25 rambling from one Inn to another.^{-b} Nor indeed is it to be wondred. For Men of Worth and Parts, will not easily admit the Familiarity of Boys, who yet need the care of a Tutor: though a young Gentleman and Stranger, appearing like a Man, and shewing a desire to inform himself in the Customs, Manners, Laws, and Government of the Country he is
30 in, will find welcome, assistance and entertainment, amongst the best and most knowing Persons, every-where, who will be ready to receive, encourage, and countenance an ingenuous and inquisitive Foreigner.^{-a}

§. 216. This, how true soever it be, will not, I fear, alter the Custom, which has cast the time of Travel upon the worst part of a Man's Life;
35 but for Reasons not taken from their Improvement. The young Lad must not be ventured abroad at Eight or Ten, for fear what may happen to the tender Child, though he then runs ten times less risque than at

9 I confess] *run on within* § 200 1   25 Inn (*so also* **Corr.**)] *June* 1
28 Stranger,] a Stranger, 1   32 ingenuous] ingenious 5   33 216] 201 1

^{b-b} *Slightly altered from* **Corr.** 999 (iii. 347, l. 33–348, l. 6)

Sixteen or Eighteen. Nor must he stay at home till that dangerous heady Age be over, because he must be back again by One and twenty, to marry, and propagate. The Father cannot stay any longer for the Portion, nor the Mother for a new Sett of Babies to play with: and so my young Master, whatever comes on't, must have a Wife look'd out for him, by that time he is of Age; though it would be no prejudice to his Strength, his Parts, or his Issue, if it were respited for some time, and he had leave to get, in Years and Knowledge, the start a little of his Children, who are often found to tread too near upon the heels of their Fathers, to the no great Satisfaction either of Son or Father. But the young Gentleman being got within view of Matrimony, 'tis time to leave him to his Mistress.

§. 217. Though I am now come to a Conclusion of what obvious Remarks have suggested to me concerning Education, I would not have it thought that I look on it as a just Treatise on this Subject. There are a thousand other things, that may need consideration; especially if one should take in the various Tempers, different Inclinations, and particular Defaults, that are to be found in Children; and prescribe proper Remedies. The variety is so great, that it would require a Volume; nor would that reach it. Each Man's Mind has some peculiarity, as well as his Face, that distinguishes him from all others; and there are possibly scarce two Children, who can be conducted by exactly the same method. Besides that I think a Prince, a Nobleman, and an ordinary Gentleman's Son, should have different ways of Breeding. But having had here only some general Views, in reference to the main End, and aims in Education, and those designed for a Gentleman's Son, who being then very little, I considered only as white Paper, or Wax, to be moulded and fashioned as one pleases; I have touch'd little more than those Heads, which I judged necessary for the Breeding of a young Gentleman of his Condition in general; and have now published these my occasional Thoughts with this Hope, That though this be far from being a compleat Treatise on this Subject, or such, as that every one may find, what will just fit his Child in it, yet it may give some small light to those, whose Concern for their dear little Ones makes them so irregularly bold, that they dare venture to consult their own Reason, in the Education of their Children, rather than wholly to rely upon Old Custom.

§ 217 *Conclusion.*

---

7 or] nor 1   13 217] 202 1

THE CONTENTS OF THE SECTIONS

[1] The italicized section-numbers indicate sections to which the topical headings apply because they are found there as marginal headings, although they were not indicated in the original contents-list. That list in **5** is also headed 'Sect.' but its references are to page-numbers. [2] *Add.* **5**. [3] *Add.* **4**.
[4] 'Hardiness' transferred to beginning of Hs in **5**. [5] 'Government' *om.* **5**.

The Contents of the Sections

⁶ Cited in error as 188?

APPENDIX I

FORMAL VARIANTS

79.3	Esq;.] Esq; **NA**
4	SIR;] SIR, **5**
7	*you*] *You* **5** *you*] *You* **5**
8	*you*] *You* **5**
11	*view*] *View* **5**
13	*you*] *You* **5** *some,*] *some* **NN**
14	*mine,*] *mine* **NN**
16	*defer*] *deferr* **NN**
18	*me.*] *me:* **1**
19	*Duty,*] *Duty* **NN**
20	*difference*] *Difference* **5**
25	*shame*] *Shame* **5**
28	*self,*] *self* **1**
29	*body*] *Body* **5**
30	*loss*] *Loss* **5**
31	*corruption*] *Corruption* **5** *Youth,*] *Youth* **5**
80.1	*Stage*] *stage* **1**
2	*matter of correction*] *Matter of Correction* **5**
4	*afterwards-incorrigible*] *afterwards incorrigible* **NN**
5	*parts and stations*] *Parts and Stations* **5**
13	*Witness,*] *Witness* **1**
15	*think,*] *think* **NN**
16	*usage*] *Usage* **5** *disciplining*] *Disciplining* **5**
18	*love*] *Love* **5** *pleasure*] *Pleasure* **5**
19	*more,*] *more* **1**
21	*Patronage*] *Patronnge* **NN**
24	*I*] *1* **NN** *Heart;*] *Heart,* **1**
26	*helping hand*] *Helping Hand* **5**
27	*shortest,*] *shortest* **1**
28	*useful,*] *usefull* **1**
29	*Calling. For*] *Calling, for* **1**
32	*it*] *it,* **NN**
34	*acceptance*] *Acceptance* **5** *thanks*] *Thanks* **5**

80.35	*pleased,*] *pleased* 1 *I can*] *1 can* **NA**
37	*remembrance*] Remembrance 5 *one,*] *one* 1
81.1	*useful,*] *usefull* **NN** *useful* **NA** *and lover*] *aud lover* **NN** *and Lover* 5
3	SIR] Sir 1
83.5–6	Description] description 1
11	Constitutions] Constitution 5
12	vigorous,] vigorous 1
13	strength] Strength 5
14	carried] carred 4
15	Privilege] privilege **NN** priviledge **NA** Constitutions,] Constitutions 1
16	Wonders:] Wonders. 5
17	Parts] parts 1
19	Difference] difference 1 Mankind:] Mankind. 5
22	Application] application 1 Hand] hand 1
24	Direction] direction 1
27	Minds] minds **NN**
84.1–2	Part . . . Care] part . . . care 1
2	inside] Inside 5 Clay] clay 1
6	also] also, 1
7	Compass.] compass 1
8	Happiness;] Happiness: 1 5
12	Consideration,] Consideration 5
14	Help] help 1
14–15	*Preservation and Improvement*] *preservation and improvement* 1
15–16	Children] children **NN**
18–19	possibly] possible **NN**
20	particularly;] particularly, 1 particularly: 5 only] Only 5
22	Constitutions] Constitutions, 1 spoiled,] spoiled 1 harmed,] harmed 1
24	first Thing] First thing 1
25	*Covered,*] *Covered* 1 Summer] summer **NN**
27	Cold.] Cold; 1 And] and 1
85.1	Snow:] Snow. 1
2	*Scythian,*] *Scythian* **NN**
3	Winter-Air] Winter Air 5
4	replied] replyed **NN**
7	purpose] Purpose 5
8	words] Words 5
12	black] Black 5
14	intermission] Intermission 5

20	ten] Ten **5**
24	inconvenience] Inconvenience **5** sense] Sense **5**
86.2	Hair] hair **1**
4	best that, by Night,] best, that by Night **1** best that by Night **5**
	one;] one, **1**
7	have said *He*] have said *he* **NN** have, said *he* **NA** aim]
	Aim **5**
9	things,] things **5**
10	*Daughters*;] *Daughters*, **1** difference] Difference **5**
10–11	treatment] Treatment **5**
11	matter] Matter **5**
13	*Shooes*] *Shoes* **5**
15	Mistriss] Mistress **NN 4 5** me. One] me; one **1** filthy;]
	filthy, **1** and the] & the **1**
16	pains] Pains **5** other,] other **5**
17	truth] Truth **5**
18	Considerations,] considerations **1** ten-] Ten- **5**
20	had,] had **5**
21	Children,] Children **5**
21–2	reconciled,] reconciled **5**
22	Wet] wet **NN**
23	wet] Wet **5**
24	difference] Difference **5** Hands and] Hands, and **NN**
26	bare-foot] Bare-foot **5** Hands] hands **NN**
27	*Hand-shooes*] *Hand-shoes* **5**
28	Custom] Custom, **1**
29	Hands] Hands, **1**
30	is,] is **4 5**
31	Shooes] Shoes **5**
87.3	Winter,] Winter **5**
6	big] bigh **5**
11	choose] chuse **5**
17	till,] till **5** days] Days **5**
21	pain,] pain **NN** danger] Danger **5**
28	Bathe] Bath **5**
29	tollerable] tolerable **4 5**
88.3	bathe] bath **5**
4	chilness] Chilness **5**
19	find,] find **5**
21	Bodies,] Bodies **5**

88.22	Water:] Water. 5 day] Day 5
27	life] Life 5
31	health] Health 4 5
32	heat] Heat 5 Summer] summer **NN**
89.1–2	caution] Caution 5
7	which,] which 1 5
8	World: And] World; and 1
9	it: It] it; it 1 early,] early 5
10	degrees] Degrees 5
12	born. There] born; there 1
13	more,] more 5
14	Sunburnt.] Sunburnt: 1
16	Way] way 5
19	prejudice] Prejudice 5
23	*Air*] *Air*, 5
90.2	This,] This 5
6	sight.] sight: 1 if,] if 5
7	sitting] Sitting 1
9	Forbearing] forbearing **NN**
11	Case; for] Case. For 5
12	Conduct;] Conduct, 1
15	care] Care 5 For,] For **NN**
17	case] Case 5
20	That] that **NN** Sons] Son's **NN**
21	Scope] scope **NN**
22	best. She] best; she 1 works,] works 1 5 self,] self 1
23	better,] better 5 her.] her: 1
25	Shapes] Shapes, 5
26	Children] children **NN**
27	*strait-laced*,] *strait-laced* **NN**
28	me thinks] me-thinks 1 methinks 4 5
30	Way] way 5
31	made. And] made, and 1
33	*strait-lacing*,] *strait-lacing*; **NA** conclude] conclude, 1
	Creatures,] Creatures 1
34	Munkeys] Monkeys **NN** who,] who 1 5 they,] they 1
35	fondness] Fondness 5
91.5	disproportion] Disproportion 5 nourishment]
	Nourishment 5
7	designs: And] designs; and 1 designs. And 5 wonder]
	Wonder 5 laid,] laid 1 5

8	can,] can **NN**
9	proportion] Proportion **5**
10	Women] women **NN** Beauty] beauty **NN**
11	Infancy] infancy **NN**
15	observed that] observed, That **1**
16	Women] women **NN** little,] little **NN** short-lived;] short lived, **NN** short-lived, **NA**
18	Sex,] Sex **1 5** are,] are **1 5** some,] some **5**
19	Feet;] Feet, **1**
23	Thigh] thigh **NN**
24	Inconveniencies] Inconveniences **1**
25	*Thorax*,] *Thorax* **5**
27	and,] and **5**
32	themselves,] themselves; **5**
33	danger] Danger **5**
92.2	danger] Danger **5**
3	healthy] Healthy **5**
5	wholely] wholly **4 5**
8	Meal.] Meal, **4 5**
9	Hunger,] Hunger **5** best;] best: **5** care] Care **5**
13	Inconveniences.] Inconveniencies. **5**
15	Things,] Things **1**
16	these,] these **1** taken,] taken **1**
17	Mixture] mixture **NN**
18	all: Especially] all; especially **1**
19	Things,] Things **1 5**
21	Meats.] Meats: **1** relish] relish, **5**
23	over-much] over much **NN** Thirst] thirst **NN**
27	wholsom] wholsome **5**
28	Delicacies;] Delicacies: **1**
30	Bread. If] Bread; if **1** hungry] Hungry **5**
31	hungry] Hungry **5**
32	eat] Eat **5** Effects] effects **NN**
33	love] Love **5**
35	Good,] Good **1 5** hereby,] hereby **1**
36	eat] Eat **5**
37	alike:] alike; **1** Some] some **1**
93.1	Stomachs.] Stomachs: **1** *Gormands*] *Gormans* **NN** (gurmands **HK**)
2	Nature: And] Nature; and **1**
3	strong,] strong **1**
4	Usage,] Usage **5**
5	five.] five: **1 5**

93.7	eight] Eight 5 ten] Ten 5
8	twelve] Twelve 5
10	bit] Bit 5
11	account] Account 5
13	piece] Piece 5
15	health] Health 5
20	bit] Bit 5
27	Reproach,] Reproach 5
30	convenient,] convenient 1
31	*Breakfast.*] *Breakfast:* **NN**
33	*England*] *England*, 5
34	that,] that 5
94.2	Hour. For] Hour; for 1
3	Stomach] stomach **NN** Hour,] Hour; 1
5	want] Want 5
6	Dinner,] Dinner 5
7	these,] these 1
8	*Meals,*] *Meals* 1 have,] have 5
9	hard] hard, 5
13	Stomach:] Stomach. 1 thoughts] Thoughts 5
17	nobody] no Body 5
18–19	dull and unhealthy] Dull and Unhealthy 5
20	Condition.] Condition: 1 Gentleman,] Gentleman 5
21	Soldier. But he that,] Soldier; but he that 1 this,] this 1
22	so] so, 1 Life,] Life 1
27	this,] this 1
29	know. Therefore] know; therefore 1
30	down;] down, 1
95.1	*drink.* At] *drink*; at 1
12	Custom. And] Custom; and 1
13	him,] him 5
16	Children,] Children. 5
20	where,] where 5
22	Twenty] twenty 5
25	settle: And] settle; and 1
96.1	reprehended,] reprehended 1
3	Court] court 5
4–5	themselves: And] themselves; and 1
6	carefully] Carefully **NN**
7	can; There] can, there 1
9	Children's] Childrens **NN**
13	it: And] it, and 1
15	Means] means 5

20	*England,*] *England.* **NN**
26	Cautions.] Cautions **NN**
27	Food.] food: **NN** Food: **NA**
31	Health.] Health: **1** *Summer-Fruits,*] *Summer-Fruits* **1**
32	Year] Year, **1**
36	them] them, **1**
97.1	satisfie] satisfy **5**
6	heard,] heard **5**
7	*dried*] dried **5** wholsome] wholesome **1**
9	It] it **5**
10	Ways] ways **5** Expence,] Expence **1**
13	*Sleep.*] *Sleep*: **1**
14	Satisfaction;] Satisfaction, **1**
18	early] Early **5**
19	has,] has **NN 5** setled] settled **5**
20	not,] not **5**
21	a-bed] a-Bed **5**
22	early] Early **5**
30	Contrary] contrary **5**
35	Bed,] Bed **1** that;] that, **1**
98.4	laziness] Laziness **5**
9	lovers] Lovers **5**
10	degrees] Degrees **5**
10–11	rest . . . healthy] Rest . . . Healthy **5**
15	though] Though **5**
18	Hour:] Hour; **5**
21	harm] Harm **5**
24	degrees] Degrees **5**
25	words, and usage,] Words and Usage, **5**
28	uneasiness] Uneasiness **5**
30	Feathers,] Feathers **1**
33	Grave. And,] Grave: And **1**
34	Wrapping] wrapping **NN** Reins;] Reins, **1**
99.1	Indispositions,] Indispositions; **1**
5	Bed,] Bed **1** order. And therefore,] order; and therefore **1**
6	amiss,] amiss **1**
8	Change] Change, **1**
11	Sleep. He] Sleep; he **1**
13	Cordial: And] Cordial; and **1**
14	not,] not **1** Boards.] Boards; **1** 'Tis] 'tis **1**
18	Bodies.] Bodies: **1**
20	it: For] it; for **1**
22	for: And] for; and **1**

99.24	Side] side 5
28	Books;] Books, 1
29	believing] believing, 1
31	Rational] rational 5
32	effect] Effect 5
33	Peristaltick] Per-|ristaltick **NN**
35	Application,] Application 1
100.3	who,] who **NN**
4	*Stool*;] *Stool*, 1
7	Quality;] Quality, 1
9	it was] is was **NN**
14	so] so, 1
18	case of necessity] Case of Necessity 5
20	Fibres;] Fibres, **NN**
23	length] Length 5
25	2.] 3. **NN**
28	effect] Effect 5
29	leisure . . . leisure] Leisure . . . Leisure 5
31	purpose] Purpose 5
32	hour] Hour 5 certain;] certain, 1
33	health] Health 5
101.1	prosecution] Prosecution 5
2	care] Care 5
4	endeavour'd] endeavoured 1
5	success] Success 5
6	habit] Habit 5
7	neglect] Neglect 5
11	day] Day 5
13	power] Power 5
14	contrary] Contrary **NN** so: And] so; and 1
15	play] Play 5 again] again, 1
16	not] not, 1
18	Play,] Play **NN** heedless] Heedless 5
20	gently;] gently, 1 degrees] Degrees 5
22	guess;] guess, 1
23	constant] Constant **NN**
25	tryal] Tryal 5
29	hours] Hours 4 5 enough;] enough 1
30	body] Body 5 much. And] much; and 1 means] means, 1
32	cure] Cure 5
102.1	*Physick*,] *Physick* 1
2	Diseases:] Diseases. 1 which,] which **NN** observed;] observed: 1 5

3	prevention] Prevention **5**
3–4	observation] Observation **5**
5	Apothecarie's] Apothecary's **4 5** care] Care **5**
8	Children;] Children, **1**
11	hands] Hands **5** tamper;] tamper, **1**
13	distant] Distant **5**
15	Children *ed.*] Children, **1 5** Children; **3 4** them,] them **5**
16	necessity] Necessity **5** cold-still'd] cold, still'd **1**
17	*Poppy-water*] *Popy-water* **1** Surfeit-water, **5**] Surfeit-water; **3 4** Ease,] Ease **5**
18	Flesh, **5**] Flesh; **3 4**
18–19	beginning] Beginning **5**
19	which,] which **NN**
23	part,] part **5** belief;] belief, **1** Belief; **5** body] Body **5**
23–4	pretence] Pretence **5**
25	you,] you **1** use] Use **5**
32	Wet] wet **NN**
33	care] Care **5**
103.1	*Mind*;] *Mind.* **1**
3	disposed] disposed, **1**
5	beginning] Beginning **5** Discourse] Discourse, **1**
6	difference] Difference **5**
7	*Education*] *Education*, **1** else;] else, **1**
8	reason] Reason **5** care] Care **5**
11	there: And] there; and **1**
18	appetite] Appetite **5**
21	care] Care **5**
22	*Season*;] *Season.* **1**
26	warily,] warily; **1** fondness] Fondness **5**
29	things;] things, **1**
30	think] think, **1**
31	irregularities] Irregularities **4 5**
32	perverseness] Perverseness **5** which, they think,] which they think **5**
34	It was] it was **5**
104.6	taste] tast **1**
10	Play-things;] Play-things, **1**
11	wilful] wilfull **NN**
13	them;] them. **1** then,] then **1** perhaps] perhaps, **1**
15	too deep root] to deep Root **5**
20	insensible,] insensible **1**
21	Indulgence] indulgence **NN**
23	why,] why **1**

104.15	suddain] sudden **NN**
26	Parent's] parent's **NN** Parents 5 indulgence] Indulgence 5
29	knit: And] knit; and 1
32	Them,] them **NN** them, **NA** 5
33	*young*;] *young*, 1
105.3	Humour; why,] Humour, why 1
6	for] for, 5 little] little, 1 5
6–7	inclinations] Inclinations 5
8	Fault;] Fault: 1
11	govern,] govern 1
12	*young*] *Young* 5
18	reason] Reason 5
25	But] but 5 notice] Notice 5
28	*blow*] *Blow* 5
34	harm] Harm 5
36	purpose] Purpose 5
106.3	finery] Finery 5
6	her *her*] her, *her* 5
9–10	fashionableness] Fashionableness 5
18	streightness] Streightness 5
20	temptation] Temptation 5
22	dislike] Dislike 5
27	share] Share 5
32	order] Order 5
33	*what*] *What* 5
34	bodies invention] Bodies Invention 5
35	want] Want 5
36	beginning] Beginning 5
37	defence] Defence 5 increase] Increase 5
38	labour] Labour 5
39	leisure] Leisure 5 humours] Humours 5
107.2	kept,] kept 5 excess] Excess 5
10	expence] Expence 5
11	title] Title 5
21	view] View 5
27	particulars] Particulars 5
33	Excellency] Excellency, 1 power] Power 5 satisfaction] Satisfaction 5
36	that,] that 1
108.7	it;] it, 1
8	Mastery;] Mastery, 1
9	others] others, 1 beginning] beginning, 1 Beginning 5
10	desire] Desire 5

14	should,] should **5**
17	mean] mean, **1**
22	took] took, **1**
24	Difference,] Difference **1**
26	less, I think,] less I think **5**
30	which,] which **5**
32	that.] that: **1**
109.1	too;] too. **1**
4	impatient,] impatient **1**
7	look,] look **5**
8	Will] will **NN**
10	Father,] Father **1**
11	awe] Awe **5**
13	Familiarity: So] Familiarity; so **1**
15	Friend] Friend, **5** methinks,] methinks **1**
17	distance,] distance **1** Distance, **5**
18	up.] up: **1** Good] good **NN**
19	*Children*: Their] *Children*, their **1**
20	Discipline.] Discipline: **1**
21	Severity] Severity, **5**
22	Children,] Children **5**
24	*die*] *Die* **5**
27	Governors;] Governors, **NN** and, as] and as **1** awe] Awe **5**
34	uneasie,] uneasie **5**
110.4	tractable,] tractable **5**
8	abated;] abated, **1**
9	them,] them **NN**
12	Settling] Setling **1**
16	dutifull] dutiful **5**
23	vertuous] vertuous, **1** within. And] within; and **1**
25	betimes;] betimes, **1**
111.1	enough,] enough **1**
3	think] think, **1**
5	Children,] Children **1**
6	*chastised*,] *chastised* **1** All] All, **1**
7	is,] is **NN**
8	used] used, **5** are;] are, **5** having,] having **5**
14	in them,] in them **1** so;] so, **1**
15	Repining] repining **NN**
17	Submission] Submission, **5**
19	Pains] pains **NN**
20	it; and] it, and **5** deferred,)] deferred) **5**

111.21	of,] of; 1
23	governed,] governed 1
27	Mastery] mastery **NN**
28	importunity] Importunity 5
30	danger] Danger 5
32	foundation] Foundation 5
34	dawnings] Dawnings 5
112.1	over-sight] Over-sight 5
3	other side] otherside 1
5	hand] Hand 5 Vigor] Vigor, **NN**
8	timorous,] timorous 5
10	thing] Thing **NN** danger] Danger 5
12	yet,] yet 1
13	things] things, 1
17	Government] Government, 1
18	Education;] Education, 1
19	Mischiefs;] Mischiefs, 1
20	hand] Hand 5
23	mastery] Mastery 5 Propensity] Propensity, 1
24	rate;] rate, 1
25	root] Root 5
29	pleasure] Pleasure 5 fear] Fear 5
30	*whiping*] *whipping* **NN**
31	*Pain.* And] *Pain*, and 1 it,] it 1
34	usefull] useful 4 5
113.2	him,] him 1
3	that,] that 1
7	about them?] about them; 1 in them;] in them, 1
8	Men] Men, 1
9	Ways] ways 1 there] there, 1
10	Recreation,] Recreation 1 *blows*] *Blows* 5
12	application] Application 5
13	so.] so: 1
14	with: And] with; and 1
15	Stomach;] Stomach, 1
18	*slavish*] *Slavish* 5 *Discipline*] *Discipline*, 1 *slavish*] *Slavish* 5
19	submits,] submits 5 fear] Fear 5
21	impunity] Impunity 5 scope] Scope 5
22	Inclination;] Inclination, 1
23	him;] him, 1
24	violence] Violence 5
25	pitch] Pitch 5

28	place] Place **5**
29	Creature: Who] Creature, who **1**
30	Sobriety] Sobriety, **1** tame,] tame **5**
31	noise] Noise **5** trouble;] Trouble: **5**
33	be,] be **5** life] Life **5**
36	those] those, **1**
114.2	Children] children **NN**
3	them,] them **NN**
4	*Apples*,] *Apples* **1** *Sugar-plumbs*] Sugar-*plumbs* **5** else,] else **1 5** kind,] kind **1**
6	love of pleasure] Love of Pleasure **5** propensity] propensitie **1** Propensity **5**
7	means] Means **5**
12	&c.] *&c.* **1**
14	fit,] fit **5** *Money*;] *Money*, **1** pains] Pains **5**
15	pleasure] Pleasure **5** Morsel;] Morsel: **1**
16	*Suit*,] *Suit* **1** performance] Performance **5**
17	Tasks;] Tasks, **1**
18	Things] Things, **1**
19	happiness] Happiness **5**
20	People,] People **1**
22	moment] Moment **5** happiness] Happiness **5** usefulness] usefullness **NN** Usefulness **5** misapplied] mis-applied **5**
23	*Punishments*] *Punishments*, **1**
27	avoided,] avoided **1**
30	Pleasures] pleasures **NN**
31	pleasant,] pleasant **1**
32	be,] be **5** enjoyment] Enjoyment **5**
35	Acceptation] Acceptation, **1**
36	Governors;] Governors, **1** them,] them **1**
37	*Performance*] *Performance*, **1**
115.4	with,] with **1**
5	Children] Childern **NN**
8	Reins,] Reins **1** work,] work **1**
13	them. The] them; the **1**
14	those] those, **1**
15	consequence] Consequence **5**
18	business] Business **5**
19	principle] Principle **5**
20	Pleasure,] Pleasure **NN** proposal] Proposal **NN**
22	purchase **4 5**] purchace **1** purchsae **3** quiet] Quiet **5**

115.23	Sweet-meat. This] Sweet-meat; this **1** Health;] Health, **1**
25	Object;] Object, **1**
26	satisfied;] satisfied: **1** root] Root **5**
26–7	Mischief: And] Mischief; and **1**
27	denial] Denial **5**
30	Spring] Spring, **1**
31	occasion] Occasion **5**
31–2	violence] Violence **5**
32	trouble] Trouble **5**
34	kind;] kind, **1**
116.1	work,] work **NA** business] Business **5**
2	difficulty] Difficulty **5**
3	incentives] Incentives **5**
4	them.] them: **1** love] Love **5**
5	apprehension] Apprehension **5**
8	appearance] Appearance **5** difficulty] Difficulty **5**
10	found,)] found) **5**
15	depend] depond **4**
16	*ill*;] *ill*: **1**
19	this] this, **NN**
20	Force,] Force **1**
24	*Disgrace*] *Disgrace*, **1**
25	weight] Weight **5**
30	may,] may **5**
30–1	possible,] possible **5**
32	Esteem] Esteem, **1**
33–4	it; and,] it. And **1** it; and **5**
34	Side] side **5** Miscarriage] Miscarriage, **1**
36	State,] State **5**
117.1	satisfie] satisfy **5**
2	Vertue;] Vertue, **1** settled] setled **NN**
4	in] in, **1** enjoyed] enjoyed, **1**
7	Punishment,)] Punishment) **5** love] Love **5**
8	love] Love **5**
9	ways] Ways **1**
10	here,] here **1**
11	Perverseness] Preverseness **5**
12	Children,] Children **1 5**
17	Countenance;] Countenance, **1**
25	which,] which **1 5**
26	found,] found **1**
28	Consideration. Only] Consideration; only **1** Importance;] Importance: **1**

29	And] and **NN**
118.3	them.] them: **1**
6	Cure. It] Cure; it **1**
11	sense] Sense **5**
13	Women;] Women, **1**
17	consider,] consider **1**
19	declared,] declared **1 5** Degree] Degree, **1**
22	reconciliation] Reconciliation **5**
24	will,] will **4 5**
25	influence] Influence **5**
27	Morning] morning **NN**
119.4	is] is, **1**
5	Reward)] Reward, **1**
6	it: And] it; and **1**
8	vertuous] vertuous, **1**
9	Encouragement] encouragement **NN**
10	find] find, **NA** right,] right **5**
14	grave,] grave **5**
19	opinion] Opinion **5**
27	established.] established: **1**
28	For, All] For all **5** *Actions,*] *Actions* **1**
28–9	left . . . and] *left perfectly free and* **5**
32	were,] were **NN**
35	natural] Natural **5**
120.1	Correction] Corection **NN**
2	force] Force **5** gaiety] Gaiety **5**
6	are,)] are) **5**
10	encouraged,] encouraged **1**
11	Health,] Health **5** curbed,] curbed **5** restrained:] restrained, **NN** restrained; **NA** And] and **1** is,] is **5**
13	leave] Leave **NN** notice] Notice **5**
15	Precepts,] Precepts **1**
21	them.] them: **1**
27	Memory,] Memory **5** Reflection,] Reflection **1**
28	Childhood;] Childhood, **1**
29	Face] Face, **5**
30	use] Use **5** Man,] Man **1**
121.1	Tenth] tenth **5** part] Part **1 5**
7	Transgression,] Transgression **1**
8	*Rules,*] *Rules* **5**
13–14	unpunished, whereby] unpunished: Whereby **1**
17	is,] is **5** practice] Practice **5**
21	practice] Practice **5**

23	when ever] whenever **5**
24	immediately,] immediately **1**
24–5	above-mentioned.] above-mentioned; **1**
34	Chid] chid **5**
126.3	concern'd,] concern'd **5**
14	vex] vex, **5**
29	Example.] Example: **1**
30	us: Nor] us; nor **1**
127.5	Civility] Civilty **5**
7	Servants] Servants, **NN**
10	Mischief. You] Mischief; you **1**
11	vitious] Vicious **5**
13	be;] be, **1**
14	*Company*] *company*
16	easy] easie **NN 5** them: They] them; they **1**
18	Restraints] restraints **1** Governor's] Governour's **NN**
	sight] Sight **5**
21	ill: All] ill; all **1** Next,] Next **1**
26	conversation] Conversation **5**
29	does,] does **1 5**
128.1	vain] vain, **1**
2	purpose. For] purpose; for **1**
19	Ancient] Antient **5**
129.21	guard] Guard **5**
36	use] Use **4 5**
130.23	Sense] Sence **5**
28	lodg'd] lodg'd, **5**
29	Master's] Masters **5**
131.6	Men;] Men, **5**
12	well-laid] well laid **4 5**
18–19	Age bred,] Age, bred **5**
23	dis-credit] discredit **5**
28	Chance] chance **5**
30	past,] past; **5**
33	Improvements,] Improvements **5**
34	retrieve **4 5**] retreive **3**
132.4	occasion **4 5**] occason **3**
12	bare-faced] barefaced **5**
18	But] but **4 5**
23	thing,] thing **5**
24	preferr] prefer **5**
25	home,] home **5**
133.7	Inconveniencies] Inconveniences **5**
9–10	Imitation;] Imitation, **1**

133.10	Parents] parents **NN**
11	him,] him **NN**
16	Example;] Example: **1 5**
20	Arbitrary] arbitrary **NN**
134.1	Ease] ease **NN**
11	Learning] learning **NN** Read] read **5**
12	Privilege] privilege **NN**
14	Way] way **NN** Things] things **NN**
21	*Task.*] *Task*: **1** proposed] proposed, **1**
23	irksome: The] irksome; the **1**
27	Rate?] Rate. **5**
28	themselves;] themselves, **1 5** Do] do **1 5**
135.4	time] Time **1**
6	Children.] Children: **1**
12	Head] head **5**
14	saved. For] saved; for **1**
16	awkardly,] awkardly **1**
29	Sides] sides **5**
31	them. The] them; the **1**
34	that, that] that that **1**
136.1	learn;] learn, **1**
2	Things] things **5**
6	first,] first **5**
10	it;] it, **NN**
21	Facility] facility **NA**
24	Children,] Children **1**
29	Employments,] Employments **5**
32	active and busie] Active and Busie **5** Age,] Age **1**
137.4	it;] it, **1**
5	*Business*;] *Business*, **1** *teazed*] *teas'd* **NN**
6	Apprehension:] Apprehension; **1**
9	Play-Games] Play Games **1**
12	themselves.] themselves: **1**
21	Assiduity,] Assiduity **1**
25	follow, more easily] follow more easily, **1**
26	Discipline. And] Discipline; and **1**
28	is] is, **NA**
32	once;] once, **1**
138.1	*Chiding*,] *Chiding* **4 5**
3	Child: For] Child, for **1**
4	Reason: And] Reason; and **1**
7	off;] off, **1**
11	Words] words **4 5**

18	asham'd,] asham'd **5**
21	What] what **1**
30	*Rebellion.* And] *Rebellion*, and **1**
139.1	much,] much **5**
2	think,] think **5**
5–6	Blows: For] Blows, for **1**
6	master'd] mastred **1**
8	obey'd;] obey'd, **1**
9	resistance. For] resistance; for **1**
12	prevail;] prevail, **1**
17	easy] easie **5**
19	ever; and,] ever, and **1**
20	*refractoriness*] *refractariness* **1**
21	Will] will **5**
23	after] after, **1**
25	so,] so **NN**
32	Beating] Beating, **1** Remedy,] Remedy **1** random] Random **NN**
35	Offender;] Offender, **1** whatever] whatever, **5**
37	contest,] contest **1**
38	Correction,] Correction **1**
140.2	Child so,] Child, so **1**
5	*humor*] *humour* **4 5**
6	Blows. A kind,] Blows: A kind **1**
7	forgetfullness] Forgetfullness **1**
9	*perverseness* **NN 5**] *perversness* **NA 3 4**
13	Orders;] Orders, **1**
14	pauses laid on,] pauses, laid on **1**
15	true] true, **4 5**
17	Whipping] whipping **NN**
18	fancy.] Phansy: **NN** phansy: **NA**
20	well,] well **1** Punishment.] Punishment: **1** But] but **NN**
22	frequent] frequentt **5**
23	useful] usefull **NN**
24	it?] it. **1**
25	slip? When] slip, when **1**
27	wilfull] willfull **NN** wiful **5**
28	Offender;] Offender? **1**
29	right?] right, **1** Which] which **1**
31	it.] it? **1**
32	Amendment] amendment **1**
34	Father] father **NN**

141.1	other] other, 1
2	Reproof;] Reproof, 1 wilfull] willfull **NN**
3–4	*perversness*] *perverseness* 5
4	Will] Will, 1 Disobedience.] Disobedience: 1
7	master'd:] master'd; 1 Only] only 1 not;] not, 1
8	Obstinacy,] Obstinacy **NN**
11	Point.] Point: 1
12	Nor,] Nor **NN**
12–13	Seriousness,] Seriousness 5
14	Growth.] Growth: 1
15	childish] Childish 5
16	them.] them: 1 Carelesness] Carelessness **NN**
20	assisted] Assisted 5
32	passionate] Passionate 5
35	come,] come 1
36	with: And] with; and 1
38	if 4 5] If 1 3
142.2	Thing] thing **NN** Things 5
5	other] other, 1 Habits.] Habits: 1
6	ways] Ways 1 them:] them; 1 And] and 1
	Persuasion] Perswasion **NN** 5
9	wondered] wondred 5
10	Children: And] Children, and 1 Way of Dealing] way of
	dealing **NN**
13	and,] and 5
17	Three,] Three 1 old,] old 1
18	Man.] Man: 1
33	Opinions.] Opinions: 1 Children] children 1
34	Principles. They] Principles; they 1
143.1	yet,] yet **NN** Temper,] Temper 1
2	Motives,] Motives 1
4	force,] force **NN** Fault,] Fault 1
7	Ways] ways **NN**
12	Beauty or Unbecomingness,] Beauty, or Unbecomingness 1
18	Things,] Things 1 Breeding,] Breeding 1
24	Occasion] Ocasion 5
27	dis-like] dislike 4 5
31	done: Whether] done; whether 1
32	And] and 1
34	it;] it, 1
36	Passion. But] Passion; but 1
144.10	Remedy: And] Remedy; and 1
15	unsuccessful: Which] unsuccessful; which 1

16	For,] For 1
17	Command,] Command 1 5
21	Improvement] improvement **NN** There] there 1
31	first] first, 5
32	then,] then **NN**
35	Fault;] Fault, 1
145.4	caused,] caused 1
5	once;] once, 1
8	out,] out 1
10	up,] up 1
11	uneasie] uneasy 1
12	Pick-ax,] Pick-ax 1
14	over-grown] overgrown 5
15	Fruits,] Fruits 1
18	Injunctions,] Injunctions 1
19	For] For, 1 Actions,] Actions 1
29	Lye,] Lye 1 Trick;] Trick, 1 The] the 1 be,] be 1
30	*strange Monstrous*] *strange, monstrous* 1
34	many,] many 1
37	Fashion,] Fashion 1
38	tried,] tried 1
146.3	Whipping] whipping 1
4	beating: Which] beating, which 1
5	unnatural,] unnatural 1
6	Methods] methods **NN**
8	too; or else,] too, or else 1
11	proposed: For] proposed; for 1 grant,] grant 1
12	Tempers: Yet] Tempers, yet 1
14	all. Nor] all; nor 1 unmanageable] unmanagable 1
16	And] and 1
17	Excuses] Excuses, **NN** obstinate:] obstinate 1
25	necessary;] necessary, 1
28	Voice,] Voice 1
29	Smart,] Smart 1
31	this,] this 1
34	Compliance;] Compliance, 1
35	*Beating,*] *Beating?* 4
37	Enemy] enemy **NN**
147.2	do,] do 1
5	such; And] such, and 1 those,] those 1
10	easie: And] easy; and 1
13	Direction;] Direction. 1
32	influence] Influence 5

147.33	Servants;] Servants, 1
34	Prohibitions] prohibitions **NN**
148.2	hearken'd] hearkn'd 5
3	say;] say, 1
4	*Sober,*] *Sober*; 1
7–8	*Diligence,*] *Diligence* 1
8	*Discretion*;] *Discretion*, 1 Persons,] Persons 1
9	Salaries;] Salaries, 1
13	principled] Principled 5
16	Addition] addition 1
22	Clothes,] Clothes; 1
25	shameful] Shameful 5
27	Pride,] Pride 1
29	though] tho' 5
32	he,] he 5
34	World] world 1
149.2	those,] those 1 able: The] able; the 1
3	Parts,] Parts 1
6	where: For] where; for 1 sorts. And] sorts; and 1
11	Terms:] Terms, 1 Terms; 5 But] but 1
13	Tutor,] Tutor 1
14	wonder.] wonder; 1
15	one. All] one; all 1 way:] way, 1 And] and 1
17	Charge;] Charge, 1
19	no,] no 1 Commendations.] Commendations: 1
22	Turn] turn 1 Curious,] Curious 1
23	Trial,] Trial 1
24	afterwards: That] afterwards, that 1
28	consider,] consider 1 Tutor,] Tutor 1
34	imployed,] imployed 4 Road;] Road, 1
150.2	Gentleman] Gentleman, 5
7	enough,] enough 1 5
20	Clothes] Cloathes 5
30	Brutality;] Brutality: 5
35	wherever] where-ever 4 5
151.19	Skillful] Skilful 5
29	Profit] profit 5
152.2	Carriage,] Carriage 5
153.1	usually] usualy 5
8	For] for 4 5
27	fashion,] fashion 5
34	Ruin] Ruine 5
154.1	those,] those 5

5	Pleasure;] Pleasure, **5**
27	skillful] skilful **5**
30	Designs,] Designs **5**
155.3	This,] This **5**
8	lanch] launch **5**
17	Figure;] Figure: **5**
21	ancient] antient **5**
157.5	principally] Principally **5**
12	*vitæ*] *Vitæ* **5**
14	those] those, **5**
15	fashion] fashion, **5**
17	prevail,] prevail; **5**
20	Men] men **5**
158.8	all] all, **5**
17	unpolish'd] unpolish'd, **4 5** ill-bred] ill bred **4**
23	choice] Choice **5**
28	Method] method **1** Though] Tho' **1**
29	setled] settled **NN 5**
31	managed; yet] managed: Yet **1**
32	along] a long **NN**
33	Pupilage.] Pupilage, **5** relaxed,] relaxed **1**
34	Good-Behaviour] Good behaviour **NN** it;] it, **1**
159.1	*Advice*] *advice* **5**
2	him,] him **1** things] things, **1**
6	*Man*, the] *Man*, The **NN**
8	Amusements] A musements **NN**
9	in.] in: **1**
10	young] Young **5**
12	would;] would, **1** Parents] parents **NN**
19	This,] This **1** T his **5**
22	Cheerfulness] Cheerfullness **NN**
23	Father. And] Father; and **1**
26	enjoy,] enjoy **1**
30—1	Doubts: But] Doubts; but **1**
36	Care;] Care, **1**
160.4-5	occasion] Occasion **5**
20	demanding,] demanding **1**
31	his;] his, **1**
33	Staff] staff **5**
35	Power] Power, **1**
161.22	And] and **4 5**
33	forbidden,] forbidden **1**
34	necessary;] necessary: **1**

161.35	When, (by] when, by **1**
162.2	gayety] gaiety **1**
3	Sleep)] Sleep, **1**
4	him,] him **1**
8	When] when **1** Tenderness,] Tenderness **1**
14	Ways] ways **1**
15	Vertue,] Vertue **1**
17	done,] done **1**
19	Lying,] Lying **1**
26	was,] was **1**
28	it,] it **1**
31	Habit;] Habit, **1**
35	*Timorous,] Timorous* **NN**
163.1	*Tractable] Tractable,* **5** *Curious] Curious,* **5**
1–2	*Careless,] Careless.* **1**
2	Men's **1**] Mens **3 4 5**
4	Minds; Only] Minds, only **1**
8	Deformities,] Deformities **NN**
10	§.102.] §.97 [*recte*], **NN** Temper;] Temper, **1**
11	that,] that **1** restraint,] restraint. **1**
12	*predominant*] Predominant **5** *Passions,] Passions* **1**
13	*Inclinations;] Inclinations,* **1**
14	Open] open **NN**
17	prevalencies] Prevalencies **4 5** Constitution,] Constitution **1**
18	Contest;] Contest, **1**
19	fear,] fear **1**
21	Byass] Byas **NN**
22	Nature] nature **NN**
23	Mind,] Mind **1**
24	judge] judge, **1**
27	before,] before **1 5** *Liberty;] Liberty,* **1**
164.3	more;] more, **1** *Dominion:* And] *Dominion,* and **1**
4	Habits] habits **NN**
5	Dominion] dominion **NN** early,] early **NN** Things.] Things: **1**
6	born, I *ed.*] born (I **1 3 4 5**
9	compliance] complyance **NN**
10	them;] them, **1** near,] near **1**
13	is **5**] is, **1 3 4**
16	have,] have **1** them,] them **1**
17	He,] He **5**

20	humane] Humane **4 5**
165.1	Nature;] Nature, **1**
20	Nature,] Nature **5**
166.3	should,] should **5**
7	lose] loose **5**
14	is,] is **5**
16	all,] all **5**
24	awe,] awe **5**
167.3	consider'd,] consider'd **4 5**
15	Submission,] Submission **5**
16	them,] them **5**
20	them;] them: **1**
27	useful] usefull **NN**
29	liberty;] liberty, **1** Reason] reason **NN**
30	hearken'd] hearkn'd **5** speak] speak, **5**
168.8	deni'd] deny'd **4 5**
169.1	course] Course **5**
5	mastery] Mastery **5**
6	rest:] rest; **1** Whoever] whoever **1**
7	crossed] Crossed **NN** it.] it: **1**
9	This,] This **1**
9–10	love and esteem] Love and Esteem **5**
11	pleasure] Pleasure **5**
13	Clamors] Clamours **5**
14	to.] to: **1**
21	*Complaint*] *Compliant* **NN**
22	notice] Notice **5**
24	pardon] Pardon **5**
25	were,] were **5**
26	strengthned] strengthened **NN**
27	custom] Custom **5**
30	Experience] experience **1** *liberal*] *Liberal* **5**
170.4	Covetousness,] Covetousness **1** desire] Desire **5**
5	possession] Possession **5**
6	root] Root **5**
7	readiness] Readiness **5**
10	freeness,] freeness **NN** Freeness, **5**
11	interest] Interest **5**
12	others] others, **1** husbandry] Husbandry **5** himself;] himself, **1** return] Return **5**
14	way: And] way; and **1**
15	means] Means **5** practice] Practice **5**
17	habit] Habit **NN 5** pleasure,] pleasure **1** Pleasure, **5**
18	*kind, liberal,* and *civil*] *Kind, Liberal* and *Civil* **5**

170.21	occasion] Occasion 5
24	wonder,] wonder 5
25	measures] Measures 5
26	result] Result 5
28	slip] Slip 5
29	notice] Notice 5 weight] Weight 5
30	moment] Moment 5
32	danger] Danger 5
33	dishonesty] Dishonesty 5 *Injustice,*] *Injustice* 5
34	shew] Shew 5
171.5	gift] Gift 5
6	take,] take 5
8	Rules,] Rules 5
9	act] Act 5
10	mistake] Mistake 5 perversness] perverseness 4 Perverseness 5 wills] Wills 5
11	rebuke and shame] Rebuke and Shame 5
13	take,] take 5 something,] something 5
14	somebody] some Body 5
18	Vice] Vice, 5
21	interest; habits] Interest; Habits 5
21–2	constantly] constantly, 5
22	facility] Facility 5 reason] Reason 5
24	fault,] fault 1 Fault, 5 Children;] Children, 1
26	Reasons,] Reasons 1
27	themselves;] themselves, 1 aim] Aim 5
28	*Crying*] Crying 1 *stubborn* and *domineering*] *Stubborn* and *Domineering* 5
29	*querulous* and *whining*] *Querulous* and *Whining* 5
30	*Crying*] crying 1
31	declaration] Declaration 5 Obstinacy:] Obstinacy, 1 When] when 1
32	power] Power 5
172.1	*Crying*] crying 1 effect] Effect 5
2	*bemoaning*] *Bemoaning* 5
3	Two,] Two 1 observed, may,] observed may 1
4	Crying,] Crying 1
4–5	distinguished;] distinguished, 1
6	*crying*] *Crying* 5
6–7	permitted;] permitted, 1
10	it.] it: 1
18	ill] Ill 5 Humour,] Humour 1
21	use] Use 5 For] for 1

22	extremity] Extremity **5** Whip,] whipp **NN** Whip **NA**
	it,] it **1**
23	find,] find **1 5**
24	Correction;] Correction, **1**
25	*crying,*] *crying* **1** *Crying*, **5**
26	them;] them, **1**
27	mere] meer **5** Cruelty,] Cruelty **1**
30	For if,] For if **NN** when-ever] whenever **5**
31	Smart,] smart **1**
34	penitent,] penitent **1 5**
35	careful] Carefull **NN**
37	much;] much, **1**
173.1	perceived] perceived, **1**
4	measure;] measure, **1** Measure; **5**
6	*Cry*,] *Cry* **1**
7	suffer;] suffer, **1** befalls] befals **1**
8	avoid: For] avoid, for **1**
11	incourages,] incourages **1**
13	hurt] Hurt **5**
16	harms] Harms **5**
17	feels,] feels; **1**
19	tenderness] Tenderness **5**
20	sence] Sence **5** Inconveniencies] Inconveniences **4**
22	hurt] Hurt **5** impression] Impression **5**
23	harm] Harm **5** suffering] Suffering **5**
24	brawniness] Brawniness **5** insensibility] Insensibility **5**
25	Armour] Armour, **1**
27	practice] Practice **5**
28	effeminacy] Effeminacy **5**
30	*Crying*] *Crying*, **1** nothing,] nothing **5**
32	harms] Harms **5**
33	again;] again, **1**
34	heedlesness] Heedlessness **5**
35	tumbling] Tumbling **5**
36	hurts] Hurts **5**
174.1	quiet and ease] Quiet and Ease **5**
2	future] Future **5**
6	comply,] comply **1**
7	latter,] latter **NN** softness] Softness **5**
10	*Whining*] whining **1**
11	Circumstances of the Thing] circumstances of the thing **NN**
12	considered: No] considered; no **1**
14–15	discountenancing] Discountenancing **5**

174.15	Father,] Father **1**
16	it;] it, **1** roughness] Roughness **5**
18–19	*whimpering*] *Whimpering* **5**
21	notice] Notice **5**
25	insensibility] Insensibility **5**
26	evil] Evil **5**
28	approaches] Approaches **5** apprehension] Apprehension **5**
30	hazard] Hazard **5**
31	use or consequence] Use or Consequence **5** resolution] Resolution **5**
175.1	dislike] Dislike **5**
2	body] Body **5** fear] Fear **5**
6	body] Body **5**
7	reach] Reach **5**
8	choice] Choice **5**
11	heat] Heat **5**
21	hands] Hands **5**
24	heart] Heart **5**
24–5	management] Management **5**
25	resolution] Resolution **5**
28	notice] Notice **5**
29	fear] Fear **5**
35	degrees] Degrees **5**
37	neglect] Neglect **5**
38	reason] Reason, **5**
176.1	face] Face **5**
5	places] Places **5**
6	Disgrace,] Disgrace **5**
7	looks] Looks **5**
10	be,] be **5**
12	cannot,] cannot **5**
14	Industry,] Industry **5**
15	use] Use **5** execution] Execution **5**
17	steadiness] Steadiness **5**
18	frights] Frights **5**
19	kinds;] kinds, **5**
21	shatters,] shatters **5**
22	suggestion] Suggestion **5** appearance] Appearance **5**
25	action] Action **5**
27	alteration] Alteration **5**
28	way;] way, **5**
29	lives] Lives **5**
30	effects] Effects **5** every-where] every where **5**

177.2	kind;] kind, **5**
3	about,] about **5** happen,] happen **5**
18	Usage] Usuage **5**
24	annex'd] annexed **5**
31	it.] it **5**
35	Occasions;] Occasions, **5**
178.4	Souldier] Soldier **5**
32	Pain;] Pain, **5** Reason;] Reason, **5**
179.2	Lacedæmonian] *Lacedæmonian* **5**
5	Foundation] foundation **5**
8	Pain,] Pain **5**
17	degrees] Degrees **5**
21	course] Course **5**
22	degrees] Degrees **5**
23	usage] Usage **5**
24	Day,] Day **5**
28	degrees] Degrees **5** humour] Humour **5**
28–9	with him;] with him, **5**
30	amends] Amends **5**
31	marks] Marks **5**
34	assistance] Assistance **5**
35	timorousness] Timorousness **5** weakness] Weakness **5**
36	grows bigger, **5**] grows, bigger **3 4**
37	him to;] him to, **5**
38	flinch,] flinch **5**
180.1	Undertake] undertake **5**
2	degrees] Degrees **5**
3	mastery] Mastery **5**
6	apprehension] Apprehension **5**
13	possession] Possession **5**
14	*torment*] torment **1**
17	*Cruelty*,] *Cruelty*; **NN**
18	custom of tormenting and killing] Custom of Tormenting and Killing **5**
19	degrees] Degrees **5**
20	suffering and destruction] Suffering and Destruction **5**
21	compassionate] compassionate, **5** benigne] benign **4 5**
22	notice] Notice **5** exclusion] Exclusion **5**
24	abhorrence] Abhorrence **5** *killing*] killing **1**
25	*spoil*] spoil **1**
25–6	preservation or advantage] Preservation or Advantage **5**
27	Mankind,] mankind **NN** preservation] Preservation **5**
28	persuasion] Persuasion **5**

180.29	World] world **NN**
31	Business;] Business, **1** Prudence] prudence **NN**
33	Birds,] Birds **NN**
34	with:] with. **1**
181.1	well] well, **1**
2	used.] used: **1**
3	Fault;] Fault, **1**
7	*waste*] waste **1**
8	delight] Delight **5** *Mischief*] *mischief* **NN**
12	habit] Habit **5** Custom] custom **NN**
18	Youth] youth **NN**
22	Thus,] Thus **1** Opinion,] Opinion **1**
23	neither] [t inverted]**NN**
25	contrary,] contrary **1**
32	damage] Damage **5** gently,] gently **1** notice] Notice **5**
33–4	miscarriage] Miscarriage **5**
34	guilty] Guilty **5** consequence] Consequence **5**
35	notice] Notice **5** only] only, **1** root] Root **5**
182.1	habit] Habit **5** And] and **1**
2	punishment,] punishment **1** Punishment, **5**
3	harm] Harm **5** play] Play **5**
4	such,] such **1**
5	habits] Habits **5** from; The] from the **1**
6	by] by, **5**
7	Animadversion] animadversion **1**
9	folks] Folks **5**
10	Language,] Language **5**
13	domineering] Domineering **5**
19	distinction] Distinction **5** authority] Authority **5**
21	esteem] Esteem **5** share] Share **5**
23	level] Level **5**
24	feet] Feet **5**
25	shufflings] Shufflings **5**
31	will,] will **5** degrees] Degrees **5**
35	appetite] Appetite **5** Knowledge;] Knowledge, **1**
36	sign] Sign **5**
182.36–183.1	Instrument] Instrument, **1**
183.1	Ignorance,] Ignorance **1 4 5**
6	*answer*] *Answer* **5**
7	so] so, **1**
8	capacity] Capacity **5**
10	it;] it, **1** variety or number] Variety or Number **5**
15	imagine.] imagine: **1**

16	Eyes:] Eyes; **1**
18	desire of Knowing] Desire of Knowing, **5**
19	reason] Reason **5**
24	satisfaction;] satisfaction, **1** Satisfaction; **5** not] not, **1**
25	pleasure,] pleasure **1** Pleasure, **5** learning and improving] Learning and Improving **5**
26	newness and variety] Newness and Variety **5**
28	answering] Answering **5** *Questions*] Questions **1**
29	matter] Matter **5**
31	faces] Faces **5** knowledge,] knowledge **NN** Knowledge, **5**
34	their] thier **NA**
35	advantage] Advantage **5**
36	spur] Spur **5**
184.1	eldest] Eldest **5**
4	taken,] taken **1** *Deceitful* and *Eluding*] *deceitful* and *eluding* **1**
5	deceived;] deceived, **1**
6	trick] Trick **5** Dissimulation,] Dissimulation **5**
7	use] Use **5**
13	Conscience] conscience **1**
15	For] for **1**
16	*Enquiries*] Enquiries **1** making;] making, **1** moment] Moment **5** those,] those **1**
17	ignorant] Ignorant **5** strangers] Strangers **5**
19	us: And] us; and **1**
26	thousand] Thousand **5**
28–9	importance] Importance **5**
33	Stranger:] Stranger, **1**
185.1	is:] is, **1**
2	directly: The] directly; the **1**
4	it.] it: **1** about it;] about it, **1**
5	satisfaction] Satisfaction **5**
12	road,] road **1**
16	way,] way **1**
17	occasion] Occasion **5**
19	know;] know, **1**
25	make] mak **NN**
26	suppose] suppose, **1**
27	useful,] useful **1**
29	say,] say **1** pleasure] Pleasure **5**
31	Judgment,] Judgment **1**
33	And when] and when **1**
186.4	The . . . improvement,] the . . . improvement **1**
5	Perfection,] Perfection **1**

186.9	*Sauntring*] Sauntring **1**
10	on,] on **1**
11	cured,] cured **1**
13	*trifling*] trifling **1**
16	*listless* **1 4 5**] *listess* **3**
19	time,] time **1**
20	Study,] Study **1** away;] away, **1**
21	*sauntring*] Sauntring **4 5**
22	Study,] Study **1** on: And] on; and **1**
25	Study,] Study **1** Inclinations;] inclinations, **NN**
	Inclinations, **NA**
26	see] See **5**
29	Book] book **NN**
30	Temper,] Temper **1**
32	play,] play **NN** else] else, **1**
33	Hours] hours **1**
35	negligent,] negligent **1**
187.2	time,] time **1**
3	diversion:] diversion; **1**
4	prevails,] prevails **1**
9	Business; And] Business, and **1** it,] it **1**
11	it;] it, **1** chiding;] chiding, **1**
12	reform;] reform **1** Tutor,] Tutor **1**
17	do;] do, **1**
18	Play] play **NN**
22	some-body] some body **4 5** imploy'd] employ'd **NN**
24	him;] him, **1**
25	Two or Three] two or three **5**
25–6	Mischief,] Mischief **1**
27	*Idleness,*] *Idleness* **1**
29	examine,] examine **1**
30	does] does, **1**
188.2	rellishes] relishes **5**
8	somebody,] somebody **5**
10	imploying] employing **NN**
11	discern] discern, **1**
23	Praise, or Play,] Praise or Play **1**
24	Cloths,] Cloaths, **5**
24–5	Displeasure;] Displeasure, **1**
28	it.] it: **1**
189.1	way,] way **1**
5	Mind.] Mind: **1**
6	tell] tell, **1**

9	worse;] worse, **1**
13	idle.] idle: **1**
16	Labour;] Labour, **1**
18	*sauntering*] *sauntring* **NN 4 5**
19–20	that that] that, that **1**
21	thing] thing, **1**
22	*as*] as **5**
23	And] and **1** impatience] Impatience **5**
25	it: But] it; but **1**
28	end.] end: **1**
29	play] Play **5** course] Course **5**
30	with;] with: **5**
31	punishment for playing] Punishment for Playing **5**
32	business] Business **5**
34	preferr] prefer **5** thing] think **4** to it;] to it, **1** to it: **5**
35	task of play] Task of Play **5**
190.1	time] time, **1**
3	Forbidding, (which] Forbidding (which **1** forbidding, (which **4 5**
4	Punishment,] Punishment **1**
13	make,] make **5**
16	that] that, **1**
17	them,] them **1 5** other,] other **1**
18	Top] top **5** scourge] Scourge **4 5**
19	Enjoin] Enjoyn **5** Hours] hours **5**
21	*a*] a **NN**
23	do;] do, **1**
25	Top,] top **NN** Top **NA** long] long, **NA**
26	eagerness] Eagerness **5**
30	difference] Difference **5** doing: The] doing; the **1** esteem] Esteem **5**
33	choice] Choice **5**
36	them;] them. **1**
191.1	Parents] parents **NN** others] others, **1**
3	example] Example **5** them,] them **NN**
4	earnestness and delight] Earnestness and Delight **5**
6	fashion] Fashion **5**
10	sorts;] sorts, **1** custody] Custody **5**
11	power] Power **5**
13	careful] carefull **NN**
14	have: Whereas] have, whereas **1** keeping] Keeping **NN** variety] Variety **5**
15	careless] carless **NN**

191.16	things,] things **NN**
17	Governour: But] Governour; but **1**
20	Attention] attention **1**
21	Consequences] consequences **NN**
33	Play-games] Play games **4**
192.28	want,] want **5**
193.6	scarce] scare **1** it.] it: **1**
7	mother] Mother **5**
13	Lye;] Lye, **1**
17	Reputation in] Reputationin **NN** World.] World: **1**
29	them:] them. **NN**
30	shame] Shame **5** roughness] Roughness **5**
31	thing] th ing **NN**
32	truth] Truth **5** And] and **1**
34	And] and **1**
194.2	love] Love **5**
3	practice] Practice **5**
4	inconvenience] Inconvenience **5** But] but **1**
9	possible: For] possible; for **1**
15	when ever] whenever **5** notice] Notice **5**
16₅	been] beeu ['n' inverted] **NN**
17	perversness] Perversness **5**
18	Chastisement] chastisement **1**
20	Gentleman; Which] Gentleman, which **1**
21	influence] Influence **5**
22	particular] Particulars **5**
24	place] Place **5**
28	contain'd (I suppose)] contain'd, I suppose, **1** Things;] Things, **1 5** *Breeding,*] *Breeding* **NN**
29	self,] self **1** names] Names **5**
31	turn] Turn **5** use] Use **5**
32	Words; which,] Words, which **1**
33	difficulty] Difficulty **5**
195.2	Gentleman;] Gentleman, **1**
4	himself.] himself; **NN** himsef; **NA** Without] without **1** that,] that **5**
9	Things. And] Things; and **1**
12	farther;] farther, **1** least,] least **5**
17	those] those, **1**
19	him;] him, **1**
20	right.] right; **1**
21	And] and **1**
23	incomprehensible;] incomprehensible, **1**
25	can] can, **1**

196.1	setled] settled **5** *pray*] pray **1**
4	way,] way **1**
5	Scripture-History] Scripture-history **5**
9	*Goblins*] *Goblings* **5**
12	*Bloody Bones*] *Bloody-Bones* **1**
17	Disease;] Disease, **1**
21	so] so, **1**
22	again;] again, **1**
25	young;] young, **1**
26	Idea's] Idea's, **1**
27	in,] in; **1**
28	Light,] Light; **1**
197.5	him] hin **NA** *Cutler*'s] *Cutlers* **1**
7	Boy;] Boy, **1**
8	Strength] Stregth **NA** Srength **5**
9	him.] him: **1**
10	latch'd; And] latch'd, and **1**
12	up,] up **1**
19	thither,] thither **5** Mad-man] Madman **4 5**
22	in.] in: **NN** in; **NA**
23	them,] them **1** Discourse,] Discourse **1**
24	other: But] other; but **1**
25	think,] think **1**
26	must] must, **1**
27	can;] can, **1**
31	Good] good **5**
32	mention;] mention, **1**
198.3	to him;] to him. **1**
4–5	imaginable] imaginable, **1**
6	forgiven,] forgiven **NN** *Truth*,] *Truth* **1**
12	Child. As] Child as **5**
13	observed;] observed, **1**
14	side,] side **1**
17	Temper,] Temper **NN** Business] Businuss **4**
18	counter-balance:] counter-balance; **1** counterballance: **5**
	But] but **1**
24	*Wisdom* I take,] *Wisdom*, I take **1**
29	*Cunning*; which,] *Cunning*, which **1** Ape] ape **1**
30	be: And] be, and **1**
32	Understanding;] Understanding, **1**
199.2	a *cunning*] a*cunning* **5**
3	hinders] hinders, **NN** big,] big **1**
4	Body] body **5**
5	so: And] so; and **1** Body] body **NN**

199.6	Men;] Men, 1
7	them:] them. 1
8	Business] business **NN**
10	them;] them. 1 Thoughts;] Thoughts, 1
11	Falshood,] falshood **NN** Falshood **NA** Cunning,] Cunning **NN**
12	it;] it, 1
15	Designs] designs **NN**
17	is,] is 5
19	and,] and 5
21	ill *Breeding*:] ill *Breeding*, 1
22	*Bashfulness*: And] *Bashfulness*, and 1
23	Carriage; Both] Carriage, both 1
26	Assurance.] assurance: **NN**
27	Value;] Value, 1
29	Modestly] modestly 5
31	Actions] Actions, 1
32	disorder;] disorder, 1 are;] are, 1
200.1–2	shamefac'dness] shamefac'dness 5
3	themselves] themselves, 5
9	*Ill-breeding*] Ill-breeding 1
15	secondly] Secondly 4 5
16–17	*Well-fashion'd*] *Well fashion'd* **NN**
18	is] is, 1 gracefulness] gracefullness **NN**
21	Language] Language, 1
25	Observation] observation **NN**
26	*well-bred*] well-bred 1
27	Good-will] Good will 5 People] people **NN**
28	Carriage] carriage **NN**
29	express,] express **NN** Way] way **NN**
201.29	entertainment *ed.*] enterainment 5
35	entertainment *ed.*] entertainment: 5
202.2	carrying *ed.*] caryring 5
23	it. *ed.*] it, 5
37	jarring *ed.*] jaring 5
203.6	recommends *ed.*] recomends 5
13	another] another, **NN**
18	*Good-Breeding*] *Good Breeding* **NN**
19	People] people **NN**
22	*mistaken*] *Mistaken* 5
25	Regard] regard **NN**
29	well,] well 5
30	Name] name 1 *Good-Breeding*] *Good Breeding* 4 5

32	Hats,] Hats **4 5**
204.3	Discourses] discourses **5**
4	impertinent,] impertinent **5**
10	Language,] Language **1 5** Carriage,] Carriage **1**
25	over-look'd,] over-look'd **NN**
28	*Ill-Nature*] *Ill nature* **5**
32	ceremonious] Ceremonious **4 5**
205.3	young] Young **5**
19	this,] this **5**
206.7	Forwardness] forwardness **5**
8	arguing] arguing, **5**
22	minding,] minding **5**
28	over-look] overlook **4 5**
207.2	possibly,] possibly **NN**
3	Morality,] morality **NN** Morality **NA**
6	Practice] practice **1**
8	think,] think **4** *Company*] Company **1**
9	Life,] Life. **5**
15	Children;] Children, **1**
17	consider] consider, **5**
20	School-masters] School-master's **4 5**
21	Education;] Education, **1**
23	Life,] Life **1**
24	Two] two **5**
25	playing?] playing. **1**
26	cannot] can not **NN**
29	Classes, **4 5**] Clasles **3**
30	Read?] read? **5**
208.3	*Learning*] Learning **1**
5	Vertuous,] Vertuous **1** Scholar.] Scholar: **1**
6	*Learning*] Learning **1**
8	foolish,] foolish **1**
11	*Learning*] Learning **1**
12	Qualities.] Qualities: **1**
14	possible,] possible **5** Innocence,] Innocence **NN**
15	correct,] correct **1**
17	*Learning*] *Learning*, **NN** in to] into **NN**
19	talk,] talk; **NN**
25	injoyn'd] enjoyn'd **NN**
32	to] *to* **1**
209.1	*Read*] *read* **5**
25	Minds,] Minds **1**
26	Books,] Books **NN 4 5**

209.27	has,] has **5**
32	*Read,*] *read* **5**
210.2	D.] D? **5**
5	Letter] letter **NN**
7	throw] throw, **5**
8	Play] play **NN**
10	Play] play **NN**
11	Play] play **NN**
21	Pains] pains **1** which,] which **NN**
25	Language] language **NN** remaining] remainding **5**
26	Dice,] Dice; **5**
27	Play] play **NN**
211.4	employed] employ'd **1**
7	where,] where **5**
8	parts] Parts **5**
12	Letters:] Letters; **1** Letters, **5**
16	variety,] variety; **5**
23	for:] for; **1**
24	him. 'Tis] him; 'tis **1**
28	Teach] teach **1**
212.8	*has*] has **NN** in it,] in it. **5**
11	vain,] vain **NN**
13	Sounds;] Sounds, **1** Things] things **NN**
17	knowledge.] Knowledge **1 4 5** *Reynard*] *Raynard* **1**
20	will, besides **4 5**] will besides, **3**
21	finds] finds, **5**
23	Reading] reading **5**
24	amuzements,] amuzements **NN** Amuzements, **4 5**
25	troubles] Troubles **4 5**
28	some-body's] somebody's **5**
29–30	*learning*] *learniug* [2nd 'n' inverted] **3**
30	not, I think,] not I think **1**
32	him,] him **1**
34	fit *to*] fit to **5**
213.5	considered] consider'd **1**
9	lie] lye **5**
20	Scripture:] Scripture; **4 5**
24	all,] all **1**
26	indifferently] indifferently, **1** God,] God **1**
28	Life-time] Life time **5**
37	together;] together: **1**
214.11	Scripture, a **5**] Scripture. A **3 4**
13	learn; **5**] learn, **3 4**

14	Commandments **4 5**] Commendments **3**
16	Understanding] understanding **NN**
20	best] Best **NN**
21	him,] him **1** hand] hand, **1**
25	Paper.] paper: **NN** Paper: **NA**
215.1	*Paper*] *paper* **NN**
5	degrees] digrees **NN**
7	Writing-Paper] Writing-paper **1**
8	do,] do **1**
26	young] Young **5**
216.6	Imploy] imploy **4 5**
18	Language,] Language: **NN**
22	living] Living **NN**
217.1	preserved] preserv'd **1**
4	Gentleman;] Gentleman, **1**
9	it,] it **1**
12	*Latin*,] *Latin* **5**
17	Course] course **1** to;] to, **1**
218.1	Commerce] Commerce, **1**
2	Grammar-Schools] Grammar Schools **1** Gentlemen **5**] Gentleman **3 4**
3	Trades;] Trades, **5**
7	has,] has **NN**
9	it,] it **NN**
10	Education,] Education **1**
11	thought] Thought **NN**
13	Learning] learning **1** Grammar-School] Grammar School **1**
14	about,] about **NN** incourage] encourage **NN**
16	success] Success **5**
17	that,] that **1** imagine] Imagine **NN**
18	short] Short **NN** this.] this: **1** all,] all **NN**
19	perplexity] Perplexity **5** Rules,] Rules **1**
23	some-body] some Body **5**
24	*French*-Woman] *French* Woman **5** *English*-Girl] *English* Girl **5**
27	over-seen] over seen **5**
219.9	Memory.] Memory: **1**
13	Knowledge.] Knowledge: **1**
16	themselves;] themselves, **1**
24	young] Young **NN**
25	*Euclid*,] *Euclid* **1**
30	easy] easie **NN**

219.31	*Æsop*'s] *Æsop's* **NN**
220.1	Fable,] Fable **1**
4	exercise] Exercise **5**
6	formation] Formation **5**
7	declensions] Declensions **5** Nouns] Nouns, **NN**
	heart] Heart **5**
8	acquaintance] Acquaintance **5** genius] Genius **5**
9	signification] Signification **5**
19	Knowledge] Knowledge, **5**
26	effect] Effect **5**
29	habits] Habits **5**
30	use] Use **5**
221.3	entrance] Entrance **5**
5	learning] Learning **5**
6	occasion] Occasion **5**
16	reason] Reason **5**
19	narrow,] narrow **5**
22	skill and art] Skill and Art **5** Teacher] Teacher, **5**
23	learning] Learning **5**
30	delight in change and variety] Delight in Change and Variety **5** contradiction] Contradiction **5**
31	state] State **5**
32	temper] Temper **5** quickness] Quickness **5**
33	instability] Instability **5**
222.19	Governors] Governours **5**
33	has that, **5**] has, that **4** fast,] fast **5**
223.32	free,] free **5** him, **5**] him **4**
224.2	easy] easie **NN**
12	Language, **4 5**] Langage **3**
14	do] do, **5**
19	other Words] others Word **NA**
25	so, *ed.*] so **5**
33	Well-bred *ed.*] Well-bread **5**
226.13	were *ed.*] where **5**
21	Grammar *ed.*] Garmmar **5**
227.8	reasonably *ed.*] reasonable **5**
17	Grammar *ed.*] Gammar **5**
33	*Anatomy*] *Anotomy* **NA**
228.9	on it,] on it **NN**
17	*and*] and **5** *Verses.*] *Verses* **NN**
18	pretence] Pretence **5** useful] usefull **NN**
19	Which,] which **1**
20	advantage] Advantage **5**

22	occasion] Occasion **5**
24	jot] Jot **5**
25	'tis,] 'tis **NN**
26	Speech] speech **NN** *Latin*] *Latin*, **5** *Amor*] *amor* **4 5** or,] or **4 5**
28	things,] things **1**
229.3–4	Materials.] Materials: **1**
7	capacity] Capacity **5**
8	Subject] subject **NN**
10	Man] man **NN**
11	crack'd,] crack'd **NN**
12	what,] what **5**
13	understand] understand, **5** matters] Matters **5**
14	*Themes*] Themes **1**
16	place] Place **5**
19	occasion] Occasion **5**
20	lives] ltves **NN**
25	pretence] Pretence **5**
27	*extempore*] *Extempore* **5**
32	meditation] Meditation **5**
34	effects] Effects **5** learning] Learning **5**
35	occasion] Occasion **5**
230.1	debate] Debate **5**
10	invention] Invention **5**
10–11	signification] Signification **5**
15	Boys Invention] boys invention **NN**
16	quicken'd] quickn'd **NN** *English*,] *English*; **NN**
17	facility] Facility **5** command] Command **5**
20	Mind] mind **NN** imployment] Imployment **5**
23	weight] Weight **5**
24	sort.] sort: **1**
26	that,] that **1**
30	be: And] be; and **1**
31	Son] son **NN** defiance] Defiance **5**
32	Business:] Business, **NN** case.] case; **1** Case. **5** For] for **1**
33	Reputation] reputation **NN**
34	considered,] consider'd **NN** considered **NA** like] Like **NN**
35	too:] too. **1**
231.1	instances] Instances **5**
4	advantage] Advantage **5**
6	losers] Losers **5** rate] Rate **5**
10	idly] idlely **4 5**

231.12	care] Care 5
13	Versifying] Versifyng **NA**
14	desireable] desirable 1 study] Study 5
18	design] Design 5
20	vulgar] Vulgar **NN** 5
26	heart] Heart **NN** 5 parcels] Parcels 5
27	advantage] Advantage 5
28	reading] Reading 5 talking] Talking 5
29	scraps] Scraps 5 heart] Heart **NN** 5
30	stuff'd] stuffed 1 5
32	Gentleman.] Gentleman: 1
34	grace] Grace 5
35	thread-bare] thread-bare, 1
232.2	matter] Matter 5 remembrance] Remembrance 5
	expression] Expression 5
6	School-boys] School-Boys 5 learning] Learning 5
7	choice or distinction] Choice or Distinction 5
9	disgust and aversion] Disgust and Aversion 5
18	afresh *ed.*] a fresh 3 4 5
24	reteins] retains 4 5
26	Lead] Lead, 5
28	Strength] Strength, 5
37	help and amendment] Help and Amendment 5
233.1	pretence] Pretence 5 Grammar Schools]
	Grammar-Schools 4 5
4	learning his Lessons] Learning his Lessons, 5
5	method] Method 5
10	share] Share 5
14	help] Help 5
16	train] Train 5 Peoples words] People's Words 5
20	Childrens] Children's 5 imploy'd,] imploy'd 5
22	Lesson] lesson 5
234.8–9	disposition: which,] disposition, which 1
9	rest:] rest; 1
11	setled] settled 5
13	indeed,] indeed 5
31	skill] Skill 5
235.11	point,] point 1
13	Straits] Strait 5
20	insensibly] in-|ensibly **NA**
24	Countries,] Countries 5
28	*Arithmetick,*] *Arithmetick* 5
30	to: And] to; and 1

31	it.] it: **1**
32	perfectly: He] perfectly; he **1**
236.3	*parallel*] *Parallel* **4 5**
7	entred] entered **5**
237.12	think,] think **5**
14	Rule,] Rule **1**
17	*Æquator*,] *Æquator* **NA**
23	hand. I] hand, I **1**
26	two,] two **1**
28	World;] World, **1**
29	Geography] *Geography* **NN**
238.5	Importance] importance **1**
6	inquir'd] enquir'd **NA**
12	learner] Learner **4 5**
19	Grown Men] Grown-Men **1**
26	read,] read **1**
239.19	*Civil-Law*] *Civil-law* **5**
22	*Civil-Law*] *Civil-law* **5**
240.16	Arts,] Arts **1**
18	them.] them: **1** is,] is **5**
19	them.] them: **1**
27	Speculation.] Speculation: **1**
28	what] What **5**
30	*Eloquence*;] *Eloquence*, **5**
31	writ] write **5**
241.1	Notions,] Notions **1**
2	Wrong;] Wrong, **1** accordingly:] accordingly; **1**
4	others:] others; **NN**
9	Gentleman] Gentlemen **5**
25	Arguing:] Arguing, **1**
27	fallacious] fallacius **5**
28	way] Way **1**
31	think,] think **5**
242.1	think] think, **5**
13	thing,] thing **5**
37	Letters.] Letters, **5**
243.14	scape] escape **5**
23	School-master] School-Master **5**
25	*English*] *Englsh* **5**
28	out-does] out does **5**
33	Stile] Style **5**
34	talk'd] tal'd **5**
244.36	imagin] imagine **5**

245.1	say,] say 1
6	Properties,] Properties 1
9	*Metaphysicks*: But] *Metaphysicks*, but 1
14	World,] World 1
15	Revelation.] Revelation **NN** [*period dropped in most copies*]
16	*Spirits,*] *Spirits* 1 God,] God 1 Souls,] Souls 1
17	Heaven, by Revelation;] Heaven by Revelation, 1
	Information] information 1
19	well,] well 1
20	Bible,] Bible 1 read:] read, 1
26–7	notion and belief] Notion and Belief **NN**
27	Transactions] Trans-|ctions 5
28–9	*Bodies.* For] *Bodies*, for 1
29	notion] Notion **NN**
33	well,] well 1
35	in,] in 1
246.4	Maids,] Maids 1 them,] them 1
7	Superstition;] Superstition, 1
10	load,] load 1
18	prejudice,] prejudice 1 Principles,] Principles 1
20	*Beings*] *Beings*, 1 *natura*:] *natura*, 1
21	Phænomena] Phœnomena 1 5
23	Matter,] Matter 1
28	which,] which 5
247.5	Floud] Flood 5
8	bye] by 1 5
10	Motion,] Motion 1 Nature;] Nature, 1
12	Preparative,] preparative 1
13	Opportunity] opportunity **NN** Explication] explication 1
	Application] application 1
15	Flood,] Flood 1
18	Young] young 1
19	Truth and Certainty] truth and certainty 1 is,] is 1
24	also,] also. 1
25	*Philosophy,*] *Philosophy* 1
28	comprehensive, scientifical,] comprehensive scientifical 1
30	talk,] talk 1 Things,] Things 1
31	*Peripateticks*] *Peripatteicks* **NA**
248.13	imploy'd] imployed 1
17	little] litle **NN**
24	Matter of Fact] matter of fact 1
28	*Phænomena*] *Phœnomena* 1 5
249.3	examin'd] examined **NN**

5	who] who, **5**
6	Masses] masses **5**
12	Original] Original, **1** Learning,] Learning **1**
22	liberty] Liberty **5**
27	Business] business **5**
29	knowing,] knowing **5**
30	Mind] mind **5**
33	He says *ed.*] Hesays **5**
250.13	when the *ed.*] whenthe **5**
251.23	avoid.' *ed.*] avoid. **5**
29	Learning *ed.*] Larning **5**
34	order] order, **5**
36	Sorts] sorts **5**
252.9	accustome] accustom **4 5**
10	distinguish] Distinguish **5**
21	graceful] gracefull **NN**
26	Country-Gentleman] Country Gentleman **5**
27	little,] little **1**
28	nothing,] nothing **1**
31	valued. But] valued; but **1**
32	it;] it, **1**
34	esteemed,] esteemed **1 5**
35	things,] things **1**
253.3	learn'd.] learn'd: **1**
4	requires,] requires **1**
5	unbent:] unbent, **NN** unbent; **NA** And] and **1**
11	things] Things **1**
13	perhaps,] perhaps **1**
18	Study] Study, **1**
25	great] Great **NN** Grert **NA**
26	Luxury: And] Luxury; and **1**
27	account,] account **1**
29	Horseback] Horse-back **5**
30	Hanches] Haunches **1**
33	time,] time **1**
254.2	parts] Parts **1**
3	that,] that **1**
5	Life,] Life **1**
7	apt **4 5**] apt, **3**
8	those,] those **1 5**
12	courage] Courage **1 4 5** Duel:] Duel, **1**
18	that,] that **4 5**
23	*Wrestling.* And] *Wrestling*, and **1** therefore,] therefore **1**

254.25	*Wrestler,*] *Wrestler* 1
33	allow,] allow 1
255.1	Nations;] Nations, 1 Force,] Force 1
2	those,] those 1
4	which,] which 1 4 presume,] presume 1 persume, 5
14	Shame] shame 5
24	nay,] nay 5
25	Children] Children, 4 5
256.4	things] Things 1 Children,] Children 1
7	health] Health 1 Reading, and Writing,] Reading and Writing 1
10	got,] got 1
20	profitted] profited 1
27	that;] that, **NN**
257.8	Way] way 5
15	Though] though 1
258.1	Grandeur] Granduer 5
2	Fruit-trees] Fruit trees 5
7	*Diversions*] Diversions 1
8	Idle] idle 1
9	And] Bnd 5
11	hunger] Hunger **NN**
259.2	Reputation.] Reputation 5
5	be,] be 1
8	produce,] produce 1
13	that,] that 1
14	*Drinking*] *Drinking,* 5 away] a way 5
19	all:] all, 1
20	themselves,] themselves; 1
24	Gentleman] Gentlemen **NA**
260.5	farther,] farther 1
7	vicious,] vicious 5
8	them,] them 5
10	some,] some 4 5
15	before-mentioned;] before-mentioned, 1 lazy] lazie 1
17	Sick] sick 1
24	pollish] polish 4 5
24–5	pollishing] polishing 4 5
31	worse.] worse: 1
261.4	*Merchants*] *Merthants* 5
6	efficacy] efficasy 5
10	runs] rnns **NN**
11	advise] advice 1

17	Father] Father, **1**
18	Concernments.] Concernments: **1**
19	Money;] Money, **1**
20	enough: Nor] enough, nor **1**
24	same,] same: **NN** same; **NA**
31	Son] Son, **5**
34	received] recived **5**
36	Money] money **1**
262.4	Pains] pains **NN**
6	a good] good **5**
10	Part] part **5**
13	abroad,] abroad **1** is,] is **5**
20	One] one **5**
24	may,] may **1**
25	Languages,] Languages **1**
27	themselves] themselves, **5**
31	boistrous] boisterous **NN**
32	Authority:] Authority. **1**
33	conduct,] conduct **5**
35–6	himself] himselfe **5**
263.5	Wise] wise **NN**
12	after-part] after part **NN**
16	for;] for: **1**
17	Governour;] Governour, **1**
24	*Travel*] *Travel*, **4** otherwise] otherwise, **5**
28	abroad;] abroad, **1**
36	Enquiries] Enquires **5**
264.1	Pleasure,] Pleasure; **NN**
2	controul'd:] controul'd; **1**
4	Tempers,] Tempers **1**
5	comport] Comport **1**
7	Briars;] Briars, **1** Miscarriages] Miscariages **5**
11	*travel*] *Travel* **4 5**
23	it:] it, **5**
25	wondred.] wondred; **1** For] for **1**
27	Tutor:] Tutor; **1**
30	welcome,] welcome **1**
31	Persons,] Persons **1**
33	fear,] fear **NN**
265.2–3	twenty, to marry,] twenty to marry **1**
4	with:] with; **1**
5	on't,] on't **NN**
15	Subject.] Subject: **1**

265.16   things,] things 1   consideration;] consideration, 1
18   Children;] Children, 1
19   Remedies.] Remedies: 1
22   there 4 5] there- 3
23   Besides] Besides, 1
26   to] ro 5   End,] End 1   aims] Aims 1
33   find,] find 1
35   little Ones] Little Ones, 1

APPENDIX II

LETTERS OF TRANSMITTAL TO EDWARD CLARKE

A. Late November 1684, following on from draft in **H** (Harvard MS Eng. 880); cf. *Corr.* 791 (ii. 648)

Thus you have my first Chapter on this subiect calculated to the age your son is now of. Upon reading it over all togeather I find some [things] repetitions which might have been spared which might well happen to one who (haveing soe bad a memory as I) writ it ⟦and⟧ at soe many days and miles distance as I did. I have not troubled my self to mend this fault, whereby you will perceive what things were setled on my minde. And since I write not as an Author to the publique but as to a freind in private I hope you will pardon me if I have been lesse carefull of giveing it the forme of a treatise, then the usefulnesse which I designe it for. And therefor have been content to give you my thoughts in as plain words as I could [......] as they offerd themselves without [any] ornament or order. I cannot be confident but that [...] many things may be omitted in it which deserve consideration. I can only say I have set downe all I thought on as necessary and when any thing else comes into my minde I shall take the liberty to mention it to you. And now though I tell you that I send it to a freind yet doe not you looke on it as comeing from one. Let it be to you as a discourse that fell into your hands by chance. Consider not the author nor his affection to you but the reason and truth of what you finde in it. Soe far as they appeare and convince you soe far follow them and where any thing sticks with you pray let me know. For though [the] I could forwardly venture to write on a subiect a litle out of my way where I thought it might be any way serviceable to you yet I am not soe vain as to thinke my self infallible in what I have written. I aime at noething but the advantage of your son and family · what you finde may conduce to that end receive for its owne sake not mine · what you doubt or [d] condemne pray tell me freely, and when we have setled this first chapter, we will if you thinke it worth while proceed on to the next step and looke two or three years forward · If I thought you not sufficiently assurd of the sincerity where with I write I should beg your pardon for the confidence and liberty I have usd in it but know I am

Sir
Yours
J LOCKE

B. 5 January 1685, following on from draft in **K** (British Library Add. MS 38771); cf. *Corr.* 804 (ii. 677)

Sir

   You will perceive by the carelesse stile of these papers that I have minded usefulnesse more then ornament and by these repet⟨it⟩ions and disjoynted parts observable in them it will easily appeare they were not writ all at a time. I began them before my ramble this sommer about these provinces, and thinking it convenient you should have them as soon as might be I writ severall parts of them as [I] stay gave me leasure and oportunity any where in my journey · soe that great distance of place and time interveneing between the severall parts often broke the thread of my thoughts and discourse · and therefor you must not wonder if ⟨it⟩ they be not well put togeather and yⁱˢ must be my excuse for the faults in the method order and connection. But that which I cheifly beg of you concerneing them is that though they were writ with the best intention and sincerest affection in the world yet that you would not looke on them under that character. Let not kindenesse interest it self at all in the judgm⟨en⟩t you shall make of them. For it being in soe great a concernm⟨en⟩t as your son let noe thing but evident reason guide you · I had much rather [f] you should finde I mistake in my advice to you, then that you should mistake in your application to him · Be therefor both you and your Lady as severe as may be in examining these rules doubt as much as you can of every one of them and when upon a scrupulous review we have setled this part and supplyd what possibly you may finde wanting I shall be ready to talke my minde as freely to Madame concerning her daughters if she continue to be of the minde that it may be wo`r'th her patience to heare me · I am

   Deare Sir

   Your most humble and most obleiged servant

   JOHN LOCKE

APPENDIX III

'Mᴿ LOCKE'S EXTEMPORÈ ADVICE &c.'

BL MS Sloane 4290, fos. 11–14. The title is Samuel Bold's. As noted in the introduction, it was first published in Pierre Desmaizeaux's *Collection of Several Pieces* with the title 'Some Thoughts concerning Reading and Study for a Gentleman', by which it is usually known. (Letters enclosed in half-brackets ⌞ ⌟ have been lost in mounting for binding.)

Reading is for the improvement of the Understanding.

The Improvement of the understanding is for two ends; ffirst, ffor our own increase of Knowledge. Secondly, to enable us to deliver and make out that knowledge to others.

The latter of these, if it be not the chief end of study in a gentleman, yet it is at least equal to the other, since the greatest part of His business and usefulness in the world, is by the influence of what He say's, or write's to others.

The extent of our knowledge cannot exceed the extent of our Idea's. Therefore He who would be universally knowing, must acquaint Himself with the obiects of all sciences. But this is not Necessary to a Gentleman, whose proper calling is the service of His Countrey; and so is most properly concerned in Moral, and Political knowledge; and 'thus' the studies which more immediately belong to His calling, are those which treat of virtues and vices, of Civil Society, and the Arts of Government, and so wil take in also Law and History.

It is enough to be furnished with the Ideas belonging to His Calling, which He wil find in the sorts of Books above mentioned.[1]

But the next step towards the Improvement of His Understanding, must be to observe the connection of these Ideas in the propositions, which those Books hold forth, and pretend to teach as Truths; which, til a man can iudge whether they be Truths or no, his understanding is but little improved; And He does but think and talk after the Books that He hath read, without having any knowledge thereby. And thus, men of much reading, are greatly Learned, and but[2] little knowing.

The third and last step therefore in improving the Understanding, is to find out upon what ffoundation, any proposition advanced bottom's; And to

---

[1] In making a textual comparison of the text and manuscript, only substantial variants in the printed edition have been noted. Capitalization, spelling (e.g. 'minde' or 'mind', 'ffor' or 'For', etc.) and in paragraphing have been ignored. Variants in Desmaizeaux's edition are indicated by the letter D. Here the printed text reads: 'in the Books that treat of the Matter above mention'd.'

[2] D: 'greatly learned; but may be little knowing.'

observe the connection of the Intermediate Ideas by which It is ioyned to that ffoundation, upon which It is erected, or that Principle from which It is derived. This, in short, is Right Reasoning, and by this way alone true knowledge is to be got by Reading and studying.

When a man by use hath got this ffaculty of Observing and Iudging, of the Reasoning and Cohere⟨n⟩c⟨e⟩ of what He reades, and how It proves what It pretends to teach, He is then, and not til then, in the Right way of improving His Understanding, and enlarging His knowledge by Reading.

But that (as I have said) being not all, that a Gentleman should aim at in Reading, He should further[1] take care to improve Himself in the Art also of Speaking, that so He may be able to make the best use of what He knows.

The Art of speaking wel, consists chiefly in two things, viz. Perspicuity. And Right Reasoning.

Perspicuity, consists in the using of proper Terms for the Ideas or Thoughts which He would have pass from His own mind into that of another man's. 'Tis this, that gives them an easie entrance, And 'tis with delight that men hearken to those whom they easily understand; whereas, what is obscurely said, dying as it is spoken, is usually not only lost, but creates a preiudice in the Hearer, as if He that spoke knew not what He said, or was afraid to have it understood.

The way to obtain this, is to read such Books, as are allow'd to be writ with the greatest Clearness and Propriety in the Language that a man uses. An Author excellent in this ffaculty, as well as several other, is Dr Tillotson late Arch Bishop of Canterbury,[2] in all that is published of His. I have chose rather to propose this Pattern, for the attainment of the Art of Speaking clearly, than those who gives[3] Rules about it, since we are more apt to learn by Example, than by Direction. But if any one hath a minde to consult the Masters in the Art of speaking, and writing, He may ʻfindeʼ in Tully *De Oratore*, and another Treatise of His, called, *Orator*, And in Quintillian's Institutions, and Boileau's discourse *Du Sublime*,[4] Instructions concerning this, and the other parts of speaking wel.

Besides Perspicuity, there must be also Right Reasoning; without which Perspicuity serves but to expose the speaker. And for the attaining of this, I should propose the constant reading of *Chillingworth*,[5] who by his example wil

---

[1] D: 'farther'.

[2] John Tillotson published many sermons. There were several in Locke's library (LL 2902–2920a).

[3] D: 'give'.

[4] Locke owned the Gulielmus edition of Cicero's *Opera* (LL 711) and separate editions of *De officiis* (LL 714, 721h). Marcus Fabius Quintilian's work on rhetoric, *Institutiones Oratoriae*, was a major work on educational theory and literary criticism (LL 2424–5, 2426a). Nicolas Boileau-Despréaux published a translation of the *De sublimitate*, long attributed to 'Longinus', *Traité du sublime* (Paris, 1675; LL 1806).

[5] William Chillingworth, *The Religion of Protestants* (Oxford, 1638). Locke owned the 4th and 5th edns. (London, 1674 and 1684; LL 685–6). Cf. § 188 (p. 240).

teach both perspicuity, and the way of Right Reasoning better than any Book that I know; And therefore wil deserve to be read upon that account over and over again, not to say any thing of his Argument.

Besides these Books in English, Tully, (the best edition of Tully, is by Gulielmus and Gruter, printed at Hamburgh 1618.[1] Elziver's edition of Tully in ix. vol: in 12° is also an excellent good one) Terence[2] (the late edition at Cambridge) Virgil,[3] (at the same place lately) Livy (Elzever's edition)[4] and Cesar's Commentaries (Stephen's edition)[5] may be read to form one's minde to a relish of a right way of speaking and writing.

The Books I have hitherto mentioned have been in order only to writing and speaking well; Not but that they wil deserve to be read upon other accounts.

The study of Morality I have above mentioned as that, that becomes a Gentleman, not barely as a Man, but in order to his business as a Gentleman. Of this, there are Books enough writ both by Ancient and Modern Philosophers; But the Morality of the Gospel doth so exceed them all, that to give a Man a ful knowledge of true Morality, I should send him to no other Book, but the New Testament. But if he hath a minde to see how far the Heathen world carried that science, and whereon they bottom'd their Ethicks, he wil be delightfully and profitably entertained in Tully's Treatises *De Officiis*[6]

Politicks contains two parts very different the one from the other. The one containing the Original of Societies, and the Rise and Extent of Political power, The Other, the Art of Governing men in Society.

The first of these hath bin so bandied amongst us for this sixty years backward, that one can hardly miss Books of this kind. Those which I thi⟨n⟩k are most talked off in English, are the ffirst Book of Mr Hookers Ecclesiastical Polity,[7] and Mr Algernoon Sydney's Book of Government;[8] The latter of these

---

[1] In Desmaizeaux's *Collection*, all the parenthetical matter in this paragraph is omitted. Locke owned many editions of Cicero's works (LL 711–721q).

[2] Terence, or Publius Terentius Afer, was considered the greatest Roman comic dramatist after Plautus. Locke owned many edns. of his comedies, including Farnaby's (LL 2852–2856b).

[3] LL 3089–95.

[4] Titus Livius; LL 1770–1772a.

[5] The Stephanus, or Estienne, family were great scholarly printers from Paris, who specialized in printing reliable edns. of Greek and Latin classics. Locke owned several edns. of Caesar's *Commentaries* on the Gallic and on the Civil Wars (LL 559–562a).

[6] See § 185 (p. 239).

[7] Richard Hooker, *Of the Laws of Ecclesiastical Polity* (2 vols., London, 1593–7). Locke owned the 6th edn. (1632; LL 1492) and his *Works* (1676; LL 1490). Unless otherwise indicated, the place of publication of these and other works cited is presumed to be London.

[8] Desmaizeaux changed this citation to the exact title: *Discourses concerning Government*, by Algernon Sidney (1698; LL 2666).

I never read. (Let me here add, Two Treatises of Government,[1] printed 1690. And a Treatise of [Polity] Civil Polity,[2] printed this year) To these one may adde Puffendorfe *De Officio Hominis et civis*, and *De Iure Naturali et Gentium*,[3] which last, is the best book of that kinde.

As to the other part of Politicks, which concern's the Art of Government, That I think is best to be learned by Experience and History, especially that of a man's own countrey. And therefore I think an English Gentleman should be wel versed in the History of England; takeing his Rise as far back as there are any Records of It; joyning with it the Laws that were made in the several Ages, as he goes along in his History, that He may observe from thence the several Turns of state, and how they have bin produced. In Mr Tyrrel's History of England[4] He wil find all along those several Authors which have treated of our Affaires, And which He may have recourse to concerning any point which either his curiosity or Judgement shal lead him to enquire into.

With the History He may also do wel to read the Ancient Lawyers (such as are Bracton, ffleta, Henningham, Myrror of Justice, My Lord Cook on the Second Institutes, and Modus tenendi Parliamentum,[5] and others of that kinde, whom He may finde quoted in the late controversies between Mr Petit, Mr Tyrrel, Mr Atwood, &c. with Dr Brady,[6] as also I suppose in Sadler's

---

[1] Locke's anonymously published work. His authorship was revealed after his death, in his will (LL 1293).

[2] Peter Paxton, *Civil Polity, a Treatise concerning the Nature of Government* (1703; LL 725). The publication-date enables us to date this manuscript 'on reading and study' to 1703.

[3] See § 186 (p. 239). *De officio hominis et civis* (Lund, 1673; LL 2403). *De jure naturae et gentium* (Lund, 1672; LL 2401). The latter also published in Amsterdam (1698; LL 2407).

[4] James Tyrrell, *General History of England* (1697–1700; LL 3002). It 'was written with the view of confuting the monarchical opinions expressed by Robert Brady . . . in his "Compleat History of England," and of establishing the historical continuity of the representation of the commons in the English legislature' (*DNB*). Locke also owned Tyrrell's *Patriarcha non Monarcha* (1681) written against Sir Robert Filmer (LL 2999).

[5] Henricus de Bracton, Bratton, or Bretton (d. 1268), an ecclesiastic and judge who wrote a comprehensive treatise on the law of England, *De legibus et consuetudinibus Angliae*; first printed in 1569. *Fleta, seu Commentarius juris Anglicani* (1647; 2nd edn., 1685): an anonymous work of *c.* 1290, a summary of Bracton, whose 'title is thought to conceal some reference either to the Fleet Prison or to Fleet Street' (*DNB*). 'Henningham' is Samuel Bold's phonetic spelling for Ralph Hengham, or Hingham, a judge (d. 1311), 'the reputed author of a register of writs, which perhaps formed the basis of the great compilation entitled "Registrum Cancellariae," or "Registrum omnium Brevium," first printed in 1531, and styled by Coke 'the most ancient book of the law' (*DNB*). Andrew Horne, *The Booke called the Mirrour of Justices* (1646), a translation of *La somme qu'appelle Miroir des justices* (1642), both published anonymously. Sir Edward Coke, *The Second Part of the Institutes of the Lawes of England* (1642). William Hakewel, or Hakewill, *Modus tenendi Parliamentum, or The Old Manner of Holding Parliaments in England* (1659); published anonymously.

[6] William Petyt, *The Antient Right of the Commons of England Asserted* (1680). It was answered by William Atwood, *Jus Anglorum ab antiquo* (1681; LL 144), and by Dr Robert Brady, *A Full and Clear Answer* (1681, published anonymously) and further in Brady's *An Introduction to Old English History* (1684). Brady also wrote a *Complete History of England* (2 vols., 1685, 1700), answered by James Tyrrell: see n. 4 above.

Treatise of the Rights of the Kingdom, and Customs of our Ancestors,[1] whereof the first Edition is the best) wherein He wil finde the Ancient Constitution of the Government of England. There are two volumes of state Tracts[2] printed since the Revolution, in which there are many things relating to the Government of England.

As for General History Sir Walter Rawleigh, and Dr Howel[3] are Books to be had. He 'who' [which] hath a mind to launch further into that Ocean may consult Whear's M⟨e⟩thodus legendi Historias[4] of the last edition, [which] wil direct him to the Authors He is to read, and the method wherein He is to read them.

To the reading of History, Chronology and Geography are absolutely Necessary.

In Geography we have two general ones in English, Heylin and Moll;[5] which is the best of them, I know not, having not bin much conversant in either of them; But the last I should think to be of most use, because of the new discoveries that are made every day, tending to the perfection of that science; tho I believe that the countries which Heylin mentions, are better treated of by Him, bating what new discoveries since his time have added.

These two Books contain Geography in general; [But whether,] But whether an English Gentleman would think it worth his time to bestow much pains upon that, tho without It, He cannot wel understand a Gazette, This is certain, He cannot wel be without Cambden's Brittan⟨n⟩ia;[6] which is much enlarged in the last edition. A good collection of Maps is also very necessary. To Geography Books of Trav⟦el⟧ may be added. In that kinde the collections made by our [own] countrey-men, Hacklute,[7] and Purchase[8] are very good.

---

[1] John Sadler, *Rights of the Kingdom, or Customs of Our Ancestours* (1649); D: 'Sedler'. Locke owned the 1682 edn. (LL 2525).

[2] *State Tracts: Being a Collection of Several Treatises Relating to the Government Privately Printed in the Reign of K. Charles II* (1689; LL 2759). Another edn., *State Tracts, in Two Parts*, was published 1692–3.

[3] Sir Walter Raleigh, *The History of the World* (1614; LL 2435); many edns. were published. William Howell, *Elementae Historiae* (1671), translated under the title *The Elements of History* (1700).

[4] Diggory Whear, *De ratione et methodo legendi historias dissertatio* (1623), published in English with the title *The Method and Order of Reading Both Civil and Ecclesiastical Histories* (1685; repr. 1694, 1698, and 1710).

[5] Peter Heylyn, *Cosmographie in Four Bookes, Containing the Horographie and Historie of the Whole World* (1652), an enlarged edn. of *Microcosmus, or A Little Description of the Great World* (Oxford, 1621); both titles were frequently reprinted. Herman Moll, *A System of Geographie* (1701; LL 2009).

[6] William Camden, *Britannia* (1586). Locke owned an Amsterdam (1645) edn. (LL 574), and a translation published by the Churchills in 1695 (LL 575).

[7] Richard Hakluyt, *The Principall Navigations, Voiages and Discoueries of the English Nation* (1589). Locke owned the enlarged edn. (3 vols., 1598–1600; LL 1374).

[8] Samuel Purchas, *Purchas His Pilgrimage, or Relations of the World and the Religions Observed in All Ages* (1613). Locke owned the 1625 edn. with the title *Hakluytus Posthumus, or Purchas His Pilgrimes* (LL 2409). Desmaizeaux correctly spells 'Hakluyt' and 'Purchas'.

There is also a very good collection made by Thevenot in fol: in ffrench,[1] and by Ramuzio in Italian,[2] whether translated into English or no I know not. There are also several good books of Trav⟦e⟧lls of English men published, as Sands, Roe, Brown, Gage, and Dampier.[3] There are also several voyages in ffrench which are very good, as, Pyrard, Bergerone, Sagard[e], Bernier,[4] &c, which, whether all of them are translated into English I know not. There is at present a very good Collection of Travels never before in English, and such as are out of print, now printing by Mr Churchill.[5] There are besides these, a vast number of other Travels; A sort of Books that have a very good mixture of delight and usefulness. To set 'them' down all, would take up too much time and room; Those I have mentioned are enough to begin with.

As to Chronology, I think Helvicus[6] the best for common use, which is not a book to be read, but to lye by, and be consulted upon occasion. He that hath a minde to look further into Chronology may get Talent's Tables, and Strauchius's Breviarium Temporum,[7] and may to those add Scaliger De Eme⟨n⟩datione Temporum, and Petavius;[8] if he hath a minde to engage deeper in that study.

---

[1] Melchisédech Thévenot, *Recueil de voyages* (8 parts, Paris, 1681); Locke lacked part 8 (LL 2890). He also owned Thévenot's *Relations de divers voiages curieux* (4 vols., Paris, 1663–72; LL 2889–2889a).

[2] Giovanni Baptista Ramusio, *Navigationi e viaggi* (3 vols., Venice, 1595–1665; LL 2438). Many edns. published.

[3] George Sandys, *A Relation of a Journey Begun A: Dom: 1610, Foure Bookes, Containing a Description of the Turkish Empire* (1615); Locke owned the 7th edn. with the title *Travels Containing an History of the . . . Turkish Empire* (1673; LL 2553). Sir Thomas Roe, *Mémoires de T. Rhoë, ambassadeur du Roy d'Angleterre auprès du Mogol* (Paris, 1663); later included in the Churchills' *Collection of Voyages and Travels* (n. 5 below). Edward Browne, *A Brief Account of Some Travels in Hungary, Servia, Bulgaria* (1673; LL 498); also a French translation, *Relation de plusieurs voyages faits en Hongrie, Servie, Bulgarie . . .* (Paris, 1674; LL 499). Thomas Gage, *The English-American His Travail by Sea and Land, or A New Survey of the West India's* (1648); Locke owned the 3rd edn. with the title *A New Survey of the West Indies* (1677; LL 1205). William Dampier, *A New Voyage Round the World* (1697; LL 910).

[4] François Pyrard, *Discours du voyage des François aux Indes orientales* (Paris, 1611); Locke owned the new edn. with the title *Voyage aux Indes orientales* (Paris, 1679; LL 2411) and his *Voyage concernant sa navigation* (3rd edn. of the *Discours*, Paris, 1619; LL 2411a). Pierre Bergeron, *Relation des voyages en Tartarie* (Paris, 1634; LL 280). Gabriel Sagard Théodat, *Histoire du Canada* (Paris, 1636; LL 2526); and Sagard's *Le Grand voyage du pays des Hurons* (Paris, 1632; LL 2527). Locke owned several works by François Bernier, including *Voyages . . . contenant la description des Etats du Grand Mogol* (2 vols., Amsterdam, 1699); cf. LL 284–9.

[5] *A Collection of Voyages and Travels*, published by A. and J. Churchill (4 vols., 1704; LL 3118). Its general preface is sometimes attributed to Locke.

[6] See § 183 (p. 238).

[7] Francis Tallents (D: 'Tallent's'), *A View of Universal History* (1685?; LL 2829). For Strauchius, see p. 238 n. 80.

[8] Joseph Justus Scaliger, *De emendatione temporum* (Frankfurt, 1593). Locke owned Scaliger's *Elenchus Trihaeresii* (The Hague, 1703; LL 2558). Dionysius Petavius, or Denys Petau, *Rationarium temporum* (Paris, 1662).

Those who are accounted to have writ best particular parts of our English History are Bacon of Henry 7th. And Herbert of Henry 8th.[1] Daniel[2] also is commended, And Burnet's History of the Reformation.[3] Mariana's History of Spain,[4] and Thuanus his History of his own time,[5] and Philip de Comines[6] are of great and deserved reputation.

There are also several ffrench and English Memoirs and Collections, such as Rochefoecau, Melvil, Rushworth &c[7] which give a great Light to those who have a mind to look into what has past in Europe this last age.

To fit a Gentleman for the conduct of himself whether as a private man, or as interested in the government of his Countrey, nothing can be more necessar‿y‿ than the knowledge of Men; which tho it be to ⟨be⟩ had chief‿ly‿ from experience, and next to that, from a judicious reading of History, yet there are books which of purpose treat of Humane Nature, which help to give an insight into it. Such are those which treat of the passio‿ns‿ and how they are moved, whereof Aristotle in his second book of Rhethorick has admirably treated, and that in a little compass. I think this Rhetorick is translated into English, if not, It may be had in Greek and Latin together. La Bruyer's Characters[8] are also an admirable piece of painting, I think, It is also translated out of ffrench into English. Satyrical writings also, such as Juvenal, and Persius,[9] and above all Horace,[10] tho they paint the Deformities of Men, yet thereby they teach us to know them.

There is another use of Reading, which is for Diversion, and Delight. Such are poetical writings, especially Dramatick, if they be free from Prophaness, Obscenity, and what corrupts good manners; ffor such pitch should not be handled. Of all the Books of ffiction, I know none that equals Servantes his

---

[1] Francis Bacon, *The Historie of the Raigne of King Henry the Seuenth* (1622); Locke had the 1641 edn. (LL 162). Edward Herbert, Baron Herbert of Cherbury, *The Life and Reigne of King Henry the Eighth* (1649).

[2] Samuel Daniel, *The Historie of England* (1612), later published with the title *The Collection of the Historie of England* (1618).

[3] Gilbert Burnet, *The History of the Reformation of the Church of England* (2 vols., 1679–1715).

[4] Juan de Mariana, *Historiae de rebus Hispaniae* (Toledo, 1592). Locke possessed his *De ponderibus et mensuris* (Toledo, 1599; LL 1905).

[5] Thuanus, or Jacques Auguste de Thou, *Historiae sui temporis* (2 vols., Paris, 1604–6). It went through many edns., including French translations.

[6] Philippe de Comines, or Commynes, *Mémoires*, first published Paris, 1524.

[7] François, second duc de La Rochefoucauld (D: 'Rochefoucault'), *Mémoires*; Locke owned the Cologne edns. of 1662 and 1664 (LL 2492–3). Sir James Melville, *Memoires* (1683). John Rushworth compiled *Historical Collections of Private Passages of State* (7 vols., 1659–1701); Locke owned vol. i (LL 2514).

[8] See § 195 (pp. 249–50); D: 'La Bruyere'.

[9] Decimus Junius Juvenalis; Locke owned several editions of his works (LL 1604–1608b), including an edition of Juvenal and Persius combined, with Farnaby's notes. Aulus Persius Flaccus was a Stoic satirist.

[10] Many editions of Horace were in Locke's library (LL 1494–1512a).

History of Don Quixot[1] in usefulness, pleasantry, and a constant Decorum; And indeed no writings can be pleasant which have not *Nature* at the bottom, and are not drawn after Her Copy.

There is another sort of Books, which I had almost forgot, with which a Gentleman's study ought to be wel furnished. viz. Dictionaries of all kinds. ffor the Latine Tongue, Cole, Cooper, Calepine,[2] and Robert Stephen's The-saurus Linguae Latinae,[3] and Vossii Etymologicum linguae latinae.[4] Skinner's Lexicon Etymologicum[5] is an excellent one of that kinde for the English Tongue. Cowel's Interpreter,[6] is useful for Law Terms. Spelman's Glossary[7] is a very useful and Learned book. And Selde⟨n⟩'s Titles of Honour,[8] a Gentleman should not be without. Baudrand has a very go⟨o⟩d Geographical Dictionary.[9] And there are several Historical ones which are of use; as Loyd's, Hofman's, Moreri,[10] And Bayle's Dictionary[11] is something of the same kinde. He that hath occasion to looke into books written in Latine since the decay of the Roman Empire, and the purity of the Latine tongue cannot be wel without Du Cange's Glossarium.[12]

[1] Locke owned a French translation of Cervantes' tale (LL 2428) and T. Shelton's translation, *The History of . . . Don-Quixote of the Mancha* (1652; LL 651). D: 'Cervantes'.

[2] Elisha Coles, *A Dictionary English—Latin and Latin—English* (1677 and 1679 edns.; LL 808–808a). For Coles, Desmaizeaux substitutes 'Littleton': Adam Littleton, *Linguae Latinae liber dictionarius quadripartitus, A Latine Dictionary in Four Parts* (1678). Thomas Cooper, *Thesaurus linguae Romanae et Britannicae* (1565); Locke owned the 1573 edn. (LL 842). Ambrosio Calepino, *Dictionarium septem linguarum* (Geneva, 1516); Locke owned the Lyon edns. of 1663 and 1681 (LL 569–569a).

[3] R. Stephanus, or Robert Estienne, the elder, *Thesaurus linguae Latinae* (2 vols., Lyon, 1573).

[4] Johannes Gerardus Vossius, *Etymologicon linguae Latinae* (Amsterdam, 1662 and 1695 edns.; LL 3107–8).

[5] Stephen Skinner, *Etymologicon linguae Anglicanae* (1669). Locke owned the third edn. (1678; LL 2689).

[6] John Cowell, *The Interpreter, or Booke containing the Signification of Words* (Cambridge, 1607). Locke's library contained the 3rd edn. (1687; LL 868).

[7] Sir Henry Spelman, *Archaeologus, in modum glossarii ad rem antiquam posteriorem* (1626). Locke had the 3rd edn., published with the title *Glossarium archaiologicum* (1687; LL 2739).

[8] John Selden, *Titles of Honour* (1614; LL 2608).

[9] Michel Antoine Baudrand, *Geographia ordine litterarum disposita* (Paris, 1682; LL 224).

[10] Nicholas Lloyd revised a dictionary by Charles Estienne of the publishing family (see p. 321 n. 5): *Dictionarium historicum poeticum . . . auctum et emaculatum per N. Lloydium* (Oxford, 1671); Locke owned the 1686 edn. (LL 1773). Johann Jacob Hofmann (D: 'Hoff-man'), *Lexicon universale historicum* (2 vols., Basel, 1677); Locke owned this and the 1698 edn. (LL 1468–9). Louis Moreri, *Grand dictionnaire historique* (Lyon, 1674); Locke had the 6th edn. (Utrecht, 1692; LL 2051).

[11] Pierre Bayle, *Dictionnaire historique et critique* (4 vols., Rotterdam, 1697; LL 237). Presumably Bayle and Desmaizeaux were friends: the latter has emended the text to read: 'and Bayle's incomparable Dictionary'.

[12] Charles du Fresne, sieur du Cange, *Glossarium ad scriptores mediae et infimae Latinita-tis* (3 vols., Paris, 1678; LL 579). Du Cange also published a similar work devoted to 'Graecitas' in 1688. Desmaizeaux gives the 'Latinitas' title more fully.

Among the Books above set down, I mentioned Johann: Gerh: Vossii Etymologicum Linguae Latinae,[1] all his works are lately printed in Holland in six Tomes, They are very fit Bookes for a Gentleman's Library, as conteining very learned Discourses concerning all the Sciences.

---

[1] See p. 326 n. 4. Desmaizeaux omits Vossius' Christian names.

INDEX